VICTORIAN
EPIC

VICTORIAN EPIC

THE LUCKNOW CAMPAIGNS
1857–58

WILLIAM WRIGHT

AMBERLEY

For My Family –
Emma, Affie, Erik & Diego

Page 1: Havelock's grave and the Alumbagh picket house.

First published 2024

Amberley Publishing
The Hill, Stroud
Gloucestershire, GL5 4EP

www.amberley-books.com

British Library Cataloguing in Publication Data.
A catalogue record for this book is available from the British Library.

ISBN 978 1 4456 8469 7 (hardback)
ISBN 978 1 4456 8470 3 (ebook)

1 2 3 4 5 6 7 8 9 10

Typeset in 10.5pt on 13.5pt Sabon.
Typesetting by SJmagic DESIGN SERVICES, India.
Printed in the UK.

Contents

Introduction

On a hot March day in 1858 at Lucknow, northern India, an old Scottish general with a mop of curly grey hair and a grizzled walnut of a face trotted out on a horse to inspect his assembled troops. These men were, in the main, English and Irish lads red-faced from the sun, kilted and bearded Scots and fierce-looking turbanned Sikhs. Swords, epaulettes and bayonets glittered in the sunshine, a blaze of scarlet and khaki, blue and gold, the largest host ever assembled by the British in India to do battle – over 33,000 officers and men and over 3,500 impatient horses supported by 165 cannon drawn by dozens of elephants, bullocks, horses and sailors. This huge assembly was supported by upwards of 50,000 Indian camp followers – cooks, grooms, washerwomen, mistresses and others.

The battle that followed, generally not well known, involving over 130,000 combatants, has been ignored in many histories of the Great Uprising, or merely given a glance in others, yet it was the turning point of the whole terrible war, once described by a British pro-consul as "the epic of the race". It was also the culmination of no fewer than three attempts by the British to re-capture Lucknow which, until that time, had been the fairest city in India. After the battle it can be said that the Victorian Raj, made possible by the transfer of India from the control of the East India Company to the Crown, was a reality.

Facing the British were over 100,000 armed insurgents and a hostile population led by two remarkable people – an ex-dancing girl who had risen to become a queen and a soft-spoken, absolutely incorruptible religious zealot who wanted to take his jihad to the shores of England. Behind them were regiments of ex-EIC sepoys who now served and were led superbly by their Indian officers. These men had fought under the Union Jack in Burma and the Punjab, but events had exploded in 1857 and they wished to rid the sub-continent of English rule and the Christian religion. Allied with them were the ordinary people of Oudh (Awadh), of which Lucknow was the capital, many of them drafted into war in obeisance to their landowners. All were willing to die that March day, for the shirkers had long gone, all were determined men – and women – though for most of them it was their kingdom they fought for and not some airy concept of Hindustan.

Forty years after the Uprising, a participant, James McLeod Innes VC, wrote an overview of the whole Lucknow series of campaigns based on his own experiences and perception of events, a very Victorian book for military historians. What you are now reading is the first attempt since then to re-tell the whole saga in detail using the letters, diaries, journals and printed memoirs of those who were there, to view those times fairly but objectively, to try and understand the fears and thrills, joys and sadness of many of those involved. Unfortunately, almost all documents written by the rebels at Lucknow were destroyed during the last battle, but I have tried to examine the detailed British intelligence reports to construct where possible a narrative. While my story is seen largely from the perspective of British men, women and children, I have tried where possible to tell you all that I can about their Indian opponents.

Women (and to a lesser extent children too), play a remarkably important part in this narrative. I cannot think of a single other series of battles where they figure so much. Sieges of cities invariably involve lots of civilians but famous old ones like Rorke's Drift and Mafeking usually seem to be the tales of heroic men. This story is different in that it tells of ordinary people caught up in extraordinary circumstances. When the Siege of Lucknow began, the garrison included 240 British women and 320 children and young people. By its close more than 20 of the women were dead and at least 53 children and babies. Many of these women were in their twenties, newly arrived in India. Most were the wives of officers and NCOs. The former group – the memsahibs – had been used to servants and had never really had to fend for themselves. The shock and horrors of war were to have a profound effect; a few went mad, but most somehow found the courage and fortitude to make the most of a terrible situation. Their stories make harrowing reading, but humour also flashes through the darkness. The children coped better than their parents, at least on the surface, as children often do.

Their chief foes were a young queen and her son. It is fair to say that if Begum Hazrat Mahal had not been so good at holding together her coalition of arguing Hindu and Muslim VIPs, then the insurgency would have collapsed much sooner. A brilliant speaker, her speeches inspired her soldiers and poured scorn on everyone from deserters to Queen Victoria and her empire. Resolute to the end, this remarkable woman, beautiful and dynamic, refused to give in and died as one of the last unrepentant and free rebels of the Uprising.

Among those who rallied to her cause were a regiment of Amazons who fought and died to the last woman in November 1857. The British found these "hellcats" especially difficult to dislodge in the inner city fighting. By that stage, even ordinary peasant women were playing their part and we find an old lady in the last battle trying to lay a trail of gunpowder to a store that would have blown up half the city!

The Lucknow Residency and its defence, the first chapter in the drama, became, as Jan Morris wrote, "the supreme temple of British imperialism". This part of the saga is well-known, aided in part by the printed memoirs of many who suffered during the 141 day siege (30th June–17th November 1857) It is a remarkable story and testament to human endurance. To save these men, women and children, a little-known old soldier called Henry Havelock was tasked with leading a small army to relieve Lucknow. His military genius and the tenacity of his soldiers became the stuff of legend and won him a statue in Trafalgar Square. For a brief time he was world famous, though today not one in a hundred Britons, or the tourists happily snapping selfies, have a clue who he was or what he did.

Havelock's men were in turn besieged and so a second army set out for Lucknow. Its commander, Sir Colin Campbell, did not hurry nor waste the lives of his men unnecessarily. Finally, he reached the city and fought one of the bloodiest battles in British history; more VCs were won on that day than any other. His first concern was the women, children and wounded soldiers, so he had to arrange a hurried evacuation in the teeth of seemingly insurmountable odds, a remarkable feat, getting all to safety down-country to Cawnpore, where another unexpected battle against a well-trained rebel army awaited him.

So it was that in March 1858 Campbell returned to finish the job and restore British rule in the city. This whole long series of fights and battles cost over 100,000 lives, British and Indian, and probably three times that number in wounded. The bravery and the strategic and tactical skills demonstrated by the Indians who opposed Havelock and Campbell's armies, or day after day tried to dream up ingenious ways to assault the Residency, cannot be overstated. The British may have shown much hate, especially after the Cawnpore Massacres, but they also quickly came to respect their enemies' fighting abilities and spirit. Frequently in their letters and diaries British officers noted the courage shown by the insurgents. H.E.I.C. officers who had once commanded some of them were somewhat proud of the Indians' mettle and there is one glorious instance of Havelock actually cheering and yelling jibes at a rebel regiment that he had been proud to lead into battle years earlier.

The majority of Indians and the largest part of India did not revolt; the uprising affected only parts of northern and central India. Further south and over to the east there was no violence. While most of the landowners and lords of Oudh took part in the revolt, a few sat on the fence and many of them suddenly supported the British again, once it was clear they were winning. Most of the Bengal Army regiments mutinied, but the Sikhs, such as Brayser's Regiment, stayed loyal and it is worth remembering that some ordinary Indian sepoys stayed true to their salt at Delhi, Cawnpore and Lucknow. I can understand the view that these Indians should have deserted their imperialist masters, but it might be fairer to say that they preferred to stay true to the honour and fidelity of their regiments, not some Queen in a faraway land.

To tell my story I have drawn on the help of a wide range of libraries, published and unpublished sources. Details can be found in the bibliography. I must especially thank the cheerful staff of the Asian and African Studies reading room at the British Library, who never lost patience with this dotard trying to understand their somewhat complex system of files online. Similarly, the archivists at the National Army Museum were helpful as always in their new, cold and barren Templar Study Centre (one misses the old library and its stacks of useful reference books). Praise, too, for the Wellcome Medical Library that has digitised most of its collection, making a researcher's job a joy. In places as diverse as Northallerton and Norwich, archivists were always helpful.

Books on Victorian India face the problem of transliteration – there are sometimes six different spellings of one town or place. Today Oudh is spelled Awadh, but in 1857 it was generally known by the former and so I have stuck with it here. I hope purists, especially Indian ones, will forgive me.

The events of 1857-59 are usually lumped together in modern Indian history books as the First War of Independence. Not everyone agrees with this title and debate still rages on the causes of the cataclysm – was it a "mutiny", a "military insurgency", an "uprising" – you can take your pick, though I favour the latter since it covers a lot of ground. Almost monthly, new books in India get published on the events, though many are not well-researched and have limited bibliographies. I consulted a great number before writing this book and the best can be found in the bibliography. I would particularly like to thank the doyen of 1857 historians, Rudrangshu Mukherjee, whose essays and books, notably his ones on Mangal Pandey, the Cawnpore Massacres and most especially his ground-breaking *Awadh In Revolt* are all essential reading. The Hindu historian Smita Pandey has written intelligently on the revolutionarry governments. I owe a debt to Roshan Taqui, a Lucknow resident whose great grandfather, along with 13 of his brothers, all died fighting the

British in the city; Mr Taqui published in 2001 a day-by-day account of events during the Uprising, based to a large extent on the British intelligence reports but also Urdu sources. No one can write about 1857 without first reading the two finely balanced general accounts by Professor R.C. Majumdar and Surendra Nath Sen; the latter's book was the Indian Government's centenary publication and on its publication aroused some ire for taking such a balanced, unemotional line, but it is for exactly this reason that it remains such a fine work. Most especially I want to thank a Lucknow resident, Eva Schawohl, in 2021 Mrs Eva Chatterji, whose fascination for the Residency and accumulated knowledge on its defenders make her a treasure trove of information.

I must thank my friend, Tibor Nagy, for helping supply many of the illustrations, along with the staff at Amberley who also drew the plans. A final thank you to my editor, Shaun Barrington, who has helped me with this giant as well as all of my previous books.

Today, among many academics and students, the British Empire and all it stood for seems to stink in the nostrils of its own people. This is particularly true in the case of India's Great Uprising 1857-59, the most brutal colonial conflict in the British Empire's history. It seems a precursor to the wars of the 20th century in ferocity – a cruel campaign, with no quarter given or asked for, and atrocities committed by both sides. The British routinely shot or hanged almost all prisoners, burned villages and committed scores of what today would be termed war crimes. Their enemies had not quite the same opportunities to be so cruel, but committed one of history's most infamous massacres and, in a little reported outrage, indiscriminately butchered Sikh women. I have tried not to censor the writings of the British soldiers but let them speak for themselves.

This book has a few heroes but also plenty of villains. In the case of one of the worst – General Neill – I find it fascinating that a man who displays the traits of a narcissistic sociopath was also insistent that his troops should carry sugar plums to give to the children. My own opinion, after a wide reading on the subject, is that neither side should be sanctimonious about this foul war.

Yet there are lessons to be learned from a reading of this period and how people back then lived, laughed, fought and died. If, indeed, it was for the Victorians the epic of their race, it begs a whole series of questions. Personally I am still searching for answers and have simply tried to tell the tale as fairly as I can. I trust you to reach your own conclusions and hope, as you turn the pages, that you gain a better understanding of those who fought on both sides.

William Wright
Budapest

Prologue

British Residency, Lucknow, 30ᵗʰ June 1857

It stood on a hill dominating the skyline, much to the annoyance of the local potentates, an oddly shaped building that blended the East with more than a hint of the Mediterrenean. From any point in the city one could see the red, white and blue of its flag fluttering in the breeze. Eccentricity and incongruity had long been staple ingredients of architecture in British India; the splendid doric columns of Government House, Calcutta, were modelled on Kedleston Hall, Derbyshire, while the cosy bijou villas sitting on top of a Himalyan mountain at Simla would not have been out of place in the Home Counties. So it was that the British Residency at Lucknow in the princely state of Oudh (Awadh), its walls a soft and cheery yellow wash, with brightly coloured awnings, turrets and a balustraded flat roof looked like a villa from the lakeside at Como or Maggiore that had somehow dropped from the skies onto the hillock where it dominated the surrounding buildings and looked down upon the sluggish River Gumti below.

The building had been started in 1780 and grown piecemeal over the years. It stood three storeys tall constructed of brick and stucco: along its west front was a wide and lofty colonnaded verandah; the principal entrance which was on the east side was beneath a handsome portico; twin turrets on the north and south sides led by spiral staircases to the flat roof and an Italian balustrade. Here, the most recent addition to the Residency in the shape of a signalling telegraph post had been constructed to communicate with troops stationed about one mile away to the west in the old Macchi Bhowan citadel, which commanded a bluff near the stone bridge. Finally, of course, there was the Residency flagstaff on the roof from which at all times flew the Union Jack.

The view from the roof or, indeed, the first view of the city from a distance, usually took a visitor's breath away. Emily Eden, sister of one Governor-General, called it an "Arabian Nights" vista. Earlier that June, Adelaide Case, young wife of Lt-Colonel William Case of HM 32nd Regiment, had climbed to the roof early one morning to enjoy her *chota hazree* (early breakfast). She described the view as "truly beyond description beautiful ... when the sun begins to shine on the gilded mosques, and minarets, and towers, it is like a fairy scene."[1]

Lofty windows at all levels, many with coloured blinds set at an angle to give some protection from the sun, let in the light to well-proportioned rooms including a billiard room, though visitors remarked on the Residency's rather basic furniture. While the view towards the poorer "native city" showed the rooftops of squalid dwellings and a maze of muddy streets, a visitor looking to the city's north east was invariably captivated by Lucknow's gleaming gilded or white domes, cupolas and minarets. These buildings included the Kaisarbagh – the main palace of the nawabs of Oudh – the Chutter Munzil and others, along with many mosques including the Great Imambara, at one time the largest vaulted hall in the world. The vista was made even more pleasing by great splashes of green – formal gardens, parkland and clumps of trees breaking up the scene. From the Residency roof or the main rooms on the top floor one could see across the river, where floated the fish-shaped Royal barge and the King's steam yacht, past more native quarters and an iron bridge of fairly recent construction to open countryside beyond.

Below ground the Residency had a series of large, cool rooms called *tykhanas*. There was even an underground swimming pool. Close to the Residency was an ornate two-storied building called the Banqueting Hall, a classic late Georgian edifice with a suite of "spacious salons furnished with costly chandeliers, mirrors and silk divans" intended to wow the Kings of Oudh at formal gatherings. Now the ground floor had been turned into a hospital. Outside, the Residency grounds had once been full of mango and cypress trees, roses, oleander and scarlet hibiscus though, many of these were now uprooted or flattened to make way for piles of ammunition and other accoutrements of war.

Lucknow was the capital of Oudh, one of the most dazzling cities in India and home to over 300,000 souls. It was considered the most enigmatic city on the sub-continent with its own distinctive architecture, cuisine, customs and fashions, a place known for its pleasure-loving rulers, its sophistication and beauty. Oudh itself had dropped like a cherry into the hands of the British-owned East India Company, the trading company that now ruled India through its Governor-Generals, when one of them, Lord Dalhousie, has set his sights on the state. It fell into the British lap in February 1856. Oudh was also the principal recruiting ground of the sepoys who made up the E.I.C's native army.

To say that the British community was expecting the worst that late June was not an understatement. The Residency itself and the private houses nearby were packed full of men, women and children. Rudimentary defences, some better than others, had hastily been assembled around the perimeter of a 33-acre site now called the Residency quarter. Things had gone bad since Sunday 10th May when the native regiments at Meerut had mutinied, burned their cantonment, slaughtered many of their officers and marched to Delhi. Here they had declared the elderly and infirm Moghul emperor, Bahadur Shah II, their leader, and captured the city. Nearby, a token British garrison held out on the ridge overlooking Delhi. As the days passed the spectre of insurgency reared its head at military stations large and small across the Ganges plain. On 30th May a major outbreak had occurred in the military lines at Lucknow. It had been squashed but soon there was tumult at smaller posts in the province. Then mutiny broke out at Cawnpore, the most important place near Lucknow and just 48 miles away. News from Cawnpore had seemed bleak and everyone feared that the garrison might have surrendered to the rebels. All prayed that Lucknow might be spared a similar calamity.

One of the early risers that Tuesday morning was the Reverend Henry Polehampton, the 33 year old vicar of the city church. He and his young wife, Emmie, had been very comfortable at Lucknow in "a very fair house, with the best garden in Cantonments. There are plenty of strawberries for breakfast every morning and there are orange and lemon-trees and ... a nice verandah all round."[2] The Polehamptons had been just over 14 months at Lucknow and very happy. Now they were temporary refugees in the Residency, like so many others. Henry was up by 5.30 a.m. and watched as a small army set off for Chinhat, about 9 miles away, where a rebel force had been sighted. The British had 10 9-pounder guns and one 8-inch howitzer drawn by an elephant. With the guns marched 300 officers and men of Her Majesty's 32nd Foot commanded by Lt-Colonel William Case, 150 of the 13th Native Infantry under Major Bruere, 60 men of the 48th Native Infantry under Colonel Palmer and 29 men of the 71st Native Infantry, a Sikh regiment, commanded by Lieutenant Birch. There were 84 sabres of the Oudh Irregular Cavalry, a Sikh regiment, under Captains Forbes and Hardinge and 36 sabres of Radcliffe's European Volunteers. In overall command (in theory) was Colonel John Inglis of the 32nd, but he was accompanied by Sir Henry Lawrence, Chief Commissioner of Oudh, recently appointed a Brigadier-General, an old time soldier with vast political and diplomatic experience and considered one of the most astute men in India – wiry, small, bearded, gaunt, made older than his 51 years through hard work and sickness.

By eleven that morning Polehampton was out on the verandah straining his ears for the expected gunfire. He had heard nothing when suddenly the sound of horses galloping hard and disturbed voices reached him. He rushed up to the Residency's roof and looked around; down below he saw to his horror a wounded officer being assisted off a horse covered in foam by two Sikh soldiers. Henry rushed back down the stairs to see if he could help. The injured man was Lieutenant C.W. Campbell of the Volunteer Cavalry. He was shot through the left thigh and looked exhausted. To his dismay Polehampton now learned that the Chinhat affair had gone badly; the troops had been completely beaten by the rebels, many in the British force had been killed and the remainder were now scurrying back towards the Residency. Within the next few minutes Captain James of the commissariat arrived, shot through the knee-joint,[3] Thompson of the 32nd, mortally wounded, and worst of all, a poor artilleryman bleeding profusely from the stumps of both hands that had been blown off.

Other wretches began arriving, most gasping for water, some lying lifeless on artillery wagons or the limbers of guns. By noon a bloody and shocked little army had stumbled into the Residency lines. The news was quite dreadful; 5 guns had been lost apart from the mighty howitzer. Some 118 European officers and men were killed, 182 native troops killed and missing, while 54 Europeans and 11 natives had returned wounded. A dejected Lawrence was left with only 1,720 men to man a two thousand yard perimeter. "My God, my God," he was heard to exclaim over and over, "and I brought them to this!"

How had it all gone so wrong? Lawrence's modest force – representing one-third of the garrison – had set off in fair spirits, though there were some grumbles from the ranks of the 32nd as the men had not had time to eat a breakfast and soldiers do not like marching on empty stomachs. They were also heading directly towards a rising sun. The soldiers plodded along until they were four and a half miles along the Chinhat road. Ahead of them they thought were about 5,000 rebels who were expected to turn tail at the sight of their opponents, especially one of Her Majesty's line regiments. Near a small bridge over the Kokrail stream Lawrence halted his men in order that they might get some rest and organize a meal. He rode on a further quarter of a mile with some of his staff and a cavalry escort to a patch of rising ground amid a clump of tall trees. Here the brigadier spoke with some native travellers who had come from the direction of Chinhat. These men insisted they had seen no rebel army. In retrospect, this was a lie and it is likely they had been sent on ahead by the wily rebel commander, Burkut Ahmad, to mislead the British. The lie effectively sealed the fate of Lawrence and his soldiers because Sir Henry was convinced that the enemy did not intend to advance and were probably just a reconnoitring party. Minutes earlier he had sent his D.A.A.G., Captain T. F. Wilson, galloping back to the column to tell Inglis and Case that he was not proceeding any further and intended to return to Lucknow, but now, spurred on "by the ardour of the younger members of his staff", according to one of his A.D.C.'s Captain Birch, the general decided to advance.

Neither Inglis, Case or Wilson were consulted about this momentous decision. Birch rode back to ask the former officer if the troops could press on? Inglis felt he could hardly say no to his superior and so replied, "Of course they could if ordered." So it was that the column hastily re-assembled without the troops taking refreshment of any kind. Colonel Case and one of the 32nd's regimental surgeons protested; the men were emphatically unfit for action and the two officers felt that Inglis, not always the wisest of men, ought plainly to have told Lawrence the same. Birch later noted: "The elephants were up with commissariat stores, and it would have been easy to give them their breakfast; but this useful opportunity was lost, and the force advanced with empty stomachs under a burning sun." In her memoirs Julia Inglis suggested that Lawrence had assumed the troops had been given some food, (but we only have her word for this, and she wasn't there).[4]

The column began trudging along a raised embankment of loose sand. This slowed down the steps of the men while the sun rose inexorably higher in the sky. One and half miles further on, the soldiers approached the village of Ismailgunge, which lay off the road to their left. Skirmishers thrown out were soon under sporadic musketry fire from some of the houses. The British vedettes retired and the 8-inch howitzer commanded by Lieutenant Bonham and christened the "Turk" by the men, was ordered forward. While this was happening enemy roundshots started to be lobbed into the column and an artillery driver had his head taken clean off by one incoming cannon ball. Several of the dooly-bearers (stretcher and ambulance men) were also killed.

Pressing on, the British saw ahead of them the village of Chinhat lying by the banks of a very extensive shallow lake. Lined up in battle array in front of the village was an imposing sight; line upon line of native soldiers, cavalry and guns, armaments gleaming, uniforms and shakos all parade ground correct. The size of this force has been the subject of some debate. One observer wrote that it was "not four or five thousand, as the spies had reported, but numbering at least fifteen or sixteen thousand men, with not merely two batteries of field pieces, but six or seven consisting of more than thirty-six cannon of various calibre."[5] Private Henry Metcalfe of the 32nd put the number of rebels at "nearer 10,000". These figures all seem to be exaggerated; Lieutenant Bonham later noted: "I feel quite sure they had nothing like 36 guns. I put the number at 13....This is the number given me by the Subahdar of my battery, who was a prisoner with the mutineers during the action, and it is, I believe, quite correct."[6] Martin Gubbins, one of the civil commissioners of Oudh (but not present at Chinhat) concluded the enemy had twelve 9-pounder guns and some lighter native guns. He also ascertained that the enemy consisted of the 2nd, 3rd, 5th, 6th, 8th and 9th Oudh Irregular Infantry supported by cavalry from the 15th Irregulars at Seetapore and the three Oudh local regiments of horse – Daly's, Gall's and Hardinge's – with some police troopers. The remaining mutineers were from the 22nd Native Infantry and the 1st and 2nd Police Regiments. Gubbins reckoned the infantry at 5,500 men with 800 cavalry and 160 artillerymen. In command were two men about to give the British a nasty lesson in generalship; Khan Ali Khan, a rich landowner, had helped assemble the 9th O.I.I. and 2nd M.P. from Seetapore, though probably the genius on the field that day was *Ressaldar* (troop cavalry commander) Burkut Ahmad of the 15th Irregulars.

With cannon balls falling amongst them, the British cavalry swiftly deployed. The "Turk", with Lieutenant Bonham sitting on top, was left in the middle of the road. Lieutenant Cunliffe moved his 4 guns of No 1 Horse Light Field Battery (the "European" guns) to the right slightly in advance of the howitzer. The 32nd at the same time took up positions on the left between Ismailgunge and the road while the native infantry moved towards the scattered houses of a small hamlet on the right.

At first all seemed to be going well for the British. "'Turk' returned the enemy's fire with effect, and the field-pieces played vigorously. The centre of the enemy was seen to give way; the day seemed ours." Captain Wilson galloped up to the gunners urging them on with shouts of "That is it! There they go! Keep it up!"

It was all a feint to draw the British on as the wily rebel commander extended his men around the British flanks. Soon puffs of smoke showed that the rebels were approaching Ismailgunge, literally leaping from tree to tree. The Oudh Field Batteries were ordered to stem them. Now it was that the native gunners turned traitor; they overturned their guns into the ditches by the embankment, cut the traces of their horses and abandoned them. Sir Henry Lawrence with drawn sword tried to remonstrate with some of them, but to no avail. Captain Wilson managed to spike two of the guns using a bayonet before he had to make a hasty retreat.

The rebels were steadily advancing. "They came on in quarter-distance columns," wrote an awed observer, "their standards waving in their faces and everything performed as steadily as possible. A field day on parade could not have been better."[7]

Bringing his cavalry forward, Lawrence ordered them to charge. Captain Radcliffe's volunteers obeyed immediately, pushing back for a time the enemy infantry, but most of the Sikhs of the Oudh Irregular Cavalry turned their horses and fled in the direction of Lucknow. Her Majesty's 32nd were now commanded to take Ismailgunge at the bayonet's point. Immediately they ran into a fierce hail of lead. Lt-Colonel Case, out in front, was first to fall. Well-liked by the men, William Case was in the words of one of them, "as nice an officer and as good as ever drew a sword."[8] Captain Steevens assumed command and ordered his men on, but they refused. Soon the 32nd were slipping back, at first in ones and twos, then dozens, before a general rout. Despite the entreaties of their officers nothing would stop them.

With almost textbook precision the rebel gunners now unlimbered their guns and swept the British ranks with grape and canister shot while the swarming skirmishers pressing on the flanks rained bullets on their stricken foes. Sir Henry did all he could to rally his soldiers but he was out-gunned, out-flanked, out-numbered and, frankly, out-generalled. A retreat was ordered; Captain Bassano refusing to do so at first, found Case and offered to carry him. Choking in his own blood, knowing his wound was fatal, Case gave his last order, "Leave me sir and rejoin your company!" Poor Case! His young wife, Adelaide was waiting anxiously for him back at the Residency. Just eleven weeks earlier he had written to his mother: "How I have always prayed for coolness and presence of mind under whatever circumstances of difficulty and danger."[9] He saw little of that in his dying moments as his men deserted the field. A few remembered their last sight of him – clutching his sword, his dead eyes wide open. Bassano shortly afterwards shot himself through the foot. He refused the offer of a ride and hobbled back to the Residency with his men.

Retreats under fire are always nightmare experiences; parched with thirst, worn out by exertion and fatigue, men fell down to get a little rest and were killed by the rebel cavalry. Others collapsed with heat apoplexy. Dying men hauled themselves onto the gun limbers and waggons. Private Metcalfe recalled the sights:

I saw one fine young fellow who was wounded in the leg. He coolly sat down on the road, faced the enemy, and all we could do or say to him would not urge him to try and come with us. He said – "No, you fellows push on, leave me here to blaze away at these fellows. I shan't last long and I never would be able to reach Lucknow. He remained, and was very soon disposed of, poor fellow… A bonny young man, by name Jones, was being conveyed back on a gun carriage after being wounded.

He saw his brother struck down with a bullet from the enemy, and without the least warning, he jumped off the limber on which he was riding and joined his brother to be killed with him. Another man, maddened by the heat and fatigue, charged single-handed into the ranks of the enemy and was soon put to rest.[10]

In all the 32nd left 4 officers and 111 of its men on the battlefield. Besides Case and Lieutenants Brackenbury and Thomson, one of the dead was Captain Steevens who had tried to rally the men; he was shot through the leg and limped along for 5 miles, gradually slipping further and further behind, until he was overtaken by the enemy cavalry. Some of the sepoys stayed loyal; men of the 13th B.N.I. helped to carry wounded British soldiers to the gun carriages, even leaving their own wounded comrades on the ground to do so. Among the British wounded was Major Bruere, though the strangest invalid was Lieutenant Farquhar, 7th Light Cavalry, who was shot in the cheek. The doctors probing his fractured jaw could not understand what had happened to the bullet until it was found that in all the excitement Farquhar had swallowed it. Ten days later it exited his body in the usual manner. He later said, "The ball, on going through my jaw, must have taken the direction of my throat and I must then have swallowed it, together with the blood collecting in my mouth. The ball, when it struck me, must have been getting spent. Otherwise it would probably have gone through both jaws, and come out on the opposite side."[11]

In the midst of all this action Lieutenant Bonham was in a pickle: he wanted to get off the "Turk" but the terrified elephant bolted at the sound of the firing and had to be brought back; then the howitzer's wheels got stuck in the mud and the big gun refused to budge; without warning the elephant suddenly moved forward and snapped the gun's limber rope; finally, to top it all, the gallant young officer was knocked over by a bullet in his side and had to be carried to the rear by some of his gunners. With the enemy fast approaching Sergeant Suttle had no time to spike the gun; he broke off the priming wire in the touch-hole, hoped for the best and made a fast getaway.

One of the most courageous acts in the battle happened when one of the 9-pounders was saved by a man called Johnson, a former trooper in the 9th Lancers (he appears to have joined the 32nd but was serving that day with the volunteer cavalry). He galloped up to an abandoned gun, jumped off his horse, climbed onto the lead battery horse and rode the 9-pounder, its carriage and horses all the way to Lucknow.[12]

Despite being beaten by the mutineers and in retreat, one Victoria Cross – the first of many for Lucknow – was awarded for an action that day; it was won by Lieutenant William Cubbitt of the 13th B.N.I. who managed to save the lives of three soldiers of HM 32nd by seating one man behind him on his horse while two others hung on to his stirrups. This meant, of course, that Cubbitt had to travel very slowly. In some respects it seems an odd award since, despite his bravery, several others on horseback tried to help wounded or exhausted men, including some of the volunteer cavalry.[13]

When the mass of retreating British had reached the Kokrail bridge the rebel cavalry were seen gathering in the far rear to the left of them. Then in a loud voice Captain Radcliffe bellowed "Three's right! Trot!" His small squadron of less than 40 sabres gathered speed. Two light guns blazed away at them, luckily doing no damage, as Radcliffe bellowed, "Charge!" Trumpets blared forth and the British volunteers thundered forward on their horses. The shock of the charge was too much for the rebel cavalry who turned and fled. Radcliffe lost two men but was able to cut down some of the skirmishers before re-joining to some applause the slowly moving British troops.

By now Lawrence had a new problem – his ammunition was running low. He ordered his guns halted, their portfires lit. The rebels did not fancy meeting such a hail of shot and the column stumbled into Lucknow. The water-carriers had mostly vanished but native women, seeing the distress of the British troops and sepoys, ran across to pour water or milk down parched throats. It was one of the acts of kindness that restored a common humanity in this brutal war. When the iron bridge was reached, Captain Edmonstone of the 32nd was ordered to hold it with 50 men so that the mass could get across. Meanwhile the British guns in the Macchi Bhowan stopped the enemy from crossing at the stone bridge. The insurgents were not however cowed; they simply planted their guns by the banks of the Gumti, "and with astonishing rapidity and well-directed aim" lobbed shot and shell into the Residency compound. Later that afternoon they crossed the river below the two bridges, seized houses and key positions in the city, swiftly loopholed them and began musketry fire on the British entrenchments.

Lawrence had galloped back to the Residency to take charge of things. The place was one of chaos. Michael Joyce expressed it best:

Barricades were being thrown up, walls loopholed, guns dragged into position. Clothes and furniture were being thrown about. Men were hastening to their posts, women seeking out the safest places for their families, children crying and all the Europeans shouting for their Indian servants, many of whom had run away. The hospital was full of shattered men. They had been taken off the wagons and limbers at the iron bridge and brought the rest of the way on litters. They lay in rows, pale, bloody and groaning, while the surgeons amputated, probed and dressed. Women flocked round fanning the wounded and offering iced water and stuff for bandages; the horrors of war were new to most of them.[14]

Eerily, outside the entrenchments not a living soul was seen for a time; elephants and camels had been hurried away by their masters; a few riderless horses galloped about in terror from the guns; the river boatmen and their craft had vanished. From the upper windows of the Residency the rebels could be glimpsed fording the river downstream. Soon the walls of the native gaol just outside the Baillie Guard gate were covered with the prisoners making their escape by ropes from the windows. Shots began smashing into the masonry of the Residency and surrounding houses.

Then, as if to add insult to injury, the 8-inch howitzer the "Turk", abandoned by the British but captured by the insurgents, now began to lob its large shells into the compound. Terrified women and children screamed and ran for their lives. None of the garrison – soldiers, sepoys, male civilians, women, children and native servants – nor even their well-organised and defiant foes could have guessed the ordeal they were all about to face, but the great siege of Lucknow had just begun.

Maps

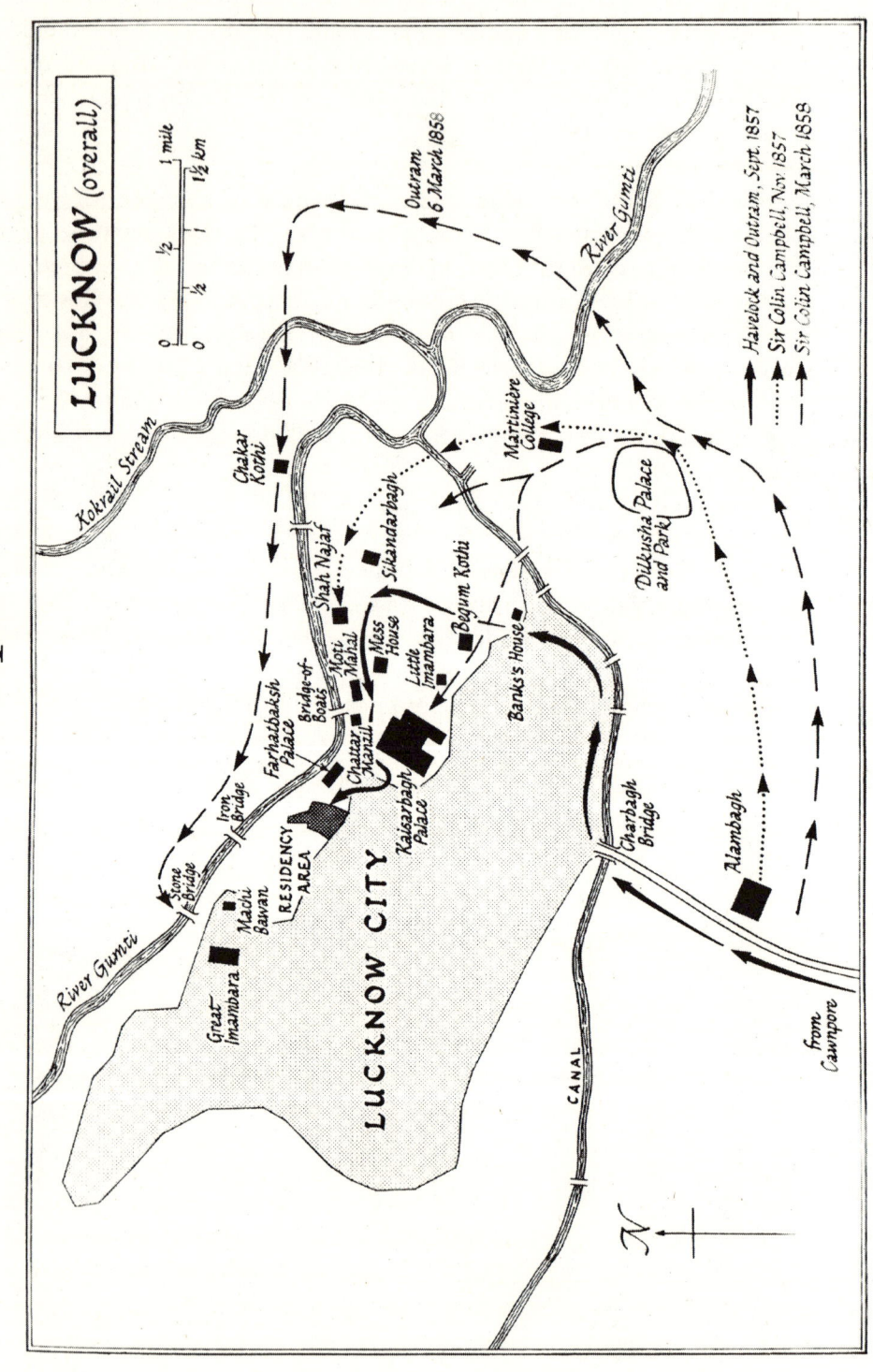

LUCKNOW (overall)

Kokrail Stream

River Gumti

Chakar Kothi

Shah Najaf

Sikandarbagh

Martinière College

Outram
6 March 1858

River Gumti

Dilkusha Palace
and Park

Iron Bridge

Farhatbaksh Palace

Bridge-of-Boats

Moti Mahal

Mess House

Little Imambara

Bagum Kothi

Banks's House

Stone Bridge

Machi Bawan

RESIDENCY AREA

Chattar Manzil

Kaisarbagh Palace

Great Imambara

LUCKNOW CITY

Charbagh Bridge

Alambagh

CANAL

from Cawnpore

Havelock and Outram, Sept. 1857
Sir Colin Campbell, Nov. 1857
Sir Colin Campbell, March 1858

N

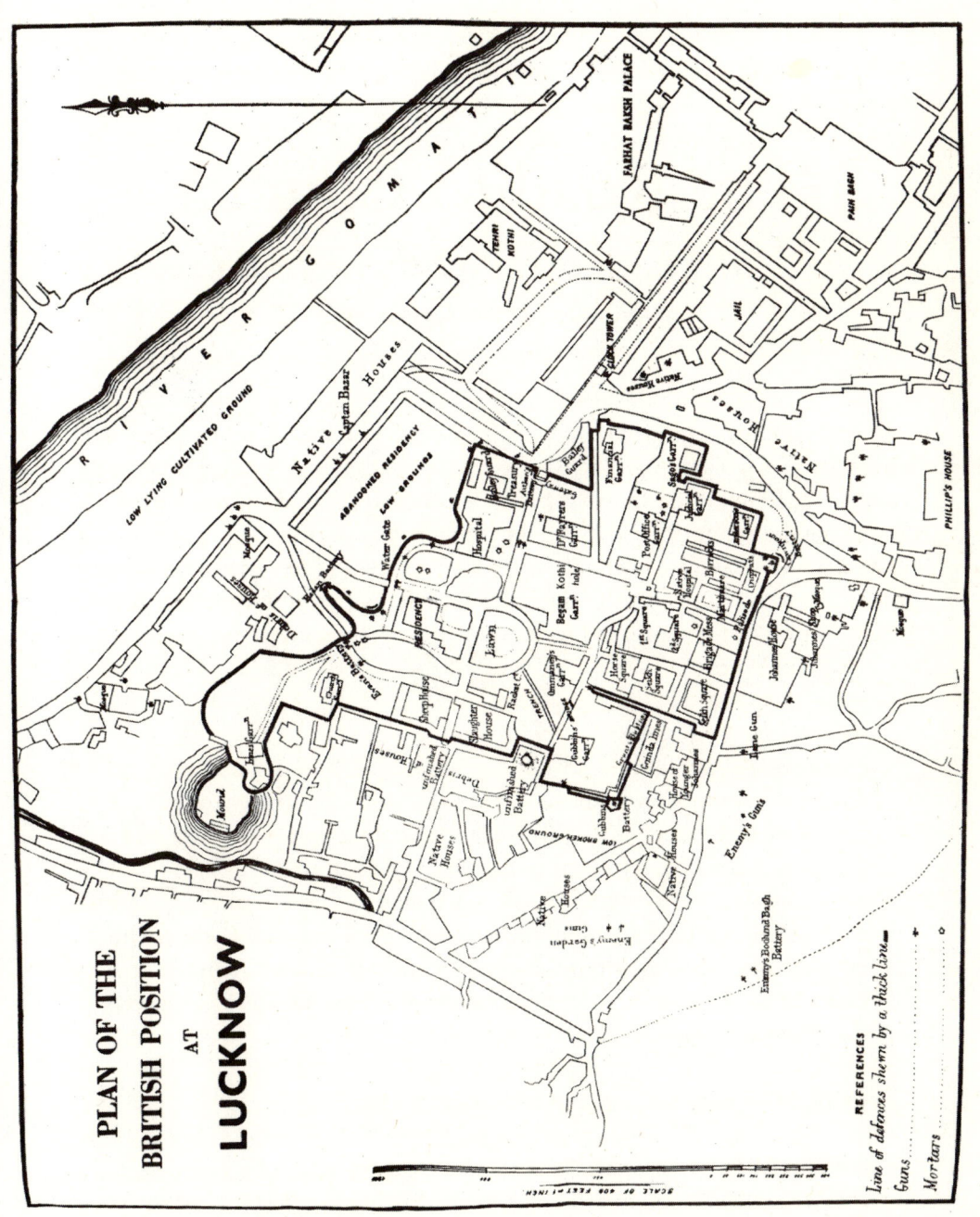

PLAN OF THE
BRITISH POSITION
AT
LUCKNOW

1

The Road to Chinhat

Lucknow and Northern India,
1856 to 30th June 1857

To trace a path leading to the British disaster at Chinhat let us first track back to 1843. That year, Henry Lawrence, then in his prime but already considered one of the sharpest brains in the E.I.C.'s administration, hard-working, conscientious and intelligent to a remarkable degree, penned a scenario affecting the Bengal Army that 14 years later made uncannily prescient reading. Drawing back the curtains of complacency he began by pointing out the precarious state of British rule after the disasters of the Afghan War:

> Dissensions among our enemies have raised us from the position of commercial factors to be lords over emperors. Without courage and discipline we could not thus have prevailed, but even these would have prevailed little had the country been united against us... Our sway is the sword, yet everywhere our military means are insufficient... If stores are ready they may rot before carriage is forthcoming. If there are muskets, there is no ammunition. If there are infantry, there are no muskets for them. In one place we have guns without a man to serve them. In another, we have artillery standing comparatively idle, because the guns have been left behind.

Then Lawrence spelled out the nightmare scenario:

> Is Delhi ... better prepared than Kabul was, should 3,000 men arise tomorrow and seize the town? Let all this happen in Hindustan on 2nd June ... and does any sane man doubt that twenty-four hours would swell the hundreds of rebels into thousands and that if such conduct on our part lasted for a week, every ploughshare in the Delhi States

would be turned into a sword. And when a sufficient force had been mustered by bringing European regiments from the hills and native troops from every quarter (which could not be effected within a month at the very least) ... should we not then have a more difficult game to play than Clive had at Plassey or Wellington at Assaye? We should then be literally staking our existence at the most inclement season of the year, with the prestige of our name vanished.[1]

Lawrence was of course talking in general terms about a rising of malcontents and not, as it turned out, almost the entire Bengal Army. He also had no specific year in mind, yet oddly enough, when the great uprising came, it was only eight days later than his suggested date.

It was on the last day of 1600 that the Honourable East India Company got its royal charter from Queen Elizabeth I. An emphasis solely on commerce ended in the 18th century as a reaction to French expansionist policy in southern India. While Robert Clive's brilliant victory at Plassey on 23rd June 1757 made the British masters of Bengal, they did not exploit their new power to the full, and it was another 15 years before they began to govern the province themselves. The power of the Moguls, India's previous rulers, was fast waning; various nobles fought amongst themselves. The E.I.C. was able to exploit these weaknesses through a series of military victories and diplomatic guile until by the 1850s they ruled the whole sub-continent, from the gleaming sands of Kerala in the south to the snow-topped Himalayas in the north. By this time there were three presidencies – Madras, Bombay and Bengal – and of this trio Bengal was by far the most important. There were also three presidency armies and of these Bengal was by far the largest. Central government was exercised through a Governor-General and his Council at Calcutta. Despite immense power, the Governor-General was in turn appointed by, and responsible to, a committee, its chairman and 24 directors in faraway London.

The growth of British power across India was, for over a century, a source of much pride. Schoolboys at home could see the red mass of India in their geography books and hear of generals with odd names like Sir Eyre Coote, defeating vast armies of Mahrattas and others with but a handful of stout redcoats. One can loathe imperialism and see the British as the villains in this tale, but that expansion across the sub-continent was a remarkable story and much blood was shed on both sides. Today, revisionist historians such as William Dalrymple denounce Clive, for all his military prowess, as evil incarnate, the worst of the nabobs, for his greed and financial rape of Bengal. Successive British Governor-Generals were a mixed bunch; some, like Wellesley, were decidedly expansionist, though their Indian rivals for power were every bit as wily. Others had a more pacific view of things – wars, after all, cost money, and the East India Company, did not like wasting its revenue. They also felt a growing affinity with Indians, though this well-intentioned rule might appear paternalistic and condescending to 21st-century tastes. By 1857, after a century of expansionist rule by the East India Company, everyone was aware of the gaps in the seams of this creaking old vessel. During the disastrous Afghan War 1838-42 an entire army of 16,000 men and camp followers had been massacred – the worst defeat in British history – a disaster due to the imperial arrogance of a governor-general, and appalling military and political leadership. It was also the first death knell of E.I.C. rule.

The main recruiting ground for the Bengal Army was the Kingdom of Oudh. This fact helps partly to explain why in 1857-58 the centre of rebellion shifted from the ailing and defunct figurehead of a doddery Mogul emperor in Delhi to a state that had very recently been independent and where a combination of factors led to a strong resistance to the *feringhees* (foreigners). Oudh occupied an area of 23,923 square miles (about the size of Belgium), yet had only 18 towns with a population over 10,000. The vast majority of its 10 million or so inhabitants lived in hamlets, some 70,000 of them, communities of mud and brick with thatched roofs, usually with three or four to the square mile, each one surrounded by its own cultivated fields and often sheltered by a glade of peepul or banyan trees, under which the village elders might sit to talk or the children play away from the blazing sun.

While the province in 1857 was one of the most recent jewels in Queen Victoria's imperial crown, its rulers, the Nawabs of Oudh – though they liked to be called Kings – had a long association with the British as friendly allies. Oudh was one of the most fertile regions in northern India, yet it had been termed "a disgrace" by successive Governor-Generals and their advisors. Back in 1801, when Governor-General Lord Wellesley had forced a treaty on its ruler, he had predicted that one day "John Company" (the East India Company), would have to take control of the place. The 1801 treaty gave the British a slice of Oudh and greater control; they demanded that Nawab Sadat Ali agree to rule in a manner "conducive to the prosperity of his subjects". In reality nothing changed. "Successive Nawabs, resisting British advice (which was not always wisely given), ignored or evaded it" wrote the Raj historian, Sir Penderel Moon. He explained: "The majority of the Nawabs were profligate spendthrifts; two of them were avaricious misers; most of them were careless of their people's welfare; and under all of them revenues were collected at the point of the bayonet and were expended, sooner or later, not on works of public utility, but on the pleasures, amusements and foibles of the Nawab and his Court."[2]

In 1847 the destiny of Oudh fell into the hands of two very different young men who were, oddly enough, both to fall from office in1856. Neither of them seemed very likely at first for a station in life that would bring them into conflict; one was a second son and never expected to be a king while the other, a younger son of a Scottish Earl, could easily have had a dull career as a back bencher in the House of Lords.

The latter individual was James Andrew Broun-Ramsay, 10th Earl of Dalhousie (he liked it to be pronounced "Dalhoosie"), 35 years old, a handsome, self-assured and egotistical man of intellectual brilliance and energy, yet with a sensitive skin that could be easily pricked. While at Oxford he had written, with a royal "We", "We certainly are immensely cocky, but then, hang it, we have reason."[3] He had decided quite early on in life never to play "second fiddle" to anyone and on becoming Governor-General this philosophy was soon made plain. His dynamism and vision would extend the British Empire after two wars with the Sikhs of the Punjab, acquiring their kingdom, while a conflict with Burma also led to an enlargement of territory. During nine years at the helm of Indian affairs his administrative reforms included the foundation of a legislative council in Calcutta, a separate provincial government in Bengal and reforms of the Indian Civil Service and the E.I.C. Army. He oversaw the construction of the Ganges Canal, longer than "all the irrigation lines of Lombardy and Egypt", and planned post offices by their hundreds all across India, so that "A Scotch recruit who joins his regiment at Peshawar may write to his mother at John O'Groats House and may send it for sixpence."[4] He pushed ahead the electric telegraph, one of the wonders of the age, so that at a click Calcutta was connected to Bombay and Delhi with Madras. Railways, that other wonder of early Victorian Britain, now began their march across India and Dalhousie was delighted to see the first section of the Bombay line opened in 1853. In short, with dynamism and flair he was saying to all the traders and industrialists in mid-19th century Europe that the Indian sub-continent was now open for business.

Dalhousie had many supporters in his lifetime (and some critics), but his legacy today is tarnished by his annexations of native states – seven were said to have "lapsed" during his time. The Doctrine of Lapse related to his lordship's refusal to accept the rights of native princes to pass their title, lands or wealth to an adopted heir. The past ways of the easy-going Moguls did not suit Dalhousie; he wanted government done according to international law as defined by treaty. Two states where Dalhousie challenged the wishes of the rulers were Hyderabad and Jhansi.

It was not until his final two months in India before sailing home a sick man that Dalhousie turned the full glare of his formidable intellect on Oudh. Here the ruler was a man in his thirties called Wajid Ali Shah, an effeminate, sensitive and aesthetic soul whose greatest delight was writing poetry (some of it very good indeed). The King was a teetotaller, an easy-going Shia Moslem with a court of many Sunnis, though he prayed five times a day. He was just 27 years old when he had ascended the throne and the novelty of kingship made him try for the first three months to be a diligent ruler, working at his desk in daytime, while on evening drives two splendidly dressed Turkish sepoys rode ahead with a silver casket into which complainants were invited to place their petitions, which Wajid Ali, like the good monarch he wanted to be, read later.

Very quickly the King lost interest. Ennui had always been his problem. While it was true that he enjoyed donning a tight-fitting military uniform and riding out to review his soldiers at drill, the King also loved dressing up for erotic ballets (*rahas*) and playing the leading part of the star-crossed hero to his dancing-girls (*gopis*) as they all swayed to the intoxicating strains of the sitar. After those first three months rule Wajid Ali gave himself over entirely to music, dancing, writing poetry, philandering and his imagined illnesses. In the words of historian John Pemble: "State affairs were abandoned to the new minister, Ali Naqi Khan, while the King passed his time secluded with minstrels, poets and paramours, on whom he bestowed lavish gifts and sinecure appointments."[5] Insulated by a doting mother and a bunch of flattering sycophants, a court full of singers, artists, dancers, eunuchs and pimps, the King was allowed to do anything his heart desired, such as spending a fortune on his private zoo, or walking through the streets of Lucknow banging a big drum. He later admitted that the animals gave him more pleasure than his children. He had 60 wives and concubines and 72 children, evidence of another of Wajid Ali's hobbies.

For several years Dalhousie watched Wajid Ali and his libertine court with mounting horror. He told himself that it was "ambitious and hypocritical humbug" to think of annexing Oudh, yet something had to be done to "the wretch of Lucknow" whose regime was one of "disorder, self-indulgence, sensuality, stagnation". In 1847 the retiring Governor-General, Lord Hardinge, had given the Oudh King two years to clean up his act or incur the risk of forcing the British to assume the government of his country. Wajid Ali played on. He was probably emboldened by the thought that for decades the British had threatened his predecessors with the same words and done very little. Enter Lord Dalhousie.

The impetus to British interference in Oudh came in the form of a report Dalhousie received from William Sleeman, the British Resident (political officer and advisor to the King) at Lucknow. Sleeman remains best known for his work in the 1840s suppressing the notorious cult of Thugs (*thagi*) who had, up until that time and for hundreds of years, strangled thousands of Indian travellers each year. Under Sleeman's direction these 'religious' murderers (some had killed more than 900 persons), were imprisoned or executed. He had spent 40 of his 61 years in India, spoke several native languages and dialects and especially admired village communities. Indian rulers he detested as parasites feeding off the rural classes. Sleeman was convinced that ordinary Indians supported British rule because "they never had a government so good as ours, and that they could never hope for another so good, were ours removed."[6] The Lucknow court Sleeman lambasted: "Such a scene of intrigue, corruption, depravity and neglect of duty and abuse of authority I have never before been placed in and I hope never again to undergo."[7]

It has been suggested that Sleeman was more deluded than prejudiced. He certainly was an odd, volatile man, highly paranoid, who convinced himself that his assistant was plotting to get rid of him and that he had survived three assassination attempts in Lucknow during his five years there. Contemporaries noticed that he was quirky, puritanical, prone to exaggeration and bias. One writer noted how Sleeman's "descriptions of the misgovernment and sufferings of the country itself were laid on with somewhat pronounced exaggeration of colouring." Sleeman was quite content to reproduce bazaar gossip on the Lucknow court as fact.[8]

One thing the Resident did not advise was the annexation of Oudh; he adopted an approach suggested by Sir Henry Lawrence a few years earlier, namely that the British should assume the country's administration as trustees of the royal family and people.

When Sleeman left India on sick leave in 1854, Dalhousie appointed James Outram – a far more likable man – as Resident, and ordered him to report on the kingdom. During this period a scurrilous book was published in England called *The Private Life Of An Eastern King*. This "journalistic concatenation" vicariously thrilled the mid-Victorians, especially the evangelicals, with its racy record of the lavish excesses and lurid eccentricities of the Oudh king and his court. Outram meantime, a man who had many sympathies with Wajid Ali, was given two months to prepare his report, which had to rely to a great extent on Sleeman's evidence. Despite many years living among Indians, Outram found that the situation in Oudh left him in a quandary; he had famously denounced the British annexation of Sind a decade earlier, he was no supporter of expansion just for the sake of it, yet this brightest of political agents found that Oudh's affairs were "in the same state, if not worse, in which Colonel Sleeman from time to time described them to be." The new Resident reported that the King devoted himself solely to "debauchery, dissipation and low pursuits".[9] Once Outram's report was made public there were many in the British Parliament as well as the East India Company who now thought that Britain had a moral duty to take over Oudh, by force if necessary.

Governor-General Dalhousie had always tried to cover his actions in legal niceties, but during his last days in office he decided to push for a new treaty with Oudh's ruler. He demanded that Wajid Ali give over the administration of his country to the British in return for a liberal pension, but he added a nasty sting in the tail – an ultimatum that gave the King three days to comply or Oudh would be taken by force and Wajid Ali lose all his rights and privileges. Before setting off to Lucknow to present this treaty, Outram held talks with the Governor-General. Outram thought a war was very likely. Dalhousie disagreed. The Resident "croaks a good deal" he wrote in a letter and held to the view that "my own motives are pure." Outram was piously told that "the British Government would be guilty in the sight of God and man if it were any longer to aid in sustaining by its countenance an administration fraught with suffering to millions."[10]

Outram arrived back in Lucknow on 30th January 1856 and presented his new treaty. Aghast at its contents, the King's Minister and the Queen Mother read it with what must have been mounting horror and both stalled for time. Outram even tried to bribe the Queen Mother but with no luck. On 4th February came the showdown with the King. A consummate actor, Wajid Ali laid on a remarkable display of theatrics; he had disarmed all his soldiers and taken his big guns off their carriages as if to advertise his helplessness. After reading the treaty attentively, he replied:

> Treaties are necessary between equals only: who am I, now that the British Government should enter into treaties with? For a hundred years this dynasty has flourished in Oudh. It has received the favour, the support and protection of the British Government. It has ever attempted faithfully and fully to perform its duties to the British, who are able to make and unmake, to promote and degrade. It has merely to issue its commands to ensure their fulfilment; not the slightest attempt will be made to oppose the wishes of the British Government; myself and my subjects are its servants.[11]

Bursting into tears, the King took off his turban and presented it to the embarrassed Resident.

Yet still Wajid Ali refused to sign the treaty; thus at noon on 7th February 1856, on the expiration of the ultimatum, the British became the masters of Oudh. It was, as Pemble says, "*de jure,* as well as *de facto* an act of aggression". Dalhousie, on hearing the news, wrote on the same day: "So our gracious Queen has 5,000,000 more subjects and £1,300,000 more revenue than yesterday."[12] Twenty-six days later he sailed for England.

Historians have not looked kindly on Dalhousie's annexation of Oudh – "a scurvy tale" is a comment repeated many times. The problem has always been, as one woman pointed out in 1856, that "the humanity of the act was soiled by the profit we derived from it ... the good of the people ... was nothing more than pretext and sham."[13]

Wajid Ali went into a rich exile at Calcutta where he plotted to regain his throne and wrote an erotic autobiography of sorts (now held in the library at Windsor Castle). His love of the arts and animals continued unabated. This artistic lifestyle led one British official to write sniffily how Wajifd Ali, "emasculated to the point of childishness ... turned to the more harmless delights of dancing and drumming, and drawing, and manufacturing small rhymes."[14] At Lucknow, 7,000 animals from the royal menagerie were sold in a single day and a vast array of palace servants, from peacock fan bearers to dancing girls, bookbinders to royal boatmen, suddenly became jobless. The people of Oudh generally missed their King for the simple reason that, despite all his faults, he had been one of them; many of the British who followed had good intentions but they failed to grasp this simple fact. One dirge (*nana*) at the time went:

Noble and peasant all wept together
and all the world wept and wailed
Alas! The chief has bidden adieu to
his country and gone abroad.[15]

One contributor to a Lucknow newspaper wrote rather beautifully: "Lucknow was once a garden that saw the autumn. Whoever lived there was like a nightingale in a garden of flowers... The angels used to dance in ecstasy. These days it appears deserted, reminding all that this world is a place of warning."[16]

British officials now descended on Oudh to re-assess the revenue and run the new administration. Pemble writes:

Civilian and military officers poured into Lucknow, where they lived temporarily in the Residency while being briefed. Then they were packed off in palanquins to their Districts, where they often had to live under canvas. Many had to leave their wives and families in the capital for lack of suitable accommodation in the out-stations. Once arrived, they plunged into the work of fixing District boundaries, organising courts, jails and police, planning essential roads and postal communications and gathering the land revenue.[17]

Top of the British hit-list were the *taluqdars* (landowners) who had exploited their own peasantry for generations. Besides making thousands of royal servants penniless, the British quickly demanded the disbandment of the royal army as well as those private armies used by the taluqdars. Some 60,000 men lost their jobs and the British only had room for 15,000 of them in the newly raised Oudh Irregular Force and the Military Police. So 45,000 sullen men sat in the bazaars frittering away (in the case of government soldiers) a small gratuity, or they took themselves off to their villages where their voices helped to swell a growing rumble of discontent.

Then there were the sepoys of the East India Company's Bengal Army, almost all of them recruited from either high-caste Rajput peasants – the traditional warrior class of Northern India – or Bhumihars, the military wing of the priestly caste of Brahmins, and almost all of these men came from Oudh (with a few extra from Bihar and the Doab). In 1857 the strength of the Bengal Army was 135,767 soldiers (representing about 60 per cent of the total East India Company Army), with 74 Bengal Native Infantry regiments, 18 regiments of Irregular Cavalry and 10 of Light Cavalry. There were also 4 horse troops, 18 foot companies of Bengal Artillery and 12 companies of sappers and miners.

For many years the bond between the officers, especially colonels, who ruled their regiments almost paternalistically, and their sepoys had been eroding. Discipline had never been more lax and officers often had to flatter and coax their men to maintain influence. Colonel Henry Durand, told a committee in 1858 how bad things had become:

He could neither flog for insubordination, nor dismiss for general bad character; he could not give extra duty to the negligent soldier, nor refuse furlough to an habitual offender; he could not send a non-commissioned officer to drill, nor reduce without formal trial, and he was even prohibited from confining one before trial, and required to put him simply under arrest. When to all these restrictions is added the facility of direct appeal through the post office of any sepoy to the commander-in-chief, and even the reception of anonymous petitions, we can understand how such a system in course of years undermined the legitimate influence of commanding officers, and gradually reduced them to the ciphers which they were found as in 1857.[18]

Yet the sepoys grumbled continually; their basic pay of seven rupees a month had not changed for many years and was less than half that earned by a private soldier in a Queen's regiment. A sepoy was expected to pay for all his own uniform and food, as well as his transport on the march. All native officers whatever their rank were considered subordinate to all British officers, even the most yellow of "griffins" (newcomers to India), and NCOs. Oudh sepoys were no longer able to submit petitions for legal redress via the Resident, they worried about their diminishing pensions and a new order for them to serve overseas. "I used to be a great man when I went home," bemoaned one Oudh soldier speaking for many, "The rest of the village rose when I approached. Now the lowest puff their pipes in my face."[19]

Some historians dispute whether the memoirs of Sepoy Sita Ram Pande, first published in 1873 in English, are genuine or not. Most think they are. Here is what he said of the causes of the mutiny:

> It is my humble opinion that this seizing of Oudh filled the minds of the sepoys with much distrust and led them to plot against the Government. Agents of the Nawab of Oudh, and also the King of Delhi, were sent all over India to discover the temper of the army. They worked upon the feelings of the sepoys, telling how treacherously the foreigners had behaved towards their king. They invented ten thousand lies and promises to persuade the soldiers to mutiny and turn against their masters, the English, with the object of restoring the Emperor of Delhi to the throne.[20]

In Oudh itself, the revenue collectors set to work and many of them were determined to break the power of the taluqdars; as a fairly dramatic start they demanded the wholesale destruction of most of the landowners' traditional mud forts, then hit them with high revenue assessments. The taluqdars soon came to the conclusion that the British were bent on destroying their power and prestige. Some great landowners were gaoled for not paying their revenue assessments, a terrible humiliation, while others such as Raja Man Singh of Mahdauna fled to Calcutta; on his return he found most of his villages had been confiscated for default. Some of the British commissioners were zealous in the extreme; Colonel Philip Goldney of the Fyzabad Division soon acquired a reputation as a bigot and, as Pemble notes: "A taluqdar was to Goldney as a red rag to a bull."

As 1856 drew to a close, the taluqdars had lost 10,000 villages out of some 23,500 prior to annexation. The intentions of such men as Goldney were, of course, good; it was widely thought that by sweeping away the remnants of feudalism and abolishing the crippling taxes the taluqdars had imposed, a contented peasantry would be grateful to the British for a new and carefully regulated land revenue system. They were wrong. A young I.C.S. man, William Edwards, hit the nail on the head when he outlined the bond between landowner and peasant farmer: "Although the old families are being displaced fast, we cannot destroy the memory of the past, or dissolve the ancient connection between them and their people ... in the event of an insurrection occurring, we should find this great and influential body, through whom we can alone hope to keep under and control the masses, ranged against us on the side of the enemy, with their hereditary followers and retainers rallying around them, in spite of our attempts to separate their interest."[21]

The annexation witnessed a rise in the price of essential commodities in Oudh, giving further cause for discontent; the departure of the royal court, for example, affected the demand for certain goods and the cotton weavers of Oudh were especially affected. While some old taxes were abolished, these reforms brought no great joy to the man in the street as taxes were now applied to opium, stamps, petitions, food, houses and ferries. Many of the poor in Oudh used opium and this tax in particular led to murders and suicides by those desperate for the drug.

Self-styled religious leaders and zealots were not slow to denounce the British takeover; Maulvi Ahmadullah arrived in Lucknow that November and called for jihad. Another firebrand, Qadir Ali Shah, posed as a saint and raised a force of 12,000 men. He demanded that his followers rise against the British on 11th September 1856, but his plot was foiled.

In the countryside as well as the bazaars there was more and more talk that people might soon have to fight in defence of their religion. The British were not unaware of this but tended to be dismissive of the dangers, though men such as Martin Gubbins, financial commissioner of Oudh, considered the perceived threat to caste and religion was the chief cause of the great uprising. His view is echoed by many other soldiers at the time; one of these was a Bengal officer, S. Dewe White, himself a zealous preacher, who declared that loss of caste and forcible conversion to Christianity was "the ostensible and immediate cause" of the uprising. It was in his opinion an "absurd idea" cunningly engineered by Moslems "who religiously and politically regard us with far more dislike than the Hindoos."[22] Many officers in E.I.C. regiments, such as Surgeon James Thornton of the 67th B.N.I., agreed with him.

In the early days of "John Company", missionaries had been positively discouraged as part of official policy, but a change can be discerned from the 1830s onwards as the Evangelical Movement, with its call to go out and take the word of God to the heathen, grew in power under the intellectual domination of such men as John Stuart Mill and Thomas Babington Macaulay. In his *Minute on Education*, written while law member of the new legislative council, Macaulay declared that the British had to strive to create "persons Indian in colour and blood, but English in tastes, in opinions, in morals, in intellect".[23] The missionaries met with a mixture of indifference and disgust from most Indians. Generally speaking, Indian Army officers did not like missionaries either (as distinct from a good Anglican chaplain who preached a mercifully short sermon to the regiment on a Sunday and did good deeds the rest of the week). Though a Queen's officer, Captain H. A. Ouvry, spoke for many when he declared that clergymen in India were either lazy or narrow-minded fanatics, while the missionaries were all of two sorts – rogues or fools. A few army officers held proselytising views; one such was Colonel Henry Wheler of the 34th B.N.I. who was an unapologetic evangelical Christian. Despite being reprimanded by the new Governor-General, Lord Canning, Wheler declared that in 20 years he had tried to spread the word of God among "sepoys of my own regiment, as also other regiments at this and other stations where I have been quartered… As to the question of whether I have endeavoured to convert sepoys and others to Christianity, I would humbly reply that has been my object."[24] Soldiers such as Wheler, despite good intentions, did irreparable harm to the relationship between sepoys and their British officers, seeming to prove that the *feringhees* had a hidden agenda to turn Hindus and Moslems into Christians. Officialdom did not help; even Lord Canning gave donations to the Calcutta Bible Society, the Baptist Serampore College and the Free Church Mission.

Into the glare of Oudh affairs as they simmered with discontent that spring of 1857 stepped a new Resident. He was 50-year-old Sir Henry Lawrence, a man described by one who knew him as "Above the middle height, on a spare, gaunt frame, and a worn face bearing upon it the traces of mental toil and bodily suffering, he impressed you, at first sight, rather with a sense of masculine energy and resolution."[25] Another Victorian wrote: "His eyes, overhung by massive, craggy brows, looked out with an expression in which melancholy was strangely blended with humour: his thin wasted cheeks were scored down their whole length by deep lines; and a long ragged beard added to his look of age."[26] Sons of a tough Irish colonel, Henry was one of a bevy of brothers who stamped their mark on the British Raj (younger brother John would rule the Punjab during the great uprising and older brother George would be political agent in Rajputana). At school he was quiet and reserved, not the most gifted scholar, but a hard-working and religious student with obvious signs of integrity. A fellow pupil at the E.I.C.'s training establishment at Addiscombe, Surrey, noted how "Anything mean or shabby always aroused his ire."

Until well into his thirties Lawrence was a dull, conscientious soldier until he fell in love with and married Honoria Marshall, his cousin, daughter of an army chaplain. She helped develop a warmth previously hidden in her husband. He served with distinction in the 1st Afghan War, moving into political work, and in 1847, on the close of the 1st Anglo-Sikh War, Henry was made Resident at Lahore. From here he sent out his "young men", a loyal band of trusted young lieutenants to bring law and order along the marches of the north-west frontier with Afghanistan. His reputation grew as his young men made names for themselves. A workaholic, Lawrence still had a happy family life and found time to father two sons and two daughters (there is a wonderful drawing of him from this period sitting in a wooden tub washing his hair, with a naked toddler nestling on his shoulders). Knighted, he became involved in a bitter feud with his brother John, an associate on the Punjab Board of Administration. Despite some pleasant years as Resident in Nepal and Rajputana, Sir Henry also had a spat with Dalhousie, who thought he was too big for his boots. By the start of 1857, his health wrecked and still grieving over the loss of Honoria who had died three years previously, Lawrence was planning to return to England when Lord Canning asked him to go to Oudh. The summons came on 19th January. Sir Henry offered to be there in 20 days, but actually entered into his new duties on 20th March.

The first thing Lawrence noticed at Lucknow was that relations between his own officials were at a low ebb. The acting chief commissioner after Sir James Outram's departure on sick leave had been a man of ill-temper and hasty judgment called Coverley Jackson. He had feuded non-stop with the equally short-tempered financial commissioner, Martin Gubbins, a pushy and egocentric young man. The judicial commissioner, Manaton Ommaney, was, in Sir Henry's words, "not a wise man, jealous of interference, and yet fond of interfering".[27]

Lawrence saw his biggest task as trying to win over the people of Oudh whom he realised were far from happy with their first year of British rule. He had always been sympathetic to Indians and spoke several of their languages and dialects, so he set to work with a will to improve things. Now he opened the doors of the Residency to both native nobles and traders, holding large *durbars* (meetings), and encouraging the individual members of each class to visit him daily. His basic policy towards the inhabitants was simple:

Ten men in an hour quell a row which, after a day's delay may take weeks to put down. Time is everything just now. Time, firmness, promptness, conciliation and prudence... A firm and cheerful aspect must be maintained. There must be no bustle, no appearance of alarm, still less of panic. But at the same time there must be the utmost watchfulness and promptness. Everywhere the first germ of insurrection must be put down instantly.[28]

To the taluqdars he sent out a message that he would maintain them in possession of their villages pending a full investigation of rights and claims. These promises, "delivered in Hindustani with patriarchal dignity and authoritative assurance", calmed the worst fears of the landowners. It was the disbanded soldiers that worried him the most. As he rode through Lucknow he observed "angry looks", as he told Lord Canning. One morning in April "a clod was thrown at Mr Ommaney and another struck Major Anderson while in a buggy with myself."[29]

Rumours began reaching everyone's ears of "polluted cartridges" for the new Enfield rifle (a weapon so far not issued to the E.I.C. Army), smeared with the fat of pigs and cows, and thus anathema to both Hindus and Moslems. It was all nonsense. Then there was a story that the ground bones of cows had been mixed with flour and served out as rations to the sepoys. Sir Henry had a talk with an old artillery *jemadar* (an Indian officer equal to a lieutenant), who dismissed the ground bones theory as silly, but he argued that it was in keeping with the East India Company, who ruled by fraud. Lawrence could not convince the old soldier that he was mistaken, and this conversation rankled with him, since it showed that even Indian soldiers of long and meritorious service had little faith in the British. In a letter of 2nd May to Lord Canning he wrote that Indians – especially sepoys – needed to be treated "as having much the same feelings, the same ambition, the same perception of ability and imbecility as ourselves".[30]

Fine words, but the die had been cast. A small mutiny took place at Berhampore, 110 miles north of Calcutta, where sepoys of the 19th B.N.I. refused to touch the copper caps for firing exercises. By March the discontent had spread to the Musketry Depot at Ambala where detachments of the 41st B.N.I. were being trained in the use of the new Enfield rifle. It became apparent that the sepoys' objections were steadily growing; incidents occurred across northern India in March and April. It was no longer the grease used on the cartridges – the sepoys now complained about the paper on them and finally to the paper on the old musket cartridges. Fear of caste pollution and a religious panic swept through the native ranks.

Many Bengal Army officers were unsympathetic to their men's fears, which they considered simply foolish or irrational. A typical response was that of Lieutenant Robert Danvers of the 70th B.N.I. who thought the colonel at Berhampore ought to have "peppered" the mutineers with grapeshot, "and given the order for the Irregulars to charge them".[31] He thought the sepoys were getting "impudent", even demanding pay increases before using the new cartridges. Lt-Colonel William Case at Lucknow blamed HM Govt for reducing the number of Queen's regiments in India. Even his beloved 32nd was below strength. In a letter to calm his mother's fears he wrote: "We are peaceful here, yet, at any rate, and I rather hope we shall remain so. I mention this as you may see all sorts of exaggerated reports in the Papers."[32]

Matters came to a head at Barrackpore on 29th March when a *bhang*- (hemp-) intoxicated sepoy of the 34th B.N.I., barefoot and improperly dressed, went rampaging about with a loaded musket, calling upon his comrades to join him and yelling at the bugler to call assembly. He is supposed to have shouted: "From biting these cartridges we shall become infidels. Get ready! Turn out all of you!"[33] In an incident that was half-farce and half-drama, attempts to disarm the man, whose name was Mangal Pandey, led to officers, both British and Indian, being wounded. The sepoy then tried unsuccessfully to kill himself. He was executed on 8th April, but his name became synonymous with mutiny and all rebels in the coming months would be called "Pandies" by the British. Of course in India the sepoy's actions have made him a nationalist hero, yet in a seminal book about the incident the historian Rudrangshu Mukherjee concludes that the event was blown out of all proportion to its reality – and this was largely due to the British themselves:

> The myth that surrounds the name Mangal Pandey is a British creation… Mangal Pandey had no notion of patriotism, or even of India. For him *mulk* was his small village in Awadh, his *watan* a plot of land that his father and forefathers had cultivated. To bestow patriotism on him is to wrench him from his time and context. If love of country drove him he would not have become a sepoy in the first place.[34]

Strange things seemed to be happening across the land. That spring, before the heat of summer and the drenching monsoons, the Lucknow Residency surgeon, 32-year-old Joseph Fayrer, decided to go tiger-shooting in the steamy jungles of northern Oudh with Commissioner Gubbins. Six other Englishmen went with them and all save Fayrer and Gubbins were destined to die in the great uprising. It was at one of their first camp sites out in the Oudh countryside that they were told of *chupattis* – flat, round cakes of unleavened bread – being passed from village to village at night. The cakes seemed to be a signal or caution of some kind, but the villagers insisted that they knew not what, other than "a warning that they were to be on the look out for something."[35]

One visitor to Lucknow in mid-April was Nana Sahib of Bithur, whose palace was not far from Cawnpore. With him came his English-speaking, oily secretary, Azimullah Khan, who had visited England and been much feted there in 1854. Gubbins found the Nana to be "arrogant and presuming". History does not record, but one suspects, the Nana and Azimullah thought the same of him. It seemed just a casual visit. Yet the two men found time to meet with Mirza Bedar Bakht, a grandson of the Mogul Emperor at Delhi. Under discussion was the printing of a seditious pamphlet called *Rissalah Jihad* (Officers Jihad), a call for Moslems to arm and fight the British. Azimullah had arranged the printing on a press he had brought back from France. When Sir Henry heard about the pamphlet he had the press stopped. "Nana Sahib by now was safely back in his palace at Bithur,"[36] writes Rosie Llewellyn-Jones. In his definitive study of the Cawnpore Rising, the American historian Andrew Ward concludes that Azimullah Khan was a leading plotter in the 1857 revolt, weaving webs across northern India for his master. Visits had been made by him to the ex-king of Oudh's house at Calcutta and it is clear that members of the disgruntled royal court had talked sedition with him. We will never know for sure but it does seem likely, following the Lucknow trip by Nana Sahib and Azimullah Khan, that the sepoys in Oudh were encouraged to mutiny.

In late April Dr Walter Wells of the 48th B.N.I. stationed at Lucknow stupidly took a sip from a bottle of medicine, thereby rendering it obnoxious to all his Hindu sepoys. They complained to the commanding officer, Lt- Colonel Palmer, pointing out it was an insult to their caste. Palmer gave Wells a telling-off and smashed the bottle in the presence of the sepoys. Under the cover of darkness some men got their revenge by burning down the Wells's bungalow. A day or two later, a mysterious fire also burned down the huts of the 13th B.N.I.

On Sunday 3rd May the Reverend Polehampton found he had an unusually thin congregation for his evening service. To make matters worse, several officers slipped away as their servants crept in and gave them messages. The ladies started to look uncomfortable and a few left the service while others crossed the aisle and began whispering with their friends. "Altogether, I had not a very attentive congregation," wrote the slightly aggrieved padre. That morning the 7th Oudh Irregular Infantry had mutinied and threatened to kill their officers, but some order finally prevailed and the men dispersed. At evening parade each company was asked if they would bite the new cartridge. "Yes," they replied sullenly. Lawrence, wasting no time, assembled as many European troops as he could muster, thus depleting Polehampton's congregation, and rode over to the ranks of the 7th. When the men saw the lit portfires of Sir Henry's heavy guns they broke ranks and fled, some laying down their arms in submission. Other fugitives slunk back next morning, cowed but not contrite. Alarmingly, a letter misdirected into British hands showed that the 7th O.I.I. had been conspiring with the 48th B.N.I. "for the faith and awaited their orders". It all sounded horribly ominous.

Rumours abounded and it was whispered among the British, as Polehampton recorded, "that parties had been appointed in the three sepoy regiments to go round and murder us all in our beds and set the houses on fire." The chaplain personally thought the alarms were exaggerated and jokingly told Sir Henry so, but he replied gravely, "I can assure you it is no laughing matter."

Martin Gubbins, a man who was never short of ideas or slow in making his voice heard, now urged Lawrence to order some of HM 32nd Regiment to protect the Residency. Sir Henry was reluctant, "lest by displaying alarm a new crisis might be precipitated". Finally he relented and in addition, on 25th May, requested that all the women and children at the cantonments three miles away, as well as the families of civilians in the city itself, should immediately move to the Residency compound. Some families of officers were accommodated at Mr Gubbins' house, others with Dr Fayrer and Mr Ommaney. One of these women was Maria Germon, wife of Captain Richard Charles Germon – "Charlie" – of the 13th B.N.I. She wrote:

I desssed and packed up what I could and at half past seven the Harris's and Mrs Barwell came for me and we drove down the City, passing on our way innumerable coolies with beds and luggage of all descriptions – carriages and buggies all off to the Residency with ladies and children – such a scene – when we drove up the Residency looked everything so warlike – guns pointed in all directions, barricades and European troops everywhere – such a scene of bustle and confusion – we then heard there was hardly a room to be got – ladies had been arriving ever since gunfire, so Mr Harris went over to see if Dr Fayrer could take us in – he came back saying yes, and away we went, thankful to get into such good quarters – two ladies were there already and five came after us with three children, so that every room was full. This house as well as Mr Gubbins' and Mr Ommaney's (both also full) are within the Residency compound and are barricaded all round... The heat is intense... I cannot sleep at nights for it. Our beds are all under one punkah. I and Mrs Fayrer and Mrs Anderson – the others are as thick, but it is nothing to the Residency – our party here is a very agreeable one – we meet at chota hazree and then after dressing, eat an agreeable breakfast at ten, then have working, reading and music (there are good performers amongst our party), tiffin at two, dine at half-past seven and then the Padre reads a chapter and prayers and we retire.[37]

How to defend the Residency? Sir Henry Lawrence was faced with what must have seemed almost insurmountable problems. For one, the position of the troops was "as bad as bad can be – all scattered over several miles, the Infantry in one direction, the Cavalry another, the Artillery in a third, the magazine in a fourth and almost unprotected".[38] Escaping Lucknow did not seem an option. To get so many people to safety through territory swarming with rebels without having a large and loyal body of troops for protection was logistically and militarily unfeasible. Lawrence decided to make the Residency compound as defensible as possible. A second defence would be the only other commanding position in the city – the old fortress of Macchi Bhowan. He was also keen to retain the cantonments as a third defence, though others advised against it.

Surrounding the Residency and its Banqueting House were a number of other buildings – a church, civic offices and some large private houses. There was a post office, the city hospital and telegraph office. The Residency itself and the large houses such as Gubbins' and Fayrer's had extensive private gardens. Major John Anderson, the chief engineer and his second-in-command, Captain George Fulton, were ordered to prepare a line of defence. Meantime the Macchi Bhowan was to be repaired and re-stocked with arms and ammunition. The engineers had to work quickly, not knowing if or when an attack might come. They drew the outer defences as a line; where walls did not exist the gaps were to be filled with palisades, earthworks and trenches of all kinds. Outside this rampart were sown a field of obstacles, as described by historian Michael Edwardes: "Great iron spikes, some of them with four points, were set in the earth. Pits were dug and lined with sharpened stakes. All this was designed to hinder a storming party before it reached the main defence. The whole area was roughly diamond-shaped, with each of the faces about a quarter of a mile in length."[39]

The Residency position was not a bad one. One of the engineers later wrote:

> It was sufficiently extensive, healthy and well-supplied with water. It had an ample amount of house accommodation and shelter. It commanded the river face and the adjacent ground for half its circle. Nowhere was it commanded by artillery sites, and the higher portions of the buildings in its immediate neighbourhood could be demolished, and so depirived of any command. The features along its trace allowed of good defensive sites and batteries. It was already one of the three posts that were being held in close connection with each other; and lastly, it would be readily accessible to relief by a force advancing through the comparatively open country on the north of the Goomtee.[40]

Like some fearsome monsoon waiting to break, the great uprising finally burst forth on the evening of Sunday 10th May at Meerut, about 375 miles north of Lucknow and 45 miles from Delhi. The mutineers burned their cantonments, killed several officers and their families and marched in the darkness towards Delhi (though a few deserted and set off for their homes in Oudh). At Delhi they and more mutineers managed to wrest control of the city from the British, indulge in more killing and proclaim old and fragile Bahadur Shah II, the Mogul Emperor who had lived quietly for years under the watchful eyes of his British masters, as their leader. "The dates of the mutinies after the massacre at Delhi seem to indicate a pattern," writes Mukherjee. "It was as if the mutinies were travelling down the Ganges valley from Meerut and Delhi with a time-gap between the various stations required for the news to travel from one place to another."[41]

Lucknow's Hindu and Moslem inhabitants seemed to sense that something was about to happen and that when it came it would do so suddenly. Traders who had always given the British goods on credit now refused unless paid in cash. "Government paper notes were selling as low as 37 rupees for the hundred and even less," noted Captain R. J. Anderson of the 25th B.N.I. Proclamations were pasted up – by whom no one knew – urging citizens to unite and exterminate all Europeans. Late on the night of the 20th a message came from Sir Hugh Wheeler commanding at Cawnpore; he begged for help and said that he daily expected that a mutiny might break out in his garrison. Sir Henry swiftly despatched 54 men of HM 32nd along with 240 troopers of the Oudh Irregular Cavalry. Anxious to know the exact state of affairs at Cawnpore, he also sent his Military Secretary, Captain Fletcher Hayes, who was instructed to return to Lucknow after meeting with General Wheeler.

It seemed as if the discontented were waiting to see how events would progress at Delhi. With a small British force made to hold out on the ridge overlooking the city, it seemed as if in this centenary year of the Battle of Plassey, the *feringhees* might at last be ousted from India. On 21st May some stables in the Lucknow cantonments were set on fire, but the storm so long in coming finally struck on the night of 30th May. Lawrence's staff officer, Captain T. F. Wilson, had warned him, on the evidence of a loyal sepoy, that the firing of the 9pm gun would be the signal for a general mutiny. Sir Henry found this hard to believe and ate dinner that night with some friends at his house in the cantonments. When the gun was fired all in the room listened expectantly. There was silence outside. Then Lawrence said with a smile to his aide, "Wilson, your friends are not punctual." A moment later came the sounds of shouting and musket shots. Lawrence leapt to his feet. "I am going to drive those scoundrels out of cantonment," he said. With bungalows blazing and shots firing all round he ordered his guard to be resolute, then galloped off towards the action. Wisely, a company of HM 32nd, supported by two guns, were ordered to patrol the road that led to the city so that the mutineers could not join forces with any trouble-makers approaching from Lucknow (this had been one of the mistakes made at Meerut). The rest of the British infantry and artillery under the command of Lt-Col. John Inglis of the 32nd took up a position on the right of the lines of the 71st B.N.I. For a time there was a sharp fire-fight with the rebels but they withdrew into the cantonment. Here they ransacked and burned homes, set fire to the officers mess and looted all they could take.

A few loyal sepoys stayed with Lieutenant Grant of the 71st, who was commanding the main piquet in the centre of the lines. They tried to hide him under a bed. He was soon discovered and besides being shot was bayoneted no fewer than 15 times. Brigadier Handscomb rode out to remonstrate with the rebels but was shot fatally in the chest. Cornet Raleigh, 7th Light Cavalry, was shot by a trumpeter and then hacked almost to pieces with swords. "Our men found his body still warm," wrote a civilian, L. E. R. Rees, "and the blood yet oozing from his wounds… A lock of the hair of some lady love, to whom perhaps he had plighted his faith, was found round his neck. One of his fingers, on which there had been a ring, was cut off."[42] A British sergeant's wife and her children were bayoneted, although Mrs Bruere, wife of Major Bruere of the 13th B.N.I., along with her four children, were hidden in a ditch by loyal sepoys of her husband's regiment and survived the carnage. Three of Mrs Case's servants were butchered and it is clear that the mutineers dealt ruthlessly with any Indians they found loyal to the feringhees. In total about 700 sepoys remained loyal, mostly from the 13th and

48th Regiments. Fundamental to their actions was the respect many had for Charles Bruere who had served with the 13th for twenty years. Interestingly, Colonel William Halford of the 71st – the most disaffected regiment – had been in command only 18 months.

From the roof of Mr Gubbins' house the Reverend Polehampton and others watched the cantonments blazing. The bungalows, one after another, burst into flame. It was a miserable moment; many of the women at the Residency now knew that they had lost all their belongings. Adelaide Case worried about her husband, who was with Lawrence and Inglis. She recalled the blaze as one of "tremendous fury", while "The stillness in the city was very remarkable, not a sound was heard."[43] At 11.30pm a *sowar* (native cavalryman) galloped up with a message from Sir Henry saying that the incident was nearly over and Adelaide heard that William, as well as Julia Inglis's husband, John, were both unhurt.

One young subaltern who watched 50 of his troopers desert was Lieutenant Ashton Warner of the 7th Light Cavalry. He wrote home:"The same confidence can never be put in natives again. I know I will never serve with the treacherous brutes again. All our candles in the air about native army are gone for ever." He hoped that regiments would soon arrive from England "and rule these brutes with a rod of iron".[44]

Sir Henry was up early on the 31st and marched out with some British infantry and artillery towards the city race course where the mutineers had gathered. He opened fire on them with his guns, then pursued them for six miles but only managed once to get within range. Martin Gubbins, with his usual verve, pursued them four miles further. In total that day, 60 prisoners were taken. Lawrence disliked Gubbins, but was forced to admit that he was a hero and had done "the work of a regiment". The troopers who had stuck with Gubbins were given 600 rupees as a reward. Sir Henry seemed mildly elated after the incident. He told Canning: "We are now positively better off than we were. We now know our friends and enemies."[45]

Lucknow braced itself for a riot. That Sunday afternoon thousands of Moslems marched through the old city beneath a banner of the Prophet, Christians were attacked, the rioters broke into stores and shops, looting and ransacking them, "smashing earthenware pots, tearing down mat doors, slitting open sacks of flour and beans and kicking the contents across the ground".[46] It was pandemonium. Captain Anderson noted that men were seen "with figures dressed up as European children, and much to the amusement of the mob, the heads of these dolls were struck off with sword cuts."[47]

Early the next morning and unaware what had happened in Lucknow over the past 24 hours, Captain Hayes, who had been sent 12 days earlier to Cawnpore, was cantering across country on his way back. He was accompanied by Lieutenant T. Carey of the 17th B.N.I. The pair had the bad luck to run into some mutineers from Lucknow. Hayes, a poor rider, did not gallop very far before a native officer cut him down from the saddle with a single blow.[48] Carey rode for all he was worth as the "pings" of musket balls whizzed past his ears. Two sowars galloped after him for quite a long way and at one point Hayes's terrified and riderless horse raced across his path, but Carey kept on going. Eventually the cavalrymen gave up the chase. "Never did I know a happier moment," Carey wrote later.

Mutinies were now breaking out at all the outlying stations; the sepoys rose on 4th June at Sitapur, barely 51 miles from Lucknow; Fyzabad followed, then Durreabad and Sultanpore. The latter, a town on the Gumti, was on the main road to the capital. Further risings followed at Secrora, Salone, Pershadipur and Gonda. By 11th June British control of Oudh "had virtually ceased to exist". The death toll of British civilians, soldiers and their families kept rising. People also had various hair-raising adventures and escapes from the mutineers. Two who got away from Sitapur were Lieutenant James Ruggles, 41st B.N.I. and his wife. The day after reaching Lucknow Ruggles went to see Inglis who ordered him to turn the church into a granary. He later recalled:

It was not at all nice work, having to pull everything to pieces – the pews, pulpit, everything had to come away – but it had to be done, and when all was clear the whole space inside was filled with sacks of grain. Meanwhile I had taken up my quarters in the vestry. A few days after this another officer was sent to help, a Captain Barlow, who had been major of brigade to the Oudh force. A more excitable man I never met; it seemed that he could not stand all that was happening; he was in the vestry with myself, but he had such disturbed nights I could hardly get any rest. At last the idea seized him that I wanted to murder him, and his yells were awful. Then I thought it was time a doctor should see him, and he was ordered to the hospital… Poor Captain Barlow! He did not live long, but retained his hallucinations to the last.[49]

Over in the Residency the underground swimming pool was also filled up with grain.

In the city things had gone quiet; a holy man who menacingly drew his finger across his throat in front of a British sentry was placed in irons and given 150 lashes. A second native who was accused of tampering with one of the entrenchment guns was hanged and so were several of the mutineers from the walls of the Macchi Bhowan. Some of these rebels hurled curses at their foes and reminded those watching that they were dying for their faith, but would be avenged, "by their children – and children's children!" Despite problems with traders it was still possible to get goods, and people like Gubbins laid in stocks of arrowroot and flour, ghee and dhal, sugar, rice, beer, wines and spirits, tobacco, soap and candles.

A Scotsman, 27-year-old Lieutenant James McLeod Innes, Royal (Bengal) Engineers, had been put in charge of the Macchi Bhowan. He described the place as "uninhabitable from filth and want of ventilation, and the roofs were weak, and in many cases had fallen in."[50] It had not always been so; a visitor in 1782 wrote of how the fort "reminded me of what I had imagined might be the style of a Baron's castle in Europe about the twelfth century."[51] Nineteen years later another traveller spoke of "beautiful gardens", white marble floors inlaid with red and black mosaics and internal fountains of hot and cold water. But within a short space of time the Macchi Bhowan had fallen into disrepair as palaces such as the Kaisarbagh and Chutter Manzil came into favour.

From 17th May to 2nd July Innes never left the place, except for two half-hour visits to see his wife at the Residency. He had the rubbish cleared away and paths made, reinforced the gateways, put loopholes in the walls, supervised the cleaning of wells, built parapets and then made them musket-proof. One of the buildings was turned into a magazine and filled with barrels of gunpowder. Soon Innes had six companies of Sikhs and one of HM 32nd besides a complete field battery holding the fort. Seven 18-pounder guns, eight 9-pounders and eight 8-inch mortars were in position. The fort with its heightened parapets, breastworks and flanking defences had taken on a new lease of life. Constantly, Sir Henry told Innes to be on his guard; he had no illusions about what might happen and on one occasion told his lieutenant, "As sure as you and I stand here, we will be long and closely besieged." Whether a lone garrison cut off from the Residency could survive in the old fort troubled Lawrence. Innes later recalled: "He even came over in the middle of the night to see what we were about."[52]

Some state prisoners were quietly housed in the old fortress; they included two sons of the Mogul Emperor, along with Mustapha Ali Khan, a brother of the King of Oudh, and the Rajah of Toolshepore, one of the most powerful Hindus in the country.

Two of the Macchi Bhowan's defenders were L. E. Ruutz Rees, a Calcutta merchant now stuck in Lucknow and his friend, Monsieur Deprat, a wealthy French merchant. Deprat tried to take his stock of consumables with him when he left his house that lay on the main road towards the cantonment, but Lawrence prohibited him. So he and Rees moved as much food as they could into the old fort and decided to eat a decent portion of it; for several days they lived exclusively on tinned salmon, Cambridge sausages and other delicacies, washed down with bottles of Deprat's best burgundy. "We seemed to have a presentiment of what privations we had afterwards to undergo," wrote Rees, "for we enjoyed ourselves as much as good living could effect."[53]

Work on the Residency defences had begun before the 30th May mutiny, but from that date on, its defenders worked frenetically. The neat flower beds, green lawns and flowering shrubs were quickly trampled and destroyed as men got to work. On 16th June it was estimated that 3,000 local native labourers, soldiers and volunteers were digging ditches, raising palisades, moving stocks of ammunition and food, positioning guns, strengthening barricades. From dawn until nightfall all was bustle and noise – from shouts of command to the bellowing of elephants, from the crackle of rifle practice to the cries of infants. Captain Anderson, whose house was exposed by the Cawnpore road, pulled down his garden wall, erected a wooden stockade in its place and dug dry ditches, then filled them with sharp bamboo stakes. Martin Gubbins turned his villa into "a fort which would not have disgraced Marshal Vauban himself..." He broke up his library and tried some experiments, finding that a volume of *Lardner's Encyclopaedia* could stop a musket ball at page 120, while Finden's *Illustrations Of Byron*, a thick quarto book, although completely destroyed by its impact, successfully blocked a three-pound shot.

The civilian volunteers were untrained yet enthusiastic defenders. There were tall, thin officials of the Bengal Civil Service; small, fat European clerks; noisy French and Italian merchants and several doctors, including Dr Fayrer who was reckoned a "first-rate" shot, and Dr Hadow whose Enfield rifle would soon claim 19 victims. Captain Anderson thought many of the volunteers were "quite hopeless" soldiers and the laughing stock of the regular troops. One night he heard a volunteer asking how on earth one presented arms. Back came the unmistakable voice of Signor Barsatelli, one of the merchants, who replied: "Never mind, sir, make a *leetle* noise. Who's to see in the dark?" Drill practice left Anderson in tears of laughter as "Some dozen pairs of very *indifferent* legs simultaneously jerked out to their full stretch, and then as quietly dragged back again, as if the owners of these said legs had all made a terrific kick at some very dangerous reptiles and then thought *better* of it." Barsatelli, who claimed to have fought alongside Garibaldi, was to be one of the heroes of the siege, always fantastically over-dressed and over-armed, "with a musket in one hand and a double-barrelled rifle in the other; at his side a huge cavalry sword and pendant; over his breast hung his ammunition pouch resembling an Italian hand-organ." One volunteer asked Anderson very seriously, "What are we to do, sir, if we are charged by elephants?"[54] He could hardly answer for laughing.

Not least among the defenders were the senior boys and their masters from La Martinière School under headmaster George Schilling. They took up positions on the south-eastern face and, when not practising drill, grinding corn or tending to the sick, even had time to do a few Latin declensions and vulgar fractions. Led by Schilling were six masters, the estate superintendent and 67 boys, some as young as six.

While all this work was going on Lawrence was visited by a number of deputations from the city, all suggesting that his defensive preparations were not necessary. One Hindu gentleman suggested a pack of monkeys should be let loose in the Residency grounds, since they would not only propitiate the gods but help to make British rule popular again. "Your advice is good, my friend," said Sir Henry, putting on his hat, "Come and I will show you my monkeys." He led his visitor over to a newly completed battery and a gleaming 18-pounder gun. "See here," he said, "Here is one of my monkeys; *that* is his food," indicating a pile of cannon balls, "and this is the man who feeds him," pointing to a private of HM 32nd, "There! Go and tell your friends of my monkeys!"[55]

Everyone saw that Lawrence never seemed to rest. He was in the saddle at daybreak riding about the compound, giving advice and encouragement. He even had his bedding "spread out near the Baillie-Guard Gate, not to sleep, but to plan and meditate undisturbed".[56] Mrs Wells, the doctor's wife, loathed Colonel Inglis, but thought Sir Henry was "a most affable old gentleman", while Mrs Georgina Harris, wife of the new assistant chaplain, James Parker Harris, said he was "vigilance itself". An officer who visited Lucknow that spring wrote in a letter that he was "a most charming person; his manner is so kind, so cheerful, so affable, it sets everyone at his ease; he is full of life and animation, ready to talk on every subject... He is worked *hard* from morning to night, and often looks sadly weary, but he is hospitable and sociable in disposition and likes to collect people around him."[57] Food did not interest Sir Henry but good conversation did. Sometimes he invited 30 people to dinner when his poor servants were expecting only fifteen. Exuberant children made him laugh.

Nothing was overlooked; one day in early June one of the deputy commissioners, Simon Martin, was summoned to see Sir Henry who told the astonished official to lay in supplies to last 3,000 people for up to six months. Working day and night meant that Lawrence "lost appetite and sleep and his changed and careworn appearance was painfully visible to all",[58] wrote an eye-witness. On occasions the staff, when entering his room, found the gaunt, long-bearded man on his knees praying for wisdom and asking God to be merciful "to the poor people committed to my charge".

Far from well, Sir Henry secured an agreement from Lord Canning that if he was too ill to carry on then Major Banks, Commissioner of the Lucknow Division, should succeed him as Chief Commissioner. Command of the troops would go to John Inglis of HM 32nd, who was raised to the local rank of brigadier. "They are the right men," wrote Lawrence, "In fact they are the only men for their places." Soon after this he delegated his authority to a provisional council with Martin Gubbins as its president. Sir Henry was very wary of Gubbins, whom he had deemed a hero; as Financial Commissioner he had exacerbated the situation with the taluqdars, he constantly criticized Lawrence's policies and he had a bee in his bonnet about sending out sorties against the rebel forces in the district. Gubbins, Sir Henry told the Governor-General on 13th June, "would be continually sending 50 men on elephants forty, fifty and more miles off. He is perfectly insane in what he considers *energetic, manly measures*. His language has been so extravagant that were he not really useful I should be obliged to take severe measures against him." Lawrence ended this character assessment with the harsh words; "He is the one *malcontent* in the garrison."[59]

A handsome man in his forties with a trim moustache, Gubbins was the third son of Major-General Joseph Gubbins. He had two brothers, John and Frederick, also working in India. His sister, Elizabeth, managed to catch a duke for her first husband and a viscount for the second, so the family were generally wealthy and had pretensions. Martin had gone out to India aged sixteen in 1830 and gradually worked his way up the civil service ladder. He was undoubtedly brave and energetic, but "most strange" – at times sympathetic to Indian grievances, yet "inconsistent and unreliable", with strong prejudices and flawed judgment.

Just how awkward Gubbins could be was proved a few days later when Dr Fayrer, alarmed at the state of Sir Henry's health, insisted he must rest in bed for two or three days before he dropped from fatigue. Gubbins seized the occasion as a chance to send away all the native troops that Lawrence desperately wanted to retain. He even cheekily wrote to Canning that the Chief Commissioner "is no longer, I think, firm, nor his mental vision clear". When he found out what Gubbins had done Sir Henry was furious and it was with some difficulty that 150 sepoys returned on his personal assurance (and most of these remained loyal to the end of the siege). He also invited all pensioned sepoys to return and quite a few, some limbless, sightless or on crutches, responded to the call;

the infirm were thanked and sent home, but of the rest some 80 remained to help swell the defenders around the perimeter.

By mid-June the Residency was filling up with families including a number from the outlying stations. Life for everyone was getting more and more uncomfortable. "There's not one hole or corner where one can enjoy an instant's privacy," complained Mrs Case. "The noise of the children in this house is something dreadful... The coming and going, the talking, the bustle and noise inside as well as outside, the constant alarming reports, and at times the depressed expression on some of the countenances, baffle all descriptions."[60] Mrs Ogilvie, another doctor's wife, kept insisting that hot air was better than no air; she opened all the windows in the Residency so that a scorching wind accompanied by "great, cold, clammy flies" and hordes of mosquitoes soon made life even more unbearable.

On 9th June Mrs Katherine Bartrum arrived at Lucknow from the small station of Gonda. She was 23 years old, a shy girl, daughter of a Bath silversmith. When the order came for the women and children from the outlying stations to go to Lucknow, Katherine argued with Robert, her assistant-surgeon husband, but he was adamant, for the sake of their 15-month-old son, Bobbie, that she must go. He accompanied his wife and child for the first 16 miles of the 80-mile journey, but after that Katherine had to rely on an escort of sepoys whose loyalties seemed daily more doubtful. Collecting some stragglers along the way, this little band moved through a countryside full of rebels, marauders and burning buildings.

When Mrs Bartrum arrived at Lucknow she was shocked by the room she was given in the Begum Kothi (literally the "Begum's Mansion", built for one of the royal wives, Queen Malika-i-Ahad, in 1844), which was "a most uninviting-looking place, so dirty, having neither a punkah to cool the air or a scrap of furniture to set it off." Katherine knew no one and had no servants to help her. "On that first night we slept, fifteen in one room, parked closely together... How great a change after the comforts of our homes!" She got news of Robert's escape from Gonda, but would receive only one more letter from him. By 20th June Mrs Bartrum found it impossible to get hot food and was grateful to the wife of a British soldier who brought her hot water for breakfast and tea. Each day she was "fully occupied in nursing, and washing our clothes, together with cups and saucers, and fanning away the flies that become a fearful nuisance". When the children at last fell asleep, the ladies would gather around a chair "that formed our tea-table", and drink their tea by the light of a candle stuck in a bottle. On 29th June one of the women, Mrs Hale, died of smallpox leaving a little daughter. "Poor little lamb," wrote Katherine, "how unconscious was she of her sad loss; a motherless babe amongst strangers and her father far away."[61]

"The idea that our rule in India has come to an end seems firmly to have possessed all the natives,"[62] wrote Mrs Harris on 16th June. "Our servants seem to be deserting daily." Three days later smallpox broke out in the Residency itself and one of those stricken was Julia Inglis, aristocratic wife of Colonel Inglis (she was a daughter of Lord Chelmsford and sister to soldier Frederic who would play a major role in the Zulu War 22 years later). Until her illness, Julia, along with her friend, Adelaide Case, as the wives of the senior officers of HM 32nd, had tried to help the other women of the regiment by taking them puddings and soup, tea, sugar and other niceties to their billet in the cooler but no less packed and darkened tykhana below ground.

Certainly, for all their privations, life was a little better for Adelaide and Julia than for Katherine Bartrum and many others; at 9.30pm the Reverend Polehampton normally held prayers in Mrs Ogilvie's room, then everyone tried to sleep, though it was not easy. Adelaide and Julia got into the habit of sleeping on the roof. Mrs Inglis thought the view of the city and countryside was very beautiful. "Everything used to look so calm and peaceful, it was difficult to think it could ever be a scene of war; but looking down into the Residency garden, we could see the guns placed in position ready to be used at a moment's notice and soldiers sleeping amongst them."[63] When, at dawn, other women and children came up to the roof for some fresh air, Julia would go down to her room for a little peace and quiet before morning prayers again with the chaplain.

On 11th June the cavalry of the military police rode out of the city and next morning the infantry followed suit. Their Superintendent, Captain Gould Weston, rode to stop them. During the ensuing dialogue one man raised his musket to kill the officer but another knocked the muzzle to the ground saying, "Who would kill such a brave man as this?" Colonel Inglis told his wife privately: "Our position is a bad one and we shall have a hard struggle."

During the last week of June the rains came, first with a heavy shower and a good deal of thunder, but three days later the monsoon began in earnest as torrents poured from grey skies. The women were getting very depressed and it was up to their menfolk to try and revive their spirits. William Case could only make occasional visits to see Adelaide, as Inglis was now acting brigadier and so he was in charge of the 32nd, but he did his best to fill his wife with hope and courage. The pair exchanged letters daily. William wrote: "Still I live in hope that ere long I shall be able to pay you a visit ... don't despair, you'll see we will pull through with the Almighty's aid… I feel that no cause like that of the mutineers, supported by murder, fire and everything that is savage and inhuman will be allowed to prosper."[64]

Every day Sir Henry Lawrence sent off a stream of letters. The hardest to write were those to Sir Hugh Wheeler besieged at Cawnpore. "Surely we are not to die like rats in a cage," Wheeler had asked. Martin Gubbins urged action and suggested a feint attack on Bithur. Banks and Inglis told the Chief Commissioner that even if men could be spared from the Residency to head towards Cawnpore, and get there safely, it was impossible to cross the Ganges as the rebels had destroyed the bridges and seized all the boats. "Husband your resources and do not accept any terms from the enemy," was the best advice Lawrence could send in a *cossid* (a tiny note that could be hidden by a native messenger), to Wheeler. As late as 23rd June he was still being typically optimistic and telling Lord Canning that if Delhi fell quickly and Cawnpore held out, then "I doubt if we shall be besieged at all." On 29th June he was writing to Agra that "We shall not do badly if we hold out for a month."

On the morning of 28th June soldiers were sent to the Kaisarbagh Palace led by Major Banks. They were able to take away a brass 24-pounder gun complete with its equipment, but the real object of the expedition was to seize the royal regalia, a fabulous collection of jewels including emeralds as big as duck eggs, diamond necklaces and a silver crown set with amethysts. The soldiers also discovered plenty of muskets and other arms which were taken in carts to the Residency. Later, on the front lawn, some of this treasure was buried along with 23 lakhs of rupees.

About 10.30am on the morning of 29th June spies reported to Gubbins, who was in charge of intelligence, that an advanced guard of Cawnpore mutineers were at Nawabganj and that a small party of these men, estimated at 500 infantry and 50 cavalry, with one small gun, were at Chinhat collecting supplies for the main force. With his usual ardour, Gubbins was all for an immediate attack. Sir Henry listened politely yet hesitated to take action. Gubbins shouted at him, "Well, Sir Henry, we shall all be branded at the bar of history as cowards!"[65] Later that day cavalry patrols brought information directly to Lawrence. He concluded (in a written note attached to Gubbins report), "The force now (at 4pm) *almost certainly* does greatly exceed 500 foot and 50 horse," and he was satisfied "that now there are 2 or 3 thousand men at Chinhat and that in the morning there will be many more."[66] Later meetings with Inglis, Captain Wilson, DAAG. and Captain A. P. Simons commanding the the Artillery convinced Sir Henry to try a reconnaissance the next morning. He told Wilson that a successful sortie would have "a good effect" on Lucknow's inhabitants. The Mutiny historian George Forrest also suggested that Lawrence wanted to test the temper and fidelity of his native troops. "We must try and blood them," he had told an aide, meaning commit them to the British side. If so, then he was taking a terrible gamble, as events were to prove.

Julia Inglis spent the 29th sick in bed as she slowly recovered from the smallpox. She did not see John in the early hours of the 30th to bid farewell, though Adelaide Case had been delighted on the night of the 29th by a surprise visit from William, who seemed "as cheerful as ever". He looked in on Julia as he left and remarked:"I hope we may meet under happier circumstances." He did not tell his wife of the march due at dawn (in fact orders were not given out until 3am), towards Chinhat. When she awoke, Adelaide saw that the whole place was astir, cavalry were trotting through the gate, HM 32nd were marching away and an elephant-drawn howitzer was lumbering off into the distance.

2

'Neath Shot and Flame

The Residency Compound, Lucknow,
30ᵗʰ June–15ᵗʰ August 1857

If there was a Hell on Earth that last day of June 1857, it most certainly was Lucknow, northern India. As the afternoon wore on over 10,000 insurgents surrounded the Residency and bombarded it with a colossal display of firepower; hundreds of cannon balls with their low, rushing sound slammed into the compound and its buildings, smashing through brickwork and masonry, causing large portions to crumble; with screams of defiance and the pop-pop of their muskets, thousands of ex-E.I.C. sepoys, townsfolk and *budmashes* (a unique Indian term for rascals), hurled themselves towards the scanty British defences.

Inside the compound all was pandemonium: shouts and military commands mingled with the screams of horses and bullocks (some of them blundering down wells and polluting the drinking water); wounded, dying and in pain, men rushed hither and thither, heavy guns boomed their discharges, bullets whizzed through the air like a thousand angry bees, while down in their darkened tykhanas the women and children of the garrison prayed quietly for a ceasefire and "tremblingly listened to every sound". The defences, everyone knew, were imperfect and incomplete.

The return of the troops around noon from Chinhat had roused Julia Inglis from her sickbed. Her friend, Adelaide Case, told her to rest since a groom had brought the good news that both their husbands were safe. A few minutes later Brigadier Inglis arrived and kissed his wife. Turning to Adelaide he said, "Poor Case." The colonel's wife gave "a pitiable cry" and would have lapsed into hysterics had not Mrs Polehampton taken her into another room and comforted her. Later that night Inglis had his wife, Mrs Case, her sister and their three children moved to a small, freshly white-washed room near the Brigade Square, "a most bare-looking place".

As if a portent of the many deaths that would soon follow, two women, Mrs Watson (whose husband commanded the 7th Oudh Irregular Infantry), and Mrs Soppitt, wife of Lieutenant Arthur Soppitt, 4th Oudh Infantry, each lost a child overnight to cholera. Erina Soppitt was just 18 years old and heavily pregnant with a second child.[1]

In the midst of death though there is always hope – and life. At Captain Anderson's House on the compound's east face the defenders were engaged in a sharp fire with the enemy when a roundshot carried away some of the pillars. They fell with a huge crash and pile of dust burying Mr Capper, a deputy commissioner who was fighting as a volunteer. As the dust settled he was heard calling, "I'm alive! Get me out! Give me air, for God's sake!" Someone said loudly, "It's impossible to save him!" Capper, on hearing this, shouted back, "It *is* possible, if you try." There was just enough wall remaining to cover the bodies of a rescue party from the enemy fire. After three-quarters of an hour, covered in dirt and sweat, they had freed Capper's head and trunk. Huge blocks of masonry had to be shifted, rubble still kept falling and the insurgents, aware that something curious was going on, peppered the place with musket balls. Finally, Mr Capper was pulled free and to everyone's surprise and the victim's delight was found to be uninjured save for a few bruises and a feeling of faintness.[2]

Another happy person that afternoon was Mrs Germon who with six other adults and seven children was destined to spend much of her time in Dr Fayrer's dark and mice-infested tykhana. Yet she was happy because a few hours earlier word had reached her that husband "Charlie" had survived Chinhat, though suffering from sunstroke, and had been brought into the Residency on a gun carriage.

Grimy and exhausted, Sir Henry Lawrence sat down to put pen to paper. In dejection he wrote a letter to General Henry Havelock at Allahabad. He knew its contents would be sent on to the Governor-General in Calcutta:

This morning we went out to Chinhat to meet the enemy, and were defeated, and lost five guns through the misconduct of our native artillery, many of whom deserted. The enemy have followed us up, and we have now been besieged for four hours, and shall probably tonight be surrounded. The enemy are very bold, some Europeans very low. I look on our position now as ten times as bad as it was yesterday; indeed it is very critical; We shall have to abandon much supplies and blow much powder. Unless we are relieved quickly, say in 15 or 20 days, we shall hardly be able to maintain our position.[3]

As the night wore on the firing ceased, but it started again at daybreak on 1st July, another cloudless, dry and hot day. It was difficult for the Reverend Polehampton to get a grave dug for the two dead infants. Bullets zipped about the churchyard. Only at gunpoint did he stop five coolies who were on the point of deserting. It was a quick service and one of Mrs Soppitt's servants was shot in the arm as they departed.

One who had a lucky escape was Sir Henry when an 8-inch shell crashed into one of the upper rooms of the Residency where he was giving dictation to his secretary, George Couper. Neither man was injured and Lawrence joked that the rebels did not have an artilleryman good enough to put another shell into his small room. Throughout the day, shots and shells continued to pepper the Residency's upper storeys and Sir Henry reluctantly agreed to move down to a room on the ground level.

Within Lucknow itself, according to the later evidence of Sayyid Yusuf, a police official, "the confusion and looting went on for six days" as the ex-sepoys and civilians argued over who should head the new administration. Gangs looted many shops, generally rampaging mindlessly across Lucknow, killing Christians and the servants of Europeans who had lived in the city. The initial attacks on the Residency were planned by Raja Ali Khan. With sepoys and servants fleeing the Residency, it was very easy at first for the attackers to get a clear idea of where, for instance, Lawrence slept and worked, as well as a good description of the British defences. The flight of their servants infuriated some British, but in all fairness, many servants had families living in Lucknow and it was natural that they wished to be with them in wartime instead of their employers.

It was generally agreed by the insurgents that their revolt needed a figurehead. The soldiers initially offered to set up the son of Queen Malika-i-Ahad, provided that she paid them lots of rupees. The lady refused saying she was not that rich! For the first week or so the attackers were fighting in an un-coordinated manner, "the Cavalry on their own account, so on with Artillery, and Infantry".[4] Yet the defenders quickly realised that their foes deserved a great deal of respect. Mr Rees explained:

> With incredible rapidity, with remarkable ingenuity, and with indomitable perseverance, they had, in the very first week, made batteries in positions where one would have fancied their erection impossible – some having actually been moved to the tops of houses, and others placed most cleverly in places where our own batteries could not effectively open on them, and which were well-protected

from musketry fire… Many of these batteries were not further off than fifty to a hundred yards, and told tremendously on our buildings.[5]

Lawrence was everywhere that first day of July, taking great risks in exposing himself to enemy fire as he urged on his men. His big worry was the situation at the Macchi Bhowan; messages sent there had not got through, all the native runners had deserted and one letter received from Colonel Palmer, 48th B.N.I., commanding at the fort, said the garrison had plenty of gunpowder and small arms ammunition, but were low on food and shells. Sir Henry decided no time should be lost in somehow evacuating the garrison to the Residency. The semaphore on the Residency roof now took on some importance, though it was an odd contraption – a lone post "with a crossbar, from which hung a row of black bags each attached to a separate pulley". By the time Captain Fulton, whose dreamchild the device was, had attracted the attention of the Macchi Bhowan garrison the insurgents were also aware that something was happening. Fulton and two other officers spent three hours at he task, while "it rained musket balls," as cords broke and pulleys jammed. It was physically hot work, too, with the sun high overhead in the sky, but at last their message – "Blow up and retire at twelve tonight. Bring prisoners guns and treasure"[6] – was received and acknowledged.

It was thought best not to tell Colonel Palmer that his 19-year-old daughter, Suzanne, was fighting for her life. She had been carrying some china to a cabinet in a second storey room of the Residency when a 9-lb shot passed through the wall and took off one of her legs. The china crashed to the floor as the stunned girl cried out, "My leg is shot off! I know I shall die!"[7] Several other women who were in the room tried to stanch the bleeding. One of them, young Mrs A. E. Huxham, whose husband was serving with the 48th B.N.I., called out for Dr Wells and noticed how Miss Palmer had turned "deadly pale". Wells pressed the arteries to quench the flow of blood and bound the wound. Suzanne was carried into a ground floor room above the tykhana. "Poor soul, her screams were fearful," noted Mrs Huxham. Oddly enough, Miss Palmer had whispered to Mrs Huxham only five minutes before the accident that she had a presentiment of death that day. Dr Fayrer ran a gauntlet of bullets on the way from his house to the Residency. With Wells's help, he administered chloroform and amputated above the knee. Both doctors were hopeful Suzanne might live, but it was known that amputations of this kind were almost always fatal.

Across the city at the old fortress-palace, Colonel Palmer carefully wrote down his orders and handed them to officers so that everyone knew his job. Any guns that could not be removed were to be spiked, but not until the last few minutes before departure. Women, children and the sick were to be conveyed by bullock carts. The state prisoners were bound, gagged and blindfolded. If there was any attempt to rescue them they were to be shot. Some 240 barrels of gunpowder and 594,000 rounds of ball and gun ammunition could not be conveyed. Lieutenant Thomas, Madras Artillery, Deputy Commissary of Ordnance, was personally commanded to fire a 25 minute fuse as the rearguard left the fort. Time for departure was midnight from the eastern gate, "in perfect silence", ordered Palmer, "under penalty of death".

At 11pm the garrison assembled; only five heavy guns could be taken, but the convoy included vast quantities of small arms stores, horses and bullocks. At twelve the gate opened and the British marched out in silence, followed by the State prisoners and then the guns – the horse limbers ridden by British officers as the native drivers had bolted. "I rode one of the leaders of the first gun, "wrote Lieutenant David Hay, 28th B.N.I., "and was slightly taken aback on finding the gun stick fast in the gateway. For quarter of an hour we were delayed, and at last got out. Then came all the camp-followers, and last of all the rearguard of Sepoys." Hay had loaded his nine servants with his clothes and other personal belongings, but all of them deserted on the journey, "stealing *everything* I possessed, with the exception of what I had on, which consisted of a suit of linen and my sword."[8]

Too busy that night celebrating and drinking, the Oudh rioters did not notice the column as it made its way uphill to the Residency Water Gate in 15 minutes without a shot being fired. The suspense got worse when the column found the Water Gate locked. "Open the gate" was almost mistaken for "Open with grape" and some defenders were about to fire when an officer stopped them. Finally the key was found and the Macchi Bhowan column marched inside. Seconds later the old fortress exploded "with a great quake of the earth, a thunderous retort, and a brilliant glare."[9] The noise was colossal; Mrs Inglis thought the Residency had been hit by a shell as doors rattled and china jumped. Down in her dark tykhana Mrs Bartrum thought the rebels had entered the city and was so terrified that she sprang up as bricks and mortar fell down from the ceiling and little Bobbie stood on his bed and cried for his mama. In Dr Fayrer's House the concussion covered some of the ladies in glass splinters and blew one of the doors off its hinges.

An immense black cloud of dust and fragments spread over the city and was wafted on the wind towards the Residency, "darkness covering a bright starry firmament," wrote an observer. It was now that Colonel

Palmer learned about the fatal injury to Suzanne. She passed away at 4am, but by this time was calm and perfectly lucid, begging the chaplain to take care of her papa when she was gone.

After the explosion, some of HM 32nd had given a cheer. This was echoed across the city by the insurgents who thought at first that one of their shells must have hit the Macchi Bhowan's powder magazine. The explosion had rocked the chandeliers in the Great Imambara and put out its candles. Only later did the rebels find out what had taken place and they were far from happy. Yet their "capture" of the old fortress had its advantages; next day, when the riots got worse, a small gun was towed to the Macchi Bhowan, lifted to the battlements by a rope and pulley and fired on the budmashes.

Meantime the garrison's last man had gotten safely through the city. This was a drunken Irish soldier of HM 32nd who had missed the roll call and evacuation. The explosion had thrown him in the air and ripped off his clothes, but he was so inebriated that he went straight back to sleep. At dawn he awoke naked and alone amid a pile of smoking ruins. Somehow he acquired an ammunition cart and a pair of bullocks and gingerly walked through the sleeping city. Arriving at the Water Gate he bellowed, "Arrah, be Jasus, open yer gates!" The guards collapsed with laughter when they saw naked Paddy. Asked if he had seen any of the mutineers, he replied: "Sure, I didn't see e'er a man in the place."[10] It was a comic miracle and some wondered if the begrimed Irishman must have been spotted, yet mistaken by the rebels for a naked wild fakir.

Sir Henry Lawrence's relief at getting the Macchi Bhowan garrison safely into the Residency was perhaps one of his last joys on Earth. By 8am on 2nd July it was already turning into a hot day. Lawrence, "greatly exhausted" was resting on the top of his bed with his clothes on giving some dictation to Captain Wilson, his aide, who was standing over him. His nephew, George Lawrence, was also lying on his bed parallel to his uncle's. Wilson later explained what happened next:

A coolie was sitting on the floor pulling a punkah. I read what I had written ... and he was in the act of explaining what he wished altered, when the fatal shot came – a sheet of flame, a terrific report and shock, and dense darkness is all I can describe it. I fell down on the floor, and perhaps for a few seconds was quite stunned. I then got up, but could see nothing for the smoke and dust. Neither Sir Henry nor his nephew made any noise, and in great alarm I called out, "Sir Henry are you hurt?" Twice I called out without any answer; the third time he said in a low tone, "I am killed."[11]

Outside on the verandah Lieutenant Hay was standing and recalled Sir Henry's shrieks as "most pitiable". Dr Fayrer administered some chloroform and the dying man was moved under fire to the greater security of the surgeon's house. Moving in and out of consciousness, Lawrence was visited by a stream of tearful friends. Even Martin Gubbins, now forgiven for his behaviour, was moved to write afterwards that he had never witnessed "such a scene of sorrow". Sir Henry tried to see any man he felt had been spoken to harshly during his time at Lucknow and begged their forgiveness. He spoke "humbly of his own merits and dwelt on his shortcomings." He worried about the fortunes of the Lawrence Schools established by him across India for the children of British soldiers, and he was heard to mutter, "I forgive everyone – I forgive my brother, John," a reference to the rift between the two men that had taken place years earlier.

It was, as Mrs Harris wrote, "a wretched day". When a roundshot smashed into the Post Office Battery it caused a fall of bricks that mortally wounded Lieutenant Dashwood, 48th B.N.I. His wife tried to comfort the dying young officer, who was laid near Lawrence. Captain Power of HM 32nd was also shot and killed on the front verandah.

On 3rd July, Mrs Harris, who seems to have been Lawrence's chief nurse, wrote: "His screams are so terrible, I think the sound will never leave my ears."[12] Yet later in the day Sir Henry seemed to rally a little, drinking large drafts of arrowroot and champagne. Outside, the enemy kept up a continuous barrage. Another fatality was Mr Ommaney, the judicial commissioner, who was mortally wounded on his way home from visiting Lawrence. At 8.15am on the 4th, Sir Henry finally passed away. His dying words were said to have been to Brigadier Inglis – "Dear Inglis, ask the poor fellows whom I exposed at Chinhat to forgive me. Bid them remember Cawnpore and never surrender. God bless you all!"[13] Major Banks, the new Chief Commissioner, jotted down haphazardly into his diary a final set of intelligent and explicit instructions:

(i) Reserve fire, check all wall firing. (ii) Carefully register ammunition for guns and small arms in store. Carefully register daily expenditure as far as possible. (iii) Spare the precious health of Europeans, in every possible way, from shot and sun. (iv) Organise working parties for night labour. (v) Entrench, entrench, entrench. Erect traverses, cut off enemy fire. (vi) Turn every horse out of the entrenchments, except enough for four guns. Keep Sir Henry Lawrence's horse, Ladakhi, it is a gift to his nephew, George Lawrence. (vii) Use the state prisoners as a means of getting in supplies, by gentle means if possible, or by threats. (viii)

Enrol every servant as *bildar* or carrier of earth. Pay libetally – double, quadruple. (ix) Take an immediate inventory of all natives, so as to know who can be used as *bildars,* etc. (x) Turn out every native who will not work (save menials who have more than abundant labour. (xi) Write daily to Allahabad or Agra. (xii) Take an immediate inventory of all supplies and food etc. Take daily average expenditure. (xiii) Sir Henry Lawrence's servants to receive one year's pay. They are to work for any other gentleman or they may leave if they prefer to do so. (xiv) Put on my tomb only this: "Here lies Henry Lawrence who tried to do his duty. May God have mercy on him."[14]

Half an hour before his uncle died, Mr George Lawrence was shot through the shoulder on Fayrer's verandah, a nasty wound but not life-threatening. George truly seemed to have a charmed life since he had already had a lucky escape from the shell that killed Sir Henry, and in the coming days would have two more incredible brushes with death. His uncle was now wrapped in a sheet and buried under the cover of darkness. He had asked for no fuss and was put to rest with some gunners who had died that day. Before being lowered into the grave dug by the Reverend Harris, as no coolies were available, the soldiers of the burial party each bent down and gently kissed the great man's head.

As the first week of the siege started to draw to a close "a feeling of calm resignation seemed to steal over most of us,"[15] wrote Mrs Huxham. This sentiment was mirrored by Adelaide Case six days after losing her husband (and not even with a body she could mourn over), who wrote in her diary: "Our courage feels renewed when daylight appears. I hear that the enemy's force round the Residency are in great numbers, and that they have a great many guns; but our brave little handful of Europeans, scarcely numbering 800, are holding out nobly."[16]

Banks and Inglis had only 1,640 active men, along with 80 or so at various stages of sickness, to man a perimeter of more than one mile around the 33-acre Residency site. There were 103 British officers including several doctors, 671 British non-commissioned officers and men, 51 Christian drummers, mostly Eurasians (called "Anglo-Indians") and 153 white civilian volunteers. The largest proportion of British troops were men of HM 32nd Foot, but it is sometimes overlooked that there was a company of the 84th Foot comprising two officers and 48 men under Lieutenant David O'Brien (they had been originally sent by Lawrence to Cawnpore with another company, but returned to Lucknow under Wheeler's order, thus avoiding the fate of their comrades who were massacred on 27th June). Rees gives an oft-quoted figure of 712 Indian troops who had stayed loyal after Chinhat; according to a roll taken on 1ˢᵗ July 386 Indian officers and other ranks came from just four regiments of the Bengal Army: 189 from the 13ᵗʰ B.N.I.; 16 from the 41ˢᵗ B.N.I.; 73 from the 48ᵗʰ B.N.I. and 108 from the 71ˢᵗ B.N.I. The Oudh regiments supplied the rest, especially the Sikh troopers of the Oudh Irregular Cavalry.

The non-combatants numbered 510 women and children at the start of the siege with a further 67 boys from La Martinière School. It was estimated on 1ˢᵗ July that about 680 Indian servants, coolies and camp followers also remained, but in the coming days their number fell dramatically. The defenders were a disparate bunch, and who they all were and where they came from still bedevils researchers and is the subject of debate. The "British" soldiers came from all over the United Kingdom with a goodly number of Irishmen in the lower ranks of HM 32ⁿᵈ. The civilians included French merchants such as Deprat and Geoffroi, as well as Italians like Barsatelli (who traded in alabaster). There was an American, Mr J. Soule, and the Polehamptons had a black American servant called Ramsey. Besides the two Anglican padres there were two Catholic priests, both Capuchins, Father Bernard of Pistoia and Father Adeodatus of Perugia. Some sources say Bernard was French (though Pistoia is in Tuscany). He was an unsmilingly strict prelate who refused to administer to any except his flock. Father Adeodatus, in contrast, was "a saintly old man of sixty-eight" who had served continuously in India since 1822 and hoped one day that his bones might lie in the church of St Mary which he himself had built (gout would keep him bedridden through most of the siege). Two of the British gentlemen – George Couper and John Inglis – had been born in Canada, the former to an army father serving there and the latter to a bishop. Another Canadian was drummer John James Parsons.

Each little post around the perimeter was regarded as a separate garrison. Officers and men alike took their turn at guard duty. There were no reliefs. Each unit tried to keep its defences in a good state of repair, helped by advice from the engineers, and each small band used their own initiative to repel attacks.

Across the palisades and trenches the regiments that had mutinied were also cohesive to a remarkable degree. Their British officers had gone but they stayed true to their regimental traditions; every morning their bugles sounded assembly and regimental calls could be heard all through the day. In the evenings their bands played as if back on parade in East India Company days. The British across the divide heard the enemy serenading them with old musical favourites such as "See The Conquering Hero Comes" and "The Girl I Left Behind Me". Most incongruous of all – in fact almost bizarre given the circumstances – was that these evening recitals invariably ended with "God Save The Queen". One can only imagine how this must have galled the listening British defenders; it suggested cherished institutions were somehow being mocked.

At this juncture, with Sir Henry Lawrence gone and both sides accepting the likelihood of a long siege, let us take a walking tour of the Residency perimeter. We will start at the Water Gate in the middle of the northern curtain. This area was given to Lt-Colonel Palmer, who had so recently lost one of his daughters. He had two other children at Lucknow (his wife had died years earlier). His son Charles, aged nine, a La Martinière pupil, helped carry ammunition and messages to the battery of his brother-in-law, Ralph Ouseley, who was married to sister Annie. Colonel Palmer's task was perhaps the easiest position in the defences since the guns of the Redan Battery commanded this stretch of the river front. A winding road from the city led up to the gate, which was never seriously assaulted.

Just behind the Water Gate stood the Residency itself, at the compound's highest point. It was a difficult building to defend and after a week's bombardment was starting to look a wreck, though the Union Jack still flew from the roof. Cannonballs continually slammed into it or whizzed through its large open windows. By 11th August the structure would be so fragile that a gale collapsed the north-east wing, burying six men of HM 32nd and killing four of them.

The hospital next door, formerly the Banqueting Hall, was commanded by Lieutenant Langmore, formerly adjutant of the 71st B.N.I. The building had no tykhana and the upper storey was too dangerous for invalids, so the front rooms of the ground floor were used by officers, the interior rooms for the men, and the back of the building was a dispensary. A battery of three guns – an 18-pounder, a 13 inch howitzer and a 9-pounder – were placed between the Water Gate and the Hospital.

Walking eastwards one came to the Baillie Guard and its gate, beyond which a road wound down to the richest part of Lucknow. Many people got the name wrong thinking it should be spelled "bailey" – as in motte and bailey castle – but it had been coined by a former Resident, Colonel Baillie. It was a "single-storied, verandahed building, of no particular merit, that had been used partly as a storeroom and office, partly as a treasury, and partly as a barracks for the native soldiers."[17] The guardroom lay in a no-man's land beyond the wooden gates, which were now blocked up by earth. Two 9-pounders and an 8-inch howitzer sat ready to shower any invaders with grapeshot and canister. During the siege the post's commandant, Lieutenant Aitken, 13th B.N.I., with some of his men, constructed an 18-pounder battery to the left of the gate.

Robert Hope Moncrieff Aitken was to be one of the most courageous defenders. A contemporary wrote of him: "Here from summer into winter, until of his two hundred musketeers he had buried 85 and sent to hospital 76, earning his cross in ragged flannel trousers and a jersey of dubious hue, burly Bob Aitken bore the unequal fray."[18]

Standing behind the Baillie Guard and also facing east was Dr Fayrer's House. The post was commanded by Captain Weston of the Oudh Military Police. Fayrer has left us this description:

> My house in the Residency was a large, oblong building, with a flat roof surrounded by a parapet about 3 feet high. On this bags of earth were piled, and the side which overlooked the city was used as a breastwork for riflemen. The house was built on a slope with a garden on both sides, one higher than the other. On the Residency side there was one floor, on the city side two floors, owing to the lower level of the ground on that side. There was a suite of rooms from which doors opened into the garden... In one of the rooms was a swimming-bath ... there was also a tykhana, or underground room for hot weather.[19]

One 9-pounder loaded with grape was placed in a north-east direction to command the Baillie Guard gateway. A disadvantage of Fayrer's House was that the clocktower of the nearby Fureed Buksh Palace gave a splendid vantage point for the insurgents to pot-shot anyone moving outside.[20]

Walking south-easterly but closer to the perimeter and on lower ground was Sander's Post, sometimes called the Financial Garrison. It was rather weakly barricaded with furniture on all sides and inside with boxes. The house was a big one and had two verandahs. In command was Captain Sanders, 41st B.N.I., aided by several soldiers of HM 32nd and volunteer civilians. The only way into the post was by sliding down a slope of loose gravel to the rear. Even worse was leaving, and more than a few good men were shot climbing back up the slope.

Slightly lower but separated from Sander's Post only by a wall was Mrs Sago's House. The good lady before the uprising had been mistress of a charity school. Little is known about her but she survived the siege, though not in her home, which was a particularly dangerous place. Both Sander's and Sago's posts were commanded outside the defences by a building known as Azimullah's Kothee and a small brick building that had once been a gambling den. Though Sago's was exposed, it at least had the support from above of two 18-pounders and one 9-pounder at the Post Office. Sago's was commanded by Lieutenant Clery of HM 32nd with some of his regiment and a few civilian volunteers.

Another 32ⁿᵈ officer, the very popular Bernard McCabe, commanded at the Post Office. Also fighting here was Postmaster William Forder and his supervisor, Mr J. Marshall. Being relatively safe, several families were quartered there including Marshall's wife and child (all three survived the siege), Bandmaster Martin and his wife, and Mr W. May of the uncovenanted civil service. In addition to its three guns, the garrison had three mortars to lob shells into the Cawnpore Road and the Moti Mahal Palace. The post was also headquarters for both the garrison engineers and artillery, with workshops for both services including the preparation of shells and fuses.

Right of the Post Office was Germon's Post commanded by Mrs Germon's husband, "Charlie", of the 13ᵗʰ B.N.I. It was garrisoned by some of his Sikh troops and civil service volunteers. The building was a commodious two-storied villa, once the home of a British official of the King of Oudh. A wall of stakes and a bank of earth protected it from the roadway to the east. This meant that the enemy was only 12 yards away and so it was to witness more hand-to-hand fighting than anywhere else in the defences. A high turret of a building outside called Johannes's House also exposed the garrison to enemy fire.

Finally, in the south-east corner was the garrison's most exposed position – the home of Captain Robert Anderson, one of the civil commissioners. Built on high ground and two-storied, the place was totally exposed and by the end of the siege would be completely destroyed. At the start of July it was still well loopholed and staunchly defended. Anderson was to lose his wife and one of his children during the siege. He commanded a mix of HM 32ⁿᵈ and civilian volunteers; one of these was the brave Mr Capper who had such a lucky escape on the first day and went on through the siege to perform heroically. Others, such as clerk Mr J. Brown, were to be less fortunate. The captain described the position as "fairly box'd up... A man could not show his nose without hearing – whiz – whiz – of bullets close to his head." Sometimes the bullets danced on the walls, "like a handful of peas in a frying pan".[21]

In the south-eastern corner was the Cawnpore Battery, specially constructed of earth and palisades to dominate the main road out of the city. At this stage it had three guns but was overlooked from Johannes's House. Three officers would die trying to hold this place – Lieutenant Arthur and Captain Radcliffe of the 7ᵗʰ Light Cavalry and Lieutenant Lewin of the Artilllery – in fact, so dangerous was the battery that it had no regular commandant. Later during the siege, it was decided to remove the guns and hold the post with sharpshooters.

Further along the south side was what was called Deprat's House, "an undistinguished building" with a verandah overlooking the wall of

Johannes's House which it faced, single-storied, unstockaded, but with a nine-foot-high mud wall. Deprat, who had served under Canrobert in Algeria as a *Chasseurs d'Afrique*, was foolhardily brave and also generous. Frequently, his Latin temper would well up and he would yell, "Come on ye brave, ye rascals, cowards, scoundrels." A flurry of musket balls was the normal reply, along with taunts of, "Cursed dog of an infidel, I know thee! Though art Deprat, the Frenchman living near the iron bridge... We'll yet kill you. Be sure of this."[22] Within six weeks the building was a heap of rubble and not long after, the gallant Frenchman also lay dead.

A short distance from there walking westwards along the south curtain led to what was called the Martinière Post. This was formerly the home of two wealthy Indian gentlemen; it was built of sturdy brick (unlike many of the houses which were constructed of small Roman-style tiles) and furthermore defended by a stockade of massive wooden beams. The older students and the teaching staff of La Martinière School had taken over this vacant building, aided by men of HM 32nd, headmaster George Schilling acting as commandant. The Martinière boys armed with muskets were enthusiastic but tended to blaze away at anything.

Further along the south side was a former hospital now re-named the Brigade Mess – an officers mess for all the Native Regiments. Rather uniquely, its garrison consisted almost entirely of officers. The cooking for all the troops was also done here and distributed by Indian cook-boys who ran a gauntlet of fire every day to deliver the meals. Several of these youngsters were killed and some of them deserted. One of the garrison's best marksmen, Lieutenant Sewell, 71st B.N.I., was based at the Brigade Mess with his double-barrelled Enfield rifle. His firing was effective up to 750 yards and so enraged the insurgents that they had to build a special screen to protect themselves at the bottom of the lane running into the city. Commanding the post was Lt-Colonel Masters, 7th Light Cavalry, Inglis's deputy, a man "liked a great deal, but not much respected". He had a tendency to hail people from the flat roof of the Brigade Mess and soon got the nickname of "Admiral".

Lying adjacent were a group of low buildings in an area called Sikh Square. Just beyond lay another square full of artillery bullocks and another of cavalry horses. At the start of the siege, the Sikh soldiers were greatly distrusted after their shameful behaviour at Chinhat. Passionately loyal to them was Lieutenant Hardinge of the 3rd OIC who commanded the post. Several of the men sat around sulkily that first week, doing little or nothing, and a bunch deserted on 8th July (creeping back on some nights to try and get others to do the same).

A broad path led from the Sikh Square to the south-west corner of the defences and Mr Gubbins' House. This large villa was protected by a 9-pounder battery paid for by Gubbins himself. It was a useful gun since it could be traversed to command in three directions. A second 9-pounder was set up in a garden nearby. The commissioner frequently interfered with the military men sent to command this post; these included Captain H. Forbes of the OIC, who was wounded, Major Banks and Major Apthorp of the 41st B.N.I. Poor Apthorp in particular had a difficult task since the highly strung Gubbins was also his host and had made room in the house for the major, his wife and child. Gubbins had spent several weeks and a small fortune preparing for the siege by laying in stocks of basic foodstuffs, wines, spirits and some tinned goods. He admitted that "Our garrison was the best provided for." His Indian cook and butler stayed loyal along with several servants. He described how he used his supplies:

We possessed some supply of bottled beer. This which was esteemed the greatest luxury during the siege was reserved for the nursing ladies and for the sick. One glass of sherry and two of champagne or claret was served to the gentlemen, and less to the ladies at dinner. One glass of light wine, Sauterne, was provided at luncheon... A cold luncheon only was served and we made an early dinner at four. By these timely precautions the supplies which we had husbanded, and the wants of our numerous guests were provided for during the siege. Besides, we were often able to render assistance to persons in other garrisons ... and to the wounded in hospital... At dinner our chief luxury were rice puddings. Occasionally a plum pudding or jam pudding was made. One cup of tea was made for each person at six in the morning, our English maid, Chivers, presiding at the tea-table. Another cup at the ten o'clock breakfast and another at night. We enjoyed both milk and sugar in our tea, a luxury which few possessed... Our greatest want in the way of food, was that of bread... The flour was therefore kneaded with water, and beaten thin and flat, thus forming what are called "chupatties". They were not, however, wholesome.[23]

As the siege wore on, the upper storey of Gubbins' House had large holes in the walls and an occasional shot went through the dome of the drawing room.

Behind this was Ommaney's House, not strictly in the front line, yet far from safe. A bridge built by the engineers linked it over the road to Gubbins' House in case the latter garrison needed to escape. Large and double-storied, it was soon full of refugees. Here Brigadier Inglis made his own HQ and night quarters. The handful of men from HM 84th Foot were billeted here as a final reserve.

In a kind of triangle on this side of the compound between Fayrer's, Ommaney's and the Residency itself were a few lesser buildings, one of which, the Begum Kothi, had been Mrs Bartrum's first abode during the siege. Its magnificent green and yellow upper storey served as a store room while its deep foundations were a safe retreat for several families. Close by, in this relatively safe area, was the Native Hospital. Further walking along the west curtain one came to the Sheep and Slaughter Houses, all loopholed, facing an area of ruins occupied by the enemy. Captain T. F. Boileau, 7th Light Cavalry, commanded all this area supported by a battery in the Sheep Pen. The stench from the slaughterhouses and the millions of flies made garrison duty here a hard job. Several members of the Sequera family of civil servants served here; one of these, Edwin, had fought nobly at Chinhat, but was killed during the siege along with his mother.

Sitting in a small declivity in the ground was the Gothic-style Residency church, dedicated to St Mary, with its 20 low steeples. Near the descent to the church were placed one 18-pounder and two 9-pounder guns commanded by Captain Evans, Deputy Commissioner of Poorwah (his wife died of disease during the siege). The church was one of the weakest points in the defence line and in August the garrison was withdrawn on Inglis's orders. At the gate to the east was a mortar battery capable of shelling buildings on the western and northern sides as far as the iron bridge. The small churchyard had not been designed as a cemetery, but it was now destined to receive many of the garrison. Due to the constant sniping, burials were usually done at night and rather hastily; in time, the fact that many people were given shallow graves would cause the place to have a most unholy stench.

Further north was Innes's Post, home of Lieutenant James John McLeod Innes, assistant to the civil engineer of Lucknow. Despite the post bearing his name, Innes was not one of the garrison. It was commanded by Lieutenant Loughnan of the 13th B.N.I. supported by a mixed band including a dozen uncovenanted gentlemen commanded by Mr J. C. Parry, secretary of the Delhi Bank. From the building one could see across low land all around on the enemy side, but this vantage meant that the position was very exposed, a situation made worse by its only defence being a wooden palisade. Innes's Post came under fire or was attacked frequently. The building itself was low with verandahs and a sloping roof. A low mud wall separated it from the churchyard on one side and a Moslem cemetery on the other.

Finally, walking northwards on the west side one reached the great Redan Battery, built by the engineers to overawe the Captain's Bazaar district of Lucknow that lay below it and all of the city and river as far as the iron bridge. It was "the best, most strongly fortified and most complete battery of the whole garrison".[24] Its two 18-pounders and one 9-pounder gun could move on their platform three-quarters of a circle to threaten attackers north, east and west (and across the river). A trench gave shelter to the gunners. Captain Sam Lawrence of HM 32nd commanded the garrison, a big, genial fellow who was in action every day yet somehow survived without a scratch.

Examining the whole perimeter, Innes thought the weakest aspect of the defences was their lack of flanking fire except in the northern sector and before Baillie's Gate. He also thought it was a bad mistake not to have blown up Johannes's House, or included it in the defences. But it was not all gloom; thanks to Sir Henry Lawrence's foresight the garrison had large quantities of basic foodstuffs (excluding fresh fruit and vegetables), there was enough rum for the British soldiers to have a daily ration throughout the siege and enough wells to provide sufficient drinking water.

As the first week of the siege drew to a close, the monsoon rains poured down from leaden skies to drench both defenders and attackers leaving both sides equally wet and miserable. On 7th July, despite heavy enemy fire all day, a sortie was made from the Residency by 50 men of HM 32nd and 20 Sikhs led by several officers. The object was to see if the insurgents were driving mines from Johannes's House. The British managed to shoot fifteen or more of the enemy with a loss of only three men wounded. That day, a heavy attack was made on the Brigade Mess where a cannonball took off both the legs of Major Frances of the 13th B.N.I. He died next day along with Mr Ommaney.

Next morning the Reverend Polehampton had just finished shaving and was rolling up his bed mattress when he was shot. The ball very obligingly exited his body and rolled across the floor. Doctors bound him up and said the wound was not life-threatening.[25]

The new regime of the garrison was noted by Captain Wilson, who wrote in his diary on 8th July: "Very few servants remained and most of the officers had none. All were on duty thirteen and twenty hours a day; and constant alarms took place at night."[26] In all duties, the officers shared with the men, manning guns, shooting through loopholes, carrying loads and digging pits for putrid animals that had to be buried under darkness; and all this work done in heavy rain or blistering heat.

Each day brought more adventures for the officers, some of which never found their way into despatches. In a letter home not written until December, Lieutenant W. Fletcher, 40th B.N.I., recalled one such incident:

About the 7th of July the Enemy set fire to a lot of tents standing near one of our powder magazines containing, I heard, 140 barrels, and there was of course a chance of us being blown to the deuce, if by any circumstances they they could have fired them three feet or so into the magazine and made a communication with loose powder. It was in the garden of the Residency and they had possession of the garden wall – so Aitken, 13th, Green (ensign) 13th and I volunteered to go and cut them down (the tents). I had a very sharp tulwar and after cutting down all the empty tents (some were so full of things that they stood after every rope had been cut) we came back – some two or three shots passed over us, but whether from the enemy or our own men I can't say as it was at night.

He concluded with a sigh: "This will never be mentioned in Orders – so much for volunteering!"[27]

On the 9th and 12th July the insurgents tried to storm the Baillie Guard gate at night, sounding a general advance on their bugles. Shelling from the guns and musketry fire drove them back. Then they tried to storm Gubbins' House "and were frequently heard abusing each other for not advancing," but after 30 minutes their attack wavered and they contented themselves with shelling the Cawnpore Battery.

Next day, the monsoon heat left everyone exhausted. Yet the attackers still showed great dash, re-occupying Johannes's House, firing down the street, killing two sepoys and wounding a conductor; they also got close to the Redan Battery. Captain Wilson marvelled at the "excellent" Indian marksmen, one of whom, with a crack shot through a hole in the church wall, managed to plug Lieutenant Charlton of HM 32nd in the head. The garrison noticed how the insurgents seemed to be running low on roundshot and now started firing other objects such as carcasses or logs bound up with iron. Captain Birch noticed among the attackers some Oudh villagers armed with traditional bows and arrows; several arrows were found in the entrenchments, some with oiled wicks intended to set fire to the grain stacks. Indeed, the Residency caught fire on the 8th but the conflagration was soon extinguished. The British soldiers found the large blocks of wood fired into the compound rather comical and would yell out, "Here comes a barrel of beer at last!" Two expert enemy marksmen were nicknamed "Bob the Nailer" and "Jim the Marksman". The notorious "Bob" was thought to be a former black slave of the King of Oudh; he used a double-barrelled rifle and hardly ever missed. The dangers posed by such men would have been even greater if the troops had worn white clothing, but their garments had been dyed a dingy-brown khaki before the siege. One officer from the provinces, in despair at the state of his uniform, cut up the Residency billiard table's felt and donned a suit of thick Lincoln green.

Some officers remained upbeat; Lieutenant Hay wrote:

I look upon the garrison as perfectly safe for a month longer. The hospitals are very full, and the cholera has been taking its share of useful men away, but at the present rate of mortality, I think we can hold out at least thirty days from this time… I get on wonderfully without servants. The washing is terribly uphill work, and dreadfully unsuccessful. However, I am not much worse off than my neighbours. The poor ladies with children have much to put up with.[28]

Not used to cooking their own food or washing their dishes – in fact not used to doing any menial work at all – the siege came as a nasty shock to the officers' wives. Many of them had children in tow and more than a few were heavily pregnant. Their pampered lifestyles had been brutally transformed. Every task they now performed had to be done wearing heavy long dresses, crinolines (in some cases) and, of course, layers of flannel underwear and a tight corset. On 1st July Mrs Huxham was one of those moved from the tykhana at the Residency to quarters in the Brigade Square. "No sooner had we emerged into the open air than we were assailed by showers of bullets which were flying in all directions and whizzing closer to our ears. The bearer carried my sweet baby and little Willie [was] clinging fast to my hand." The group ran 200 yards to a lofty building on one side of the square; it was an odd structure with no doors and no inner walls, "just a huge roof supported on pillars from which hung *purdahs* (curtains) to keep out the glare of the sun."[29] Two rows of native bedsteads without any other furniture were arranged inside. Each day the women and children had a meal of sago and arrowroot cooked in a huge pan in the Brigade Square. Willie Huxham never complained and the baby was fed on sago and boiled rice. For a time there was even some milk for the infant, since Annie Ouseley's cows had been brought into the square and each day she kindly sent the nursing mothers a soda water bottle of warm nourishment.

One of the curious sights was the children at play, especially the little boys, who seemed to accept the horrors around them with a cheerful equanimity. Julia Inglis noted how "they would make balls of earth, and throwing them against the wall would say they were shells bursting." One grimy urchin of four or five years of age was heard by Captain Anderson telling his chum, "You fire roundshot, and I'll return shell from my Battery."[30]

At Fayrer's House young Maria Germon was getting used to acting as her own servant. She thought it "a good thing, it kept our thoughts from dwelling on our misery."[31] Charlie came over, sometimes bringing milk for the children. On 10th July she and the other ladies left the darkness of their underground room to sit by the front door. It did them all some good, and two nights later they risked sleeping in the dining room, "but the mosquitoes were fearful" as the punkah did not work properly. Mrs Harris, also staying with Dr Fayrer, explained the general living conditions:

> The gentlemen sleep in a long verandah sort of room on the side of the house least exposed to fire. My bed consists of a purdah and a pillow. In the morning we all roll up our bedding, and pile it in heaps against the wall… Our usual fare consists of stew, as being easiest to cook … ladled out to each person. Of course we can get no bread, or butter, so chupatties are the disagreeable substitute. We have large stores of beer, wine, arrowroot, sago, etc which will last a long time. Our rations of meat, rice wheat, dhol etc we draw from the commissariat.[32]

Mrs Bartrum felt utterly unable to cope at first; presented with her ration of flour, salt, rice, peas and meat she had no idea how to cook them, so a native servant put the whole lot in an old copper saucepan and created a strange stew, "perfectly green". At first Katherine needed a *punkah-wallah* (a servant to push the swinging ceiling fan), but in time she learned to do most of her menial tasks, getting up at daybreak to look for bits of wood, cutting up small pieces with a dinner knife, lighting her own fire, boiling water for breakfast and washing her clothes.

On the first day of the siege Mr Parry of the Delhi Bank had left his wife and four children in the tykhana at the Residency, but Mrs Parry did not like the overcrowded place. Next day and while her husband was fighting at Innes's Post, she went looking for alternative accommodation. By luck, she met a former employee of the Bank called Macmanus who invited the Parrys to share his hut. Some time later he was killed at the Baillie Guard heroically rolling away a barrel of gunpowder. Mrs Parry now invited two more homeless families to share the hut, which was roughly eight feet by fifteen feet square and had to serve as a living and bedroom with three beds and a few chairs kept outside until nightfall. A native cook did what she could for the Europeans on a primitive store at the rear of the hut and everyone ate their meals by balancing their plates on their knees.

There were others who coped remarkably well right from the start; Mrs Harris and Mrs Polehampton, the two chaplain's wives, offered their services as nurses. Mrs Brydon, wife of another doctor, and Mrs Gubbins organised a roster so that the men on night duty got tea and brandy. Even the aristocratic Julia Inglis, daughter of an Attorney-General and future Lord Chancellor, went out and gathered firewood. Some women were creative; Mrs Boileau utilised her dress-making skills, turning bits of flannel into new shirts.

Inside the hospital the atmosphere was stifling, the windows all barricaded and hot gusts of air blowing in whenever the doors were opened. "Everywhere cries of agony were heard," wrote Rees, "piteous exclamations for water and assistance." Flies in their hundreds settled on those covered with blood. The nurses tried, largely unsuccessfully, with the aid of some of La Martinière's younger boys, to drive away the insects. One poor fellow, while smoking his pipe, was shot "in his bed, and several of our sick had narrow escapes from the bursting of shells." Cholera could take a seemingly healthy man in a few hours, as it did Captain Mansfield of HM 32nd. Some men were accidentally injured such as Captain Alexander of the same regiment who had a mortar blow up in his face, turning him into "a dreadful figure, black as ebony, and covered in blisters which afterwards suppurated."[33] Gastritis was a general complaint, as were colds and skin rashes; scurvy caused by the lack of vitamins made teeth drop out, heads to swell and left large black bruises from the lightest of bumps. Some women such as Mrs Bruere went crazy. So did Captain Graham, adjutant of the 1st Oudh Cavalry, who later in the siege shot himself in bed. Among the engineers, just as examples, Major Anderson, senior engineer, had a history of tuberculosis, Captain Fulton suffered from a liver complaint and Lieutenant Hutchinson was prone to bilious attacks and diarrhoea.

Lieutenant Innes lost all his servants except two:

These two and one other were the only kitchen & table servants for a mess of 23 of us. Not a single house except Mrs Ommaney's and the Begum Kothee were safe from roundshot and bullets which went flying thro' all the compounds, along the lanes and into the doors and windows. If a Soldier was rash enough to fire over a parapet, he was pretty sure to get a bullet in his forehead. If he darkened a loophole too long, he was sure to be covered with fragments of mud of which the parapet was made, from the bullets stirring all round. Major Banks, Major Bruere, Captain Power and Lieutenant Lester were all shot looking through loopholes. Mrs Doni, Dr Brydon, and Rev. Polehampton were all shot thro' windows. Shells of course might come anywhere but the rebels had no mortars and very little ammunition for the howitzer.[34]

On 4ᵗʰ July Mrs Harris was pleased to find a "delightful" soldier, Private Henry Metcalfe of the 32ⁿᵈ, who agreed to keep her white terrier for the duration of the siege. The animal, called "Bustle", had been given to the padre and his wife by a dying old soldier of HM 75ᵗʰ Foot when they had been stationed on the Punjab frontier. They adored the dog, but could not afford to keep feeding him, and had decided he must be shot. Henry Metcalfe was 22 years old and extremely literate by the army standards of the day. Like the Harrises, he thought Bustle was a "beautiful" dog and it was just the kind of company he needed. James Harris was so pleased by Metcalfe's offer to look after Bustle that he asked Henry if he could thank him with a gift. The private asked for a pipe. Harris did not smoke, "but instead he presented me with a box of beautiful cigars," wrote Metcalfe. "After this the dog accompanied me wherever I went, both day and night, and indeed it was a good job on some occasions, for when on sentry at night and when the least sign of drowsiness came over me, the dog was sure to notice it and catch my trousers between his teeth, and shake me to keep me awake."[35]

During the first month of the siege (Private Metcalfe excluded), the men of HM 32ⁿᵈ "showed a most disorderly spirit", wrote Innes. "They were not wanting in courage, but were in a state of complete insubordination; their language and manners to all were most disgraceful and thefts and robberies were committed openly and shamelessly."[36] Some men broke into the room where much of the Oudh regalia had been stored and items were stolen "or despoiled of jewels". On 5ᵗʰ July, according to Rees, most of the British soldiers in the Cawnpore Battery were dead drunk; earlier they had found their way into Deprat's cellar and while ignoring the merchant's claret and Haut-Sauternes, had consumed his entire stock of champagne and brandy. Monsieur Deprat's personal chests of valuables were rifled and several gold and silver watches stolen. In some ways this raid turned out not to be a bad thing since, with the main store of liquor gone, the soldiers were less intoxicated for the remainder of the siege.

On the rebel side, discontented men continued to pour into Lucknow. By 10ᵗʰ July, according to a letter from Raja Man Singh to a British political agent, some 35,000 insurgents surrounded the Residency; 10,000 of them were mutineers from different regiments and the rest were retainers of such talukdars as Goorbux Singh of Ramnuggur and Nawab Ali Khan. "Everyday their numbers increase."

The military skill of the mutinous gunners consistently impressed the British, along with their enemies' courage and determination. Martin Gubbins wrote:

Within the first week after the siege began, the enemy had established batteries all round us ... generally well placed, and very near: some guns being in position within sixty yards of our defences ... they were very clever in placing them so that we could bring no gun to bear upon them in reply. Sometimes they kept the gun concealed behind the corner of a building, ran it out, fired and immediately retired before we could return the shot, pulling back the gun with a drag rope. In other places the gun was kept at the bottom of an incline, to the top of which it was dragged to be fired, when the rope forced it down the inclined plane again... Their batteries were usually formed of strong rafters of wood stuck upright and deeply embedded in the ground, and strengthened and supported by a bank of earth; a square embrasure being left in the centre for the muzzle of the cannon... Their fire was generally precise and seldom went very wide of the object aimed at. But they rarely attempted to batter in breach: their object seemed to be rather to drive us from our works... Where our cannon could not bear upon the enemy, their batteries were shelled; and three or four shells usually caused a suspension of their firing... The ingenuity of the enemy, however, preserved them in their batteries in a great measure from injury by these missiles; for on several occasions upon which sorties were made, it was discovered that they had dug narrow trenches ten feet deep near their guns into which they could at once spring and find security when they saw a shell approaching.[37]

Gubbins garnered most of his intelligence about the enemy – and they, in turn, about the British – from the Sikh soldiers, who were never totally trusted. Deserters often crept up to the walls and passed news and gossip with their old comrades still inside the Residency.

So it was learned that the insurgents had finally found a figurehead. The ex-royal family of Oudh, of course, made an excellent rallying point and, the rebellion in Oudh was popular with all classes, and a "national" one insofar as the kingdom was concerned. The new "generals" from the army, along with influential taluqdars, finally settled on a 12-year-old boy, Birjis Qadr, as the new King of Oudh. It was assumed, though never explicitly stated, that his mother, Hazrat Mahal, would rule in his name. She had been helped by Raja Jai Lal Singh, one of the aggrieved old Court faction, a man who held great influence with the Hindu ex-sepoys. The old King of Delhi, or so it was said, had asked Birjis Qadr to rule Oudh as his representative. It was thus easy for the ordinary peasants to see the rising as a way of re-creating with pride (and nostalgia), the land as it had been in Mogul times before the British changed everything.

Some publications have suggested that Hazrat Mahal was one of the ex-king's chief wives, but they are mistaken; Wajid Ali had far too many wives and children to care about them much, and as Hazrat Mahal was left at Lucknow she can hardly have been very important. We do know that she was a remarkable woman of great beauty who had been born into a relatively poor family in Fyzabad. Her irresistible physical charms brought her to the Lucknow Court as a dancing girl and here she caught the eye of the king. As a Begum of Oudh, Hazrat Mahal would prove to be highly intelligent, a clever foe of the feringhees and in every way the equal of that other great female character of the uprising – the Rani of Jhansi. Only in love, perhaps, was Hazrat Mahal weak; she promoted her paramour, Mammu Khan to *Dewan Khana* (chief counsellor). One wonders what she saw in this illiterate man of low origin who was not well-liked in Lucknow; clearly, Mammu had a strong physical appeal and he was almost certainly the father of Birjis Qadr, which partly explains his promotion.

With a heavy rain falling, Birjis Qadr was crowned at the Imambara on 5th July with as much pomp as the rebels could muster; the British had purloined the crown, so a simple gold coronet was placed on the boy-king's head, the generals wore their best East India Company uniforms, the Begum her best jewels, and the soldiers fired a 21-gun salute that was heard at the Residency. Many of the chief taluqdars were there and the city's leading citizens but there was one significant no-show – Maulvi Ahmadullah claimed to have injured his leg leading a charge against the British at Chinhat and so did not attend. His explanation fooled no one, since it was common knowledge that he loathed the Begum and her family. The Maulvi had his own followers, fanatical like him in their hatred of all things European and Christian. Four days later, his leg would be strong enough for him to lead a charge against the Residency. In the coming weeks the rift between him and the Begum would widen.

On 11th July, the insurgents held a long assembly; Sharafaddaula Ghulam Raza was now prime minister and a sepoy called Abid Khan was appointed the senior general, with others including Mammu Khan given bodies of troops to command. The senior cavalry commander was Yusuf Ali Khan, an ex-ressaldar. The regimental commandants now appointed were Ressaldar Kasim Khan and Agha Habibi. Agents brought their intelligence about the British to a man called Abdul Rassaq, the rebels' chief spymaster.

Following the riots Lucknow's inhabitants experienced a severe shortage of grain, a situation made worse by the thousands of new insurgents pouring into the city from all over the province. Prices rocketed for wheat, maize and barley. The Begum had some wheat and peas distributed to the poor, though it was hardly enough for so many empty bellies. New supplies of ammunition, which had been running low, reached the city on 16th July.

Only one letter from this period seems to have survived in English. It had first appeared in a Calcutta newspaper and was then reprinted in the *Illustrated London News*. It had been penned by a man called Gujral Brahmin:

On Sunday July 12th about eight o'clock I left Lucknow, up to that time all was well. The Europeans were in the Residency, and the mutinous troops were attacking from the outside; great plunder was going on in the city. Outside the Residency there are many thousands of men, but they are not all fighting men. Many of them are the people of the city and lookers-on. There may be about twelve regiments and a few Rissalehs. More than 100 of the mutineers are killed daily. Of those who die, those who have relations are burnt, otherwise the bodies are thrown into the Goomtee river. The wounded are carried away in doolies and treated… The sepoys who have plundered the city are walking homeward with their spoils. The mutineers are searching the city for saltpetre. Provisions are plentiful and the Bunneahs have been told to keep their shops open, and sell for ready money. All the mutineers have put up in the gardens of the city people, of which they have forcibly taken possession.[38]

The nights of heavy rain and stiflingly humid days continued. On 14th July Captain Wilson wrote in his diary: "We threw up a traverse near the Post Office gate, in order to save our people from the fire from Johannes's house, which was very sharp. Our sharp-shooters killed four of the enemy in Johannes's house. Still no information of any kind."[39] To the defenders it seemed after almost three weeks as if the whole world had forgotten them. The enemy were ominously seen erecting new batteries; about 5pm a 9-pounder opened on the gable end of the Brigade Mess, causing a soldier of HM 32nd to lose a leg.

Two days later the attackers could be seen making batteries in the garden of Johannes's House and they tried a feint attack at 11pm but were repelled. The Brigade Mess was shelled heavily on 18th July until Lieutenant Bonham dislodged the attackers with a few well directed shots from the Post Office's 18-pounder. That night, the defenders realised with heavy hearts that their enemies now had more guns, as they opened fire simultaneously on Dr Fayrer's House, Gubbins' House, the Brigade Mess and the Post Office. Next morning at breakfast one ball whizzed through a room in the Residency and fractured the leg of Lieutenant Harmer,

HM 32nd Foot, who was breakfasting. A short distance away at the Cawnpore Battery, Lieutenant Arthur, 7th Cavalry, was shot through the heart. Around noon the insurgents sounded an advance at the Redan, but some hard lead from the gun battery made them think twice. During the day Henry Polehampton, whose wound had been doing so nicely, died of cholera. The padre had known he was failing and did not fear death but went peacefully with a smile, telling his wife all was well, as he "entered into the joy of the Lord".[40]

On the morning of 20th July while Mr Rees was cleaning his musket and whistling merrily to himself, the call to arms sounded. A large body of the enemy had been spotted marching about in different directions close to the perimeter defences. It was 8.30am and ominously quiet, apart from the bugle calls of the mutinous regiments. At 10.15am there was a terrific explosion and a mine detonated inside the Water Gate, but still 75 feet from the Redan Battery. The result was "a large crater and a great deal of dust, but no breach in the defences".[41] Bravely rushing through the smoke and not realising the mine had not done the job for which it was intended, hundreds of Indians attempted to storm the Redan and Innes's House. Their leader, cap on the end of his sword, tried to rally his men, but they were mown down by grapeshot and musketry fire from the defenders. Courageously they rallied but to no avail.

Hurrying to the Water Gate amid a shower of shot, Rees started to pick off attackers, one by one, with his musket. Brigadier Inglis, standing at the Redan, was shouting "Bravo! Bravo!" to encourage the defenders. Nearby, Lieutenant Loughnan said: "Give me a shout, boys, a loud one and a strong one." His soldiers bellowed for all they were worth and the insurgents temporarily faltered – but not for long. On they came again, right up to the walls, and there were calls for scaling ladders. From the roof of Innes's House two civilian volunteers hurled down bricks, lumps of mortar, logs, stones "and other missiles of a very impure nature" on their screaming foes. At Innes's a Eurasian (Anglo-Indian) called Bailey (his father had been a Christian captain in the King of Oudh's service), got into an animated conversation with some of his attackers: "Come over to us and leave those cursed feringhees, whose mothers and sisters we have defiled, and whom we shall kill this day. Come over to us, what have you to do with them? Will you be made a Christian too (pop, pop), or have you already lost your caste?" An enraged Bailey replied, "Take that!" He fired his musket and yelled back, "Do you think that I have eaten pig's flesh like yourselves. Do you think that I too shall disgrace myself, by proving unfaithful to my salt. Take that, thou son of a dog! (pop, pop) Thou whose grandfather's grave I have dishonoured!" More gun shots and threats – "My sword is sharp," yelled one rebel. "Is it," cried Bailey, "but thy heart is craven. Come along then, boaster. My bayonet is ready. Scale the wall."[42]

Commanding 11 other uncovenanted gentlemen at Innes's House, Mr Parry of the Delhi Bank recalled in his diary how the enemy bugle that morning sounding the advance had been "something terrific – dreadful – and hellish". He wrote:

On came the sepoys with shouts; not a moment to be lost. Lieut. Loughnan hurried with his men to one face, while I placed my Volunteers on the other face. We had hardly taken up our positions when down came a part of the stockading and we could see and hear some hundreds. Three volunteers only stood behind a loopholed wall ... my men are good shots ... and 3 men bite the dust... Now is the opportunity of the enemy... They seem to be hesitating and they have actually given the volunteers time to reload and once more we are ready ... at last, sword in hand, a great corpulent fellow appears almost filling the gap. He is allowed to enter and 2 or 3 others; steady is our aim and all are down.[43]

The fighting that day was also fierce at Fayrer's House, where the insurgents came swarming through the stables into the garden. The doctor later recalled: "I and the other officers kept our guns and rifles going as hard as we could ... many were knocked over and their bodies lay all night when they were dragged away ... the 18- and 9-pounders were pouring in shot and bags of bullets into them, but I certainly thought our time had come.[44]

The green flags of the Prophet were seen at times being waved in the attack. Shouts resounded of "The Faith! The Faith! Kill the Europeans!" A standard bearer came on and fell pierced by seven bullets. Two courageous ex-sepoys got right up to the wall of the battery before Captain Greene, 48th B.N.I., shot them both in the face. At Anderson's Post a mutineer officer had shouted, "Come on, brothers, there's nobody here!" Mr Geoffroi, one of the civilians replied; "There are plenty of us here, you rascal!" He shot the man dead and the one following him. At Gubbins' House, where the main attack was against an unfinished bastion, Lieutenant Grant leaned over the rampart throwing grenades until one exploded prematurely and blew off his hand.

The fighting all around the garrison lasted seven hours and the defenders stood to arms another three hours until 8pm. The enemy, it was discovered, had been using some 20-25 guns of large calibre. Yet all in all it had been a good day for the defenders; they had repelled countless attacks with a loss of just four Europeans killed and twelve wounded, besides about a dozen sepoys. The insurgents had lost upwards of 1,000 men. Lieutenant Hay fighting at the Cawnpore Battery counted some 300 enemy dead and wounded lying outside his post. It was also reassuring for the Residency Europeans to see that their sepoys, especially those of the 13th, 71st and 48th regiments had behaved in exemplary fashion. When the attackers asked for a truce to carry away their dead and wounded it was agreed – after all, it made sanitary good sense. Brigadier Inglis issued an order praising everyone for their actions during this, the first general assault. Only Major Banks got a reprimand – a strong note telling him that as Chief Commissioner he should not expose himself to so much enemy fire.

At last there was a quiet night as both sides recovered from the stresses of the day. Yet at 10am on the 21st the insurgents broke through some buildings between Gubbins' House and the Sikh Square. Never short of courage, despite his other failings, Martin Gubbins met the enemy head on as he fired two double-barrelled shotguns. Around noon, Major Banks, again in the thick of the fighting, reconnoitring on the top of an outhouse, was shot cleanly through the head and died instantly. He had once told Dr Fayrer that he never wanted to suffer "when my time comes". Now his wish had been granted. Eventually a mortar was brought up and the rebels turned tail. Major Banks' body was sewn up in a sheet and he was given a simple burial by the Reverend Harris. In the case of his colleague, the Reverend Polehampton, his widow had begged the chaplain to find a coffin. Eventually, after searching, one was located under some stairs at the hospital. Harris buried his associate in the coffin and, as a mark of respect, also dug a separate grave for him.

During the attack, Dr William Brydon, in charge of the native hospital, was shot in the groin. Despite intense pain for a time, Brydon would make a complete recovery. He was a remarkable man and must have felt more than a touch of *déjà-vu* about the siege, since it was not his first; 15 years earlier he had been besieged at Kabul during the 1st Afghan War, then taken part in the nightmarish retreat and been immortalised as the solitary horseman who reached Jalalabad on 13th January 1842 with the news that an entire British army had been annihilated in the Afghan passes.

Chief command now devolved on Inglis, who declared that there would be no successor to Major Banks and that his military authority would henceforth be paramount. This information, as one might expect, went down very badly with Commissioner Gubbins, but he was forced to accept the decision. Despite his thick, dark wavy hair and full bushy beard, John Eardley Wilmot Inglis looked older than his 42 years. He had served with HM 32nd Foot since joining as an ensign in 1833. Four years later he saw service in the Lower Canadian Rebellion and fought in the actions at St Denis and St Eustache. He was a Canadian, having been born in Nova Scotia, son of the colony's third bishop. During the 2nd Anglo-Sikh War he had served with distinction at the Siege of Multan and Battle of Gujerat. While unquestionably brave, Inglis was not liked by all his troops; Private Robert Waterfield in his memoirs wrote that Inglis "was no favourite with the men", due to his strictness, and was nicknamed "Scaly Jack". One of his worst traits was a tendency to harangue his soldiers, making long-winded speeches and often administering flogging punishments. Henry Metcalfe thought that Inglis's marriage to Julia Thesiger, a lady liked by the men, helped turn him into a warmer human being.

Classic histories of the Indian Mutiny by authors such as Kaye, Malleson or Forrest paint Inglis as a true hero. He certainly had a lot on his plate to worry about and many less well-disciplined men might have succumbed to the strain of the command (just as Colvin did at Agra). The recent Mutiny historian, P. J. O. Taylor, called Inglis "a man of limited ability and dull personality", which is a far cry from Thomas Rice Holmes' description of "a plain, honourable Christian gentleman, a tender husband, a staunch friend, a lover of all that was high and noble, a soldier of unsurpassable gallantry respected by all those who served under him."[45] One of the garrison who did not view Inglis as a parfit gentil knyght was Lieutenant McLeod Innes. He authored two books on the Uprising and also wrote some magazine articles. In none of them is he critical of Inglis. Yet in a hitherto unpublished and highly critical account of the siege, written contemporaneously, he castigated Inglis:

> A man who possessed not one single quality except energy to fit him for his position... He was brave, no doubt, but not cool or calm in difficulty; he had no control over his temper, no military knowledge beyond drill, and no natural capacity to compensate for his ignorance. He gave orders without making inquiries as to the possibility of carrying them into expectation... His ridiculous and braggadocio speeches were the laughing stock of the garrison. His men despised and disliked him. To us Engineers, who had always enough of necessary and useful work, he gave twice as much that was useless and unnecessary.[46]

The rains continued with an incessant hard downpour every night. Drains overflowed, excrement and effluvia mingled with the commissariat stores lying about, and the bodies of the dead horses and bullocks killed every day. Add to this noxious brew the sick and dying in the hospital and one can understand how the flies bred in their millions.

The ground was sometimes black with them, they swarmed over tables, up people's noses, into their mouths and eyes, they stopped sleep and made eating a nightmare. The boiled lentil soup and chupatties that were a soldier's daily meal was so studded with flies that one ate several with every mouthful, while more fell into the soup and floated about like "impromptu peppercorns".

Feelings of despair were dispelled on 23rd July when – at last – a native messenger got into the lines from Cawnpore. His name was Ungud, one of the pensioners recalled by Lawrence and he had been sent out on 29th June to observe the movements of Nana Sahib's army. After 13 perilous days detained by the mutineers he had gotten away to Cawnpore and the camp of a relief column that was battling its way gradually towards Lucknow. Now, just two days later, he was back with no letters, but the great news that General Havelock, with a small army and just 12 guns, had defeated the mutineers in three battles, retaken Cawnpore and was about to march on Lucknow. Gubbins, as head of intelligence, could hardly believe his ears. Hastily he sent Ungud over to Inglis to see if the brigadier wanted to send Havelock a letter. The reply came back that he did not, so Gubbins prepared his own despatch for the Governor-General under cover via Havelock. It was raining heavily that night and Ungud was keen to get away while the storm kept the rebel sentries indoors. Inglis meanwhile changed his mind and prepared a despatch. "Aid is what we want, and that quickly" ran one of the lines. Ungud grew impatient and eventually Gubbins let him depart without receiving Inglis's document. When the brigadier found out this had happened he naturally felt slighted and lost his temper. When Gubbins restated his claim for the Chief Commissionership it was all too much for Inglis, who seethed. Wilson, his AAG, was ordered to write in the following terms:

Lucknow, July 23rd, 1857.

Sir

I am directed to acknowledge the receipt of your letter No 1 of this date, in which you report that you have assumed charge of the office of Chief Commissioner of the affairs of Oudh, and in reply to state that Sir Henry Lawrence superseded you in the post by the late lamented Major Banks, and he also expressed to Lord Canning and to more than one living member of this garrison that you should on no account be permitted to hold the office of Chief Commissioner. Under the above circumstances, the Brigadier, with the entire concurrence of Anderson, thinks it is duty to inform you and to publish in this day's Orders, for general information, that the office of Chief Commissioner is for the present vacant, and that Martial Law and the highest Military Authority will be paramount in Oudh until a successor to Sir Henry Lawrence shall be duly appointed by the Governor General in Council. The Brigadier therefore requests that you will for the future abstain from sending any message to the relieving force, or performing any act whatever connected with the public service without previously communicating what you propose to do for his information. As your messenger was despatched without waiting for the Brigadier's letter to the officer commanding the Relieving Force, he requests you will furnish him with a copy of your communication.

T. F. Wilson, Capt Offg.a.a.Genl.[47]

The news that a relief army was on its way delighted everyone. "You have no idea what a change it has made in every person here," wrote Lieutenant Hay. "The enemy, we suppose, are gone to meet our reinforcements," he noted after a day of little firing, "which ought to be here in four days if they are not seriously opposed." Hay had fought and slept in the same clothes for 58 days. He felt well, but admitted how "A refreshing odour of carrion pervades our entrenchments: the cattle will get shot, and there is no one to bury them. In the compound close by where I live there are three dead horses and a bullock, and three sepoys down the well into the bargain close to the verandah."[48]

At night on the 25th Ungud returned with a letter from Lt-Colonel Fraser-Tytler, DAQMG with Havelock's army, saying that "We have ample force to destroy all who oppose us," and that he expected that "In five or six days we shall meet." Not all the news was good; now, at last, Ungud confirmed that the women and children held prisoner at Cawnpore by Nana Sahib had all been massacred. This was bitter news for those who had loved ones there. The defenders also heard how the first general appointed by the insurgents at Lucknow had been killed by a bullet from the garrison as the fellow was peering through a loophole, and that one of the sons of the King of Oudh had been placed on the throne.

Early next morning another runner set off, this time with a letter from Inglis:

Lucknow, 26th July, 1857.
1 a.m.

My dear Tytler,
Your note to Mr Gubbins has been received. We are inclined to believe that but a small force has gone out to meet you but that the enemy are disposed to meet you here and will make a final assault on our position.

Our Europeans being now little more than 300 we shall be able to afford you little assistance except by shells. The bearer of to-day's letter will start from this to-morrow with a completed plan of the entrances to the city with a memo by the engineers.

J. Inglis, Brigadier[49]

After one day's rest, Ungud set off with this second Inglis letter and a set of plans and a memorandum drawn up by the engineers. For carrying this important package he was offered the phenomenal sum of £500 (about £50,000 today).

A few relatively quiet days were spoiled at about 10pm on Sunday 26th July by a sudden attack along the whole of the city front. Lieutenant Shepherd, 7th Cavalry, was shot by someone on the roof of the Brigade Square, an example of death by friendly fire. More typical was Lieutenant Lewin killed at the Cawnpore gate (leaving a pregnant widow and baby daughter). By now the insurgents were trying more and more to dig and lay mines. On the 28th a new weapon – stink bombs – were used by the ingenious attackers. These made a "fearful hissing noise and great stench", but were relatively harmless. The Indians, ever inventive, also made shells of brass and stone, which gave off a high shriek. They were called "Whistling Dicks" by the soldiers. When, one Sunday, a huge block of wood landed near Dr Fayrer's House a young Irish soldier of HM 32nd rushed into the room where Chaplain Harris was conducting a service and blurted out, "By Jabers, the devils are firing cook houses at us!"

After 20th July, the doctors decided that the hospital was no longer safe for Mrs Polehampton, Mrs Gall and Mrs Barbour to work in. The three women, all widows, were given three-quarters of a room in the Begum Kothi, the other quarter screened off for the use of Lieutenant Thomas, Madras Artillery, and his little girl. (Mrs Thomas had died of smallpox a few days earlier.) The widows never left their quarters except at night when, despite a stinking drain nearby, they enjoyed a short stroll. Mrs Polehampton developed a kind of death wish and took great risks, walking alone on starlit nights, "listening to the bullets flying overhead, and longing sometimes for the summons to join her husband".[50]

Mrs Harris kept herself busy knitting flannel jumpers for her favourite officers. She had grown used to the miraculous escapes experienced daily by her husband; on 16th July she noted how James was going down to the graveyard when "a roundshot fell between him and the doolie next to which he was walking and threw up earth all over him." When a cannon ball whizzed through the house she hardly noticed it, though like many of the women the attack on the 20th had left her "paralysed with terror".

James Harris had been in the bath when that attack began and was smothered in plaster when a great piece of the wall and ceiling fell down. The poor padre, it seemed, could not even enjoy a bath in peace; he never rested, always aware of the fact that he was the only chaplain now that Polehampton had gone. Georgina got used to the fact that "we don't see much of each other."[51]

Also making do was Mrs Germon, though her husband called in at Fayrer's every day and sometimes brought luxuries, such as a saucepan of soup, or a bottle of port wine. Like everyone else, she found Ungud's news to be "glorious", but as the days passed and the promised relief did not arrive, she grew very disheartened. By 31st July, when the enemy cavalry were seen moving about and the firing, slack for a few days, started to increase again, Mrs Germon was forced to write: "We feel like a ship becalmed. The future is a perfect blank."[52]

Mrs Inglis and Mrs Case strained their ears and fancied they heard heavy guns firing a long way off, but no one else did. It was 4th August. Just as they all sat down to dinner, a shell exploded in the courtyard. It was feared that some of the children might be injured but all were fine. On going out to check, Mrs Couper found a shell on her doorstep still fizzing, though it had failed to explode for want of sufficient powder.

Dr Fayrer was also anxious for any news from the relief column. Supplies, he realised, were running out, especially for the natives. On 2nd August he wrote: "The wounded are not doing well. How could they under such circumstances? Everything is against them. Sharp firing was going on all day and they are now firing rockets which make a fearful noise... A Sikh sowar of the 3rd Cavalry deserted this morning. The wonder is that any of them remain!"[53] Many of the men were now on duty twenty hours each day, bruised and filthy, crawling with lice – "light infantry" as polite ladies called them. When an exhausted private at the Post Office threw down his musket and refused duty, Captain McCabe simply shouted, "Put him to bed!" A well-liked officer, McCabe had risen from the ranks, commissioned from sergeant for conspicuous gallantry during the 1st Sikh War. He knew the taunt would goad the man to pick up his musket again and soldier on. Many officers and rank and file equally suffered now from scurvy, spitting out teeth and rotting membrane, or were doubled up with dysentery, or suffering from sores. When a minor wound turned nasty, 15-year-old Edward Hilton from La Martinière was given a stark choice by the surgeon: lie still or he would be forced to amputate. In the foul hospital Hilton lay very, very still for two months.

On 6th August, the insurgents fired several rounds at the Residency from a big 24-pounder. One projectile hit Ensign Studdy of HM 32nd.

An eye-witness recalled: "Strangely enough, in its passage, it swept off the fringe of the punkah hanging there, which swathed his body round and round; it then struck him in the arm and chest, the wounds having the appearance of violent contusions. The arm was amputated and he died under the operation."[54] The Residency had become so dangerous, its walls pockmarked everywhere by shell holes, that it was decided to vacate its token garrison. Oddly enough, one of the turret staircases still made it possible to reach the roof and keep the flag flying.

The lucky escapes of George Lawrence continued: at 5.30pm on 2nd August a shell smashed through the wall of a room in the Begum Kothi shared by him and another invalid, Lieutenant James of the Commissariat. They both survived without a scratch. Four days later the same two men, along with Ensign Keir (who was sick), were in their beds when an animal carcass fired by the insurgents came crashing into their room. No one was hurt, but a candle was overturned and the room set on fire for a few minutes. This made four occasions when young Lawrence had cheated death and three for James.

On the 10th the insurgents launched their second major attack on the garrison. Around 1,500 of them were seen on the Residency's left flank assembling behind their trenches near the Cawnpore Road about 7am. Thirty minutes later, a shell fired into the Begum Kothi seemed to be the general signal for an attack. A mine was blown by them near the Martinière Post, smashing its wooden palisade to matchwood. One timber spar landed on the roof of the Brigade Mess, so huge was the blast, which created a 60-foot gap in the defences. It took some heavy shooting from the defenders and the hurling of several grenades to drive back the attackers, especially after 30 of them got into the trench of the Cawnpore Battery. Another Indian mine blew up some outhouses near Sago's Post and threw two soldiers out into the road, but the men got safely back inside under a hail of bullets. Sander's Post was attacked by men who may have been fanatical ghazis; one of them tried to wrest a bayonet out of the hands of a private of HM 84th but was shot dead. Makhdoom Baksh, Ghamandi Singh, Ausan Singh and Umrao Singh with their regiments under General Hisam Uddaula attacked at Sander's Post, Raghunath Singh, Gajadhar Singh and Rajmand Tewari's ex-sepoys, under the overall command of Raja Jia Lal and Khan Ali Khan, attacked Sago's Post. Groups of insurgents using scaling ladders attacked Anderson's, Gubbins' and Innes's posts about 9pm that night, led by Bande Ali.

The sky was lit up by exploding shells and grenades, the air riven by the cries of men in battle and in pain. The "Turk" howitzer seized by the insurgents after Chinhat now sent shells crashing into Innes's Post, bringing down beam after beam of the building. Mr Blenman, a volunteer firing through a loophole, was blinded when a ton of bricks temporarily buried him (he regained his sight about a month later). Once again, the garrison did remarkably well, losing only three Europeans and two sepoys killed and just twelve men wounded. Enemy losses are not known but they ran into the hundreds (Captain Anderson quoted a figure of 470 enemy dead).

Next day came the sad news that Major Anderson, chief engineer, a man who had done so much to prepare the Residency for defence, was dead of dysentery. Captain Fulton now became senior engineer; he stitched up his chief in an old quilt and helped to bury him, marking the place with a stick. On the 11th, Inglis himself led a sortie into the enemy lines south of Gubbins' House. Julia Inglis decided to cook some potatoes for dinner, the first anyone had seen for a month (they had been discovered accidentally in an obscure corner). Mrs Bartrum's child, who looked ready to die for a time, was now getting better, as she was at last able to procure some milk. She was getting used to cooking for herself and found that after half an hour of beating the commissariat beef with a big stick it was tender enough to be cut up using her nail scissors.

On the night of the 15th, the pensioner Ungud crept into the compound bearing a letter dated 4th August, addressed to Gubbins from Fraser-Tytler at Mungulwar. It was written in minute letters, partly in Greek characters and folded inside a quill:

> DEAR SIR – We march to-morrow morning for Lucknow, having been reinforced. We shall push on as speedily as possibly. We hope to reach you in four days at furthest. You must *aid us in every way*, even to cutting your way out, if we can't force our way in. We have only a small Force.[55]

It all sounded very different from the last upbeat letter from Fraser-Tytler. Ungud was able to explain that for some days he had been taken prisoner again by the mutineers but, after gaining his release, courageously re-traced his steps to Mungulwar to discover that Havelock had crossed back over the Ganges to Cawnpore, where the general advanced a second time to Busherutgunge and defeated his enemies, but had decided to retire after routing them.

An anxious Inglis wrote a letter to Havelock on 16th August. It was a note of despair. "It is quite impossible with my weak and shattered force that I can leave my defences. You must bear in mind how I am hampered, that I have upwards of 120 sick and wounded, and at least 220 women, and about 230 children, and no carriage of any description... In consequence of the news received, I shall soon put this force on half-rations." After explaining something of the enemy attacks the general concluded: "If our Native force, who are losing confidence, leave us I do not know how the defences are to be manned. Did you receive a letter and plan from me? Kindly answer this question."[56]

Bleakly, Inglis made it plain that he thought the garrison could hold out no longer than 10th September, by which time he assumed the food stocks would be exhausted. Little did he know that no help would reach him for 40 more days – and it would be a further 53 incredible days after that date before he, the gallant defenders, their wives, children and servants would eventually leave Lucknow!

3

A Fossil Turned into Pipe Clay

Calcutta, The Ganges Valley and Oudh, 7th July–15th August 1857

At half-past three on the sultry afternoon of 7th July 1857 a slightly built man with a chest full of glittering medals had ridden out, attended by his staff, onto the parade ground at Allahabad Fort, 125 miles from Lucknow, to inspect a little army drawn up in marching order. Steam still rose from the ground after a night of torrential rain that had turned the place into a quagmire. Despite his small stature, the general rode "neat and erect. His face was older than his years, and much tanned by the Indian sun; his moustache, whiskers and beard bring rather long and perfectly white."[1] He was wore a general's "undress blue frock coat, a forage cap with a large white cover which draped down to shelter his neck, and drab-coloured waterproof leggings which also covered his feet." The man's name was Henry Havelock and within a few short months he would rise from complete obscurity into becoming to the British people a kind of demi-god worthy of a statue in Trafalgar Square.

On the right of the general's line was Captain Francis Cornwallis Maude, a 28-year-old bearded Royal Artillery officer with six guns – two 6-pounder guns, two 9-pounders and two 24-pounder howitzers – and "a scratch force of gunners", 51 Royal Artillerymen, who, like their commander, had rushed over from Ceylon (Sri Lanka) as soon as news of the uprising reached there. Nearby stood 31 other gunners, volunteers from British regiments, mostly men of HM 64th Foot (all received extra pay as gunners and behaved with exceptional gallantry), who had a smattering of gun drill. There were also 22 veterans from the invalid depot at Chunar and a few loyal *golundaz* (native gunners), mostly Moslems. The cavalry nearby were a laughably small unit; just 21 officers and volunteers under 41-year-old Captain Lousada Barrow, with a detachment of Native Irregular Horse. Drawn up to the left of the cavalry were 381 officers and men of HM 64th Foot who had just returned from war service in Persia. So, too, had the 78th Highlanders, the Rosshire Buffs, a further 294 officers and men; its four companies had served at the Battle of Mohumra under Havelock. "All came from the Highlands and nearly every man carried a Bible in his haversack, as Havelock knew." Left of the 78th were two companies of HM 84th Foot, 190 officers and men who had been brought over hurriedly from Burma. These men were aware that 50 of their comrades were besieged at Lucknow and 50 more had died with General Wheeler at Cawnpore. Next came a detachment of the 1st Madras Fusiliers, one of the few white regiments in the East India Company's army, some 200 officers and men whose ranks included a number of hard-drinking, tough ex-gentleman rankers. Finally, on the extreme left were 150 of Brayser's Sikhs, tall men with long beards in tight-fitting white pantaloons and sandals.

Havelock trotted to the front centre "on a natty arab" as a bank of dark storm clouds threatened to dispel the oppressive heat with yet more rain. He surveyed the 1,200 officers and men under his command. Most of the British wore white cotton or linen, all forage caps were draped and curtained in white like the general's, except for the Fusiliers whose caps were curtained and covered in their customary blue. The Highlanders were perspiring in their red woollen jackets, though they had discarded their Mackenzie kilts in favour of loose white trousers. Most of the Fusiliers had the new Enfield rifle, as did flank companies of the 64th, but there were only 499 of these superior weapons in the whole force and some had gone to an advanced detachment sent on ahead. The rest of the troops had the old Brown Bess musket or the Minié rifle introduced during the Crimean War.

Those who had served under Havelock in Persia could guess what was coming next. He liked nothing better than a Napoleonic-style oration. Sure enough, he did not disappoint them:

> Soldiers! There is work before us. We are bound on an expedition whose object is to restore the supremacy of British rule and avenge the fate of British men and women ... we have a common aspiration that knits us together as one man... I know you will give me no cause to waiver in the implicit confidence I have in you.

When the general stopped speaking the men of HM 64th and the Fusiliers gave him a cheer, but from the ranks of the Highlanders came only a grim muttering. Riding over to their old colonel, Havelock said with a smile, "Your men like better to cheer when the bugle sounds 'Charge' than when it sounds "General Parade". We'll try their throats by and by."[2] Hearing these words the centre companies of the 78th broke into some cheers and soon the sound was picked up and carried down the line. At exactly 4pm, the troops moved off in column of route for Lucknow via Cawnpore. The great Relief had begun.

Havelock was in many ways an odd choice for a British hero. He had been born on Easter Day, 5th April 1795, second son of a wealthy Sunderland shipbuilder. At 19 he was just five feet tall and was hoping to become a lawyer, but suddenly the family fortunes crashed, so he followed his brother William into the army, gaining a commission in the Rifle Brigade in 1815. From the start he wanted to learn all that he could, not just pipe clay, but the finer details of tactics, strategy and military history. Transferring to HM 13th Foot, he sailed for the East in 1823; on the voyage he came under the spell of an evangelical lieutenant, James Gardner, and Havelock found his Saviour. It was a life-changing experience.

When the 1st Anglo-Burmese War broke out in 1824, Havelock volunteered and was then made D.A.A.G. of the British troops. No chaplain had been sent with the men so he started prayer meetings. One night an outpost was attacked and word was sent to General Archibald Campbell that most of the troops were too drunk to fight. "Then call out Havelock's saints," he replied, "they are always sober and can be relied upon."[3] After the war Havelock expanded his proselytising alongside temperance work. It was clear to him that sober soldiers made better fighters.

Not being rich, his climb up the promotions ladder was agonizingly slow; by 1838, when the 1st Afghan War broke out, he had just obtained his captaincy without purchase. He served with distinction at the Siege of Jellalabad and authored a book on the war. Soon he was noted as an officer always in the thick of a fight; at Maharajpore in the short 1843 Gwalior War he galloped straight at the enemy guns to inspire his men; his horse, "Feroze", was shot from under him at Mudki, the first battle of the 1st Anglo-Sikh War; at Sobraon he had another horse killed, the cannon ball striking the saddle just an inch from his thigh. He made friends with the Governor-General, Lord Hardinge, himself a soldier. He praised Havelock as "Every inch a soldier and every inch a Christian". With Hardinge as a kind of mentor Havelock's career started to blossom and he was made D.A.G. of the Queen's troops at Bombay. In 1855 came promotion to Adjutant-General of all the Queen's troops in India, a perfect job for a man with a strict sense of discipline. Then, in

1856, he was offered a divisional command in a short war with Persia. "Old as I am I did not hesitate a second," he told his adoring wife, Hannah, daughter of a Baptist minister.

With Havelock in Persia had been his son, Harry, a reluctant aide to his father, though the general thought "his value is already felt as a staff officer." Father and son had a difficult relationship due in many ways to Harry's temperament; while undeniably bright, he had also been "idle and rebellious" at school (a loathing of authority lasted all his life, as did his mood swings). On joining the army in 1846, the younger Havelock was foolishly extravagant and naive about money matters. Several times his father, who always had money worries of his own, had to bail him out of financial mishaps. After shorts spells in HM 39th and 86th Regiments young Harry became in 1852 adjutant of the dreaded 10th Foot – dreaded not for the behaviour of its men, but its paranoid and ill-tempered colonel, Thomas Harte Franks, a courageous soldier reckoned to be the toughest martinet in the British Army. In Persia, father and son had slept together in a small tent on iron camp beds. Over the years they had grown apart but now, in close familiarity, the pair began for the first time to truly get to know one another.

With Harry in tow, Havelock landed at Bombay on 29th May 1857 to hear the astounding news that the Bengal Army had mutinied. As Adjutant-General of the Queen's troops he knew that his place was with the C-in-C, India, General Anson, who was somewhere in the Upper Provinces "and is marching on Delhi, but waits for a battering ram". The Havelocks set off by ship for Calcutta, but off the coast of Ceylon the *Erin* hit a sandspit on the night of 5th June. Harry had been sleeping on deck but went below to his father's cabin and calmly said, "Sir, sir, get up, the ship has struck!" On deck it was blowing a gale and the captain and crew "had lost their wits and obeyed no orders", in Havelock's own words. So he took command and in his parade ground voice said: "Now my men, if you will obey orders and keep from the spirit cask we shall be saved."[4] Four long wet hours of suspense followed with no reply from the shore, despite the firing of distress rockets, until at last an answering signal came.

As soon as he was on land Havelock made his boatload of survivors get down on their knees and thank their Maker for deliverance. Personally, he and Harry had lost several trunks and both their horses. Quickly getting passage on another ship, the *Fire Queen*, they steamed into Madras on 13th June. The flag flying from Fort St George was at half mast; General Anson had died of cholera at Umballa 17 days earlier. Havelock now took a carriage to the home of the C-in-C, Madras Army,

General Sir Patrick Grant, an old friend from Sikh War days. Harry, in a big sulk because he assumed his regiment was already in action, slunk along after his father "with the worst grace possible".

Next day the *Fire Queen* left Madras with both Havelocks and Grant on board bound for Calcutta, where Governor-General Lord Canning had asked Sir Patrick to assume the role of interim C-in-C India. All but forgotten today, Grant was a good choice: an East India Company officer who had joined the Bengal Army as an ensign 37 years earlier.[5] He had married a daughter of a previous C-in-C India, Lord Gough, and acted as aide to his father-in-law in several Sikh War battles where the white-haired old general liked his troops to go at the enemy with the bayonet. At Mudki in 1846 Grant had been wounded. Proud of the E.I.C. Army and its sepoys, Sir Patrick blamed the mutiny on "feelings of dissatisfaction and distrust" within the ranks of the Bengal Army, caused by "a want of officers in whom the sepoy could confide". The task before him as C-in-C was enormous: Agra, Cawnpore and Lucknow were all surrounded by mutineers; rebels were threatening the British camp on the ridge at Delhi; insurrections were breaking out at scores of smaller posts between Benares and the Punjab, which also had rumblings of disaffection; telegraph links had been severed; not a single field gun was available; no horses for cavalry or artillery; no field hospitals created or ordnance ammunition prepared.

During a two-day passage up the Bay of Bengal, Grant and Havelock spent much of the time in conference. Harry selfishly moaned all the time and childishly railed at his "ill-luck". While on the *Erin*, Havelock had written a memorandum originally intended for General Anson. With ice in his veins, he noted:

> It is clear that no Native Infantry regiment can be trusted... All must henceforth be jealously watched by British troops... No piece of cannon must be henceforth entrusted to a native... The whole of the Enfield rifles must be given over to theBritish troops ... there must be no more disbandments for mutiny. Mutineers must be attacked and annihilated and if they are few in any regiment, and not immediately denounced, to be shot and hanged, the whole regiment must be deemed guilty and given up to prompt military execution.

Tactically, Havelock recommended movable columns. Two such columns had already been formed and Grant concluded that Havelock would be the best person to command a third. Sir Patrick remembered how Lord Hardinge had once told him, "If ever India should be in danger the Government have only to place Havelock at the head of an army, and it will be saved."[6] When Canning walked up the gangway at the Fort William Ghat on the night of 17th June, Grant led Havelock forward with the words, "My Lord, I have brought you the man!"

There were of course some dissenting voices. The Indian press labelled him an "old fossil dug up and only fit to be turned into pipe clay." A friend who respected Havelock's abilities admitted that he was a "cold" man. Others thought he acted too much "the saint". A civil commissioner who served in the uprising (but seems not to have known Havelock personally), wrote that "He was unpopular with his soldiers to an extraordinary degree. He was a martinet, very formal and precise, and seems to have maintained a rigid and perhaps somewhat sour discipline which they could not bear."[7] Francis Maude, who served very closely under the general, wrote how Havelock was "a good rider, quick of speech, too, and ready to retort, grandiloquent and Napoleonic in his style both in writing and conversation. He knew infantry and brigade movements thoroughly well. Everybody knows that he was God-fearing." But Maude concluded, the general "was sterner and more severe than seems to be generally understood."[8]

Havelock was aware that his critics thought him a dinosaur or fossil, yet it seems not to have bothered him. He knew that people joked about his "saintly" ways but was neither angry nor embarrassed. At sixty-two he was "aloof, argumentative, ambitious and censorious", concealing "a deep need for affection behind a manner at once reticient and ruminative".[9] A saucy officer's wife had chaffed him just before the uprising: "It's no use asking you to dinner, Colonel Havelock, as you do not like champagne; but if you will come and take a cold bath with me some morning I will be delighted."[10] Charlotte Canning (one of the few people who were not impressed by James Outram), liked Havelock, who made her laugh wearing all his medals at dinner, "like five-shilling pieces, looks almost ridiculous, as if he carried his money tied up in a bunch on his shoulders."[11] Yet "his little old stiff figure looks as active & fit for use as if he were made of steel. We believe he will do well."[12]

Havelock felt that he was the right man for the job. Now he was to embark on his first ever independent command and was ready to entrust all to his Saviour. "May God give me wisdom to fulfil the expectations of Government and to restore tranquillity to the disturbed provinces,"[13] he wrote to Hannah. His orders were clear that after quelling all discontent at Allahabad he should hurry to support Wheeler at Cawnpore and Lawrence at Lucknow. All mutineers and insurgents were to be dispersed or utterly destroyed. These were, however, loose guidelines. It was impossible to be more precise, but Canning had every confidence in Havelock's energy and proven fighting abilities.

After much persuasion, Harry agreed to go with his father as an aide. For his A.Q.M.G. and D.A.A.G. roles the general selected two Scotsmen. The former position was filled by Lt-Colonel John Bannatyne Fraser Tytler, something of an action man who liked to lead from the front; as a result this 36-year-old Bengal Army officer had been denied his Afghan War medal after rushing into a cavalry skirmish; later he had two horses shot from under him at Ferozeshah against the Sikhs while serving as an aide to Lord Gough. During a second Sikh War he swam a river to convey his chief's orders to the cavalry, a feat that so impressed Gough that he made Tytler a brevet major even though he was only a lieutenant. His regimental commanding officer, John Christie of the 9th Bengal Irregular Cavalry ("Christie's Horse") said Tytler was "almost constantly in the saddle" during the war and "daily on outpost duty". Havelock's D.A.A.G., William Stuart Beatson, was a well liked officer with numerous kith and kin in the East India Company's service; he was himself the son of a former Bengal Army Adjutant-General.

Formidable were the tasks facing Havelock and his troops. He knew that his soldiers would have to fight at the hottest time of the year. More troops would be hurried up to him, so he was told, but he was expected to press on with all speed against an enemy whose numbers were clearly high but unknown and growing daily into thousands. Every hamlet, every village and every town was liable to be fortified and defended by well-trained sepoys as well as local peasants, all ready to die for their soil and their faiths. The general no doubt mulled over all these obstacles and problems as he and his staff rode the smoky train the 120 miles from Calcutta to the railway terminus at Ranegunge (the railway continued in short sections here and there along the Grand Trunk Road). He transferred to horse-drawn dawk-gharries, a uniquely Indian mode of transport resembling a laundry van with a bed inside. Gharries tended to manage about six miles an hour and Havelock and his staff set off briskly up the Grand Trunk Road with a couple of Highlanders sitting on each roof as an escort. On the third day they caught up with Francis Maude and his guns travelling by slow bullock-train. The general urged his artillery officer to grab the first gharries he could find and gallop after him to Benares. Without Maude's guns, Havelock knew his task was hopeless. It had been hard going for Maude right from the start; the ponderous bullocks could only do 30 miles a day, even on metalled roads, and cholera had broken out after the first day, killing six of his 58 gunners. The bullocks had to be halted during the extreme heat of the day, watered and fed, the waggons had no springs and were "extremely uncomfortable".

On the morning of 28th June, with a great clattering of hooves and wheels, Havelock's party crossed the Bridge of Boats at the sacred city of Benares (Varanasi) and entered the cantonment. A little more than three weeks earlier an event had taken place at Benares which, in retrospect, had far-reaching and terrible consequences. Stationed there had been the 37th B.N.I., the irregular Ludhiana regiment of Sikhs, a wing of the 13th Irregular Cavalry and 2/3 battery European artillery under Captain William Olpherts. The city was not only the first major place in the direction of Lucknow but also of strategic importance. Here were housed several state prisoners from the Anglo-Sikh Wars a decade earlier. Commanding the brigade was elderly General Ponsonby, an officer in poor health, though a brave cavalryman with a fine record of service in the 1st Afghan War almost two decades earlier. The garrison had just been reinforced by 60 men of the 1st Madras Fusiliers sent on ahead by their colonel, James Neill, along with 150 men from HM 10th Foot at Dinapore (Harry Havelock's regiment).

Full of his own importance, the fiery no-nonsense Neill arrived on 3rd June. Next day came the news that the 17th B.N.I. had mutinied at Azimgarh, 60 miles to the north. Ponsonby asked Neill if he thought the 37th should be disarmed. Neill not only thought this was necessary but wanted it done that evening (Ponsonby had in mind to do it over the next few days). After listening to Neill, he ordered Colonel Arthur Spottiswoode to disarm his men. Spottiswoode was not happy with this command but did as he was told and the men were "quietly obeying" when British troops were seen approaching the parade ground. A panic now seized the regiment; some voices in No 6 Company were heard to shout, "Our officers are deceiving us, they want us to give up our arms, that the Europeans who are coming up may shoot us down."[14] The sepoys rushed for their stands of arms and began firing on the British soldiers. Some men of HM 10th returned fire. Olpherts, known throughout the army as "Hellfire Jack", poured in a shower of grape. It was later claimed that Ponsonby was possibly affected by the sun (he may have had a heart attack or a stroke), but the upshot was that he now asked Neill to take over command.

Just then the Sikhs, supporting the British rear, heard firing from behind them. Captain Guise commanding the Irregular Cavalry had been shot by a sepoy of the 37th. There was confusion in the ranks and shouts of treachery. A sepoy levelled his musket at Colonel Patrick Gordon, popular commander of the Sikhs. As the man fired, another Sikh bravely stepped forward in front of his officer and took the bullet. A second sepoy took aim at Gordon but two loyal Sikhs shot him down. Yelling and firing wildly, the Sikhs now sent shots whistling through

Olpherts' battery. Never slow to action, "Hellfire Jack" swung his guns around and opened fire at almost point-blank range. He did so, not in retaliation for the Sikhs volley, "but because they were moving towards the guns and looked as if they were about to charge them."[15] Olpherts stamped his foot and exclaimed: "I don't know what they mean, but by God they shall know what I mean. Fire!"[16] After trying to charge the guns three times the Sikhs followed the 37th in flight, pursued by the vengeful Neill.

The incident won both Neill and Olpherts much praise at the time from most civilians and officers but not all. Mr Tucker, the evangelical local magistrate, told both Lord Canning and General Havelock that the disarming had been a botched affair. Some officers of the 37th thought their men had been "foully used". The contemporary historian, Montgomery Martin, concluded that it was a mistake to attempt the disarmament and even Thomas Rice Holmes wrote that it was "certainly mismanaged". A generation later, the Indian Army historian, Lt-General Sir George Macmunn, called what had happened at Benares "a mess-up". Next day, several of the Sikh soldiers returned declaring that they had acted out of a mixture of confusion exacerbated by the 37th sepoys' threat. Witnesses stated that in running towards the guns the Sikhs were simply trying to join their own officers on the far side. Clearly, there had been a degree of disaffection among the ranks of the 37th and the Sikhs, yet more than 200 Sikhs who were guarding the treasury, along with sepoys of the 37th protecting the paymaster's compound, all stayed loyal. Later, sepoys told Spottiswoode that "the majority of the men were entirely ignorant of the intentions of the turbulent characters." Spottiswoode was another officer who did not know his men well (he had been absent from the regiment on other duties for 20 of the previous 22 years).

Matters at Benares might have been worse if one of the Sikh state prisoners, Surat Singh, had not helped to steady his countrymen at the Mint. Magistrate Frederick Gubbins (elder brother of Martin Gubbins at Lucknow) had also helped matters by showing himself about the city to instil confidence, and the local rajah also gave the British his support. Lord Canning, after sifting through reports, reached the conclusion that the whole affair had been a shambles. "It was done hurriedly and not judiciously… A portion of a regiment of Sikhs was drawn into resistance who had they been properly dealt with would I believe have remained faithful." Ponsonby had "lost his head & his nerve," while Neill "was out of his element".[17]

Needless to say, Neill would not have agreed. He had read enough of the uprising in other places, of white women raped and babies hanged from hooks. Severity, to his mind, was the only just and Godly way of dealing with miscreants, even if it meant lining the Grand Trunk Road with gibbets. With the assistance of some zealous civilians Neill had a gallows constructed near the Mint and natives suspected of the slightest treason were flogged, shot or hanged. Captured sowars and sepoys risked being blown from guns, an old Mogul custom that the British revived. British volunteers rode about the countryside conducting informal hanging parties, "stringing up Indians with as little compunction as though they had been pariah-dogs or jackals or vermin of a baser kind".[18] One gentleman boasted how he strung up his victims from trees in artistic figure-of-eight patterns. Canning wired Neill that he should push on to Allahabad. The energetic colonel wired back: "Can't do it. Wanted here." He finally left Benares on 9th June.

Havelock stayed in the city only long enough to assume formal command of his Moveable Column and inspect such new troops as could join his force. These were few, but he met some British officers from regiments that had mutinied, indigo planters and shopkeepers who had lost their homes, "all who were willing to join him". The general responded by asking Patrick Grant if he could form a volunteer cavalry from such men and the acting C-in-C telegraphed his agreement.

On the evening of 29th June by dawk gharry the general set off to cover the 70 miles to Allahabad. He travelled all night (his staff following the next day) and at about 7am entered the tall red fort built by the Moguls at the juncture of the rivers Jumna and Ganges. Shortly after this he sat down to breakfast with the man who would be his second-in-command, James George Neill. He was a tall and handsome middle-aged man with a "great shaggy moustache and eyebrows" who sat in his khaki uniform with a turbaned pith helmet placed on the chair beside him. That first meeting went well, but the *bonhomie* was not destined to last. The disharmony between the two men, whose temperaments were chalk and cheese, would soon reach epic proportions. Neill had been the first commander to lead soldiers up country towards Cawnpore and Lucknow. He had pushed on his Fusiliers, christened by some "Neill's Blue Caps", prevented (as he saw it), insurrections at Benares and Allahabad, punished wrong-doers with a terrible swift sword of vengeance and deserved to be in command of the Moveable Column. Instead, he was now supposed to kow-tow to the dictates of a stiff-shirted old "Mr Pomposity" who did not think or move half quickly enough.

James Neill was yet another Scotsman in the service of "John Company". He had been born in Ayrshire in 1810, son of a soldier, educated at Ayr Academy and then at 15 went to Glasgow University to study law. Here he had a sudden change of heart and one year later joined the 1ˢᵗ Madras European Regiment (later Fusiliers). Despite always brimming with restless energy Neill had not, unlike Havelock, seen a great deal of active service in his career; he was almost 30 years in his regiment before heading to Burma, but his appointment as AG of the Madras Army troops in a second British war with the Burmese was a staff appointment. Ill-health took him back to Britain in June 1854. Pushy, he got the second-in-command appointment of an Anglo-Turkish contingent in the Crimean War. By the time he reached Constantinople in the summer of 1855, the war was all but over. He also had a big spat with General William Beatson (a relative of Havelock's AAG), who found him to be infuriatingly insubordinate. Neill with his usual asperity had criticized Beatson's control of the Turkish troops. His regiment meantime saw action in the Persian War, though Neill was not there, but he was hugely proud of his 900 men, "fully equal to any other regiment", and it must be admitted that his soldiers adored him. On 16ᵗʰ May 1857, news reached Madras of the Meerut mutiny and the capture of Delhi by the rebels. Neill embarked his regiment two days later and reached Calcutta on the 23ʳᵈ.

The citizens of the capital, jittery about the uprising, gave Neill's men a huge welcome. It was a famously tough regiment that had helped Clive in his victory at Plassey 100 years earlier. They were also the first fresh British reinforcements. Charlotte Canning wrote: "They had a decided character in their Colonel, for when part had arrived at the railway station & the station master wanted to start the train without the rest, he fixed bayonets & held the whole station establishment under arrest until all the men were seated in carriages."[19] Neill was, wrote George Blake of HM 84ᵗʰ Foot, "the finest-looking man I ever saw. He was the sternest and, at the same time, kind-hearted and best-hearted of men."[20] In recent times the Victorian assessment that Neill was "tender and loving to those dear to him, merciful to the weak, and ever ready to sacrifice his own comfort for the well-being of his soldiers ... a staunch friend, but a terrible enemy",[21] has taken something of a beating. Saul David calls him "a religious zealot who believed himself destined for great things" and a man "utterly ruthless if crossed".[22] Neill was a soldier's soldier, ready to endure the hardships of his men, proud and stern, a loving father to them. He considered himself a Bible-reading and God-fearing man, though his God seemed to be very much that of the Old Testament. In Neill's mind, focused as it was on a Manichaean struggle between good and bad, right and wrong, his sword of justice would smite all the insurgents with a brand of divine retribution. He swore a lot, something that offended the pious

Havelock, and liked action over argument. His rush into situations had precipitated the debacle at Benares. Yet it is easy to see why his soldiers adored him. "He is worth more than a dozen Havelocks,"[23] concluded his aide, Captain Gordon, formerly of the 6th B.N.I.

No one ever doubted Neill's courage, nor his earnest desire to relieve those besieged at Cawnpore and Lucknow. What has blackened his character is the severity of some of his actions that took cruelty mightily close to the realms of sadism, stained his country's name (in the long-term), and may have fundamentally contributed to such Indian excesses as the Cawnpore Massacres. Commissioner George Campbell who followed Neill up the Grand Trunk Road a few weeks later wrote:

> Neill did things almost more than a massacre, putting to death with deliberate torture in a way that has never been proved against the natives... He seems to have affected a religious call to blood and almost gloats over the way he ordered fat Subadars and Mahommedan civil officers to be lashed till yelling... Neill is one of those people who have been elevated into a hero on the strength of a feminine sort of violence... I can never forgive Neill for his very bloody work.[24]

News of the insurrection at Benares reached Allahabad on 5th June. The sepoys there also heard how the British guns had been turned on their comrades. Next day, some few hours after protesting their fidelity, the men of the 6th B.N.I. mutinied and began killing their officers. The fort itself was saved by white-bearded Lieutenant Brayser of the Ferozepore Sikh detachment, an ex-gardener who had risen through the ranks to become commandant. He managed by sheer "force of personality to prevent his wavering troops from joining the rising".[25] The British stayed shut up in the old fort while the city was ruled by a handsome holy man called Maulvi Liaqat Ali who led "an all night orgy of death and destruction" on the feringhees. This charismatic ex-schoolmaster now declared himself, with local backing, governor of Allahabad on behalf of the King of Delhi. Liaqat Ali was about 40 years old, fair-complexioned, tall, "with a high forehead and large eyes". Interestingly, in the opinion of Indian historian, Smita Pandey, the maulvi was not a bigot. She writes: "He did not discuss doctrinal aspects of Islam, nor did he endeavour to establish fundamentalism."[26] Instead he saw himself as "a subordinate functionary under the King of Delhi" to promote war against the British who were inflicting poverty and misery on Moslems. In his writings he constantly emphasized using weapons to win.

On the evening of 7th June an advance party of Madras Fusiliers under Lieutenant Arnold reached Allahabad (though rebel control of the Bridge of Boats meant that it was two more days before these troops could enter the fort), and four days later in marched Neill with 54 more men. He wrote: "I found all wrong here: the Europeans cheered me when I came in. The sentries at the gate cried, 'Thank God sir, you'll save us yet!'"[27] Exhausted and weak from cholera, the colonel lived on a diet of champagne and water, but he had enough strength to direct a bombardment that led to the re-capture of the Bridge of Boats the next day. Further attempts at re-taking the city were limited as Brayser's Sikhs had acquired stocks of alcohol, which they sold to the British troops, and the men were rolling drunk. One day later the women and children were sent off towards Calcutta in a steamer. Neill began attacking rebel-held villages and a day later, deserted by most of his followers, the Maulvi quit Allahabad for Cawnpore.

Finally, the city was restored to British control on 17th June. With Neill in charge the sword of retribution fell swiftly. One local magistrate recalled how "The gallows and the trees adjoining it had each day the fresh fruits of the rebellion displayed upon them. Hundreds of natives in this manner perished, and some on slight proofs of criminality."[28] Neill had few doubts about his conduct – "God grant I may have acted with justice," he wrote at the time, "I know I have with severity, but under all the circumstances I trust for forgiveness. I have done all for the good of my country, to re-establish its prestige and power, and to put down this most barbarous, inhuman insurrection."[29]

To be fair to Neill, his mind was inflamed, like so many other officers, by the atrocity stories daily appearing in the Anglo-Indian newspapers. Most of these tales were lies or exaggerations; one going the rounds was that, as Neill wrote, "Miss Jennings and her father, a clergyman at Delhi, are both brutally murdered in the palace before the king, she, poor creature, subjected to the most unheard-of indignities and torture beforehand." In reality, an investigation would later show that Miss Jennings had not been raped or molested, nor killed before the king, though she was murdered by mutineers. On 20th June the Commissioner of Allahabad authorized the arrest of all suspicious persons, adding the further instruction that "in case of their offering resistance, to slay them." One civilian wrote in a letter on 6th June that a policy had been adopted of "burning villages … the aged, women and children are sacrificed as well as those guilty of rebellion."[30] This scorched earth policy is confirmed in a letter of Ensign Hugh Pearson of HM 84th Foot who wrote of how Lieutenant George Blake of his regiment "has been rescuing Europeans from villages some way off, and one night brought in 15 men, women and children, including one poor old man of 86 and 2 little orphans who had seen both parents brutally murdered before their eyes." In consequence of such massacres "our troops are burning all the villages about Allahabad, and every day 10 or a dozen ... are hanged."[31]

Colonel Neill's main concern, however, was not hanging rebels but somehow getting on towards Cawnpore. His mood was not improved by the commissariat department's failure to replace the bullocks plundered by the insurgents. On 23rd June he wrote to Canning that he could not start for at least four more days. Then cholera re-appeared, depriving him of 70 soldiers. At last, on the afternoon of 30th June, just after Havelock's arrival, an advance column of 100 Blue Caps supported by 300 Sikhs, 120 Irregular Cavalry and two 9-pounders all under the command of Major Sydenham Renaud went by road, while Captain John Spurgin with 100 more infantrymen and two 6-pounder guns set off up the river in a little steamer, the *Burrumpootra*, one day later.

Some historians have in recent years suggested that Major Renaud was given "remarkably restrained" instructions to "attack and destroy all places en route close to the road occupied by the enemy but touch no others; encourage the inhabitants to return and instil confidence into all of the restoration of British authority."[32] Yet the same set of orders included the following:

> The village of Mubgoan to be attacked and destroyed; slaughter all the men; take no prisoners... All sepoys found without papers from regiments that have mutinied to be hanged forthwith... Futtehpore to be promptly attacked, the Patan quarters to be destroyed, all in it killed, in fact make a signal example of this place... The object in attacking villages and Futtehpore is to execute vengeance, and let it be amply taken. All heads of insurgents, particularly at Futtehpore, to be hanged... If the Deputy Collector is taken, hang him and have his head cut off and stuck up on one of the principal buildings.[33]

Once again, in fairness to Neill, it must be said that Havelock had seen and approved these orders, but they gave the men he was sending up country ample scope to conduct a reign of terror. Not a lot is known about 49-year-old Renaud, who had served with the regiment in Persia, but he seems to have been one of those officers who liked to impress his superiors, and on the road to Cawnpore his zeal exceeded even his ruthless instructions. One of Renaud's officers described his executions as "indiscriminate to the last degree" and "all the villages in his front were burnt when he halted." This officer even remonstrated with the major, pointing out that his scorched earth policy made it impossible to re-supply any advancing army with provisions, since all the peasants were running away in fear. It will never be known for certain to what extent these bloody excesses added to the tales circulating among the insurgents of Neill's operations around Benares and Allahabad. Did the harsh British measures lead Nana Sahib and his advisors to massacre the feringhees at the Satichura Ghat on 27th June? The Indian historian, Surendra Nath Sen, one of the most impartial scholars of the uprising, wrote: "It was Neill's hand that signed in letters of blood the doom of Kanpur and decreed the ordeal of Lucknow."[34] Similarly, the news that Renaud's Column was marching on Cawnpore burning villages in its wake and hanging hundreds may have decided the fate of the remaining British prisoners at Cawnpore who, on 15th July, in a seeming fit of revenge, were to be butchered by the rebels.

Back at Allahabad and within hours of Renaud's men marching out, a letter arrived for Havelock from Sir Henry Lawrence at Lucknow. It was dated 27th June and, three days before the Chinhat disaster, displayed his optimism. "Once we have a thousand more Europeans here, we shall be alright. We are snug enough in the city and still hold the cantonment... This enables us to get supplies... I am very glad to hear you are coming up." Everything, Sir Henry thought, depended on Wheeler at Cawnpore, "but if he is destroyed, your game will be difficult."[35]

General Havelock spent the first three days of July collecting transport since Renaud had taken every available cart and animal. The old man did not impress the local British community nor his troops at this stage. There was "a general feeling of regret", as John Sherer, a refugee magistrate from Fatehpur put it, "that Neill should have been superseded." Even Beatson, Havelock's AAG, was rather disloyally writing letters of complaint to friends in Calcutta.

Before dawn on the 3rd the general was awoken by the arrival of a breathless rider on a sweating horse who had ridden 40 miles from Renaud's camp with the horrifying news that Cawnpore had fallen and the entire garrison had been massacred; they had been promised safe passage on the river but once there, guns and sharp-shooters had opened fire on them. Literally all the men had been killed and, after the firing stopped, a few women and children were taken prisoner. It was believed that the miscreant who had ordered the killings was Nana Sahib of Bithur.

The transport problem once again made it impossible for Havelock to start on the 4th and 5th. On Monday 6th July the rain came down in torrents but the troops knew they would start as soon as it stopped. Not all the soldiers were looking forward to the trek; Ensign Pearson of the 84th wrote how he did not have a horse and "as there is no more bullock-train travelling, we shall to march all the way." He also expected to "suffer dreadfully from the prickly heat".[36]

On the late afternoon of 7th July, after Havelock's parade-ground bombast, the Moveable Column got under way. Colonel Neill, somewhat to his chagrin, was left behind at Allahabad to supervise things, especially reinforcements, and join up with Havelock at an unspecified later date. The little body of cavalry acted as advance scouts, the band of the Fusiliers struck up a tune and the five bagpipers of the Highlanders responded, the screech of their pipes terrifying some of the watching natives. Francis Maude recalled the start of the journey:

> Although the number of fighting men was small, the cavalcade made an imposing appearance … we took the field with an equipment, in regard to tents and some other matters according to the stately fashion that is still *de rigeur* for an Indian Army on the march. The transport of these required a goodly number of admirably-trained "tusker" elephants, which for the most part were laden with our tents. There were also long strings of cross-looking camels whose guttural protests against the putting-on of their burdens in the middle of the night used to make those hours, to us, hideous indeed. Then there were bullock hackeries almost without number, besides the peripatetic meal for the morrow, which consisted of minute and skinny sheep. Lastly there were the suggestive "dhoollies", or covered stretchers, each carried by four bearers; empty that afternoon, but very soon to be filled to repletion with their ghastly load of sick, wounded and dying.[37]

As the troops set off to catch up with Renaud's Column they first passed through the native quarter of Allahabad: tall Moslem houses, squat mosques, narrow streets, souks and Hindu temples. In doorways and on rooftops the inhabitants crowded in gloomy silence. After barely a quarter of a mile the heavens opened with a deluge of rain, "one of the heaviest showers I ever was in," noted Lieutenant William Groom of the Blue Caps. For seven miles and three hours they continued marching, "night falling swiftly before the end of the second hour". Camp was made "in a swamp".

The height of the rainy season is also the hottest; reveille was at 1am and by the time a camp might be pitched around 11am "the steam from the wet ground and our sodden tents, together with the myriads of insects, put both our valises and patience to the severest test,"[38] wrote

Captain Maude. In his case a colony of white ants on the first night bored a large hole through his portmanteau and ruined his best gold-laced overalls.

During the first few days the column passed several examples of Major Renaud's handiwork. Lieutenant Swanston of the Volunteer Cavalry recalled: "The whole road was deserted, the villages empty and all in ruins, and every here and there bodies were seen hanging from the branches of trees."[39] Another subaltern, George Barker of the 78th, wrote home how the rebels hung by "half-dozens" at the roadside and "have now become so common that the soldiers called them 'acorns!'"[40] An NCO explained how a prisoner "was placed on the back of an elephant, a piece of rope put round his neck, fastened at the other end to a tree. The elephant was driven off and the prisoner left hanging."[41] Francis Maude recalled how a friend had told him that "Renaud was rather inclined to hang *all black creation.*" He noticed how "In every case, where the feet were near the ground, pigs (either wild or belonging to the villagers) had eaten the lower part of the bodies; the stench from the latter, in the moist still air, being intolerable."[42] The countryside was flat and reminded some of the men in places of English parkland, despite the paddy-fields. Yet it was a grim march. "All the police stations were unroofed, the telegraph poles cut down, the mile-stones broken, the staging bungalows gutted and burnt"[43] wrote an observer. John Sherer, accompanying Havelock's Column, painted a very dismal picture:

The swamps on either side of the road, the blackened ruins of huts now further defaced by weather stains and mould; the utter absence of all sound that could indicate the presence of human life or the employments of human industry (such sounds being usurped by the croaking of frogs, the shrill pipe of the cicada and the under-hum of the thousand-winged insects, engendered by the damp and heat); the offensive odour of the neem trees, the occasional taint in the air from suspended bodies, upon which before our very eyes the loathsome pig of the country was engaged in feasting; all these things appealing to our different senses – contributed to call up such images of desolation and blackness, and woe, as few, I should think, who were present, will ever forget.[44]

At the head of his little army, Havelock refused to be rushed, despite the heat or any other factors. He knew that the men of HM 64th and 78th regiments needed to acclimatise after their sea voyage, while the roadside was soon littered with young Blue Caps – over 300 of the men were fresh recruits. He also knew that the Cawnpore garrison was past any relief. The last letter he had received from Lawrence at Lucknow had been upbeat, suggesting that the garrison could hold its own.

A railway line ran along Havelock's route for the first 40 miles. Its locomotives had been smashed up by rebels but he was able to turn the track into a supply tramway using gangs of native labourers. Commissary-General Macbean, in charge of the baggage train, also made certain each camp was pitched quickly and efficiently using different coloured flags to point the various corps to their rest points. There was even a bazaar run by the camp followers where officers' servants could buy goods for their masters. One day Havelock ordered Maude to lob two shells into a village believed to be harbouring insurgents, but not a rebel was seen. A report came in that Spurgin's steamer had come under fire, but he had landed, routed the enemy and spiked their cannon. On 9th, Canning sent word that Renaud was not to delay just because of "rumours" of Cawnpore's fall; nothing had been confirmed officially. Havelock sent a message to the major to proceed cautiously forward.

The whole situation changed late on 10th July when the general received two alarming pieces of news. Renaud reported that an army was approaching him from Cawnpore led by Nana Sahib; it was supposed to consist of 3,500 ex-sepoys supported by cavalry, 12 guns and various native levies. If this wasn't bad enough, a native runner brought Havelock a cossid from Lawrence at Lucknow with news of the Chinhat disaster. The general dashed off a letter to his wife blaming Sir Henry for taking up "an untenable position... His own small garrison is now in extreme peril."[45]

The bugle sounded at midnight and at 1am soldiers set off on a forced march of 16 miles, five miles further than originally planned. The sun, once up in the sky, was fearfully hot that day and the sick doolies were soon busy. The doctors urged a long halt but Havelock insisted the column would march again at midnight. "We groaned when our bugles sounded the rouse," wrote Lieutenant Groom, "and the pipes of the Highlanders began "' Johnnie Cope', however, away we went and joined Renaud's force about two in the morning."[46] Despite their tiredness the men of Havelock's Column put on their best faces, the Highlanders struck up "The Campbells are Coming", and Renaud's detachment stood by the roadside and cheered, "their weapons and two guns glinting in the moonlight".

The combined force now marched together into the dawn, an army of just 1,900 men – approximately 1,400 of them British with 418 of Brayser's Ferozepore Sikhs and 50 native cavalry. At 7am the troops reached their scheduled camping ground at Belanda, "by a vast swamp four miles shy of Fatehpur". Here the general intended giving his soldiers one day of rest before assaulting the town on the morrow. "Arms were piled in line," wrote Major North, 60th Rifles, temporarily serving with the 78th Highlanders, "ground was taken up for each corps, and the weary, wayworn men, overcome by the oppressive heat and brilliant sunshine, lay down in groups, a little in the rear, anxiously expecting the arrival of the tents and baggage which were close behind."[47]

Breakfast was on the camp fires with the guns in the centre beneath a tall *tope* (grove) of mango trees when the general sent Tytler forward with 100 infantrymen and the native cavalry to reconnoitre Fatehpur. Havelock expected the insurgents to arrive there that day and take up defensive positions. Spies from Sir Henry Lawrence were waiting for him at his headquarters staff tent and the interview had just begun when the bugles sounded for breakfast. At that moment, a 24-pounder bounced into camp just 200 yards from Havelock and hit a kettle with a loud clang. Soon, Tytler galloped in to report that the enemy were advancing rapidly. The insurgents seemed to think that only Renaud's detachment lay in front of them. Coming on fast and due for a nasty surprise were the sowars of the mutinous 2nd Light Cavalry, along with two regiments of infantry and a battery of guns. Immediately the alarm was sounded and the troops quickly prepared for action. "The camp was beautifully laid out," wrote a volunteer in a letter three days later, "so they only had to move from their tents to come to the front. Out they came, eager for the fray, like so many bulldogs, and as jolly as possible, although just off a long march."[48]

Havelock had wanted to avoid a confrontation that day. His only counter-disposition had been to place 300 Enfield riflemen from HM 64th Foot in an advanced copse. "But the enemy maintained his attack with the audacity which his first supposition had inspired and my inertness fostered," wrote Havelock in his despatches later. "It would have injured the *morale* of my troops to permit them thus to be bearded, so I determined at once to bring on an action."[49] Quickly the general, fighting his first-ever independent command, made his dispositions: Maude's guns in the centre were to be protected and assisted by 100 men of the 64th; the rest of the infantry were formed in quarter-distance columns at deploying distance behind; cavalry were placed on both flanks. The advance sounded and Francis Maude described what happened next:

> We opened fire at 800 yards; our second round disabled their leading guns … they were falling back in confusion, we limbered up on the road, and advanced to the enemy's guns. But as we did so, the infantry

of the latter halted, and appeared inclined to re-form; while at the same moment a large body of cavalry advanced down the road towards us. So we came into action again at 650 yards; and, at the very first shot, the cavalry turned about and bolted, leaving in view two elephants, two heavy guns, and a large body of infantry. We peppered into these so smartly that they could not stand to their guns; which, by the way, when came up to them, we found to be loaded, and turned upon the retreating masses.[50]

This was the first occasion on which Maude, a later Victoria Cross winner, was able to demonstrate his skill and also the prowess and courage of his gunners. Sometimes his guns fired roundshot, a round iron ball "slightly smaller than the diameter of the gun barrel and its weight categorized the gun". At other times they fired "canister" or "case-shot", a mass of metal balls or slugs inside a tin or brass canister. Richard Holmes explained with his customary economy and accuracy:

Roundshot was fired with as flat a trajectory as possible, with the intention of hitting the ground ("first graze") just in front of the enemy. A British 9- pounder laid point-blank, with no elevation, would achieve this first about 400 yards from the muzzle, and would then richochet on before hitting the ground again, some 600 yards from the muzzle. It might richochet once more, to perhaps 700 yards, or simply bounce and roll onwards for a shorter distance... A British 9-pounder had a maximum range of 1,700 yards and an effective range of 8-900 yards, when roughly half its shot could be expected to take effect on a line of infantry, and cavalry made an easier target... At between 300- 500 yards gunners switched to canister... There were generally two sizes of ball, heavy and light... Light balls were about the size of a thumb-nail and heavy ones the diameter of a fifty-pence piece... When the tin container left the gun's muzzle it burst open, forming a lethal pattern 32 feet wide at 100 yards, 64 feet at 200 yards and 96 feet at 300 yards."[51]

Although many accounts from the Indian Uprising talk of "grape", it was rarely used for land battles and contemporaries are actually referring to heavy canister. "Our shot went rolling in among them just as if the old Allahabad Eleven were playing the Futtehpore"[52] wrote a volunteer cavalryman.

Protected by a shield of skirmishers, 100 Enfield riflemen gradually moved forward, shooting as they went. Captain Lousada Barrow's small body of volunteer cavalry galloped ahead. Reining their horses at

400 yards they opened fire and dropped three rebel troopers from their saddles. Shots tore into the rebels from all sides "bearing them backward like a sea to their second line of guns". It became clear to Havelock that the rebels were hurrying around to attack his rear. Maude was able to swing his guns and pound this flanking movement as Renaud's riflemen poured in a fire on the enemy's left. Maude pushed his guns on through flanking swamps where the wheels sank deep and needed every bit of muscle that weary gunners and snorting bullocks could muster to pull them out. Then the guns on both sides arrived at point-blank range and "exchanged salutations".

Seven hundred yards away from the British lines a leader could be seen moving to and fro on a richly caparisoned elephant as he shouted orders to his men. Beatson and Tytler now urged Maude to "knock over that chap on the elephant". Maude dismounted, laid a 9-pounder gun "at line of metal"[53] and fired. His lucky shot went in under the elephant's tail and came out of its stomach, promptly disembowelling the beast. As the poor creature groaned and rolled over the British troops cheered. The Indian general was seen to stagger off, seemingly unwounded, but very shaken. The insurgents, seeing their leader fall, abandoned their remaining guns and began a hasty retreat. Havelock's men were not far behind, peppering the rebels as they hot-footed it back to Fatehpur.

Ordering a general advance, Havelock strode on; HM 64th did the same on his left and Renaud cleared a hillock on the right, while Highlanders, armed with the old short-range smoothbore muskets, kept the line between centre and right. Only ten minutes had elapsed since that first cannonball, yet, as the general wrote later, "I must say that in ten minutes the affair was decided." So far, not one of his force had been struck by enemy fire and, as Maude wrote, "the rebels had been taken completely by surprise."

War is ever an ugly business. "The road was strewn with dead and dying sepoys, and bullocks and wounded horses screaming from pain and fright, and smashed carts and tumbrils." The general was in his element, never happier than when on a battlefield, apparently without any sense of fear, content on meeting his Maker when He so decided. When he saw that some of the mutineers wore the facings of the 56th B.N.I. (who had mutinied at Cawnpore), his face broke into a grin; he had led them with pride up to the Mahratta guns at Maharajpore in 1843. Shouting to them in Hindustani, Havelock yelled out, "There's some of you that have beheld me fighting. Now try upon yourselves what you have seen in me."[54]

Fatehpur came into view; in front of the place were garden enclosures with high walls, swamps lay on both sides of the road (about four feet deep in water) and in front of them were hillocks, villages and mango-groves which the enemy already occupied in force. The British pressed on, driving the insurgents from the gardens, out of a strong barricade on the main road, off the town walls, into and then beyond Fatehpur itself. At one point Havelock stopped to ask some questions of John Sherer, the town's former magistrate, as bullets pinged around them. It was discomforting for Sherer and his native bearer, though the old general seemed unbothered that he had been recognized and "some people behind the walls were plainly taking shots at him."[55]

Rebel musket fire was "wild and miserable", but the Sikhs could not resist stopping for a few minutes in the town to stuff their pouches from an overturned money-cart. This delay gave the mutineers time to re-group on the far side of Fatehpur. For a few minutes there was a chance that their cavalry might turn Havelock's right flank, especially since his own Irregular Native Cavalry were once again in a wavering mood. About a mile beyond the town the insurgents made a last stand. Captain Palliser led his Native Irregulars forward where they met a party of about 30 mutineers from the 2nd Light Cavalry. One of the British subalterns recalled:

> On seeing the enemy, Palliser called the men to charge, and dashed on; but the scoundrels scarcely altered their speed … they came round waving their swords to our men, and riding round our party, making signs for them to come over to their side… One or two came in at us, and one or two blows were exchanged. Palliser was unseated by his horse swerving suddenly, and then the row commenced. The 2nd Cavalry tried to get at him and his native officers closed around him, and they certainly fought like good men and true – the few of them… It was a regular run for our necks, for the whole of the fellows were behind our small party thirsting for our blood… I fully believed that our men were about to join the 2nd Cavalry and leave us to their mercy; you may imagine how jolly I felt… Najub Khan, a tall fine fellow, with a black beard, after saving Palliser, fell with his horse on crossing a ditch we had to pass, and was cruelly cut up.[56]

Squelching and straining through the mud, the gunners and British riflemen were soon in range of their foes. They poured a heavy fire into the 2nd Cavalry who galloped away. As Havelock wrote, "The enemy was in final and irretrievable flight."

British losses had been only five dead, four wounded and four missing – and sunstroke may have taken two of those lives. It was a lucky first victory for Havelock in several ways: many of the Blue Caps were Eurasian (Anglo-Indian) recruits from the Madras Military Orphanage who had never been under fire before; the same was true of most of the white gentleman cavalry volunteers who had never spurred their horses at anything more lethal than a wild boar; Sikh behaviour in the battle rested with Jeremiah Brayser, their sinewy, long-bearded commander, who had a real hold over his men (and had threatened to blow them all to Hades if they had defected at Allahabad); and the Highlanders had found fighting in their red woollen doublets to be sweaty, uncomfortable work.

What had shocked the Indian insurgents most was the fire power of the new Enfield rifle. It was four feet six inches in length and longer when capped by a gleaming seventeen-and-a-half-inch steel bayonet. Lethal at 1,000 yards, compared to the rebels' old muskets, which had a 200 yards range, this was a vastly superior killing machine. But the British soldiers understood the Enfield so little that 3,000 of the rifles had been left behind at Allahabad. Some soldiers liked their old muskets or the Minié rifle, which had a conical expanding bullet that left terrible wounds. With the new Enfield, some men forgot to reverse the cartridge or mistook the high numbers on the back sights to indicate velocity instead of range with the result that fire was at less effective elevation. Yet, overall, it was proving to be a most deadly weapon.

After the battle, Francis Maude was told that the rebel leader, Tantia Tope, had been the man on the elephant he had hit. This is very likely as Tope had part-supervised the Satichura Ghat massacre at Cawnpore. Maude also found a silver-mounted "chowree", or yak's tail fly whisk, an emblem of royalty, beside the stricken elephant. Near the beast a wounded ex-sepoy lay with a badly smashed thigh. A Fusilier raised his Enfield to shoot him. The sepoy clasped his hands together and piteously cried out, "*Aman, aman*" (pardon). Maude told the British soldier that a wounded man should not be shot, but Beatson interjected that there would be "no mercy shown" on this campaign, and the Blue Cap pulled the trigger. From the ordnance captured Maude was able to make up a complete 9-pounder battery, since five of the guns were of that calibre. He was also delighted to acquire one 24-pounder brass howitzer along with "ammunition wagons and stores sufficient for several weeks' campaign".

One of the wounded was Major North who accidentally got in the path of a poor bullock that had been hit by roundshot and was in extreme pain. The animal lifted him up with its horns and threw him some distance. A Highland private called Butterworth attempted to save the major and got the same treatment. Both survived after some rest on beds in the Fatehpur Gaol, which had been turned into a hospital. In

North's case, his spirits revived considerably after Lt-Colonel Tytler sent him a bottle of champagne.

Besides capturing 10 heavy guns and two mortars, with loads of ammunition, the British had acquired an immense quantity of food stores, uniforms and baggage, besides some large sums of rupees intended as payment for the rebel sepoys. A civilian serving in the Volunteer Horse made a note of his swag: "A Major-General's shabrac edged with gold lace, an English leathern valise, two good 'durries' (small carpets), a cashmere 'chogha' (long coat), a pistol, a lot of puggree cloth, some horse trappings, and a poll-parrot, proved a valuable addition to my 'property'. And this was a fair specimen of what the others got."[57] Even the country people who tagged along as syces or grass-cutters benefitted from the plunder and helped the British hunt for fugitives. Indian historians have largely ignored these folk whose more immediate concerns than "nationalism" centred around daily survival for themselves and their families. At Fatehpur, a search of the houses yielded "ladies' dresses, men's overcoats, saddles, pictures etc" from the sack of Cawnpore, including General Wheeler's own white saddle-cloth trimmed with lace. "The inhabitants had fled to a man," wrote Sherer, "so the houses and shops were ransacked without remonstrance, and next morning, when we marched away, the Seikhs were left behind to set the town on fire in several places at once."[58]

While the British troops rested a nearly naked man, exhausted and surburnt, staggered into camp. This was Ensign Brown of the Cawnpore garrison who had set off to try and get help six weeks earlier with a detachment of HM 56th Regiment. He had lost his comrades, swum the Ganges, been tortured by the sun, thirst and hunger, but been sustained by a few friendly villagers on his travels. "Half-mad from exposure" he now asked Havelock to let him join the volunteers and return with them to Cawnpore.[59]

On the day after the battle, one of rest for the troops, Havelock wrote to his wife:

> My dear Hannah – One of the prayers oft repeated throughout my life since my school days, has been answered, and I have lived to command in a successful action … but away with vain glory! Thanks be to Almighty God who gave me the victory! Harry was in the thickest of the fight, but God be praised, escaped unhurt.[60]

News of Havelock's victory at Fatehpur ran around Calcutta like electricity. For the first time in the war the mutineers had been beaten in the open field and by a much smaller army. It was a ray of hope to the British throughout India. There was jubilation unrestrained and the little old general's achievement added a lustre to his name. His biographer, John Marshman, wrote how "It was a novelty in India to see an Order of the Day ascribing victory to 'the blessings of Almighty God.'"[61]

The general permitted no slackening of his famous iron discipline; all government property looted by the mutineers was to be handed in, no officer or soldier was to leave camp without permission (snipe were plentiful in the marshes), and any ranker or camp follower caught doing so was to receive a dozen lashes. Stuart Beatson on 13th June was told: "I wish to have within an hour a return of killed and wounded… Also a return of your force now in camp. If I cannot have these without further reference I shall not form a favourable opinion of things in your department." Havelock's strictness did not sit well with all his officers. One of them later grumbled: "He was always as sour as if he had swallowed a pint of vinegar, except when he was being shot at, and then he was as blithe as a schoolboy out for a holiday."

Back at Allahabad, where Neill had been left in charge, a tough regime continued. Fearful of attacks by Gwalior rebels or others, the colonel begged Havelock to send back Brayser's Sikhs and the veteran artillerymen. The general refused; instead, he permitted 100 Sikhs to return. The old gunners were vital for his advance, especially so after the capture of the rebel guns at Fatehpur. He urged Neill to hurry along any reinforcements coming up-country. The general had permitted his Sikhs to burn Fatehpur, but he refused to sanction an indiscriminate slaughter.

His army moved off at midnight with 46 miles still separating them from Cawnpore. Dawn saw them tramping down the Grand Trunk Road, one of the engineering marvels of the Raj. The highway dated back many centuries, but from the 1830s the British had reconstructed it as a metalled road running all the way from Calcutta to Peshawar on the north-west frontier. John Pollock described the scene very well:

> The countryside was slightly less flat, though no rise of ground more than a few feet. Now and again they passed a Mohammedan tomb, or a small shrine beside the road, the god ungarlanded because travellers were scarce in time of war; two or three deserted, blackened villages, their mud walls crumbled, were seen across the fields, and trees covered the distance and stood scattered to the left and right in the fields, with bases banked up against flooding. Black and white storks flew away

at the sound of tramping feet, though large black crows and hideous vultures ("turkeys" the men called them) tore at the bodies of men and animals left by the retreating sepoys.

A false alarm led to Maude unlimbering his guns when the glint from the swords and harness of enemy cavalry were seen watching through some trees to the front and on the flanks. The column halted. All was silence, everyone expectant. Suddenly came the loud cry of a cuckoo (a bird not usually not heard that far south in India). "I say, Bill, who'd ha' thought of the likes of that," exclaimed a British soldier in a loud voice, "If it were not a damned old cuckoo!"[62]

While guarding the baggage train, the native Irregular Cavalry, who had behaved badly at Fatehpur on the 13th, now sent in a false alarm. It was too much for Havelock and when the soldiers made camp about 10am at Kallaypore he decided to disarm the corps. Loyal Indian officers were allowed to remain with Palliser. The sowars' fine horses were given to the gentlemen of the Volunteer Cavalry to replace their tired nags. It was a boost for Lousada Barrow and his men; the captain, a former political officer, was no youngster at 41 but a good soldier. His bearer followed him on a horse and was bedecked over his shoulders with a strap from which hung a kettle and teapot. Whenever the captain or his troopers felt like a cuppa the bearer would rustle up some hot tea using two small containers of milk and sugar that he carried in his cummerbund.

A spy arrived in camp with the good news that Nana Sahib had spared a large number of women and children captured at Cawnpore and now held them prisoner in the town. Among Havelock's troops the general feeling was, "If so, please God, we shall be able to save them."

At 4am next morning the column set off again with 33 miles still to go. The general hoped to cover a mammoth 17 miles that day. Yet as the sun rose in the sky near the village of Aong scouts reported that the place was fortified with an entrenchment thrown across the road, a gun battery, and cavalry and infantry in strength. Tytler was sent on to lead the advance while Havelock, with Harry and Beatson, supervised the baggage train. What followed was a tough little engagement and it took two hours before the rebels turned and fled. Havelock would have loved to pursue them but with only 20 cavalrymen this was impossible. At one point in the fight, rebel skirmishers on either side of the road worked their way around the flanks intending to attack the baggage train. A courageous Indian hospital sergeant from the 25th B.N.I. collected together all the invalids and camp followers that he could muster and formed a rallying square of about 100 men who kept the insurgents at bay under a hot rain of lead. During the fighting at Aong, Major Renaud was mortally wounded leading some riflemen on the left. A cannon ball smashed one of his legs, driving his metal scabbard deep into his thigh, thus ending the life, in Saul David's words, of "a wholesale arsonist and hangman".[63]

Another person killed during the action was Bombardier Harding, a fine young lad much liked by Captain Maude. A round-shot shattered Harding's arm, "from his fingers to the elbow", while he was loading a gun. "If you please sir, may I fall out," he asked Maude, "saluting as if on parade, and pointing to his mangled arm." He died that evening from loss of blood. During the fight Maude's horse – the "most comfortable beast I ever sat on" – turned traitor and galloped off to join the rebel cavalry. As a replacement, the general gave him "a rather sluggish brute" from the Irregular Cavalry horses. After the "skirmish", as Maude called it, he had lost two gunners killed, one NCO wounded, four bullocks killed and one native driver terribly wounded.

The fight at Aong had happy outcomes for everybody: the rebels had revenged themselves on the hated Renaud; the British troops found 25 casks of commissariat porter stored in the village which, when tasted, was found to be perfect. Officers and men that day were able to each enjoy a glass of the delicious dark beer. Later, as the soldiers poked about among the discarded flotsam and jetsam left by the mutineers on the road, they came across an abandoned palanquin. "Drawing swords and gingerly lifting the curtains," they discovered, to everyone's surprise, a young white girl cowering inside in a native dress. She was 14-year-old Amy Sutherland, a Cawnpore escapee. She had been saved from death by an Indian subardar of a mutinous regiment who took pity on the girl – though he may also have had sexual designs on her – but whatever his motives he behaved like a gentleman, cared for Amy, fed her and nursed her. Finally he deserted her (or her doolie-bearers did) as Havelock's army approached.

Aong had delayed Havelock for 120 minutes so he now pushed on his troops as hard as he could. Soon they reached a tope of tall mango trees. The shade after the fierce sun was an immense relief. It was not to be for long. After a few minutes in flew several 24-pounder balls, crashing through the branches, "which were very well-aimed", killing two or three of the infantry. With his men of HM 64th was Lt-Colonel Bingham:

The first shot went through our Regt and 84th in Column together. I saw it coming at a most fearful rate along the ground and called out, "Look out for the round shot!" The words were hardly out of my mouth when

it dashed slap into the middle of us, breaking one poor fellow's leg and
knocking down another without injuring him and pitching into another
poor fellow's legs, causing a frightful wound.[64]

Maude moved his guns out of the tope and into the centre of the road.
He wisely split them up; three forming a kind of salient bulge were in the
centre of the British line with two others on either side. The rains had
made the ground lumpy and uneven, but luckily for the British artillery
the rebels forgot to depress their guns to meet the advancing troops;
consequently their shot went high and did little damage. At 600 yards
the two sides began an artillery duel of the kind called by the British
"long bowls".

Not far off, the land dipped down to a narrow masonry bridge over
the Panda Nudi river. The bed was almost dry, though Havelock did
not know this at first and feared it might be a torrent difficult to cross
without pontoons and boats, of which he had none. Scouts brought
back the news that the rebels were busy mining the bridge with
explosives.

Marching around a bend in the road and looking downhill, the British
saw the bridge, intact, about half a mile ahead. They quickened their
pace, but they had been spotted already by the insurgents who peppered
them with rifle and cannon fire. This caused the troops to deploy. Maude
with his usual dash rushed his guns forward to within 300 yards of the
bridge where his careful aim had the desired effect, causing terror and
confusion in the enemy ranks. While an artillery duel was hotting up
Havelock stood standing with the grenadier company of the Highlanders.
A roundshot came in whistling and whizzing. It took off the head of a
Highland private. Spurting a fountain of blood from the neck, the poor
fellow dropped down dead. Totally unmoved, the general said loudly,
"His was a happy death, grenadiers. He died in the service of his country."
Down the line and with marvellous Scottish ill-humour, a voice piped up
gruffily: "For masel', sir, 'gin ya've nae objections, I wud suner bide alive
i' the service ae mae country!"

In the next moment, with a loud roar and a cloud of dust, the bridge
exploded as the insurgents detonated a mine. When the smoke began
to clear it was seen, with a British cheer, that the bridge was still there,
the mine having only crumbled part of the parapet and roadway.
The right wing of the Madras Fusiliers and the 64th surged forward,
running down the bank towards the bridge. Anyone in their path was
bayoneted. The enemy cavalry turned and fled, spurring on their horses
and leaving their own gunners to die at the hands of the Highlanders.
Among the escapees were the Nana Sahib's brother and his commander,

who fled back to Cawnpore with the news that the hated British were now across the river.

One mile further on, Havelock halted his troops. The grateful men flung themselves down exhausted. So far that day they had fought two actions and miraculously lost only 25 killed and wounded. Damage to the bridge meant that the commissariat could not get many bullocks across for the men's meals. The soldiers did not care – they just fell down and some went straight to sleep. Before sunrise the troops marched on again after eating a meagre breakfast of hard tack biscuits, a little hot tea and, if they were very lucky, another drink of porter.

In his tent during the night Havelock had written to Neill a list of requirements: "They are 1. Enfield ammunition. 2. Gun ammunition. 3. European soldiers. 4. Field artillery. 5. Commissariat stores." Despite his teetotalism, the general was also forced to admit that his soldiers also needed some more rum to keep them content.

The moon was high in the sky when the soldiers fell in again. All knew that it was 23 miles to Cawnpore and they would have to fight at least one more battle before getting there. While they were falling in Havelock surveyed his soldiers and gave them another of his martial calls to valour, yet it was from his heart and sincere in the desire to rescue the women and children at Cawnpore: "By God's help, men, we shall save them, or every man of us die in the attempt. I am trying you sorely, men, but I know the stuff you are made of. Think of our women and the tender infants in the power of those devils incarnate!"[65] Three wild cheers from 1,000 men shook the night air. Without a word of command, they turned and stepped out towards Cawnpore.

Sixteen miles further on the men fell out for breakfast at 10.30am. They had reached a village called Maharajpore, just seven miles from Cawnpore. The sun was blisteringly hot. Some men found a little shade under some mango trees and ate their hard biscuits washed down with rum grog, "all our meat having been spoiled overnight by the sun and insects".[66] Scouting in front, the Volunteer Cavalry picked up two travellers who claimed to be, and were, loyal sepoys (from mutinous regiments). Swept along with their comrades they had been at Delhi, then joined Nana Sahib's host at Cawnpore. The pair gave Havelock a full report on the town's defensive positions. Sitting under some trees the general prepared his plan of attack, well aware that just three miles away some 5,000 insurgents were positioned in a crescent formation stretching for one -and-a-half miles, its centre some 800 yards behind the fork where the road leading to the Cawnpore Cantonment left the main Grand Trunk Road. Gathering his senior officers around him, Havelock explained his plan, "the spies at the same time drawing in the dust of the road a clever sketch of the enemy's position." The general invited his officers to make comments or suggestions, but they all thought, as Maude noted, "his dispositions appeared to be admirable."[67]

The insurgents had also given a great deal of thought to their own situation. The Indian centre, between the two roads, was a mud hamlet in which they had entrenched one 24-pounder howitzer and a light horse gun. Their right flank (the left wing as approached by Havelock's men), near another mud village called Tuttea, was surrounded by a mango grove with two 9-pounders. Even further right was a steep railway embankment affording protection for sharp-shooters. Beyond some swampy ground the rebels' left flank was by a village called Beebiapore. This area had a garden enclosure and a pond. Earthworks had been thrown up to give cover to a battery of no fewer than four giant 24-pounder guns.[68] Between these villages and guns waited several thousand infantry. At the rear were hundreds of snorting horses and their riders.

A frontal attack was plain suicide in Havelock's opinion, he reckoned it would cost him upwards of 300 men. So, with the plan of Frederick the Great at the Battle of Leuthen in his mind, he had decided on a flank march through the mango trees as he advanced on what was Nana Sahib's left. He was aware that his baggage train was dangerously exposed should the enemy attack and his own cavalry consisted of just Lousada Barrow and his 20 horsemen. As one of Havelock's biographers wrote: "This was a risk that had to be taken." During the battle, rebel cavalrymen did try and swing around to the British rear to cut up its wounded. A private of the 64th whose left thigh was shattered by roundshot was one of those lying on the ground. He coolly shot the first horsemen who approached him. As the sowar fell out of the saddle his comrades hung back for a few seconds, giving the private time to reload and shoot another man. A whole group of horsemen waving their tulwars now rode towards him but he shot and killed a third rider. The group reeled round and left him. The fellow's leg was amputated the next morning, but he died of complications.

Harry Havelock never forgot the start of this battle as one of the first shots from the insurgents, a massive 24 pounder, hit Captain Currie of HM 84th Regiment just below his horses's seat, smashing the poor animal's back and carrying away the officer's backside:

I never saw such a ghastly sight. The horse died almost at once, but poor Currie lingered in agony for nearly three days... The same shot, which was deflected by Currie's sword scabbard, also struck one of his men in the chest. Another ghastly sight! Other poor fellows had their heads, legs and arms taken off by roundshot and the exploding canister shells sent shrapnel tearing into a number of others.[69]

Yet the British troops were in good spirits, some Blue Caps cheering wildly (perhaps a combination of the hot sun, the porter, or both) as they set off at 1.30pm on the three mile trek to the turning point for the flank movement. A gunner officer writing a few days later described it as "one of the most severe marches ever made in India. In the full midday heat of the worst season in the year did our troops start, each man fully armed and accoutred with his sixty rounds of ball ammunition on him. The sun struck down with frightful force. At every step a man reeled out of the ranks and threw himself fainting by the side of the road – the calls for water incessant along the line."[70] The shimmering heat seemed a living thing; the stirrups of cavalry boots glowed like grid-irons, anything of metal blistered the fingers. In this furnace some men saw trees, faces, the sky as a blur before sunstroke took over and they crashed senseless to the dun-coloured ground.

As they toiled forward, Havelock made another short oration. This one was met with only a "low growl" from the men. "They'll cheer when I show them the enemy and the bugles sound the charge," he remarked to one of his staff officers. Half a mile before the fork in the road, skirmishers of the Fusiliers moved to left and right, Barrow's cavalrymen trotting forward towards the rebel centre to draw their fire and help in the deception. General Havelock, as calm as on a regimental field day, urged his horse forward through some fields to his right and then sat to watch events from a tope of mango trees. As he heard the first gun fire at Barrow's horsemen, he took out his watch and handed it to Drummer Pearson of the 78th riding by his side. "Note the time," he said.

"Havelock's Ironsides", as the newspapers were to call them, marched on and soon came under a heavy fire. The general had ordered that at this stage in his plan they should not retaliate. Tramping through heavy marsh and ploughed land the men saw gaps appearing in their ranks as the cannonballs made their mark. The soldiers' gorge was rising as they heard the bands of the mutinous regiments serenading them with such airs as "Rule Britannia", "The British Grenadiers" and even "God Save The Queen". Havelock's true intentions continued for a time to fool the insurgents until after another mile of marching he wheeled his army into line almost opposite the rebel left flank at Beebiapore. Here, some 900 yards away, the Indian gunners could be seen loading canister and ball through a thick haze of smoke. But the position masked the Nana's guns on the centre and other flank. "The enemy was pelting into us all the time," wrote one soldier, as Havelock ordered his men to lie down under this heavy fire, a most uncomfortable thing to do. George Barker of HM 78th, a 24 year old Suffolkman, "fell down on the ground almost senseless", but his Highlanders got wet towels and bathed his head, others doing the same.

Maude now tried to silence the rebel guns but here he was unlucky; they were too well sheltered. Realizing that seconds could cost him the initiative, Havelock ordered a general advance. While HM 64th Foot and Brayser's Sikhs attacked a less heavily fortified village on the British left, the Highlanders moved with "measured tread", despite a hail of grapeshot, to within 100 yards of the enemy. Old Colonel "Wattie" Hamilton gave the order to charge and Pipe Major Alexander M'Kellar's bagpipe began the first notes of "The Pibroch of Doncul Dhu", the war tune of the 78th, his lead followed up by the pipe and drum band. The charge was done in silence, not a shout or shot was heard, but it was furious. Colonel Hamilton's big white charger was hit and sank beneath him, struck in the front right pastern by a musket ball. Unfazed, the white-haired old officer jumped clear and continued on foot. "Nothing can stop these dour Scots," remarked Havelock to his son. The Rosshire men crashed into the village; several mutineers ran up the narrow winding stairway of the village gatehouse and had to be bayoneted or pitched over the parapets. There were yells and curses from the rebels as they were driven from rooftops, shot down or bayoneted. Some of them screamed dying insults at the "red-bearded cannibals" and "devils".

The British were impressed by the bravery and tenacity of their foes; an ex-sepoy was bayoneted seven times but still fought on until an officer despatched him with a sword thrust right through his belly. One colour-sergeant of the 78th told Havelock's son that as he kicked open a shed door a rebel hiding inside slashed at him with a tulwar. Firing his Minié from the hip, the NCO hit the man with one of its ugly expanding bullets. Yet the Indian was brave enough to rush onto the 22¾ inches of the sergeant's sword bayonet. "He had to force the fellow back and pin him to the doorpost with it," said Harry Havelock, "and even then the fellow tried to cut at him, gasping out every word of abuse he could think of till another of the 78th came up and blew the fellow's brains out."[71]

The general cantered up to his Highlanders. "Well done, 78th," he shouted, "You shall be my own regiment! Another charge like that wins the day."[72] The mutinous sepoys had scattered in two groups, the larger body falling back towards their centre from where a howitzer now had a clear field of fire on the Highlanders. For a few minutes the 78th re-formed under the shelter of a causeway that took the cantonment road up to a small bridge and across a marshy stream. Havelock, on horseback, oblivious to the dangers, waved his sword. "Now Highlanders!" he yelled, riding forwards. The soldiers, like so many angry bees, surged out of the causeway and captured the heavy gun as they poured up the Grand Trunk Road, a surge of bonnets and bayonets.

While this was going on, the Sikhs with the 64th and 84th regiments had been successful and captured three guns. Brayser's Sikhs had been at the forefront, as always. "One Sikh pinned two rebels at once against a wall, sending a foot of his rifle barrel into the first man and bending his bayonet like a corkscrew."[73] These regiments now swept on and captured two more guns on Nana Sahib's right flank.

With the enemy retreating, again Captain Barrow begged Havelock to let his small band of horsemen charge the rebel cavalry. The general, deeply aware that he only had a token force of mounted troops, refused this request. But Barrow's blood was up; sitting weak from cholera nearby was Stuart Beatson, DAAG, who pointed out: "There is your enemy." It was enough of an order for Barrow. "The sheer audacity of the charge ensured its success," wrote an historian. Galloping for all they were worth, Barrow and his 18 sabres rode full tilt towards a whole regiment of cavalry who, quite bravely, held their ground. The volunteers were basically amateurs all, but if they were to die in a glorious charge, then so be it. Richard Collier described it best:

> Two hundred and fifty yards from the rebel cavalry, massed and menacing, in their silver and grey, the pace quickened. As one they kicked into a gallop, reins loosened now, rising neck and neck, the horses' rumps bunched in unison until each man rose from his saddle from the knees, right shoulder lunging forward with the point, crashing like a shock-wave amongst the cavalry. "Give points, lads," Barrow cried, "Damn cuts and guards," for against these odds only the "straight arm engage" might carry a man through alive, the sword held rock steady like a rifle, the sheer momentum of the horse's run plunging the blade home.[74]

"The bullets rained upon us," wrote Lieutenant Swanston, one of the volunteers, "How we escaped so well, God knows." The men rode back with one man killed, one wounded, two horses shot dead and two more badly injured. Havelock rode out to meet them and he was smiling for once. "Gentlemen volunteers, you have done well," he said, "I am proud to command you."

Across his wide front, Havelock's men had a short breather. Half a mile in the direction of Cawnpore lay another small village called Suktipore and here the insurgents had taken a stand across the road, which was protected by partially flooded and ploughed fields on either side. Maude's guns and his bullocks got bogged down here. The animals were so exhausted that he knew he had to rest them.

Wearily, the infantry re-formed; Blue Caps on the right, 78th in the centre, 64th Foot, Brayser's Sikhs and a detachment of the 84th on the left. As the troops trudged forward, the rebel gunners hit them with a fierce fire. The heavy canister shot reminded one soldier of a flock of seagulls as it screeched across the sky. Once again, the old general was in the vanguard and in his "peculiar voice" said: "Who'll take the village, the Highlanders or the 64th?" A participant, Lt-Colonel Bingham, said the general held the 78th back briefly and pointed out a 24-pounder and said to him, "Now 64th, lets see what you can do." "I immediately jumped to the front and led it through showers of grape," wrote Bingham in his journal. "A good many men were knocked over at every round, but I am happy to say the last two rounds were fired high."[75] During the advance Havelock's horse was hit and collapsed. Without making a fuss the general pulled himself off the stricken beast and continued on foot.

The sun was now dropping on the horizon, its fire less debilitating. The men had been marching and fighting on scanty rations all day. Ahead lay the road to the cantonment and directly in front of them a small mud-walled village on the skyline. When they reached this place a shell came streaming in from a howitzer three-quarters of a mile in front. From the village the British looked towards Cawnpore and saw to their horror the last card in Nana Sahib's pack – ahead, standing around and behind their heavy guns, was an extended mass of sepoys and thousands of the Nana's own levies, about 10,000 men in all. "The scene was magnificent, and yet overawing, "wrote the historian George Forrest, "banners were flying, bugles sounding, drums beating, as their General rode among the serried battalions of infantry and the gathering ranks of cavalry opened to make way for him. It was the Nana himself, who had come from Cawnpore to strike for victory."[76]

A 24-pounder ball slammed into No 5 Company of the 64th, killing one man and awfully mutilating five others. There were some shouts for the men to lie down but it was all confusion. Soldiers started slinking back, a few retreating, and it looked like there might be a rout. Henry Moorsom, 52nd Light Infantry, one of Havelock's staff, shouted out, "Shame, men, shame!" Appalled by his wounded, Major Stirling of the 64th, who had been hit himself by canister shot earlier in the battle, kept shouting, "Get a doolie for these poor fellows," and, according to Harry Havelock, "lamenting what had happened in a way that was in itself enough to cause discouragement. I at last spoke to him about it quietly and he left off and the men were removed."[77]

The fire from the rebels was so thick and fast that the British soldiers hardly dared to raise their heads and look forwards. Completely undaunted by this withering rain of lead, up rode General Havelock on an old nag he had acquired and gave the order, "The line will advance." All the men rose to their feet and the little army of 900 men set off on what each knew was the final advance of the day. Putting all other accomplishments to one side, this one action is enough to give them all and their indomitable leader a kind of immortality. Out front at the head of HM 78th, on a dowdy horse but with his sword held upright, the white-haired old warrior led the way, his nag trotting at walk-march pace. On the British left and right, somewhat closer to the enemy guns, marched the 64th. So fierce was the hail of lead that most officers had dismounted and were walking with their men. The distance was 1,200 yards. After the first 100 yards the 64th wanted to charge, but Harry Havelock who, like his father, rode proudly forward, stopped them, and they progressed steadily again. Four hundred yards from the mutineers, several men began firing. A furious Harry rode down the line and knocked up some rifles with the point of his sword to end this practice. Eighteen-year-old Hugh Pearson, with his detachment of the 84th and the left company of the 64th, gave his impressions in a letter home:

> For the first 400 yards of our advance, if we threw ourselves down directly we heard the report, we were in time to let most of it go over us, but as we approached the gun, of course the shot reached us sooner and if we were not on our faces as the gunner applied the match we were too late. It was in the last discharge but one that the grape shot went through my trousers and the last round was fired when we were only 100 yards from the guns! Of course we all fell down on the instant we saw the gunner raise his hand to apply the match, and when the grape was over us we rose to a man, gave them a well-directed volley from our whole line: then the General cried "Charge" and with a truly British cheer we rushed upon the brutes who, you may suppose, ran like fiends. I never heard such a cheer as our men gave: it was not a cheer of victory but a yell of revenge. The 84th gave this awful yell, screeched out the word, "Cawnpore" and rushed like madmen at the guns.[78]

During the advance Havelock had been impressed with the way the rebel gunners handled their guns and "poured in grape with such precision and determination as I have seldom witnessed." Maude at last was able to bring up four of his guns and pound the enemy. Drummer Pearson handed back the general his watch with the words, "Two hours, forty five minutes, sir."

By now it was night and the troops halted by some rising ground. Havelock rode down the line of the Blue Caps and the 78th. "You never heard anything like the cheering," recalled Lieutenant Groom. "Don't cheer me," the general said softly, "You did it all yourselves." The officers call was sounded on the bugle by mistake as the general reached the 78th and they quickly gathered around him on his horse. Havelock always enjoyed his speeches and was in an especially happy mood; he had reached Cawnpore with his men, defeated Nana Sahib who had scurried away, seen Harry behave courageously in battle and been immensely impressed by his troops, especially the Highlanders. Facing the 78th he said:

> I am now upwards of sixty years old, I have been forty years in the service; I have been engaged in action about seven and twenty times, but in the whole of my career I have never seen any regiment behave better, nay more, I have never seen anyone behave so well, as the 78th Highlanders this day. I am proud of you, and if ever I have the good luck to be made a Major-General the first thing I shall do will be ... to request that when my turn comes for a colonelcy of a regiment, I may have the 78th. And this, gentlemen, you hear from a man who is not in the habit of saying more than he means. I am not a Highlander, but I wish I was one.[79]

That night Nana Sahib departed Cawnpore and rode as fast as he could towards his palace at Bithur. News that the British were on the outskirts of the city terrified many of the citizens, who had heard what the feringhees did to rebels. The majority poured into the countryside and hid in terror among the villages, fields and woodland.

In just nine days Havelock's army had marched 126 miles at the hottest time of the year, fought and won four pitched battles and captured 23 pieces of field artillery. Each battle had involved desperate fighting, much of it at the point of the bayonet. The general told his men that he was "satisfied, more than satisfied with you... But your comrades at Lucknow are in peril; Agra is besieged; Delhi is still the focus of mutiny and rebellion." He still needed them "to obtain great results, if your discipline is equal to your valour."[80] The number of insurgents killed that day cannot be ascertained, but in it must have been more than 1,000; the Highlanders that night found a pond full of dead bodies and in just one mud-brick hamlet "they finished off three hundred wounded sepoys and sowars."

The troops bivouacked in the dark without food or tents about two miles from the blackened ruins of Wheeler's entrenchment. Havelock was in good spirits; he, too, had no dinner and made a bed of sorts out of his waterproof coat with his saddlebag for a pillow. Harry shared his father's discomfort as the couple celebrated the victory with some biscuit and a half-full flask of port. The men were all too tired to complain. Lieutenant Swanston got a little dirty water to drink and fell asleep with his horse's bridle in his hands. The British had suffered 150 casualties – six killed in action, 86 wounded and 48 disabled badly or dead from exposure, with 10 missing. Mournfully the pipers played "The Flowers of the Forest" by moonlight as the dead were lowered into graves dug with bayonets.

Not long after dawn on the morning of 17th June 1857 the streets of Cawnpore echoed to the tramping feet of 100 men, an advance detachment of HM 84th Foot under Captain Henry Ayrton. The men in grim silence marched along. Word had reached Havelock's troops that the remaining women and children of the Cawnpore garrison had been slaughtered less than 24 hours earlier. Yet hope was in their hearts. Could any man make war on innocent women and children? And to what useful purpose? So in bloodied bandages, some even limping on crutches, these soldiers entered the city. Two-thirds of the population had decamped at the British approach. Now a few sellers of milk, sweetmeats and cigars crept from their homes and were "pathetically grateful" if their merchandise was accepted, the cheroots making a few of the soldiers filthy faces put on a grin.

As Ayrton's men hurried along they met a weird sight – a spectre of a man, wiry, under-nourished, wearing filthy rags and sprouting a scraggly long beard. The fellow was shackled at the wrist and held long chains in his hands. Lurching towards them like a madman he kept shouting "Hurrah! Hurrah!" but was weeping at the same time. This turned out to be an Anglo-Indian clerk named William Jonah Shepherd who had been made a prisoner of the Nana. He gave a "breathless account" of his adventures, the siege and the massacres, and offered to guide the soldiers into Cawnpore. Walking by the side of Ayrton's horse he led the way.[81]

The men stared at the charred remains of European bungalows in compounds littered with "broken furniture and crockery and leaves of books" surrounded by blackened trees. Nearby stood the ruins of St John's Church, unroofed, its memorial slabs destroyed. The "mere furrow" that had been Wheeler's improvised entrenchment came into view and shocked them all. Ayrton and Moorsom trotted over and glimpsed two oblong buildings totally in ruins. Could men, women and children have held this place against thousands of mutineers for weeks? Engorged vultures and adjutant birds were waddling and bickering over bones, pigs were feeding on piles of human excrement and the hooves of their horses kicked up "fragments of sepoys' skeletons". As the British moved along it seemed as if everything south of the Ganges Canal had been demolished – barracks, doors, gates, windows and walls.

A detachment of Highlanders and HM 64th Foot coming from the direction of the severed Bridge of Boats and led by Lieutenant Richard McCrae now joined Ayrton and Moorsom. Their route led them, with the help of local guides, to the low adobe building known as the Bibighar (the "House of the Ladies"). This single-storied walled building had a small gated courtyard and verandah. Two main rooms, with smaller ones leading off, were supported by large pillars, and the place reminded some soldiers of an ancient Greek or Roman villa.

The burly McCrae put his shoulders against the double doors of the main entrance. As they swung open on creaking hinges "a swarm of plump flies rose like swirling cinders from the floor."[82] McCrae and Ayrton gasped and covered their mouths and noses. Blood splattered all the walls, windows and shutters. A lone mulsurri tree in the courtyard was covered in a sheen of blood and tattered bits of linen. At about eye level the bark glimmered with glutinous patches of brain tissue, where the heads of infants had been dashed on the previous morning. On the ground in the courtyard and rooms, covered in blood, lay the detritus of an appalling massacre: ladies' bonnets; children's shoes; leaves torn from Bibles; a man's index finger; women's hair a yard long pulled out from the roots; back-combs; frocks; ladies' boots; many daguerreotypes, even a songsheet, "*No Giova Il Sospirar*" ("It Helps Not To Sigh"). The gore "trailed and smeared and spattered through the pillaried rooms." One person picked up a prayer-book the flyleaf inscribed with "Read Psalm 18:41". Turning to it, the man read: "They cried, but there was none to save: even unto the Lord but He answered them not."[83]

Poor McCrae stepped backwards, congealed blood tugged at his boots. Choking and fumbling, he staggered towards the gates. Both Moorsom and McCrae had been looking for any mementoes of family or friends. Thankfully, the place was empty of all bodies. Moorsom was particularly distressed to see so many shoes of little children amid all the gore. It was not "ankle-deep" as some later accounts said, but it still looked "as if a hundred bullocks had been killed there". Slowly, some of the soldiers filed in, "with wet eyes and quivering lips". In the courtyard they found the matting "oozed spongily under their tread, for it was soaked with blood. Wherever there was a depression there stood a pool of blood."[84] A few men paused by a hook in the wall; it was drenched in blood and "around it were the gory foot and handprints of a child."

Outside in the stinking air McCrae stammered that it was "the most awful scene" he had ever witnessed. He was wrong. There was much, much worse.

Three Highlanders had been following a bloody trail through crushed grass and brush to the tangled roots of a clump of small trees and a well about 40 feet from the Bibighar. The men looked over the edge and saw, as one of Ayrton's comrades wrote, "Such a sight as I never hope to see again. The whole of the bodies were naked and the limbs had been separated."[85] Another witness spoke of "this mangled heap with an arm or a leg protruding here and there ... several children's corpses stared sightlessly at the unanswering sky."[86] The sight was too much for some of these hardened soldiers who vomited, others mumbled curses and glared with hatred at the few friendly Indians who stood nearby wringing their hands in sorrow and fear. One soldier summed it up: "I have faced death in every form but I could not look down that well again." The well was 50 feet deep; the hacked limbs of over 200 women and children, a handful of men, a native cook and at least five native servants, all in an "obscene arabesque", filled it to within six feet of the top.

What had happened to the British garrison at Cawnpore, and especially what happened at the Bibighar, transfixed the soldiers and soon the whole Empire. Whether or not it gave some excuse for later excesses or ruthlessness, this desire for revenge was heart-felt, genuine and not wholly unreasonable. "Cawnpore, you bloody murderers, Cawnpore!" would become a battle cry. "We never said a word to each other or made a remark as we passed through," wrote one medical officer, speaking for many who visited the Bibighar, as did hundreds of other British soldiers in the coming weeks and months, "but our teeth were clenched and we inwardly swore that we would have vengeance on the demons who did this deed."[87] Three months after the massacre, one officer saw strips of clothing and scraps of hair still in the bushes, the stains of blood on the floor, sword gashes on the pillars: "I felt as if my heart was stone and my brain fire... I will never again, as at Delhi, let off men whom I catch."[88]

Gradually, the facts emerged; the bares bones were that on 5th June mutiny had broken out at this very important military base. The town itself held 60,000 inhabitants and the cantonments with a military bazaar housed some 50,000 others including four infantry regiments, the

2nd Light Cavalry and natives attached to the artillery. The garrison had been commanded by 67-year-old Sir Hugh Massy Wheeler, a man who had spent most of his life in India and had an Indian wife. Indian rebel troops outnumbered the Europeans by ten to one.

After the sepoys mutinied, Wheeler was left with almost half the besieged – some 380 or so of them – being women and children, the wives and offspring of officers, British soldiers, local merchants and civilians and about a hundred or so loyal native servants. The barracks were so cramped that some officers' wives, such as Mrs Emma Ewart, had decided to live in tents. When the bombardment started and the insurgents' 14 heavy guns began playing on the British lines, one of the first shells killed seven women outright.

The siege had been one of the most harrowing in British history. The British had only rudimentary protection from the enemy cannon, little or no food and precious little water. By dawn on 23rd June, some 4,000 rebels led by Nana Sahib had at bay just 250 able-bodied British soldiers. But try as they might to overwhelm them, this tenacious little garrison fought on. Two days later the insurgents sent in peace feelers. Nana Sahib was represented by his advisor, Azimullah Khan (whom we last met at Lucknow before the uprising) and Brigadier Jwala Prasad, the rebels' military commander. They suggested that the British would be allowed safe passage to Allahabad on a flotilla of boats provided they gave up their arms, treasure and ammunition. Food would be provided for the journey. It seemed like salvation at the last minute to the exhausted garrison, after three weeks of death and destruction. Negotiations resulted in an agreement that carriage to the river, one mile away, would be provided for the sick and injured. Small arms ammunition was permitted with 60 rounds per man.

Shortly after midday on 26th June the garrison prepared to evacuate, but the Nana suddenly changed everything until the next day. In good faith the British handed over the remnants of the treasury – some 120,000 rupees – and Jwala Prasad personally told General Wheeler that he would see no harm would come to anyone. Yet as soon as the column, including some 200 wounded, besides numerous women and children, set off on the winding, wooded path down to the Satichura Ghat temple by the river, things started to go horribly wrong; some people were singled out and killed by a mob, loyal sepoys were dragged away and slaughtered. Guiding the palanquin of her wounded husband, Colonel John Ewart, a grief-stricken Mrs Ewart, who had lost her child early in the siege, watched as two sepoys near the church lifted his body in tones of mock pity, then sliced him to death with sword blows. After making Emma give them what little money she had, they killed her, too. As the people struggled to get into the boats the Nana's treachery became plain; hidden 4-pounders and scores of riflemen opened fire. Musket balls, wrote one of the few survivors, hissed around "as thick as hail". The operations were supervised by Teeka Singh, Jwala Prasad, a cavalry trooper called Nukee and Tantia Tope, all of whom sat on a specially built platform to enjoy the spectacle.

Rebel sepoys and some villagers rushed into the water to take part in the massacre. Everywhere people were dying; General Wheeler was killed when a sowar slashed open his neck with a tulwar; 22 children of the Free School were cut down in one boat next to a drum-major and his wife, Lady Wheeler, and scores more. One girl, the youngest daughter of Colonel Williams, 56th B.N.I., spoke up as a sepoy tried to bayonet her: "My father was always kind to sepoys!" The soldier turned away but moments later a villager clubbed her to death. Hundreds were shot in the boats while others, especially the women trying to save their children who had fallen overboard, drowned in the muddy waters as their heavy dresses dragged them down. Some boats caught fire and were soon blazing fiercely. Flames consumed Mrs Thomas Greenaway and her childfren, Reverend Haysocks's aged mother, Mrs Darby and her newborn baby, wounded soldiers such as Captain Kempland and Ensigns Dowson and Forland of the 53rd. "Oh why are they firing upon us? Did not they promise to leave off?" asked a little boy of one of the only four soldiers who escaped by swimming downriver, before the child was killed.

Nana Sahib did not watch or gloat over the killings, but he was not far off, and the gunfire and screams of the women and children finally unnerved him. He sent orders for it all to stop. Any survivors would now become his royal prisoners and in theory under his protection.

The women and children not killed at the Satichura Ghat were placed in the Bibighar along with a few loyal native servants, some male stragglers and 45 other prisoners from Fatehgarh. The modern Indian historian, Rudrangshu Mukerjee, concludes, probably accurately but also rather coldly, that the massacre at the river was "a collective affair, an expression of hatred and rejection of an alien order. It was a spectacle of rebel power ... in this instance as a general settling of accounts with the firanghi, or a particular urge for retribution against British atrocities in the nearby Allahabad region ... a kind of popular, communal justice at work."[89] Popular communal justice it may well have been but of a most horrifying kind.

At the Bibighar a little milk and meat was supplied for the children, some dhal and chupatties for the adults. The prisoners, it seems, were not treated badly and the Nana at this stage was clearly intending to use them as bargaining chips. Unfortunately, as Saul David writes: "The fate of the prisoners was sealed by Havelock's rapid advance." A council of war was held after Bala Rao, Nana Sahib's brother, was wounded in the shoulder at Aong on 15th July. Various options for defence were mooted and the rebels finally decided on making a stand before Cawnpore, which is what they did. The Nana's advisors, including Bala, Azimullah Khan and Tantia Tope argued for the murder of the prisoners. It was said that they knew too much about the revolt at Cawnpore and who was involved. One historian has suggested, possibly correctly, that Azimullah, who fanatically hated the British, wanted to implicate Nana in the massacres so that his master, with blood on his hands, would become totally committed to the anti-British cause. The die was cast, a decision reached, Nana agreed to the deed.

Supervising at the Bibighar was a woman of about 30, tall and fair-skinned, named Hossani Khanum, a Muslim woman and former slave girl who was known as "the Begum" because of her imperious manner. When sepoys refused to do the dirty work of killing the women and children, she called upon Tantia Tope to issue dire threats. Some sepoys confessed later to shooting through the shutters of the rooms, but deliberately aiming high. The furious Begum then created her own execution squad led by her lover, Sarvur Khan, a Eurasian member of the Nana's bodyguard. He recruited four other men, including two butchers. The terrified occupants of the house had run from room to room crying and begging for their lives and those of their children, but it was in vain. The slain included 124 children.

Euphoria at reaching Cawnpore now gave way to depression for Havelock's army. The ruined entrenchment and blackened city, the feeling that the relief had been in vain, the horrors of the Bibighar and its well all weighed heavily on everyone's minds. At dinner on the first night, Havelock sat silently with his son. Word has just come in that Lawrence was dead at Lucknow and the siege there had begun in earnest. Eighteen miles away, Nana Sahib was reportedly massing an army at Bithur. Among the British troops, dysentery and cholera were rife and Stuart Beatson, one of the victims, lay close to death (he died two days later). The general raised his head, looked at Harry and smiled. "If the worst comes to the worst," he said, "we can but die with swords in our hands."[90]

Next morning the general moved his troops to the Civil Station on the outskirts of the town preparatory to moving across the river into Oudh. Nearer Cawnpore, on a slight plateau overlooking the river, he ordered his engineers to construct a large entrenchment to protect his crossing and hold the town thereafter. Spurgin's steamer had arrived at the Artillery Ghat. Havelock went with Maude to choose 20 invalid gunners from off the boat. "My men," he began, "I have come to thank you for so nobly volunteering to assist your country in the hour of her great peril." Not quite understanding what he was going on about, the old soldiers looked puzzled. One of them stepped forward, saluted, and interrupted Havelock before he could say any more. "Beg pardon, Sir, we ain't no volunteers at all; we only come 'cos we was forced to come!"[91] The general was famous for his ready wit, but he had no comeback, the idea that men would not want to volunteer completely dumbfounded him and brought the parade to an end.

That night, while drafting despatches and field orders, Havelock recommended his son for the Victoria Cross. On finding this out Harry replied: "You cannot send that! I cannot possibly receive it at your hands!" He thought it would make him the laughing stock of the British Army as an obvious example of nepotism. Moreover, his rallying of the 64th reflected badly on the regiment, which had exhibited much bravery in the campaign. Reluctantly, Havelock crossed Harry's name out. Some weeks later, while recommending a Highland officer for the VC he included his son's name again and was successful; Harry never knew about this in his lifetime (and there was always some bad feeling in the 64th about it).

Buckets of rain descended from the skies on Sunday 19th July. Everyone was feeling miserable; besides the weather Cawnpore now had millions of black flies swarming everywhere and they were followed by a plague of large black frogs. Stuart Beatson died and the general appointed his son as the column's D.A.A.G. There was some good news; a detachment of Fusiliers returned from Bithur next day and had found the place deserted. After the usual destruction and looting, they brought back 16 more guns. The spell of inertia after so many days marching and fighting was having a bad effect on Havelock's men; there were cases of plundering and some innocent Indians had been stripped and beaten in revenge for the massacres. A Provost Marshal was appointed and Havelock announced that all soldiers caught looting would be hanged, adding, "This shall not be an empty threat."

Briskly marching into camp on 20th July was James Neill, now a brigadier-general. With him came 227 more troops, a paltry reinforcement, but enough to garrison Cawnpore under Neill once Havelock's army got on the move again. In pouring rain, the two generals shook hands and Neill was permitted an 11-gun salute. In his tent, Havelock said politely but firmly, "Now, General Neill, let us understand one another. You have no power or authority here whilst I am here, and you are not to issue a single order."[92]

Crossing the Ganges, "swollen, broad and rapid", took time; the Highlanders embarked in a torrent of rain on the night of 20-21ˢᵗ July; the general crossed on the 25ᵗʰ, leaving Cawnpore and its inhabitants to Neill's tender mercies (much to the brigadier's annoyance, who wanted to lead the force himself). Four days later, Havelock's army of 1,200 British troops and 300 Sikhs with ten light guns set off on "the desperate enterprise of relieving Lucknow". Morale was high and the general, feeling bullish after his earlier victories, telegraphed to Sir Patrick Grant in Calcutta: "We will smash every rebel force, one after another."

The sun came out as they progressed into Oudh, but after just three miles of marching, near a town called Unao, they ran into enemy troops. In his despatch the general explained the enemy position:

His right was protected by a swamp which could neither be forced nor turned; his advance was drawn in a garden enclosure, which in this warlike district had purposely or accidentally assumed the form of a bastion. The rest of his force was posted in or behind a village, the houses of which were loopholed. The passage between the village and the large town of Unao is narrow. The town itself extended three-quarters of a mile to our right. The flooded state of the country precluded the possibility of turning in this direction. The swamp shut us on the left.[93]

Using their Enfields, the skirmishers poured in a deadly fire before Maude brought up his guns. Havelock wanted to retire his Highlanders until the guns were in place but Colonel Hamilton on his horse yelled, "Pray, Sir, let them go at the place and have done with it."[94] The general consented and the 78ᵗʰ and the Fusiliers raced towards the village and Unao. The worst fighting was in the town, where the rebels stood their ground and hit the British with a concentrated fire from rooftops, doors and windows. Six Highlanders were struck down and Lieutenant Seton, the general's aide, was shot through the face.

This was the most desperate hand-to-hand fighting that Havelock's army had so far encountered and it showed how the sepoys and peasants of Oudh were ready to give their lives to eject the invaders. Storming parties had difficulty entering many of the houses; leading Highlanders into one of them Lieutenant Andrew Bogle, a 29-year-old Glaswegian, was badly injured, though his bravery won him the Victoria Cross.[95] A battery of Oudh gunners poured grapeshot into the melee from down the main street. Men of the 64ᵗʰ faltered here, but not so Private Patrick Cavenagh, who, screaming Hibernian curses at his foes, charged into a mass of the enemy who cut him to pieces. The 64ᵗʰ now recovered at the sight of this and surged forward. More guns were captured. When the British debouched from the town's narrow central street they formed up in line again.

Undaunted, the Oudh rebels had also re-formed. It was clear that they had several more cannon. Needing to avoid the swamps all around, Havelock advanced his men until he reached an area of dry ground about half a mile in extent. He put four guns in his centre and two on each wing. The men in line held steady as a huge mass of insurgents came on down the road with drums beating and banners flying.

Up rode Francis Maude, unlimbered his guns at 700 yards range and blazed away. This action effectively broke up the rebel front, who wavered and then started to roll back. They tried to deploy their own guns but to no avail, while many began floundering in the swamps. Enfield riflemen started picking them off like ducks in a shooting gallery. Three hundred or so died in this manner. Fifteen guns were taken. One observer declared that there was a general groan from the British soldiers who said, "Oh that we had cavalry to cut the dogs up."

It was 2pm. The men had two hours to rest and eat while the British dead were buried. It was 37 miles to Lucknow and eight to the next town, Busherutgunge, a walled place with wet ditches, town gates defended by a round tower with four cannon mounted, adjacent buildings being loopholed.

It was Havelock's plan that under cannon fire the 64th would, at a given moment, move round to the left flank to confuse the enemy while the Fusiliers and Highlanders made the main assault. All went well at first, until HM 64th got held up by a concentrated fire from a small building. The general ordered his son, who had just had a horse shot from under him, to give the 64th a short message: "If you don't go at that village, I'll send men that will, and put an everlasting disgrace on you."[96] This rebuke, embellished with some of Harry's hot oaths, did the trick and the regiment moved forward. But the 64th's delay had allowed many mutineers to escape across a causeway at the town's rear.

Historian Charles Ball recorded a wonderful example of the courage of the Oudh peasants in his history of the war:

The pertinacity of one of the villagers at this place was remarkable. He had stationed himself in a little mud fort at the entrance of the place (which was almost the first position carried), and had contrived to hide himself, thus escaping the fate of his comrades in the general bayoneting. As soon as the main body of the English had passed, this man emerged from his shelter, and plied his solitary matchlock with effect, at the guns, the baggage, the elephants, or anything that came within range. His bravery amused the men of the rear-guard who, as he was not a sepoy, would have spared him if possible, and they repeatedly called on him to desist; but their humanity was thrown away; and the result was, a party of Sikhs went and smoked him out of the fort, and the poor wretch was shot through the head as he was looking over the parapet for a last hit at his enemies.[97]

It was twilight. Three more guns had been captured. The line halted by the edge of the water on the far side of Busherutgunge. When Havelock returned over the causeway from placing his picquets, he was delighted to hear the shout, "God bless the general!"

The day's victories had been sweet, but Havelock knew that the odds had been rapidly stacking up against him: sickness and combat had already reduced his force to 1,364 men and it seemed likely that sickness and particularly cholera might reduce them even further without fighting; reports had arrived that a large army of mutineers from Gwalior were forming at Kalpi, just 45 miles to the south-west; one third of his ammunition had already been expended; the troops had no means of crossing the Sai River at Bunni while the bridge there was 120 yards long, heavily defended with guns and entrenchments; and his road maps of Oudh were 10 years out of date. It seemed impossible to reach the Lucknow Residency with so few troops and fight a way out again. He could not afford to leave men at Busherutgunge, which meant Nana Sahib would be able to cut his communications with Neill at Cawnpore. Neill had boasted that his guns could cover any retreat across the river, but Havelock told Tytler, "His shot would do more harm to us than to the enemy."[98] Tytler himself was a fighting man, yet he thought there was no chance of reaching Lucknow and "failure now would seal the garrison's fate." Nothing, both men agreed, ought to be attempted further without reinforcements.

Next morning news came from Neill that settled Havelock's mind, if it was still in doubt: both the 5th Fusiliers and HM 90th Regiment, which had been expected any day, could not now arrive for a couple of months due to a mutiny at Dinapore south of Benares. These hard facts clinched the general's decision to retire temporarily to Mungulwar, a strong position he had made six miles from the river at Cawnpore. He informed Sir Patrick Grant that he needed at least 1,000 reinforcements. Neill was also apprised of the retreat. To his wife Havelock ended a letter with the words, "Pray for me and trust in God."

Major North was now made the general's aide in view of Seton's injury. On 30th July, before the force retreated he watched two rebel sepoys being blown from guns. This horrible punishment, originally used by the

Moguls, was a swift death for the victim, but it was something never forgotten by those who witnessed it. North thought the fortitude of the two men was remarkable: "Both extremely fine men, in the flower of their age – tall, athletic, graceful". They approached the guns with heads erect, gazing around contemptuously, and on the word "Fire" were both blown to shreds. North followed the trail of one man's head and saw that "from the branches of an adjacent tree, two wretches who had suffered death by hanging were dangling."[99] Maude disliked having to supervise these executions (they feature in many accounts of the uprising but in fact these were the only two of this kind that Havelock ever ordered). He recalled how as the smoke cleared, he saw the legs of each victim but nothing else. Then the heads dropped straight "down amongst us"; he reckoned they had gone 200 feet up in the sky, "slightly blackened, but otherwise scarcely changed". The crowd gave a loud "Ahh" of pent-up emotion. When Maude went to report to Havelock, he realised to his horror that he was covered in minute blackened particles of flesh, some it sticking to ears and hair. Havelock, far from being shocked, took one look at Maude and half-quoted Shakespeare: "Ee'en such a man, in such a plight/Drew Priam's curtains in the dead of night."

"Always ready-witted was the Old General," commented Maude drily.

The troops were thus turned around, "dejected and sullen, sickness increasing", and marched back to Mungulwar. Here Havelock could easily send all his sick and wounded across the Ganges to Cawnpore. From Mungulwar, the young Hugh Pearson sent his parents a letter that gives a vivid picture of recent events:

I have now been in six separate actions and in every one but the first, under a heavy fire. I have seen men of my own company killed and wounded ... on the 29th ult. my right hand man was shot through the head whilst talking to me ... most of the fighting on this side of the river has been village fighting, and when those wretches are surrounded in their loopholed houses and their village is set on fire you may easily imagine how desperate they become ... our adjutant [Browne] was shot through the leg and put in a palanquin: the bearers ran away and left him, and immediately the brutes in the town fired at him, hitting him through the arm, and in the hip... An officer of the Madras Fusliers was shot dead on the spot; another of the same corps [adjutant] was shot in the lower jaw, smashing it to bits; an officer of the 78th Highlanders was severely wounded... Our list amongst the men is large. I had 1 killed and 3 wounded in my own company... We fought our way for more than half the way to Lucknow losing at the rate of 100 men every action, and our General then decided upon retreating 10 miles. Nobody knows why he has done this ... it is not by any means uncommon for me to walk for a whole day under a hot sun, wet up above the knees... As to sleeping under cover, it is a thing I have not done since I crossed the river into Oude... We are losing many men from sunstroke, but I, fortunately, have not felt anything beyond having all the skin peeled off and my face as red as a cock's comb.[100]

Later, on 1st August, Havelock received from Neill "the most extraordinary letter I have ever perused." In his scrawly hand the brigadier had penned one of the most insulting letters ever sent by a junior to his superior:

I deeply regret that you have fallen back one foot. The effect on our prestige is very bad indeed. Your camp was not pitched yesterday before all manner of reports were rife in the city – that you had returned to get more guns having lost all you took away with you. In fact, the belief among all is, that you have been defeated and forced back. It has been most unfortunate your not bringing back any of the guns captured from the enemy... The effect of your retrograde movement will be very injurious to our cause everywhere... You talk of advancing as soon as reinforcements reach you. You require a battery and a thousand European infantry ... they are not to be had, and if you wait for them, Lucknow will follow the fate of Cawnpore.

Neill, after lecturing his superior in this fashion, added insult to his hectoring by treating Havelock as if he were a schoolboy or some errant young ensign: "You ought not to remain a day where you are... You ought to advance again and not halt until you have rescued, if possible the garrison of Lucknow. Return here, sharp, for there is much to be done between this and Agra and Delhi."

It was Havelock's turn to put pen to paper:

There must be an end to these proceedings at once. I wrote to you confidentially on the state of affairs. You send me back a letter of censure of my measures, reproof and advice for the future. I do not want and will not receive any of them from an officer under my command, be his experience what it may. Understand this distinctly, and that a consideration of the obstruction that would arise to the public service at this moment alone prevents me from taking the stronger step of placing you under arrest. You now stand warned. Attempt no further dictation.[101]

To further upset Havelock's digestion, a telegram arrived from the acting C-in-C India on 2nd August saying that additional troops would not reach him for two months. But in the same letter, Grant ordered Havelock to try and force his way through to Lucknow. Next day appeared the scantiest of new reinforcements – one company of HM 84th Foot, three horse pounders and two 24-pounder guns.

"We are still in the dark about the General's intentions," wrote Lieutenant Groom on 3rd August, "Everybody is frightfully disgusted at his conduct; but he doubtless is acting on the best information." He and four other officers were living at Mungulwar "in a native mud hut. You never saw such a queer little hole in your life. If it were not for the heat and the myriads of flies we should be almost comfortable."[102]

Next day and following his new orders Havelock set off again to relieve Lucknow. Lt-Colonel Tytler gave the spy, Ungud, the letter saying "We have to reach you in four days... We are only a small force." Grimly, the general told his troops, "Tomorrow we meet the rebels again in the field." His 1,400 soldiers were as brave as ever, but Havelock and his staff knew that their chances of fighting through to Lucknow, never mind relieving the garrison and somehow getting them safely back towards Cawnpore, was a very thin hope indeed.

4

Terriers in Rat Holes

Lucknow, 15ᵗʰ August–25ᵗʰ September, 1857

Stygian darkness. Sultry, suffocating heat. Imagine yourself in an enclosed crawl space, a tunnel some 12 to 20 feet below ground level, four feet in diameter. Crawling on his belly a figure is making his way down the tunnel. He is wearing some grubby cloth wound around his head into a turban (also useful for wiping the sweat that runs down his face and soaks his clothes), an open shirt and loose trousers over his boots. Strapped to his back is an Enfield rifle while in front, as he edges along, the fellow pushes a spade. There is no light in the tunnel since it is impossible to ventilate the shaft and no pump and bellows to circulate fresh air. When light is needed the human mole resorts to briefly lighting a candle. There are also no pit props to support the tunnel because it is constructed of firm earth, but at any moment a fall-in can occur and mean an unpleasant death.

The shaft was excavated by ten men – five to work and five to relieve them at intervals. The Number One man was the miner. Michael Edwardes explained:

With a pick or crowbar, he would loosen the earth to a depth which would allow him to squat down while still leaving a few inches above his head. The earth was collected in a packing case by Number Two. When the case was filled with earth, Number Two would pull a string, and Number Three, stationed at the bottom of the vertical shaft, would drag the case towards him. Numbers Four and Five at the top of the shaft were responsible for pulling up the case, emptying the earth, and sending the box down the shaft again.[1]

Those who took part in the mining operations did so regardless of rank; there were officers working alongside private soldiers, Anglo-Indian clerks and senior British officials, Sikhs (who turned out to be excellent miners) and Cornishmen who had worked in their county's tin mines.

Our miner's name, rather splendidly (I admit a bias here), is Captain George William Wright Fulton. He is senior engineer within the besieged Residency, a man with countless responsibilities above ground, yet he admits that nothing gives him so much pleasure as to sit in the complete darkness and furnace-like heat of a tunnel and surprise the enemy. So he sits and waits. The silence is relieved only by the monotonous whine of several mosquitoes which somehow have found their way in and now flit about his head. After a long time with his back to the wall, listening intently, Fulton at last hears what he has been waiting for – the distant chipping sound of a pickaxe and shovel and the chatter of native voices. Gingerly, so as not to be heard, he eases two revolvers out of his waistbelt. One he lays on the ground, but the other, larger one, he cups in his hands and cocks the trigger. Then, without warning, a pickaxe breaks through the wall and earth scatters down. There is a hubbub of voices. Fulton fires his revolver. The native miners scurry away as fast as they can through the smoke towards their own lines. The smoke is everywhere as Fulton continues firing and shouting curses. He enters the enemy tunnel for a distance, but the miners have all fled. From his pocket he primes a grenade, throws it, and crawls back as fast as he can before an explosion brings down a wall of earth. Another enemy mine has been destroyed.

The insurgents had exploded their first mine on 20th July inside the outer line of the British defences at the Water Gate and close to the Redan. It had been the prelude to a general assault and also the start of a vigorous underground war between the besiegers and the besieged. Next day the rebels made six fresh attempts, three being lodgements at the foot of the defences, and three being galleries. Shafts were immediately dug by the British and short galleries driven out to meet the enemy. A sap by the rebels at the Sikh Square on 28th July was met successfully by a countermine; crowbars were used to break into the enemy tunnel and it was blown up using 100 lbs of gunpowder, which not only collapsed the mine but brought down some adjacent houses.

It was not long before the soul of the British mining operations was personified by Captain Fulton. He was "like a terrier in a rat hole, and not liable to leave it, either, all day",[2] in the words of a sergeant of HM 32nd. An Ulsterman, like the Lawrence brothers and John Nicholson of Delhi fame, George had been born in 1825 at Lisburn, the linen town on the borders of County Antrim and County Down. His father had been a Bengal Artillery major and George had been a bright pupil at school. "His general good behaviour and application to his studies merited the approbation of every Master,"[3] wrote his headmaster in his final report.

Fulton opted for the Bengal Engineers rather than the gunners and in 1841 entered the EIC's training establishment at Addiscombe in Surrey. He joined the Bengal Engineers as a second lieutenant on 9th June 1843 and served in the 2nd Anglo-Sikh War 1848-49, then married and had five children. The latest in the summer of 1857 was only a few weeks old, and so Sophia Fulton and the children were luckily away from the summer heat of the plains in the cooler climes of Simla. Always active, cheerful, intelligent and resolute, Fulton had succeeded to the role of Garrison Engineer on the death of Major Anderson on 11th August. He seems to have been well-liked by everybody – a rare virtue at Lucknow. Even the grumpy Brigadier Inglis thought "No one at Lucknow could hold a candle to him in any way. His energy and talent shone forth."[4]

Divine service was held by Chaplain Harris Sunday on 18th August in the Brigade Mess House for the few officers off-duty and some of the ladies. It was a typical day, thought Captain Wilson, acting D.A.A.G., with much roundshot fired during the day; fewer enemy sepoys in sight than usual, though the enemy rounded off the evening by throwing in three 8-inch shells. Improvements at the Cawnpore Battery now made the place so secure that Inglis himself slept there that night with the garrison. Next day, work began on the first major British mine – a sap running towards Johannes's House.

According to historian P. J. O. Taylor, the Indians had recruited miners from the Passis tribe – small, wiry men who seemed to relish tunnelling. He described them as "an aboriginal race of Hindus, small in stature, but well-proportioned, supple and sleek, with a quick eye and amazing dexterity".[5] A few years prior to the Uprising, some Passis had tunnelled into the treasury of one of the begums of Oudh and stolen her jewels. They were, it appears, mercenaries for hire and had no special dislike of the British (in fact in their jungles near Sitapur and Mythowlie they were said to have been kind to British fugitives).

The wily insurgents had been busy and made two mines running towards the Sikh Square defences. The western one had been detected by the British and counter-mining had begun, but the eastern one ran under the horse corral and had gone unnoticed. Both mines exploded on the morning of the 18th with a tremendous roar that threw Lieutenant Mecham, adjutant of the 7th Oudh Infantry, Band Sergeant Curtain, 41st B.N.I., Drummer Ford of the 13th B.N.I. and Captain Orr, Oudh Military Police, up in the air and buried them in debris. Curtain was killed but the others escaped with minor bruises. Less lucky were five other drummers and Sepoy Heerah Singh, 48th B.N.I., who were all buried beneath the ruins. When the smoke cleared it was seen that a clear breach in the outer defences some 30 feet wide had been made.

One brave warrior sprang on top of the ruins, brandished his sword and called on his men to follow him, but he was shot dead by British flankers on top of the Brigade Mess. Another rebel leader quickly met the same fate. Eighteen soldiers, the reserve of HM 84th Foot, now commanded the breach and kept the enemy at bay with rifle fire as others grabbed boxes, planks, doors and assorted impedimenta with which to fill the gap. Soon a 9-pounder was brought into position by the British, followed by a 24-pounder, and a major assault was averted.

The stamina of the Indian attackers was as remarkable as that of the defenders; on 20th August they used their reinforced arsenal of guns to hit the Residency with their biggest cannonade to date. For three hours, they fired continually until Deprat's House fell in ruins while the guard rooms on top of the Brigade Mess were entirely demolished by the unceasing roundshot. In the evening the insurgents tried to burn down the Baillie Guard gate by stealthily piling logs of wood at its outer base. The fire they started burned fiercely at first, but some brave native water carriers helped the defenders to extinquish the flames.

At daybreak on the 21st all was at last ready to blow up the British countermine near Johannes's House. The building was 50 feet long and some 40 feet from the British defences. Fulton had entrusted the engineering work to Innes, who had not slept in 64 hours. The explosion was to be the signal for a sortie by 50 Europeans under Captain McCabe and Lieutenant Browne of HM 32nd divided into two parties. Precisely at 5am, the mine, containing 400 lbs of powder, was sprung. The insurgents were taken completely by surprise and within minutes the British had spiked two enemy cannon, taken Johannes's House and made arrangements to blow it up.[6] Since the commencement of the siege, the building had been a continual nuisance. With a great roar the place was blown to smithereens, its walls opening outwards as it "collapsed like a house of cards". Several rebels were bayoneted and at last "Bob the Nailer", the African who had used his double-barrelled rifle to deadly effect throughout the weeks of siege, was found sitting in his elevated seat from where he had "nailed" so many men and duly executed. One of the attackers was Fulton, who besides his tunnelling activities was also an expert shot, even managing to kill two men with one bullet.

Next day John Inglis took his wife and Mrs Case for a short walk. The previous day's fighting had temporarily exhausted the attackers and things were generally quiet. Julia Inglis thought her stroll was "a great treat, though we only saw dead walls".

The defenders were now getting used to several aspects of siege life and warfare. Soldiers knew that at night if they heard noises close to the barricades that a hurled grenade would send the enemy scuttling away like ants. Women no longer jumped at the sound of gunfire. Men had learned not to show even the tops of their heads near loopholes, though one who forgot this cardinal rule was Monsieur Deprat who was shot in the jaw on the 18th. Yet daily the death toll rose. Poor Reverend Harris, who had to bury his own dead, was so overcome by the awful stench of the churchyard that on 14th August his wife noted how he came home and spent two hours vomiting incessantly.

Many of the infants were now succumbing to the poor diet and insanitary conditions; Mrs Dashwood, widow of Lieutenant Dashwood, 48th B.N.I., lost the youngest of her two children on the 18th, her other child was failing and young Bobby Fayrer was just as ill. Mrs Brydon's diary during the summer months is chock-full of misery:

> 15th August – So many poor little children are suffering and sinking...
> 22nd – Mrs Green (48th) died last night at Mrs Ommaney's, & Mrs Lewin's baby the night before. Major Bird's [of the 48th] baby was buried this evening... August – a sergeant's wife and baby both died today... 4th September – Another little girl died yesterday.[7]

For the bereaved there was little they could do but pray. In her diary Mrs Boileau, wife of a civil servant, wrote after a week of misery watching her baby daughter die on 13th September: "My little darling was taken from me at five o'clock after such a night of agony and painful watching as I pray God I may never spend again. I cannot write it... Sergeant Court made her a little coffin... I put her into it with my own hands... At twelve o'clock she was carried away to that wretched mournful churchyard... Oh, God Almighty comfort me."[8]

Yet the defenders still tried to make light of their misfortunes in that perculiar way unique to the British middle classes. Lieutenant Calvert Clarke joked how a roundshot covered him with bricks and mortar in the gentlemen's bathroom at Fayrer's House on the 21st, just about the same time as a piece of shell whizzed by young Edward Hilton's head and embedded itself in the wall as he was washing his clothes. To celebrate the victory at Johannes's House there was a dinner party and Mrs Germon's husband, Charlie, sat down with the others to enjoy a small amount of roast mutton and a tin of salmon, though the dessert was a "perfect luxury" concocted by Mrs Need, a merchant's wife – a roly poly pudding of attar and suet.

Everyone had their favourite stories of hair-breadth escapes from shot and shell. One cannon ball smashed the leg of a chair on which a lady was sitting and brought her to the ground as the ball rolled harmlessly out of the folds of her dress; another shot grazed the temple of a sleeping Engineer officer and plunged into a treasure chest; a Fusilier officer was resting when a ball cut through his pillow and broke the leg of the bed next to him. In his memoirs, Mr Parry of Innes's Post wrote that on the third day of the siege a roundshot half-buried him under bricks and mortar. Later, a bullet passed through a cooking pot in his hand. Visiting a stables one day a bullet whizzed through his whiskers and lodged itself in the wall beyond. Finally, sitting on a verandah, he was wounded, but luckily the bullet was spent and the injury healed in a fortnight.

Regardless of the dangers, several women still volunteered to act as nurses at the hospital. Indeed, since the passing of her husband Mrs Polehampton seemed to be energised by aiding the sick and wounded. Others included Mrs Birch, Mrs Barbour and Mrs Gall, widows of officers in the 2nd Oudh Cavalry, Miss Alone (whose brother was wounded in the hand at Innes's Post), Mrs Bates, wife of one of the uncovenanted gentlemen and Mrs Erith, whose husband had been mortally wounded at the attack on Innes's Post on 20th July. One of the forgotten heroines was Mrs Parry, wife of the Lucknow branch manager of the Delhi Bank. She, in turn, praised Mrs M'Donough, wife of a sergeant-major. Mrs Parry supplied the invalids with 12 quarts of tea a day from a stock she had bought prior to the siege. She also made gruel from a kind of bran. The women also tried to do all they could to comfort the patients mentally. Yet Mrs Parry, like her husband, did not suffer fools gladly. When she complained to a doctor of feeling debilitated he suggested a change of diet. "Thank you doctor," she retorted, "I wonder you have not prescribed *a change of air.* One would be about as practicable as the other!"[9]

On the evening of 26th August, Maria Germon wrote in her diary:

> We had a wretched night, with Mrs Boileau's children and the firing. I actually lay till seven. Dear Charlie sent me a beautiful bouquet of myrtle and tuberoses. I went down and got my mug of tea without sugar and milk (I use Charlie's silver mugs as cups are scarce) and a chupattie, then went and sat at the door for a little air, went and had a wash of clothes. Today our rations are reduced – gentlemen get twelve instead of sixteen ounces of meat and we get six instead of twelve – with rather less dal. A sentry was shot through the leg in our verandah in the night and Dr Fayrer was hit by a spent ball. After breakfast I mended a pair of Charlie's unmentionables with a piece of Mr Harris's habit presented for the purpose... I afterwards sat at the door making a flannel waistcoat for myself – at four we had dinner, after dinner the invalids came out and took the air on their couches at the door – at seven I went down and made tea for all, then sat at the door till half-past eight when we had prayers – then to bed and I a good night's rest, though the children were rather squabbly.[10]

While Mrs Germon got annoyed with the noisy Boileau, tempers were fraying in just about everybody. Mr Parry wrote that Inglis was "coarse of speech and harsh in his manner, and fairly led by his staff, his aide-de-camp conceited and impertinent".[11] Some of the officers were now "snappish and insolent in the extreme". Parry also accused the doctors of being "inattentive", though the medical men were clearly worked off their feet. Comparing personalities under immense pressure makes interesting reading. While Inglis had his detractors and Fulton was loved by all, opinions on the others are mixed. In his private papers Innes accuses the Ommaneys of never sharing their stocks of food with anyone, adding that the "most useless, if not mischievous people" during the siege were Birch (Inglis's aide), Barwell (the fort adjutant and major of brigade), Wilson (the D.A.A.G.), James (the D.A.C.G.) and Couper (Inglis's secretary), all of them "eulogised by Inglis", who ignored the services of Watson who commanded at Fayrer's House, Major Apthorp at Gubbins' House, Anderson, Bonham and McFarlan (the latter pair artillery officers), Hardinge and Germon (both commanding native troops). A rather different set of opinions was voiced by Lieutenant W. Fletcher, 48th B.N.I., who thought that "of the staff, Wilson was the most useful," while "the most plucky" was Birch. None of them compared in Fletcher's mind to Fulton, who was the "mastermind" of the defence.

Had they but known it, the defenders would have been cheered to discover that the tensions within their own ranks were mirrored in the forces opposing them. On 31st August, the holy day of Ashra Moharram, traditionally celebrated in Oudh as a day of mourning and prayer among Moslems, ex-sepoys loyal to Mammoo Khan clashed at the Kaiserbagh with the followers of the Maulvi, Ahmadullah Shah. It took the Begum to personally restore order, but Ahmadullah made it plain that he thought Hazrat Mahal was acting as titular head of the Birjis government and he refused to obey her orders in future. To make plain his disdain, he immediately withdrew his followers from the Residency periphery. Adored by his followers, Ahmadullah Shah had no patience with the factious political clique he felt was suffocating the Oudh revolt. Next day at an excitable meeting of the revolutionary council (*Sazman-e-jawanan-e-Oudh*), the Begum had to use all her considerable diplomatic skills to calm tempers and sooth egos. She invited Ahmadullah to join hands in fighting the feringhees.

Only a few days earlier the rebels had been forced to arrest Lalta Prasad, a close relative of the judicial commander in Oudh. It was revealed that he and 12 other persons were involved in smuggling grain into the Residency. The proceedings became confused and Lalta Prasad, perhaps through bribery, or possibly released in error, managed to escape his gaolers and vanish into the *mofussil* (the provinces).

The Birjis government was also becoming unpopular with ordinary Lucknow citizens. Short of funds to pay the troops, the authorities started raiding the houses of people it suspected of hiding their wealth. In some respects such raids were justified, but things turned sour when certain officials used the raids as an excuse to settle old scores or loot from ordinary citizens and small businessmen.

It was about this time that Martin Gubbins' intelligence department learned that Raja Man Singh, the prominent taluqdar from Shahgunje, near Fyzabad, had joined the rebels, bringing with him several thousand retainers. For weeks, Man Singh had played a game of fence-sitting, but when Havelock re-crossed the Ganges, he concluded that the British cause was hopeless and threw in his lot with the insurgents. A salute of guns heard one day in the direction of the cantonments suggested that the rebels had given the Raja a hero's welcome. More than any of the other taluqdars he was reputed to be a good soldier.

On 28th August a dispirited Lieutenant Hay wrote:

The sixtieth day of the siege! I wonder how much longer it will be, I am so tired of it! Yesterday there was a sale of stores belonging to Sir H. Lawrence. To show you how hard up for luxuries we are, I must tell you that £16 was given for one dozen of brandy, and a ham for £7, and other things equally expensive. I am clothed principally in dead men's clothes bought at their auctions. There is such a demand for them that I had to give 10 Rs. (£1) for two pocket-handkerchiefs. I had not one for two months. At the same time I got two gauze under-jackets for 12 Rs; so with my one pair of trousers, one of boots, ditto of stockings, and two shirts that were given to me, I have a considerable trousseau again. Coats are not in fashion at present, and all white articles of dress are quite gone out. The "mode" is a sort of purple colour a man in the 32nd dyes, with black and red ink powder he stole out of the Residency, I suppose, and makes our badly washed clothes look quite respectable. The poor ladies are really to be pitied; I see some wear no stockings and most of them apparently no petticoats. You never saw such objects, especially those who have lost everything in cantonments; and to do them justice, I never hear a grumble from any of them. Tomorrow is the ninth day of the "Mohurrim", a great Mussulman festival; we expect an attack in consequence – especially as all followers of theprophet that die on that day (it is said) go to heaven. I trust, if they do come on, we will give many that satisfaction.[12]

Luxury items, as Hay had noted, now fetched enormous prices; a bar of chocolate went for £3 (about £300 today), a quart bottle of honey fetched £4, the same price as two small tins of soup. Soap there was none. Wine and spirits were still obtainable at high prices but the thing most men longed for was a puff of tobacco. It had all gone. Mr Rees now resorted to tea leaves and neem leaves and guava fuit leaves instead.

The reductions in rations made everyone grumble. Mr Rees explained: "Our grand diet consists of coarse, exceedingly coarse 'attah' (ground corn with all the husks unsifted), 'mash dal' (a nasty black slippery kind of lentils), and bitter salt, with, every other day, a small piece of coarse beef, half of it bones. The whole of this, when passed under the hands of my *chef-de-cuisine*, a filthy black fellow, who cooks for three or four others, and whom I am obliged to pay twenty rupees a month, results in an abomination which a Spartan dog would turn up his nose at."[13]

On 25th August Inglis had sent out another letter to Havelock pointing out that he had not received any news beyond 4th August. Besides being desperate for some good tidings, the brigadier was now hearing "alarming reports" that his native troops, especially the Sikhs and Indian gunners, might be plotting to mutiny. The Moharram, with Lucknow's Moslem inhabitants banging drums and sounding horns at all hours, made Inglis fear that the religious fervour might peak in another general assault.

Those who criticised Inglis perhaps failed to realise the immense stress he was working under, for beneath all his tetchiness and dogmatic ways he felt a huge responsibility on his shoulders. Every day and twice daily he did a full inspection of the defences. On 26th, while at Gubbins' bastion, a 24-pound shot narrowly missed the brigadier who, covered in dust, jumped to his feet saying, "All right!" "No, its not all right sir," said a sergeant standing nearby. The shot had killed Lieutenant Webb of the 32nd and an Indian sweeper. For a time the bastion was evacuated, but by 31st August an 18-pounder had been mounted and the thickness of the parapet increased by 16 feet.

Heavy rains on the night of 27th/28th August flooded a countermine near the Brigade Mess. Next morning, Fulton was digging by himself when he broke through into an enemy tunnel. He called for powder, laid a charge 15 yards along the enemy's mine and blew it up. The insurgents were heard digging again that day near Sago's Post; a countermine was driven out from the salient angle and a second begun at the northern end.

At midnight on the 28th Ungud returned with a letter from Havelock:

My dear Colonel, I have your letter of the 16th inst. I can only say, do not negotiate, but rather perish sword in hand. Sir Colin Campbell, who came out at a day's notice to command, upon news of General Anson's death, promises me fresh troops, and you will be my first care. The reinforcements may reach me from twenty to twenty-five days, and I will prepare everything for a march on Lucknow.

Yours very sincerely, H.Havelock, Br Gen.[14]

Ungud said it had been easier to pass through the enemy's lines than to enter the British entrenchment without being shot by sentries.

Desertions continued; on the same night 11 Eurasian Christian drummers decamped (their families were in the city), leaving the outhouses near the racquet court on the west face totally undefended. A number of Indian servants then took flight, one of them stealing Captain Boileau's double-barrelled shotgun (it was rumoured that these deserters were all shot by the enemy on the iron bridge).

On 30th August, Lieutenant Bonham of the Artillery was sitting on the Post Office steps when a musket ball smashed into his collar-bone. It was his third injury and he would receive one more before the end of the siege. Next day, the enemy opened fire with two guns, one of them a powerful 32-pounder, less than 150 yards from the Baillie Guard. Some balls smashed through the gates, destroying two wagons that formed part of the barricade. Lieutenant Aitken and his men of the 13th B.N.I. began at once to construct a sunken battery designed by the engineers to accommodate an 18-pounder gun and a 24-pounder howitzer.

The tunnelling never ceased; that day enemy miners were heard near Sander's Post; a countermine was run out and fired successfully. By now the British miners were getting very proficient; they were trained by a small team of ex Cornish miners from HM 32nd – Sergeant Day and Privates Abel, Bonatta, Cullimore, Cummerford, Farran, Hunter and Kitchen.

While the garrison knew and accepted death as a daily occurrence, they also knew that the Good Book says Charity "Beareth all things, believeth all things, hopeth all things, endureth all things." Such was the case of the heavily pregnant Mrs Dashwood, who had first lost her husband and then her infant son Herbert on the 18th. Now she was rushed into labour on 31st August. "I never was more astounded in my life" remarked Mrs Harris, who acted as a wet nurse and did all she could to make the mother and newborn comfortable. Duly christened Arthur Frederick in September, he would become one of the last ten survivors of the famous siege.

Reading the diaries and journals of women like Goergina Harris, Maria Germon, Adelaide Case, Katherine Bartrum and others, one is struck by how terrible the siege must have been for them. It was hard enough for the women of the regiment, the common soldiers' wives, but they, poor creatures, had been used to hardship all their lives. Yet the officers' wives had always known servants – at home in England and numerous attendants in their Indian households. The rigours of the siege, depriving them of all their usual comforts, must have been mentally and physically exhausting. Even their clothes were a burden; despite the sweltering Indian heat they wore "a combination suit of silk or open weave flannel, then corsets made of net, a petticoat buttoned to these, and a silk camisole to cover the corsets. Over that it was suggested, a light woollen tea-gown would be suitable wear in the mornings." Some ladies also wore cork spine-protectors and flannel cummerbunds, "as it is the first importance to women to avoid anything like cold in the organs peculiar to the sex".[15] Social niceties had to be observed and when some of these were jettisoned during the siege people were upset; Mrs Germon, for instance, was disgusted by one woman who insisted on brushing her teeth in front of the others!

Heavy rain fell every night in late August and Captain Wilson recorded 1st September as a "fine breezy morning". Everyone noticed that the days were getting cooler. Desertions continued; two cook boys of HM 32nd deserted that day. Infant mortality continued to rise with the burial of five European babies. The general mood was illustrated by an aspiring poet:

No news from the outer world,
Days, weeks and months have sped,
Pent up within our battlements,
We seem as living dead.
No news from the outer world,
Have British soldiers quailed
Before the rebel mutineers?
Has British valour failed?[16]

That evening a sad event occurred when Lieutenant Birch, 59th B.N.I., attached to the engineer department (a cousin of Inglis's aide-de-camp), went out with a party to examine some ruins on the north side to see if the enemy had been mining. The sentries had been warned, but the guard changed while the group was outside. A new sentry mistook poor Birch for an enemy in the darkness, fired his musket and shot him in the belly. He died two hours later. The men who carried him in had tried to reassure him, but the young officer smiled sadly and said, "I know it's all over with me." He had been married just six months and left a young widow carrying his child along with a younger brother and sister who were his dependants. The sentry could not be blamed for doing his duty, but the corporal who forgot to pass the word was reduced to the ranks.

Each day was a mixed bag for the women and children. Mrs Huxham, wife of Lieutenant Huxham, 48th B.N.I., had some small joy on 1st September when her husband, who was recuperating from an injury received at the Cawnpore Battery, managed to get her and their young son half of a large room in the Begum Kothi. It was divided by canvas, the other half occupied by Mr Benson of the Indian Civil Service and his wife. They all managed to get a Portuguese called Mr Gomez to cook for them on a small mud *chula* (stove) which they built on the verandah. He was paid one rupee a day, "Well paid, considering what he had to do," thought Mrs Huxham. By now she was eating dry chupattis and tough beef, so tough that little Willie Huxham could not eat it, so it was agreed that most of it should be turned into soup.

Another tragic death was Major Bruere commanding the 15th B.N.I. About 4.30pm on 4th September he was hit in the chest while on top of the Brigade Mess as he tried to pick off one of the enemy sharpshooters. He died instantly. Deeply mourned by his sepoys, they insisted on carrying his body to the grave that night, though to touch it was for them an act of ritual defilement. That evening part of the Brigade Mess collapsed, shattered by countless roundshot.

Dawn next day saw a large number of insurgents, estimated at 8,000 bayonets and 500 sabres, gathering around the Residency. The garrison was quickly called to arms. Commanding the Indians was Syed Barkat Ahmad, who had led them to victory at Chinhat. He began by launching a powerful cannonade from two guns situated across the river. Then at 10am the rebels exploded two mines – one large one near the 18-pounder battery at Sago's House and a smaller one near the Brigade Mess. The former mine, despite rocking the houses, proved short of its aim, while the latter had been countermined and did little damage. A third explosion followed near Gubbins' House but here again the insurgents had made an error of distance. The defenders stared through the smoke and saw a large crater. Then, as Gubbins wrote:

The enemy soon came out in force all round, and fixing a huge ladder with double row of rungs, so as to allow of two or more men mounting abreast, at the mouth of the 18-pounder, attempted to escalade. But it was an attempt only. They did not show their faces, but thrust the muzzles of their muskets into the embrasure and fired. They were speedily dislodged by Major Apthorp and the men of the 32nd with hand grenades and musket-shots, while we kept up a heavy fire upon them from the loopholes with which our out-houses were now pierced. After about an hour and a half they fell back into the houses from whence they had issued with heavy loss.[17]

Around the perimeter further assaults took place and were repelled at the Slaughter House, Innes's, Sago's and the Financial Post. A new heavy gun near the clock tower opened fire on Aitken's battery at the Baillie Guard, but he replied with his 18-pounder. Eight sepoys of the 13th B.N.I., assisted by three artillerymen, loaded and worked the gun, of which they were very proud, having constructed the battery themselves under the guidance of the engineers. "We load it," they said, "and Aikeen Sahib fires it!"

Some defenders noticed that there were larger numbers of matchlockmen – the retainers of taluqdars – and less sepoys than usual in the attacking columns. They guessed that many of the sepoys had been sent to obstruct Havelock's advance.

A curious event that evening was an 18-pounder ball fired from across the river that traversed the whole length of the Hospital ward, crowded with patients, before rolling harmlessly to the floor. Only two men had been hurt and both only very slightly. Earlier that day, Lieutenant Graham, adjutant of the 1st Oudh Irregular Cavalry, confined to bed with fever, grabbed a revolver and shot himself in the head. He left a widow who only a few days earlier had given birth (she had lost one child earlier in the siege to sickness).

The next two days were "unusually quiet". Captain Fulton was well aware that if the insurgents were passive above ground, then it was most likely they were busily mining below ground. During the afternoon of 6th September he led a party of sepoys from Innes's Post to destroy a house nearby that the insurgents had loopholed. The group reached the house without incident, fired two barrels of gunpowder and Fulton ran back towards the bastion, but when he reached the scaling ladder he saw to his horror that his men were still near the house collecting wood. He ran back, rounded up his unit quickly and shepherded them up the ladder ahead of himself, but time had run out; the gunpowder exploded and he and one of the sepoys were buried in debris. Fortunately, neither man was seriously injured, though Fulton's arm was bruised by a falling beam.

Fulton and his fellow engineers all worried that a number of enemy mines might explode simultaneously and make a breach in the defences. With indefatigable energy Fulton was constantly directing new countermines and going out on demolition sorties. He was invariably followed by an enormous Sikh called Hookum Singh, who could carry a barrel of gunpowder on his back. Fulton, however, was usually the last man in a mine and the one who fired the train. "I never knew him to fail," wrote Captain Birch.

A shaft seen in the churchyard was opened on 11th September and a tunnel almost tall enough to stand up in was discovered. Two barrels of gunpowder brought down the walls and roof of the mine, along with an adjacent building. That morning a second countermine at Sikh Square had been fired, destroying the enemy tunnel and burying the miners. During all this time, besides the tunnelling and constant shelling, the insurgents had continued to attack the Residency with all manner of odd projectiles. That night they lobbed into the grounds a weird missile made of five hollow cylinders of iron filled with an incendiary composition and done up in a canvas cover; when it hit the ground the cylinders belched fire, but there was no explosion.

The soldiers were increasingly exhausted. "The 32nd are quite demoralised – discipline has almost vanished, "wrote David Hay. "If their grog runs short, I should not wonder if they give in altogether." But he had much sympathy for them – "Poor fellows! they have suffered frightfully, and are now *never* off duty day or night, so there is some excuse for them." He thought the sepoys had behaved well and, unlike Inglis, was impressed by the Sikhs, "who have almost universally stuck to us".[18] Rebels would often taunt the sepoys inside the Residency, but the men shouted back, "We have eaten the Company's salt – we cannot break faith with our masters as you have done."[19]

The Hindustani troops all seemed loyal to a man, but Captain Hawes, Mr Gubbins' assistant in the Intelligence Department, was worried about the Sikhs. It was known that at night they talked to the rebels outside the defences and there was a brisk trade in opium (many Sikh soldiers being users). One Indian officer told Innes that he had little faith in Ungud's news, dismissing it all as trumped-up tales. Innes pointed out that the handwriting in Ungud's letters had been identified and that he had relayed information on regiments and individual officers known only to Havelock's column. Some Sikh troopers declared that Ungud never left the Residency at all and had been hidden away by the authorities, "and trotted out from time to time with a faked despatch".[20]

Doubts were growing in the ranks of the Europeans also; one man told Innes that "Havelock may come near, but how can he make his way against the large force hemming us in?" The doubter thought the army at Delhi might have been wiped out, "and the enemy may pour down an army onto Havelock's, or any other British troops that may be keeping the field here."[21]

"Everyone is getting very dispirited," recorded Mrs Bartrum in her diary, "No news of relief. They say we are forgotten and that reinforcements will never appear. This hope deferred does indeed make the heart sick." Her son, Bobbie, had almost died of cholera but was recovering slowly. Katherine's hands, unaccustomed to heavy work and combined with the bad diet, were now covered in painful boils that needed regular lancing. There was still no news of her husband, Robert Bartrum. A soldier broke down some railings for her so she could light a fire, "but it is a difficult matter to chop them up. Since I only have my dinner knife to do it with, and this will be worn out should the siege last much longer."[22]

Doubts never daunted Captain Fulton's spirits; he remained as cheerful and energetic as ever. On 14th September he went on a reconnaissance from the battery near Gubbins' House. In the words of Birch: "He was lying at full length in one of the embrasures, with a telescope in his hand. He turned his face with a smile on it and said, 'They are just going to fire'; and sure enough they did. The shot took away the whole of the back of Captain Fulton's head, leaving his face like a mask still on his neck. When he was laid out on his back on a bed we could not see how he had been killed."[23]

Everyone was shocked and saddened by George Fulton's death. "He was 'The Defender of Lucknow' and was the heart and soul of the contest"[24] wrote Dr Fayrer. One of the most affected was his comrade and fellow engineer, McLeod Innes. Four months later, he wrote to Fulton's widow and took another swipe at Inglis:

> George Fulton had always been the *active* Engineer of the defence and, after the end of July he became the *official* Garrison Engineer, owing to Major Anderson's debility preventing him from performing his duties. He was the life and soul of the defence, foremost in every danger, quickest to observe the enemy's movements, acutest in perception of their intentions. You can imagine the difficulties he had to contend with. Outside a numerous and deadly enemy; inside a pack of alarmists, every one ready with a suggestion, or angry if it were not carried out, few men for fatigue duty ... and a worthless commandant. He triumphed over them all.

Innes told Sophia Fulton that "Everyone wished to be present at his funeral... It was the only time I ever saw Colonel Inglis afflicted."[25] It was true; Inglis had cried at the graveside proving, if any doubted it, that he was as human as the rest.[26]

The day before Fulton died, young Ensign Robert Loveday Inglis, 63rd B.N.I., sat on some bricks at the Brigade Mess and tried to balance a pen, ink and some paper in his hands. Over the next two months he would write a long series of letters to his mother in Calcutta, though he had no idea when he could post them. Each letter was written in a neat (though sometimes illegible) hand and would cover many pages. The Brigade Mess was "riddled with round shot so now a heap of ruins" explained Inglis. He began by referring to Havelock's demand that the garrison die "sword in hand" rather than come to terms. "We still have some Sikh Irregular Cavalry & about 120 of the 13th – the latter all most trustworthy and have all along behaved nobly, but of the former we are somewhat suspicious." After Fulton's death he wrote, "We were all stupefied. In our present position his loss is a real calamity for of all others he was the man."[27]

The exhausting fighting continued; on 15th September the verandah of the Residency itself fell in with a crash. Three more enemy mines were exploded by the defenders near Sikh Square and a countermine begun near the Baillie Guard gate. At daybreak on the 16th, the insurgents began a three-hour cannonade that killed one sepoy of the 13th B.N.I. and wounded a *subedar* (an Indian captain). Returning to duty after several weeks, Dr Brydon told Fayrer that the Siege of Jalalabad in the 1st Afghan War "was a trifle to what we are undergoing here!" Next morning the sentry at the churchyard had his head carried off by a roundshot.

With Captain Fulton dead the defenders were beginning to doubt that they could hold on for the longed-for relief. Lieutenant Bonham had constructed two mortar howitzers, called "ships", that were doing good work, silencing an enemy 18-pounder near Innes's Post, but at dawn on the 20th it was discovered that the insurgents had nearly completed two new batteries.

Rain fell in torrents on the 21st and 22nd. Dr Fayrer found it all dispiriting, "as everything is so leaky now, and the roofs are all injured – nothing is watertight."[28] Mrs Harris, however, was reminded of England by the "delightfully cool" rain.

Second Lieutenant John Foster Cunliffe of the Bengal Artillery died of sickness on the 22nd leaving a wife and three children. He was buried in the same grave as Monsieur Deprat, the voluble Frenchman, who never recovered from having his jaw shot away a month earlier. He had always told his friend, Mr Rees, that he would survive the siege. "I deny that there is a Providence," he had declared. "Just see the justice of your Providence. Here is a good man like Polehampton dead, and a rascal like myself still living."[29] Fate or God decreed otherwise. The sour-faced Capuchin Father Bernard did not want to give Deprat a Christian burial and finally agreed to do so with the greatest reluctance, mumbling just a few words in Latin over the grave before hurrying away. Fortunately,

Chaplain Harris was also present to bury Cunliffe and, as he spoke the full Anglican burial service, Deprat's friends thought of it as intended for him, too.

By daybreak on the 23rd the rain had stopped. At last, Brigadier Inglis got the letter he had been dreaming of for an eternity:

TO COLONEL INGLIS
North Side of the River
September 20, 1857

The army crossed the river yesterday, and all the material being over now, marches towards you to-morrow, and under the blessing of God will now relieve you. The rebels, we hear, intend making one desperate assault on you as we approach the city, and you will be on the watch in expectation of weakening your garrison to make a diversion in our favour as we attack the city. I beg to warn you against being enticed to venture far from your works. When you see us engaged in the vicinity, such diversion as you could make without in any way risking your position should only be attempted.

Yours sincerely, J. Outram.[30]

As the afternoon wore on Julia Inglis could hear the sound of distant guns. "I shall never forget the thrilling sensation of hope and joy that filled my heart," she wrote, "Each boom seemed to say, 'We are coming to save you.'"[31]

Large bodies of rebels were seen moving guns and ammunition wagons about the city. Lieutenant Hay watched in amazement:

Irregular cavalry galloping about, guns loaded with grape pointing down the streets, regiments marching in all directions, and the citizens bolting across the bridges in great haste. Hardly a shot been fired at us all day, so we were able to keep a look-out from the top of the Residency tower, and have seen everything that is going on. Towards evening for four hours heard heavy firing about ten miles off, and saw the smoke of the guns rising above the trees – the city, if possible, in greater confusion that ever, increased by our shells, which are being fired in all directions, now we know we need not economise.[32]

Ungud told Inglis: "Now I have got back three times. I will go no more, but live or die with you."[33] Considering the huge risks he had taken for the garrison that seemed only fair (he was also richer by more than £1,000, a colossal sum). Verbally, he explained that the besiegers numbered about 15,000 and the relieving force was around 2,000 Europeans and 1,000 Sikhs. Ungud also brought in a private letter for one officer from a cousin marching up with Havelock; this revealed, to the joy of readers, that regiments from England were on their way, that all was quiet in the Madras presidency and there had been only minor trouble in the Bombay one.

The sound of guns and the enemy troop movements continued throughout the 24th, leading to feelings of expectation but also uncertainty within the Residency. During the night another hero had died: Captain Radcliffe who had led the charge of the volunteer cavalry at Chinhat was hit by a roundshot at the Cawnpore Battery and died of internal injuries.

Early on 25th September guns were heard booming to the south and by 10am it was clear that the noise was getting closer. While the garrison at Gubbins' House were listening, a sepoy suddenly appeared over the parapet. A sentry levelled his musket but the newcomer held out a letter in his hand. It was a despatch from Outram dated the 16th and had been superseded by Ungud's letter of the 20th. Inglis hurriedly sent back the following reply:

Lucknow, 25th Sept. 1857
11a.m.

My dear General
I have this instant received your letter of the 16th instant. Yours of the 20th brought by my own messenger, I had before received. I regret I am quite unable to leave my position to make a sortie on your approaching the City. Were I to attempt it, I should run the greatest risk of losing my post. The enemy sepoys and matchlockmen with guns, some of large calibre, are now moving through the streets in your direction. I will shell them to the utmost. We can reach from 16 to 1800 yards down the Cawnpore road on either side, as you approach us, and are much on the alert.
J. Inglis, Brigadier, Commanding Oudh Field Force[34]

For the besieged women, their coming deliverance was a relief and an exciting event; on the previous night Charlie Germon had sent his wife a great treat – two sugar biscuits! She now enjoyed a cup of tea sweetened for the first time in many weeks. Maria's main concern was that she wanted to look her best for the relieving force, but she had no servants to help her search her hair for "light infantry". She noted how "poor Mrs Fayrer, a little delicate creature, was reduced to tears yesterday by having more discovered in her hair."[35] Like Maria, Kate Bartrum was on her last bar of soap. She wrote on 23rd: "Such joyful news! A letter is come from Sir J. Outram, in which he says we shall be relieved in a few days; everyone is wild with excitement and joy. Can it really be true? Is relief coming at last? And oh, more than all, will dear Robert come?"[36]

The most famous incident of this first relief involved a humble corporal's wife of HM 32nd called Jessie Brown. This Scots lassie had spent weeks "in a haze of candlelight and camphor in the rat-infested tykhana of the Residency building" (according to her tale as related first of all in the *Jersey Times*). No matter that by this stage the Residency had been evacuated for several weeks, for Jessie's tale is pure myth. She is supposed to have woken from a slumber to say: "Dinna ye hear it? Dinna ye hear it? Ay, its no dreamin', its the slogan of the Highlanders. We're saved, we're saved!" Others heard only the sound of guns but Jessie was convinced that "The Campbells are comin'. D'ye hear it?"[37] The tale became a sensation back in Britain and was soon reproduced in newspapers all over the world. It led to Frederick Goodall's famous painting, *Jessie's Dream*, in which a young woman points dramatically towards the relieving soldiers. The story was also turned into a ballad, *Jessie's Dream At Lucknow* by W. Shepherd. Then the enterprising playwright and producer Dion Boccicault wrote an Indian Mutiny melodrama called *Jessie Brown*. Thirty years later, a critic would write: "The Highland lassie of Lucknow made a tour of the world of print, and though there is not one word of truth in her, she probably will not receive her official and final contradiction until the Judgment Day."[38]

Just before noon on the 25th the firing seemed to die away for a while. Scores of Lucknow's inhabitants were seen making their way north across the bridges. Soon this stream turned into a river of humanity. Old men, women and children scrambled to drag away their belongings, there were carts mixed up with camels, troopers and their horses barging elephants. Every available cannon in the garrison was now turned on the bridges. Suddenly the bridge of boats split in the middle, sending everyone and everything on it into the water. Several people drowned and the rebel cavalry gripped tightly on their horses' bridles and tried to reach the northern bank.

Then the insurgents began shelling the Residency again. It was reported at about 4pm that European troops had been seen in action by the Moti Mahal Palace, less than a mile along the river bank from the garrison. Musketry and cannon fire grew louder. There was excitement when some Minié rifle balls suddenly whizzed over a few heads. At five minutes past 5pm Captain Wilson finally *saw* British troops edging towards the Residency, "though men fell at almost every step" under an intense fire. Long pent-up emotions now overflowed and from every pit and battery, every trench and bastion, from behind sandbags piled high and from the ruins of shattered buildings, the defenders began to cheer. This excitement even gripped the patients in the hospital who joined in the applause; on crutches or crawling on the ground, the invalids came outside to see for themselves and add their own voices to the clamour. The cheers grew ever more deafening. It was, wrote Wilson, "a moment never to be forgotten".

From the rooftops of the long street leading uphill from the city to the Baillie Guard the insurgents poured a withering fire down on Havelock's men. It was heavy going for the relief column, men kept dropping fast and there was little time to pick up the wounded. Yet as they got closer and closer to the Residency, the troops were buoyed up by the cheering and started to run towards the sounds. The Baillie Guard gate was heavily barricaded, though broken and riddled with shot. Havelock, Outram and their staffs entered through an embrasure to the right of the gate, followed by some 78th Highlanders and Sikhs. Inglis felt embarrassed to see the generals who looked almost immaculate in his eyes. An orderly was told to fetch his sword, which he had not worn since Chinhat. He felt like a pirate with just a brace of pistols in his belt. Stepping forward, the brigadier said, "We hardly expected you before tomorrow."

"When I saw your battered gate I determined to be in before nightfall,"[39] was Havelock's reply. It was the 88th day of the siege. Its garrison had shrunk from around 1,700 persons to 979 – 577 Europeans and 402 natives.[40]

5

Lambs to the Slaughter

Cawnpore, Oudh and Lucknow, 15th August–25th September 1857

Triumphant, exhausted, Havelock's "lambs", as the English Press dubbed them, stumbled into the Residency compound. Their efforts to get there had been herculean and, it must be admitted, the people of Oudh had resisted them every bit as valiantly.

On 4th August Havelock had reluctantly led his army, 1,415 strong, up the road towards Lucknow. Their first objective was Busherutgunge, 12 miles to his front. In another of his orations the general told his soldiers that 30,000 of the enemy awaited them, but "I command you to defeat them, and you shall do so." About 6pm the army reached a small piece of rising ground from where they saw the insurgents "shouting and tom-tomming to keep their spirits up", as they defiantly beckoned the British to come on. Both sides went to bed wet and tired that night, but the British were up at 3.30am. Hugh Pearson of the 84th Foot recalled:

> The first shot we fired was a shell from our 24 pr. howitzer; it burst over their battery, and had the effect of shutting their mouths. The next two were round shot... These two shots went through their village from one end to the other, down the road which was straight, killing 7 or 8 each ball. As soon as they felt the effect of these 3 pills they left their battery and ran into their houses, from which they opened fire with matchlocks and gingals [a type of musket mounted on a swivel]. We advanced to the village and the General gave it up to the tender mercies of the 84th, as he said, "to do as they liked with". They did clear it with a vengeance for in 5 minutes there was not one live n****r in the village. They then (the enemy) got into very thick cover the other side of "Bushseerethgunge" and there they stood firing at us, and we at

them ... so we charged bang at them, and then they went right and left to two villages on each side of the road.[1]

Once the British guns arrived, the affair became largely an artillery duel, although Pearson and 20 others of his regiment were able to charge an enemy horse artillery team who galloped away from them. The insurgents managed to escape with all their guns save two. Barrow's volunteers again did good work as they galloped up to the rear of the retreating rebels.

The troops rested for a few hours on the far side of the causeway leading out of town and ate some hard biscuit washed down with tea. Here, Havelock took stock of his position; though he had lost only 2 men killed and 23 wounded in the figh‚t his losses in sick and dying from cholera numbered nearly 100 men in just one-and-a-half days. It was painfully evident that to reach Lucknow would require at least three more such battles. He confessed: "My wearied infantry can scarcely muster strength to capture the guns, and as I have no cavalry, the mutineers resist as long as they have the power, and then retire without fear of pursuit."[2] Tytler wrote to Calcutta that "The men are cowed by the numbers opposed to them, and the endless fighting. Every village is held against us, the zemindars have risen to oppose us... We know then to be all around us in bodies of 500 or 600 independent of the regular levies."[3]

Across the wide swathe of northern India from Unao to Lucknow, the local inhabitants led by their taluqdars were on the war path. They included Rao Rambaksh of Dundiakhera, the janwars of Beangarmau led by Jasa Singh of Debi Baksh, the baiswara rajputs of Parwa Ranabirpur and Massabali, the sengars of Kantha. Nawabali Khan, taluqdar of Mahmudabad, had been the first to raise the standard of revolt in Oudh, Raja Guru Baksh Singh from Ramnagar had been the first to join the ex-sepoys attacking the Residency and Raja Loni Singh of Mithauli even fired a royal salute when he heard that the boy-king, Birjis Qadr, had been placed on the throne.

A despatch was received from Neill in which he said the Saugor rebels were mustering at Bithur preparatory to an attack on the column. So, after their brief respite, Havelock turned his weary troops back once again to Mungulwar. Both Tytler and Captain Crommelin, his senior engineer, agreed with the general that to advance further towards Lucknow "would be madness". A lone dissenting voice was Harry Havelock who was suffering one of his "periodic fits of mental excitement and eccentricity" (as one biographer termed it). Tytler was furious with the young man and, as Harry later confessed, "took me to task severely". Next day, the general wrote to Lord Canning that it was with "great grief and reluctance" that he could not allow or lead an advance since "The losses of this force in a fruitless attempt to relieve Colonel Inglis would, of course, involve his fall."[4]

Despite the retreat, Havelock wanted to keep a foothold in Oudh if he could and so moved gradually back towards the Ganges. Lieutenant Digby Barker of HM 78th Highlanders later wrote:

> At 2 or 3 o'clock we fell back again about twelve miles to our old village of Mungulwar. The next day we commenced sending the commissariat carts, extra ammunition and heavy guns, down to the bank of the river, six miles to our rear, whence we were sent across. We were thus left in the lightest marching order possible, the men not having even their great-coats and for some five or six days, we lived day and night armed and accoutred ready to take advantage of the enemy who were now moving towards us.[5]

Meantime Crommelin designed an artificial causeway across the islands and swamps of the river linked by a bridge of boats. The width needed to cross was reduced by some 700 yards. Lieutenant W. H. Moorsom and a large gang of labourers did the heavy work and it was completed on 11th August.

That same day a message came from Neill, who had so imperiously ordered Havelock to rush on to Lucknow, that he needed help closer to home as a reported force of some 4,000 insurgents with five heavy guns were getting ready at Bithur to attack Cawnpore. "I cannot stand this," he wrote, "If I am not supported I can only hold out here; can do nothing beyond our intrenchments (sic). All the country beyond this and Allahabad will be up, and our powder and ammunition on the way up will fall into the hands of the enemy."[6]

It rained hard that night but about 3am on the 12th Havelock led his army again towards Busherutgunge where the rebels were massing once more. "The men almost dropping out in tens from cholera, but with courage as high and undaunted as old,"[7] wrote Major Stephenson of the Blue Caps. About a mile and a half before the town, the insurgents were waiting. True to form, Havelock sent the 78th and Madras Fusiliers in a flanking movement to the right of the line, while his guns opened fire directly on the enemy's front. Much to the surprise of some of the British, the rebels stood firm and replied with what Digby Barker called "extraordinarily correct aim, and mowed us down; they were behind redoubts and mounds, and we on a flat open plain, partly swamp, every inch of which had been previously measured by them, and this enabled them to fire correctly."[8]

Lieutenant Crump of the Madras Artillery agreed: "I certainly was never under so heavy a fire in my life. In five minutes after we came into action every man at the gun I was laying was wounded with grape."[9] Barker described how his men thought it "too much of a joke to be slaughtered by dozens" and with a howl they charged towards the rebels, killing upwards of 200 of them and capturing two guns. "Oh, if you could have seen the Highlanders," Harry Havelock wrote to his cousin, "a handful – 120 men – overwhelmed almost with shot, shell and grape – up to their middles in swamp – rush with a cheer on two guns behind entrenchments and defended by not less than 2,000 sepoys and wrest them from them without a second's check – you would have been proud of your countrymen for ever."[10] Colonel Hamilton of the 78th Highlanders had his horse shot and killed from under him. It annoyed the old soldier greatly as it had cost him £80 only a few weeks earlier.

Next day the whole force re-entered Cawnpore and took up quarters on some high ground near the river. In his *Orders of the Day* the general offered a Victoria Cross to the first soldier of the 78th who had entered the enemy redoubt at Bushterutgunge. This went to Lieutenant Joseph Petrus Hendrick Crowe, the first South African-born man to receive the coveted gallantry medal. Thirty-one-year-old Crowe had reached the rebels just ahead of another officer and immediately jumped in, swinging his claymore. Despite the intense fighting the only wound he received was the loss of the end of a little finger sliced off by a tulwar.

Writing to the commissioner at Benares even Neill had to admit that "the force is much too weak to attempt any advance on Lucknow."[11] Havelock told the Governor-General that he had a total of 335 sick and wounded, representing almost one-quarter of his small army of 1,415 officers and men. Next day the general decided it was time to lance the boil at Bithur or, as he put it, "to look the evil in the face, for there is no chance but between reinforcements and gradual absorption by disease."[12] The superintending surgeon had told him that "at the present rate of casualties the whole force would be annihilated in six weeks."[13]

It was Sunday morning, 16th August. Havelock led his 750 Europeans and 250 Sikhs on a gruelling tramp of eight hours and some 18 miles until the column reached a wide plain of sugar-cane dotted with tall castor-oil trees. It was "flanked by villages, and had two streams flowing through it not fordable by troops of any arm, and only to be crossed by two narrow bridges, the farther of which was protected by an intrenchment armed with artillery. After passing the second bridge the road took a turn which protected the defenders from direct fire, and behind lay the town of

Bithoor, with brick houses rising one above another, surrounded by walls and buried in trees."[14] This defensive position displayed remarkable skill on the part of the Oudh insurgents, having been planned with great care, and Havelock admitted it was one of the strongest he had ever seen. The deep-flowing streams prevented him from using any flanking movement. His little army faced three rebel infantry regiments, two more of cavalry and the Nana's local levies – a total of 4,000 men, some of them rifle companies, supported by two heavy guns.

So the bloody work would have to be done by direct assault with fixed bayonets: the 64th and 84th regiments advanced steadily on the left while the Madras Fusiliers did the same on the right. Fourteen artillery pieces played on the rebel lines, but they refused to budge, their artillerymen working furiously at the two big guns. It was ferocious, gruelling work, and the men of Oudh fought bravely. Major Bingham of HM 64th observed that "the enemy fought like fiends." He was astonished as he sat on his horse that neither he nor the animal were hit by "well-aimed shots, the bullets zipping about in all directions". In the high sugar cane, Lousada Barrow's volunteer cavalry almost trotted smack into enemy horsemen who, equally surprised, spurred on their mounts and fled. At one point rebel sowars threatened the baggage train, "but our Enfields kept them at a distance," noted George Blake who commanded the Grenadier company of HM 84th.

As the British entered Bithur town, several men dropped from fatigue, their physical strength totally drained by sickness and hard work. Captain "Hellfire Jack" Olpherts cantered his Bengal Horse Artillery forward to shell the enemy. Clearing the narrow streets of insurgents took time, but it was done. Pressing on the column at last reached the British residency near Nana Sahib's palace. Here they were able to rest for a while under some leafy trees. Blundering forward and holding on for dear life to his regimental colours was Lieutenant Pearson of HM 84th. He wrote home four days later:

> The top of the color was torn off by the branches of trees, and to make matters worse, the bullets were cutting through the trees in all directions, and no enemy could be seen on account of the surrounding brushwood. Once I went behind a mud house roofed with straw to tie up the top of the color, when ping, ping came a brace of bullets through the roof... Our men actually got within 30 yards of them but the 12 mile march, the sun, and their empty stomachs had so weakened them that not only were they unable to charge, but could not even load their muskets: the Fusiliers had had their breakfasts and grog and went in at them with a will, killing a great number. We had our baggage

attacked and 2 camels taken, but the Fusiliers came up and retook the greater part of what was lost... Three servants who started 2 hours after the column with their master's grub were caught by the cavalry and their heads cut off.[15]

After the battle the men collapsed and lay about totally exhausted. The engineers mined the Nana's buildings and blew up several of them. "It was really piteous to see our fellows lying disabled in the large enclosed garden of the residency," wrote Major North in a letter. "Our doctors are quite overworked for the cases of acute dysentery are painfully numerous and generally terminate in cholera."[16] In his Despatch Havelock praised the courage of the ex-sepoys of the East India Company: "I must do the mutineers the justice to pronounce that they fought obstinately," he wrote, "otherwise they could not for a whole hour have held their own, even with much advantages of ground, against my powerful artillery-fire." But his chief praise was for his own men. He wrote in his Orders that they were "the stay and prop of British India in the time of her severest trial."[17]

On his return to Cawnpore a surprise was waiting for Havelock; he learned via the Government *Gazette* that Major-General Sir James Outram K.C.B. of the Bombay Army was being sent "to command the Dinapore and Cawnpore Divisions, which are to be combined in one command." He would also be the new chief commissioner of Oudh. This meant that when Outram arrived Havelock would no longer hold an independent command and the task of relieving Lucknow would fall on the other man's shoulders. Brigadier Neill and his friends hinted that old Havelock had been superseded as a punishment for not pressing on to Lucknow (this was later strenuously denied by the Indian Government). Luckily, a rift between the two generals seemed unlikely as Havelock had served under Outram in Persia and respected him enormously.

Public opinion, both in India and Britain, favoured Havelock over Outram, not that the old general cared a jot. By now the man they once called a "fossil" was a media sensation. His victories and the hardships endured by his soldiers were spoken of everywhere with awe, admiration and gratitude. "Havelock and his troops fought Plassey five times over between Allahabad and Bithoor," declared *The Times*, "he advances, he fights, he conquers." Another newspaper noted how the general was "evidently a Christian warrior of the right breed". British men and women of all classes, "above all the middle classes," wrote John Marshman, took the obscure old warrior in a few weeks "by national suffrage to the pinnacle of renown".[18]

During Havelock's absence, Cawnpore's Indian inhabitants had been left to the tender mercies of Brigadier James Neill. He had visited the Bibighar not long after his arrival and been appalled by what he saw. Like many of these visitors he felt a mixture of rage and pity. To the Victorians, and especially the officer class, women were a sacred caste to be mollified, coddled and treated like angels. And all soldiers were horrified by the slaughtered children. A day after arriving in Cawnpore Major Bingham of the 64th wrote: "The place was literally ankle-deep in blood, ladies hair torn from the heads was lying about the floor in scores ... poor little children's shoes ... gowns and bonnets and frocks belonging to these poor, poor creatures scattered everywhere." He looked down the well. "It was a sight I wish I had never seen, but once seen never to be forgotten."[19]

James Neill decided that he would be the Hand of Vengeance for this atrocity. "I wish to show the natives of India that the punishment inflicted by us for such deeds will be the heaviest, the most revolting to their feelings, and what they must ever remember," he wrote in a letter. On 25th July he ordered the well to be "decently covered" to form a grave, but the charnel house was not to be touched. Instead Neill made it part of a cruelly singular punishment he now ordered:

Every stain of that innocent blood shall be cleared up and wiped out previous to their execution by such of the cruel miscreants as may be hereafter apprehended and who took an active part in the mutiny, to be selected according to their rank, caste and degree of guilt. Each miscreant, after sentence of death is pronounced upon him, will be taken down to the house in question, under guard, and will be forced into clearing up a small portion of bloodstains; the task will be made as revolting to his feelings as possible; and the Provost-Marshal will use the lash in forcing anyone objecting to complete his task. After properly clearing up his portion the culprit is to be immediately hanged.

In his letter Neill said how the first victim of his remarkable order was a subardar of the 6th B.N.I., "a fat brute, a high-caste Brahmin". He was made to clean a foot square with his tongue. He "made some objection, when down came the lash, and he yelled again; he wiped it all up clean."[20]

Perhaps Neill's sadism needs to be set against the horrors of what he had seen; he admitted that he could not control his feelings. His soldiers loved the man who could blow hot or cold in two minutes and always had their welfare at his heart. The magistrate, J. W. Sherer, thought the infamous blood order was "a dead letter" used only "in two instances", though other contemporaries suggest it was used more (a corporal of the 78th saw it used on at least three occasions). George Campbell, a commissioner, simply called the order "disgusting". He may have spoken for many, but there were probably more who agreed with Major Bingham after the Nana's Collector (chief administrative official) was arrested: "We broke his caste. We stuffed pork, beef and everything which could possibly break his caste down his throat, tied him as tight as we could by the arms and told the guard to be *gentle* with him. The guard treated him *gently*. I only wonder he lived to be hung which I had the pleasure of witnessing."[21] Another officer recorded in his diary: "General Neill is determined that every sepoy caught is to have a similar punishment until all the blood is effaced. Alas! It will take several hundreds of them to do that."[22]

The Indians, as Andrew Ward says, "died with grace". One ex-sepoy of the 10 B.N.I. smiled at a crowd of onlookers and in the words of a British officer, told them that "He was satisfied to die, and we need not think we were going to beat the sepoys, because they would yet beat us."[23] Sherer wrote, "As a rule, those who had to die died with extraordinary, I was going to say courage, but composure is the word; the Mahommedans with hauteur, and an angry kind of scorn; and the Hindoos, with an apparent indifference altogether astonishing."[24]

It is to Havelock's credit that he put an end generally to the worst excesses. Soldiers were warned not to insult Hindu temples or Moslem mosques. Despite the excesses committed by the Nana, or the desecration of three Christian churches and their tombs, he insisted that "we must not imitate these wretches." In a sense Havelock was more tolerant than most, for across the troubled districts the rebellion was suppressed ruthlessly. Spies, if arrested, were doomed; from Benares on 20th August Stephen Chamier of the Madras Artillery wrote: "We are hanging men here almost every day for rebellion. One man was found 2 days ago at half past six o'clock pm writing a letter to the Lucknow rebels; telling them what our force consisted of, and saying that, if they would come down, they could easily take Benares and kill every one of us. He was immediately tried and at eight o'clock pm on the same evening he was hung."[25]

While Cawnpore's native population shivered in fear, the British troops, exhausted and debilitated, continued to die at an alarming rate. The Volunteer Cavalry lost ten men to cholera – six of whom died in 24 hours. Some lucky men had minor attacks but survived. On 29th August, Lieutenant Barker of the 78th was writing home that "Out of 300 men of my Regiment, upwards of sixty have died or been killed and seventy more sent away sick and wounded to Allahabad. The General tried to do more than could be possibly done by mortal men, and this is the result."[26]

Heavy rains thundered across the skies. Major Bingham's tent, like many others, was deluged with water. He moved to the barracks for a time but hated the place. "One long shed," he wrote, "all higgledy-piggledy, men and officers all mixed up, hospital and all, one man dying of cholera next to me."[27] Outside the muddy ground soon turned into a greasy brown morass. On 22nd August Lieutenant Pearson noted: "The 78th Highlanders have buried 25 men and 1 officer in the last 5 days from cholera. We bury about 2 per day and every other regiment loses more than we do. The Fusiliers lost 1 officer yesterday, and the cavalry 2 officers last night, all of cholera."[28]

To keep up the men's spirits, sports and races were organised. These included horse races on the flat and a second day of steeple-chasing. Pearson wrote how on the 26th "we had foot races and racing in sacks for the men's amusement. It was confined to the 84th yesterday but tomorrow a grand day comes off: every kind of amusement is got up, open to the garrison. Seikhs included. There will be mile and half-mile races, jumping in sacks, and hurdle races, bobbing in treacle, putting a 24 lb shot, running after the pig with the greasy tail, and in short every amusement that the present circumstances will allow."[29]

Gradually the sickness started to decrease. Barker got used to resting in the cavalry stables, "much cooler and dryer than living in the tents, which are all standing empty." The numbers of men were increasing as drafts trudged in – 250 extra men of the 78th arrived to cheers on the 28th and on 13th September he could write:

> The 5th Fusiliers and the 90th are within three days marches of this place, and in three or four days will increase our numbers by 1,400 or 1,500, total about 3,100 ... we shall probably cross into Oude with 2,500 in less than a week. The rebels are actively engaged in throwing up batteries to prevent our crossing, and can be seen from our side of the river in thousands, working way like ants.[30]

On the evening of 29th August, Havelock had received a telegram from Outram at Benares dated the previous day: "I arrived here this morning... I expect the 90th and 5th Fusiliers, and shall push on at once to Allahabad... My force will total 1,268, besides what I pick up at Mirzapore and Chunar. This reinforcement will, I trust, enable you to relieve Lucknow."[31] Then, in an amazing statement, Outram waived his right to command: "I shall join with the reinforcements, but to you shall be left the glory of relieving Lucknow, for which you have so nobly already struggled. I shall accompany you only in my civil capacity as Commissioner, placing my military services at your disposal should you please to make use of me – serving under you as a volunteer."[32]

This gallant gesture, which won the 54-year-old Outram many admirers, was typical of a man who had already been dubbed – much to his annoyance – "the Bayard of India". James was the son of a rich Derbyshire engineer, though his father died when he was an infant. Raised in Scotland, he did not excel in academic subjects at school, preferring sports, yet he had no truck with bullies. He seemed best suited to an army career and so joined the 23rd Bombay Native Infantry as a cadet in 1819. It was a corps he was associated with for the next 36 years. Knowing that his mother was living in impoverished circumstances, James tried to send her all the money he could and was quick to apply for active service if war arose, since a campaign meant the chances of increased pay and rapid promotion. He was 21 years old when the 1st Anglo-Burmese War broke out and applied to his general, Sir Charles Colville. The general, who may have thought Outram an arrogant young puppy, replied: "Oh no, my little general, I think we can manage it without you!"[33] This retort so infuriated Outram that he sought a second to assist him in a duel with Colville, but no one would agree to such a crazy gesture. Sent to police the wild Candeish country, a lawless area of proud Mahratta nobles and savage Bheel tribesmen, Outram created a 900-strong Bheel Corps devoted to him and pacified the region in 10 years. When war with the Afghans broke out, he served as a political officer with the Bombay Column and dealt with the wily rulers of Sind. He returned to Sind as Resident in 1840 and worked hard to protect the line of march via the Bolan Pass. He advised General Nott at Kandahar to ignore orders from weak General Elphinstone in Kabul. "Attack the enemy on every occasion" was his advice.

James was considered to be a remarkable sportsman and almost insanely brave; tigers in the Bheel country killed 30,000 cattle a year so; bored by stalking on horseback, he began hunting them on foot. One one occasion a tiger felled him and Outram's life was saved only by quick use of his revolver. On another occasion he managed to kill a tiger in a narrow ravine by being lowered down in a sling and dangling in mid-air. He noted in his journal that between 1825-34 he had been present at the killing of 191 tigers besides bears, panthers and leopards.

Outspoken and brilliant, Outram was soon seen as "a trouble-maker and an iconoclast". Governor-General Lord Ellenborough, at the close of the Afghan War, loathed Outram, as he did all political officers. He slyly removed James from the Sind post and called him "a charlatan ... no soldier ... owes his reputation to newspaper puffs." What followed was one of the most exciting periods of Outram's life; he somehow stayed on in Sind, though advising against any British seizure. When the British Residency was attacked by over 7,000 Baluchis he led a spirited retreat to the safety of river steamers. The subsequent war appalled him and he attacked its general, Sir Charles Napier, in print, calling him a liar. The war had, in his opinion, destabilised the region. It was Napier who coined the "Bayard" epithet and it was Napier who now called Outram "a damned impudent rascal".

In 1844 James went on special service to the southern Mahratta country and took part in the storming of the fortress at Samanghur. He was then asked to deal with a rebellion in the Western Ghauts. His reward was promotion to Resident at Baroda but he typically resigned in 1852 after telling the Governor of Bombay that his presidency was corrupt. Nineteen months later, he went to Oudh as chief commissioner before hastily being sent to Persia, on Lord Palmerston's orders, to command the military expedition. It was Canning who chose Outram for the Oudh command; he had toyed with putting him on his Council as an advisor or giving him military control in Central India, but Outram's military prowess beating the Persians convinced him that in his new role he would effectively combine his skills as an administrator and soldier.

Apart from Sir Charles Napier (and his roll call of serving brothers), almost everyone liked Outram. One of the few who was not impressed was Lady Canning who wrote, after their first meeting, "He is a very common looking little dark Jewish bearded man, with a desponding slow hesitating manner, very unlike descriptions ... he is not the least my idea of a hero."[34]

"We all like Sir J. Outram," was a more typical response, "he is a first-rate officer ... his conversations you can listen to at any time."[35] Another soldier who met Outram in 1857, Captain Richard Barter, recalled: "The day I called on him I found him in his shirt sleeves and a pair of old military pantaloons sitting on his bed in a small hill tent smoking a cheroot. He was not by any means a handsome man, broad and powerful-looking, with grizzly dark hair and brusque manner. I had hardly seated myself when he offered me a cigar, which I thankfully accepted and he never ceased smoking and was most liberal with them; he also gave dinner parties to which we all were invited."[36]

It was 117 miles between Allahabad and Cawnpore, and Outram pushed towards his goal with forced marches The monsoon rains were now nearing their end with, as usual, intervals of very still, close, steamy weather. Many of the soldiers found it tough going; HM 90th had been cooped up, either at sea, or on board river boats, for some four and a half months. Marching was done mainly at night, but even so, the younger men often dropped out while others were affected by heat apoplexy in daytime. Outram had chosen good rest camps always surrounded by shady trees, the men were given good rations and generally were in fine spirits.

Insurgents for a time threatened the column's flank, but a force under the command of Major Vincent Eyre (an old hero of the Afghan War who had justed beaten the rebels at Arrah), quickly dispersed them. With Eyre had been Lieutenant Charles Havelock – the general's nephew – who wrote to his cousin, Harry, that soon they would "whop everything" in their path towards Lucknow, "and I have no doubt we shall get them out safe and sound. The garrison are holding out like real heroes. And I think the accounts of their being pressed are a *little* exaggerated."[37]

It was at dusk on 15th September when Outram at last reached Cawnpore. With him came Colonel Robert Napier, Bengal Engineers, "a quiet unassuming man, modest and slow of speech", in the role of military secretary and chief of staff. Forty-seven-year-old Napier had served in three campaigns as well as conducting much civil engineering work. He had been on his way back to India when news of the rising reached him at Aden. Quickly he had been appointed Chief Engineer of Bengal, but he gave up the post to serve under Outram. The two men established a remarkable rapport and though very unlike in some ways, Outram being "impetuous, daring, sometimes foolhardy", he learned to respect the poetry-loving Napier's modesty and simplicity of character, courage and toughness, as well as his brilliance as an engineer.

In a letter to Outram dated 4th September Havelock made it clear that in his opinion, "The reconquest of the province will require a full division of British troops." Thus the relief of Lucknow was a straightforward case of getting the garrison out of the city and to safety. The general's more pressing problems were spelled out: he was in want of money and begged for three lakhs of rupees; more surgeons were needed; shafts for his elephant guns; a pair of howitzers; winter clothing for his men and 800 more Enfield rifles. He urged Sir James to write to the influential taluqdar, Man Singh, with the hope that assurances of friendship and support "might decide him to act against the rebels".

Neill was now showing such insubordination towards Havelock that the general was at the end of his tether and complained to Outram when he heard that the brigadier had been privately writing to Sir James. Havelock raged:

This is not the first, nor I think the twentieth time I have had a similar remark to make to this officer, who delights in nothing so much as evincing his independence of my control, by writing direction on all kinds of subjects to every one in the country from the Gov-Genl downwards… This general is the most meddling, assuming and in every way unsatisfactory officer with whom it ever was my misfortune to be associated. He has filled volumes with his talks and correspondence, but has never seen a shot fired under my command, so that in the hope of hearing less of his words, and seeing more of his deeds, it will be the best, I think, that he should accompany us in our next expedition towards Lucknow.[38]

Outram's great gesture of offering to serve under Havelock had started to splinter even before he arrived at Cawnpore. Because of the small numbers of his force Havelock had written to Sir James about the two "wings" of his army, one led by Neill and the other by Colonel Hamilton. Outram replied, "Of course I leave you unfettered in your arrangements," then suggested that instead of "wings" the general ought to "constitute each a brigade, with a brigade-major to each brigadier and with a field-hospital to each brigade."[39]

Havelock and his son joined Outram for dinner at 7pm on 15th September. During the latter part of the meal the usual pleasantries turned to military matters. The old general explained that at daybreak on the morrow a covering party would embark by steamer to take possession of some low, sandy hills on the opposite bank of the Ganges to protect the re-building of the bridge of boats (dismantled after the return from Bithur). Outram now told Havelock "to throw the bridge from the bank without any covering party on the other",[40] Harry recalled later. When his father remonstrated about this, "Sir James overruled him." A fuming Harry was told by his father to ride down and convey the changed plans to the engineers. Always temperamental, young Havelock grew convinced that Outram had accepted Neill's argument that the Cawnpore guns could dominate the far bank which, as a matter of distance, he thought "simply absurd". Next morning Outram issued his Divisional Order waiving his command until Lucknow was relieved. Havelock's officers were astounded and delighted (save Neill and his cronies).

Next came the problem of tents; Havelock proposed that the troops march without them but Outram wanted them taken. The problems of this divided command soon began to infuriate Harry Havelock as he watched Sir James "interfere in every detail connected with the movements of the force". Confusion over counter-orders became so intolerable that Harry advised his father "to resign back into Sir James's hands" the chief command. The general was in a quandary; he admired Outram and did not want to cause trouble. Huffily, his son wrote out a letter of resignation and asked to join his cousin Charley in the irregular cavalry. His father smiled on reading this letter and said, "No Harry, we won't send this, but I'll write to him." But the letter he sent was far too delicate and Harry doubted if Outram would even recognize that his interference was causing problems. "For a few hours," wrote Harry, "Outram refrained from interfering, but next day he was again issuing directions on all sides."[41] Privately, Harry thought that Outram had declined the overall command "so that he might get the Victoria Cross." This was a rumour that grew in the coming months (and Outram did indeed tell friends that he would love to possess the medal). Harry later wrote that the chief problem with Outram's interference was that it gradually sapped his father's self-confidence, health and good spirits until he simply started to vacillate and say, "You had better go to Sir James first."

On 18th September, the floating bridge was completed across the Ganges and during the next 36 hours the bulk of the army passed over into Oudh. In the rear came Eyre's heavy guns, which had covered the crossing and rear guard. The army this time numbered 3,179 soldiers: 109 cavalry, 282 artillery including horse artillery with 18 heavy guns; 341 Sikh infantry, 59 native irregular cavalry and 2, 388 infantry. Commanding the 1st Brigade was Brigadier James Neill with his 1st Madras Fusiliers, HM 84th Regiment and 5th Northumberland Fusiliers. Watty Hamilton, newly promoted brigadier, led his 78th Highlanders alongside Brayser's Ferozepore Sikhs and the newly arrived 90th Light Infantry. All the cavalry were under the command of Lousada Barrow, while easy-going Major Cooper commanded Maude's battery of guns led by bullocks, Captain Olpherts' horse artillery and Major Eyre's elephant battery.

Just before the crossing, a partial eclipse of the sun so terrified the insurgents that they stopped firing at working parties on the Cawnpore bank. As the sun re-appeared, "the tall grass and jungle seemed to be swarming with sepoys who kept up a continual fire"[42] wrote Captain Edward Mason, 5th Fusiliers. The crossing went relatively smoothly, though there were a few mishaps; according to Dudley Barker as the 78th prepared to cross in the middle of the night, the 90th in front of them raised a false alarm and wounded two of their own men. As a result, "We were ordered to pile arms and lay down on the wet ground." At dawn he saw rebels collecting in large numbers and there was a short artillery duel, "soon silenced by the twenty-four pounders on the Cawnpore bank".[43]

Some officers had worse memories of the crossing than others; Lieutenant Robert Danvers, late of the 70th B.N.I. and now interpreter to the 5th Fusiliers, wrote that an enemy battery was "not more than 600 or 700 yards distant, I should say. I was on horseback with Major Simmons, standing to the right of the line, when the first round shot came over our heads with a tremendous hiss. They were allowed to fire four rounds at us, when they were getting so uncomfortably close that we ordered our men to lie down, drew up our guns, and silenced their battery; unluckily, before we could get up to take their gun, they had harnessed the horses and absconded with it."[44]

A heavy rain had started to fall from leaden skies and the deluge would last the next 30 hours. Few men had overcoats and most were soaked through to the skin in minutes. Surgeon Home of the 90th never forgot "how the rain came in at my neck and, coursing down like a small torrent, found exit at my heels."[45] It appears that in their argument over tents Havelock and Outram had met in the middle; a very few were provided for the men and one only for the officers of each regiment. Most soldiers, such as Lieutenant Danvers, "awoke in a regular puddle and slept in one".

The army was travelling light – recent events and hardships also made them an odd-looking bunch. Havelock had ordered that each man pack a tunic or shell jacket with cloth trousers with their bedding, suggesting they marched in shirt-sleeves with white or dungaree trousers. The 84th had no forage cap covers, while the 78th had left their feather bonnets at Poona after their return from Persia and "they went through the first relief of Lucknow in covered forage caps, red doublets, still of the double-breasted cut, kilts and hose."[46] HM 5th Fusiliers were even worse off; they had been stationed in Mauritius prior to arriving in India (on their way to China), and had not received the back-coats issued at home. They set off for Lucknow wearing ship's smocks over white trousers. "Spare smocks were cut up to make covers and curtains for their forage caps, to which were added peaks removed from shakos."[47] Neill had made sure that his Madras Fusiliers set off at the start of the campaign looking smart in their blue forage cap covers – hence the term Blue Caps – with matching blue trousers and white frock-coats, but by now no two frocks looked the same, after attempts at dyeing, and ranged from a dingy brown khaki to grubby white.

If the soldiers were disgruntled by the weather, this was as nothing compared to the ill temper of Brigadier Neill, who saw mistakes in everything that General Havelock did. His Journal is replete with criticisms of the man he called "Old Goose Steps". On the 18th, for example, he wrote: "Genl Havelock making a great ass of himself … much ammunition entirely and uselessly wasted." After the Ganges crossing on 19th he grumbled, "Bad management as usual, no rations served out to troops and no baggage until 11am, no tents for regiments and in fact confusion and mess as must always be when things are not properly managed… Young Havelock is zealous and inexperienced."[48]

At 7am on Monday 21ˢᵗ September, after a wet halt on the Sabbath, the march resumed. "We could not have gone a mile when the enemy opened a heavy artillery fire on us,"[49] wrote Danvers. Just ahead lay Mungulwar where Havelock's "Ironsides" had slept after the Bithur battle. The British right now rested on a village and walled enclosure with good cover due to some luxuriant standing corn; the centre and left faced down the road an enemy breastworks protecting six guns. An early shot from the insurgents hit one poor British gun-elephant, carrying away the lower part of its trunk. Bellowing in pain the animal charged through the artillerymen (it later made a full recovery, noted Maude, though its trunk was reduced to the size of a Gladstone bag).

Due to this incident it was decided that Maude's bullock-drawn guns should take the place of Eyre's elephant battery. For some minutes all was confusion, matters made worse by the pelting rain, and Olpherts spluttered with indignation because the deluge kept putting out his slow matches before he could fire his guns. HM 5ᵗʰ Fusiliers were deployed on and across the road supported by the guns. For a time, Robert Danvers found himself in the heart of the action:

> The guns – Eyre's battery – which we were protecting were immediately ordered to the front, and two companies of the 5ᵗʰ, thrown out in skirmishing order, protected the guns right and left of the road on an open plain. The rain was pouring down continuously, and our men were lying down in a regular swamp. Simmons, the Major, Haig, the Adjutant, and myself were all together on the left, and the only mounted officers. The Major sent me several times across the road with orders to the officer commanding the right party. This was not a safe duty as I had to pass our artillery, and the guns of the enemy were principally directed against ours.[50]

Adopting once again his favourite flanking movement, Havelock cleared the village. Soon the British were advancing in style. Lieutenant M. Hall of the Blue Caps wrote that "no one doubted for a moment that we should carry everything before us."[51] He watched the 90ᵗʰ "clear the hills to our left, and beautifully they did it, extending as correctly as if in a Parade and skirmishing through the bushes."[52] Captain Mason led his Fusiliers down the road in a rush, until, some 300 yards from the enemy, they were ordered to take ground to the left in skirmishing order. The fire grew so heavy that for a time his men had to lay down in a swamp. The rain had left off for a while but now it re-started. Eyre and Maude's guns blazed away on the right and finally the 5ᵗʰ got the order to advance, capturing some enemy guns. Straw huts on either side of the road were blazing away and so fiercely that Mason felt "really suffocated". There was a fear the fire might ignite the ammunition wagons and they were not allowed forward until the flames had been extinguished.

General Outram, loyally followed by Colonel Napier, decided to ride with the cavalry in a charge. Despite wearing a sword, the general never unsheathed it. Instead he carried a "stout gold-topped Malacca cane, which he was wont to wave about his head." With this stick he whacked the enemy on the backs and heads with a loud thwack. "He rode a gigantic Australian horse which had a clumsy bison-like manner of galloping but ... the square-shouldered, compact man on its back was ever well out in front of the rush."[53]

"Round we went to the right and took the rebels in the rear," wrote Lieutenant Swanston, "and then commenced cutting them up in earnest. The pouring rain soon drenched us; but as it also did the same to the muskets and matchlocks of the enemy, rendering them useless, we were rather thankful for it. Down, down, went the wretches. 'Cawnpore, my lads, remember Cawnpore!' was the battle-cry; and woe to the black skin that came under our swords."[54] Sent to the cavalry just before the charge was Lieutenant William Hargood, 1st Madras (European) Fusiliers, one of Havelock's two aides. At the last moment he decided to charge with them – "It was most exciting – 80 horsemen going at full gallop among the scoundrels cutting right and left. We killed about 150, but the ground was so bad, that hundreds escaped by hiding themselves in the grass, which was 6ft high."[55] Havelock was to grow very fond of Hargood and he of him. In a letter home on 28th August the 23-year-old had written: "In 35 days I have been under fire 9 times and, most fortunately, never been hit, yet the grape has come rattling down about me, like hail."[56]

The cavalry actually killed 107 rebels. In the chase Napier, in trying to keep up with Outram, broke his sword over one man's head. Immediately after the charge Havelock rode up to Maude at his guns, who noticed that the general's horse was bleeding profusely from four or five tulwar cuts. The old man had, apparently, also fought with the cavalry. Maude had been impressed by the Oudh men, "lithe and active as cats" who flung themselves flat on the ground when pursued by British cavalry. As a horse jumped over them they would make an upward cut with their tulwars "which seldom failed to take effect upon the horse or its rider."[57]

Shortly after the fighting had ceased, Swanston was trotting along the road when he and some officers came across a native covered in a blanket. Robert Napier suggested the man should be shot, but Outram, in his usual kindly way said, "Oh do not, he is only a villager." Napier pulled the blanket off the man and exposed "a full-blown sepoy, muskets, belts and all, of the Oudh Police". Straightaway the rebel made a dash across the fields hotly pursued by a Volunteer named Erskine and also William Swanston:

> When Erskine got to him, the man turned and fired, but missed him. He then knocked Erskine off his horse with the butt-end of his musket. I dashed out to help him, and rode straight at the sepoy, who then turned his attention to me, and tried to club me with his musket, but could not reach me,and I cut him over the head and knocked him down, and there he sat looking at me. I could not get my horse to go near him (few horses will go near a human deing, whether dead or alive, on the ground; they will jump over them.)Why this man did not load his piece and fire at me, I cannot make out, but he did not. Young Erskine had in the meantime re-mounted, and just as he came up the man got on to his feet but, before he had gone two paces, his head fell forwards on his breast, having been severed from the body by one blow of Erskine's sword. [58]

Any reader can, I think, appreciate the drama of this encounter and also admire the bravery of the mutineer trying to fight off two mounted British officers.

The rebels were pursued that day through Busherutgunge, scene of so much action in the past weeks. The 78th's pipers made "an unearthly row now and the Highlanders charged up the rising ground," wrote Lieutenant Hall, who was struck by the way the road was strewn with carts full of ammunition and hackeries loaded with grain, besides scores of dead sepoys. The rain continued to pour down and the men's spirits were enlivened not just by the pipers but also a young cornet player, sole remnant of the 90th's band that had been broken up, who played cheerful tunes. Captain Mason of the 5th Fusiliers was astonished by the large numbers of native shoes strewn all over the road, the insurgents having taken off their footwear, he concluded, to run faster.

That night the men bivouacked with little food to eat. Lieutenant Danvers with the 5th was grateful to share his captain's can of corned beef, while Swanston of the Volunteers made do with some roasted Indian corn.

About 3pm next day, after an unopposed march, the army reached the Bunnee bridge on the Sai River, now fast flowing due to the rains. It was decided to rest the army here. "What a day that was," recalled Swanston, "pouring with rain in torrents, so that often we could not see 50 yards ahead of us."[59] At dusk the troops fired a salute of 21 guns from the 24-pounders in the hope that it would reach the beleaguered garrison (but the wind was in the wrong direction). The men slept where they could; Robert Danvers found some dirty mud huts reached through "ankle-deep mud and filth, which we had to wade through". Some regiments found cover in cow sheds. A little grain was found in the village, which provided a meal of sorts for some men; Danvers and Mason "had a pretty good dinner" sharing a scrawny chicken.

During the night the rains at last ceased and the soldiers awoke to a day that, as the morning progressed, grew increasingly hot. The sun made the ground and vegetation steamy and it was an oppressive and muggy heat for marching. The soldiers plodded on through sheets of water and for ten miles their trek was unmolested. Then, about 2pm, cavalry scouts discovered the insurgents three miles ahead; their centre and right rested on some mounds, while their left lay in front of the Alambagh, a small pleasure palace built by Wajid Ali Shah. This building had four battlemented turrets, large grounds surrounded by a brick wall that enclosed some beautiful gardens about 500 yards square, a mosque and various offices. Scouts estimated that the enemy line extended some two miles with 10,000 men while a body of 1,500 cavalry were massed on their right.

Havelock would have liked to turn their right flank, but the rebels had carefully planted themselves behind a morass so that any turning movement would require a wide circuit. Quickly he ordered up his 24-pounders and two 8-inch howitzers. The insurgents had watched the British movements in silence, but as the advancing column came in range a heavy fire was directed at them. Their first shot knocked over three officers and two privates of HM 90th. Surgeon Home watched transfixed as the ball skipped along after first touching the ground. He ran over to one of the officers named Graham, "a very young lieutenant, tall and handsome, whose reputation in the regiment was very high, for bravery shown at the siege of Sebastopol, when, at the assault on the Redan, he was the second officer of the assaulting force to jump into the outwork."[60] Asked if it was a bad wound, Home replied honestly that he thought it a mortal one. "Well, I am dying a soldier's death," replied Graham, begging the doctor to see that his father in Scotland received his belt and sword. Surgeon Home went to check on the others who were injured – the two officers, Major Peston and Lieutenant Preston, were both mortally wounded. By the time he returned to young Graham he was dead.

To reach the enemy on their slightly elevated ground the British crowded on the road and were sitting targets as the 1st Brigade was halted to let the 2nd Brigade pass it. Eventually they all moved forward under a hail of case-shot, until some dry ground was found to the left of the road. To reach it a deep ditch full of water had to be crossed; Brigadier Neill was almost unseated here as a roundshot grazed his horse's hind-quarters.

In the style of what reads like live 21st-century reportage, Captain Mason wrote in his journal:

> "Boom" comes the sound of the first shot & "sheesh" comes the ball, making a line through the 5th Fusiliers, killing Hay, the Adjutant & others. The troops deploy to both sides of the road, while Olpherts dashes up the road with his guns. Crump with the heavy guns fires over the heads of theBritish advance. Two well-directed shots scatter an attack on our left flank by enemy cavalry, on the left side of the road. Fusiliers advance, sometimes up to their waists in water.[61]

Poor Hay, according to both Danvers and Mason, had felt a presentiment of doom, "having asked another officer to finish a letter in the event of his death that day". The 5th were ordered to rush an enclosure to the right of the road where the enemy had for a time kept some guns. "A shell burst close in front of us, killing three and wounding four," wrote Danvers, "I was, as usual, on the right of the line, with the Major, and the dirt was sent spattering about us when it burst."[62]

On reaching the drier ground the brigades were deployed in front of the enemy, Neill's forming the centre and left, whilst Hamilton's extended further to the left so as to overlap the enemy line. Dashing up the road at full gallop came "Hellfire Jack" Olpherts and his guns supported by Barrow's Volunteer Cavalry, both units sent to cover the movement of Hamilton's brigade. "Into the deep ditch they plunged down without a check; horses and driver splashed and struggled in the water; yet the guns were landed on the other side."[63] "Forward at a gallop!" shouted Olpherts. Neill raised his solar tope to them and the soldiers cheered as the Bengal Horse Artillery swept by. Olpherts was as proud of his horses as of his men; for days the poor animals had been ridden in torrential rain with water in the fields covering their fetlocks. His own horse had not had its harness off since leaving Cawnpore, "and in common with most of the others, suffered severely from harness galls".[64] It took five or six men to serve each horse artillery gun, with six horses pulling the 12-pounders. They fired roundshot and also spherical case-shot, sometimes called shrapnel, after its inventor, Lieutenant Henry Shrapnel R.A. The gun carriages as they bounced along were notoriously unstable and must have been worrisome to the two gun lascars who sat on the axle-tree to the rear. The men thought of themselves as an elite unit; their full dress Roman helmet, with a turban of leopard skin and a scarlet mane had given them a nickname – "the Red Men".

Eyre's heavy guns soon dispersed the bulk of the enemy cavalry. The 1st Brigade they strode forward while the 2nd Brigade dealt with the rebels on their flank. One Oudh gun battery, however, refused to budge. For the last half hour it continued to bowl deadly balls down the road. "So I went at it with five-and-twenty men," wrote Lieutenant Johnson, 12th Irregular Cavalry, "Greatly to my relief they never fired a shot as we came on; and we took the gun without much difficulty. We chopped up a few of the men, and the rest ran away... I only lost one man killed, and a few men and horses wounded: my own mare got a shot through the hock."[65]

The insurgents still held the Alambagh ("the garden of the world"). Sharpshooters supported by heavy guns still kept up a smart fire on the British from behind its walls. A company of the 5th Fusiliers were ordered to clear the enclosure, which they did just as Captain Barton of the 78th charged the main gate with his Highlanders. George Blake of HM 84th, accompanied by two men of the 5th began a search of the Alambagh's towers:

On thrusting open one of the doors into a small room "Bang" went a musket inside, filling all the room with smoke so that nothing could be seen... When the smoke began to clear away a bit, the first thing I saw was a "budmash" standing in one corner, armed with a tulwar and shield. I immediately rushed at him and made a cut at his head. He put up his tulwar to guard it, but my sword being the heavier, bent it almost double and slightly wounded him on the cheek. I drew my sword back and gave him the point, which entered his mouth and came out at the back of his neck. The two men of the 5th soon polished off the other two who were in the room. On coming out of the tower, I found a man hidden in the shrubbery, and just cut off his head. I should mention that no quarter was asked or given by now.[66]

Outram and Barrow's horsemen, supported by Olpherts' horse artillery, pursued the rebels to a building called the Yellow House close to the Charbagh bridge in Lucknow. Here they found the enemy strongly entrenched and so galloped back to the Alambagh for the night. The relieving army now knew that it was just two more miles to the Residency. The monsoon returned, soaking the soldiers, many of whom had to sleep on the wet grass. It had, however, been a good day and the men cheered themselves hoarse when Outram gave out the news that Delhi had, at last, been stormed and re-taken. Olpherts said he "never slept more soundly".

Fighting alongside the 5th Fusiliers, Lieutenant Danvers had found the most unpleasant part of the engagement had been at dusk when the enemy, "though driven back, still kept up a harassing and heavy fire with their artillery and musketry; they had opened another gun upon us, enfilading the road, and their round shot and shell came ploughing up the ground on all sides, tearing through the trees."[67] Major Simmons asked Neill for permission to move his men and at last they found a resting spot in the palace garden. Captain Mason of the 5th always remembered the moment when he led his men up to the Alambagh gatehouse, which was barricaded, "with the enemy peppering us from the walls". He and another officer managed to get in via a low window with some soldiers following them. They then opened the gates, "but as we were trying to, the rest of the Company outside, getting impatient, began to fire, which nearly finished one or two of us."[68] Inside the palace, the rooms were devoid of furniture but large mirrors and pictures still hung on the walls with ornate chandeliers overhead. Danvers recalled how a tremendous rain came down, "which sent us to bed for the third night drenched to the skin." He slept fitfully, in a melancholy mood, caused by the death of Adjutant Haig who had been killed standing next to him. Captain Mason and some others lit a fire in the Alambagh's main room, its floor space littered with officers and kit. He had no food with him, but Crump of the Artillery shared his meal with Mason and two other officers, then they all stripped out of their wet clothes and hung them by the fire to dry as the group settled down on the bare boards for a snooze.

Next day the men rested and dried their clothes and kit while the generals debated on how best to attack the city. The domes and minarets of Lucknow could be seen glinting in the sun. In groups, men debated whether the morrow meant a big battle or if the rebels would take flight. What might have been a peaceful day was spoiled by the rebel cavalry who were spotted hovering outside rifle range. About 11am, as men smoked, chatted and wrote letters home, a body of horsemen, under cover of the tall trees and crops, trotted towards the baggage train. They were ex-sowars of the 12th Irregular Cavalry. Stealthily they approached Lieutenant Nunn of the 90th and shouted, "Its alright, we are friends!" Nunn was fooled because part of the 12th under Captain Johnson were loyal. He now paid for this trust with his life. Nunn's body was found, "hacked to pieces; it bore a good many cuts upon it, and there was one especially which went through the crown down towards the left side, and must have cleft the skull."[69] Major North, the deputy advocate-general, was sitting in a tin bath as his servant poured rainwater over him. He had just thrown his clothes on when sowars appeared galloping among the carts. Camp followers and servants were cut down and terrified onlookers ran for their lives. Some men of the 78th fired a volley and they were joined by some of the 90th. The enemy were finally driven off by two guns of Olpherts' battery. One of those who responded to the cry, "The enemy are attacking the baggage," was Lieutenant Swanston. He wrote:

> We were not long in getting into our saddles, and having been joined by the staunch 12th Irregulars, off we went; but we were too late… They succeeded in killing some seven or eight of our men and one officer; but they left 17 of their number dead on the road and then had to fly. While they were riding down the line of baggage, they came upon some 19 prisoners who had been taken, who called out to be released: the sowars passed the word down to some Infantry, who were supporting them, and they advanced and succeeded in releasing them. So much for taking prisoners.[70]

The most annoying aspect of the day was that six enemy 9-pounders, hidden amongst trees near the Charbagh Bridge, could not be silenced. "Fired with double charges, at a great elevation," wrote Marshman, "the balls ricocheted through the camp causing many casualties."[71] Lieutenant Hall had found a room in the archway gatehouse of the Alambagh. He was admiring the palace gardens, especially its orange trees, when he saw another officer called Warren, with whom he had once shared a cabin in 1852, shot dead through the heart. As the lieutenant fell, another Bengal Army officer, James Grant, (attached to the 78th Highlanders), ran to pick up the young man's sword to send to his mother, and in doing so a bullet took off a thumb and forefinger. He was not the only Grant who was a hero at the Alambagh; on the same day a 20-year-old Yorkshireman, Corporal Robert Grant[72] from Harrogate, saved the life under fire of a Private Deveney whose leg had been shot away.

The enemy guns on the 24th infuriated General Neill. This is the last entry in his Journal, in full:

> A fine morning, enemy bring up their guns and pound us. The enemy's fire too much for our followers and promises to be serious, the troops move back; the Artillery practice (Maude's battery) bad; 1 gun opposed to it, a 9-pounder, holds out against the whole battery. Whilst we remain I again urge that the buildings be taken by a party of infantry but it is not listened to. Another of the enemy's guns opening on us, and being well within range, I order out two companies of the Fusiliers against it, but as they were about to go, a peremptory order came for the brigade to retire, so I was obliged to give the order, and thus from Genl Havelock's want of ability, a brigade of his was placed by him in a false military position, his over caution prevented him rectifying to it

by a bold push on the guns and enemy in front, and capturing its guns, and we have been humiliated by a retirement before a contemptible enemy. A spy in, our trustworthy one, states that the enemy are bolting from Lucknow, and there will be no opposition. Yet the orders are to halt for the day in our retired position. The guns in front still pound us, and our reply, a battery and 3 or 4 large rim guns can't silence the contemptible guns on our front. I presume Sir J. Outram is negotiating; he suggested that old "Goose Steps" should send out two regiments to take the guns, but he would not agree, saying if any went the whole should. The enemy's cavalry about 11am came down on our rear and baggage, and cut up several followers, and I regret to add some of the 90th. I presume the men being "griffs" didn't know them, and from the proverbial dread of cavalry by infantry at home they must have given the cowardly scoundrels some advantage against them. Several shots came very close to me. Young Havelock comes in with orders; we move on tomorrow in two columns, one under Sir J. Outram, the 1st Brigade, the other under Genl Havelock with all the guns.[73]

Havelock and Outram had four possible routes to reach the Residency. The first was by using the Cawnpore Road to the Charbagh Bridge, then upwards through the city one and a half miles to the Baillie Guard gate. This was the route which the rebels expected the British to use and it was defended by thousands of insurgents behind specially constructed barricades, trenches and loopholed houses. A second option was to turn right, advance alongside the canal until the Dilkusha Palace was reached, then cross the canal bridge and strike the plain between the Kaisarbagh and the river. A third route was to advance to the Charbagh Bridge, seize it, then turn to the right and advance by a twisting lane along the left bank of the canal until open ground was reached, then turn to the left and advance using the plain between the Kaisarbagh and the Gumti. A last way was the route that Havelock preferred – bridge the Gumti near the Dilkusha, gain the Lucknow Road near the Kokrail Bridge, then seize the iron bridge. Unfortunately, Colonel Napier reported that the monsoon rains had made this fourth route impracticable for heavy guns; with vivid memories of what had happened at Kabul in 1842 when the British had left their cannon, Havelock had determined that his would be taken. So this last route was vetoed and the third route was settled on. Sick and wounded, with the hospital, the main baggage, and supplies of food and ammunition were to be left at the Alambagh under the charge of Colonel McIntyre, 78th Highlanders and a garrison of 298 officers and men. The troops of the two brigades would take 60 rounds of ammunition in their pouches, with an equal reserve per man to be carried by camels.

Outram objected but Havelock for once won an argument – and it was agreed to take Eyre's 24-pounders. The plan of attack had, in fact, been largely decided by Outram in consultation with Napier.

General Havelock was well aware that 25th September 1857 was the most important day of his life. All his many years of soldiering had been leading inexorably towards these hours. He rose before dawn and, as always, read his Bible and prayed. Then he went to inspect the lines. Only 48 hours rations and ammunition were being taken. No camp followers were allowed except cooks, doolie-bearers (for the wounded) and syces (grooms) for the officers' horses. The start would not be until 8am so that the soldiers could eat a decent breakfast. For many that day, it would be their last meal.

The 62-year-old general, who looked 15 years older, sat down to breakfast with Hargood, his adc, and Harry. The day had dawned clear and fine so they ate outside at a small table placed in an open field near the brick wall of the Alambagh. Shortly before 8am, Outram rode up with his staff. He dismounted and told Havelock that he had decided not to reach the Charbagh Bridge using the two brigades taking different routes, but now intended they all proceed along the same main road. It was also decided, apparently at the last minute, that Maude's Royal Artillery would lead the guns and not Olpherts' "Red Men".

Waiting patiently down the road and inside the city were over 50,000 insurgents (see Appendix A). They had expected this day for some time and fought valiantly on the road to Lucknow to deny it or delay it. Between the Alambagh and the Charbagh Bridge were hidden four new divisions of soldiers and native levies; the commanders were Rana Beni Madhao, Jai Lal Attrowlia, Mirza Baqar Ali and Hira Lal Hakim of Baiswara. The spirits of the men were high; on the previous day, besides attacking the baggage and freeing prisoners, some mahouts, under the pretence of going for food and water, had gotten away with eight elephants and about 40 bullocks.

Back at the British camp the officers spread out some maps and began examining them. Suddenly a 9-pounder shot lobbed from some 2,000 yards away near the river struck the ground five yards short, bounced over their heads and hit a gun bullock, ready limbered, a few dozen yards beyond. "The shot dropped, completely spent, at the bullock's feet," recalled Maude, "But as we looked, a large dark lump swelled out on the poor beast's white flank, and in two or three seconds it quietly sank down and died."[74]

At about 8.30am, by which time some of the officers and men were growing impatient, bugles sounded the final push to relieve Lucknow – Neill's brigade leading first, with Outram in personal command. Havelock, riding with Hamilton's brigade, would follow once the Charbagh Bridge had been seized. The troops set off sprightly downhill, marching away from the parkland and fine trees near the Alambagh towards the southern suburbs of Lucknow. Two companies of the 5th Fusiliers, in column of sections, led the way. Next came Maude and his train of bullocks and guns. With him rode Outram and the general's two aides, Lieutenants Chamier and Sitwell. At the Yellow House, on the column's right, the road bent sharply towards the canal. It was country up to about this point, but nearer the canal were "thickly wooded gardens with high walls, and long, narrow lanes with straggling lines of masonry houses and mud huts, forming excellent cover for the enemy".[75] Shortly before the bridge was the Charbagh itself on the right hand side of the road. The name means "four gardens" and it was indeed a large and attractive ornamental retreat with a smaller garden, known as Bakhtawar Singh's Garden, on the opposite side of the road adjacent to the canal.

First the advancing troops had to pass about three-quarters of a mile of open country, with a scattering of villages surrounded by fields of tall Indian corn and sugar cane, where hundreds more rebels were lurking. Henry Willock, a political officer on Outram's staff explained:

> Our first big obstacle was a two-gun battery situated about a thousand yards up the road, at the commenecement of the suburbs. It was close to the right side of the road, and could sweep the approach; and a little further on, there was another battery on the right, and one on the left; while those several thousands of the rebels who were lurking in their huts, and the high, thick crops on both sides were only from fifty to a hundred yards away.[76]

The British had only gone about four to five hundred yards towards the city when the enemy gunners got their range "and were pitching right into our ranks". The men were ordered to lie down in the road under this "most murderous fire", as Outram termed it, for upwards of 20 minutes. Luckily for the soldiers, the road was slightly elevated, and most were able to crawl into ditches on either side, which afforded some protection. It spoke volumes of the discipline of British infantry as "roundshot, grape and shrapnel literally tore the road up, cutting our brave fellows to pieces," wrote Willock, "while the bullets fell among them like a shower of hail. The thick lines of trees which overhung both sides of the road were all literally torn to pieces and how any of us survived that terrible storm I don't know. But this much I can say: that as I lay on my face among the soldiers, I never for a moment expected to see night – the fire was so dreadful."[77]

Within a few short minutes Outram, puffing on a cheroot, was shot through the arm. His two aides, Chamier and Sitwell, fussed over him; he smiled and calmly told Lieutenant Sitwell to bandage it up tightly with a handkerchief. Chamier complained that the task was difficult as the horses, agitated by the firing, would not keep still. Sitwell, who did as he was told, later said of his chief, "a more gallant officer never trod this earth," before he, too, was hit. Then Maude was struck by a spent bullet in his right hand, "which raised an awful welt and paralysed my hand for a time". Men were falling fast; Maude watched in horror as Sergeant-Major Alexander Lamont – "the finest soldier in my battery and the best artilleryman I have ever known"[78] – had the whole of his stomach and entrails carried away by a roundshot. The captain wanted to dismount and help his comrade, but the code of military conduct forbade it. "He looked up to me for a moment with a piteous expression, but had only strength to utter two words, 'Oh God!' when he sank dead in the road." Just then another roundshot took off the whole leg of Sergeant John Kiernan, a Catholic from Northern Ireland (he was carried back to the Alambagh by brave doolie bearers but died of shock). Maude also later recalled the death of "a fine young gunner; the only one, I believe, who wore an artillery jacket that day – it was so hot and humid. A roundshot took his head clean off; and for about a second the body stood straight up, spouting blood like a fountain, and then fell flat on the road."[79]

The situation was desperate; as fast as men from the leading gun detachments were swept away by the enemy's fire, Maude replaced them with volunteers from the other guns:

> Several times, I turned to General Outram and asked him to allow us to advance, as our fire was having little or no effect. He agreed with me, but did not like to take the responsibility of ordering us to go on. "General Havelock commands today!" he said, alluding to his noble gesture of letting Havelock lead the column. At last General Havelock … sent the welcome order to advance. Had he been at the front, instead of sending his aides and orderlies to report on the situations we should not have had the destructive delay; but so much for military courtesy! Fortunately, however, our advance caused the enemy to withdraw their two nearest guns down a lane to the right of the road, which there took a bend to the left about a hundred yards from the canal. Our infantry were soon able to take those guns before they could fire at us; but as soon as we turned the corner we got it again – from a battery on the other side of the canal – only this time we were close enough to do some damage ourselves.[80]

Riding at the very head of the British advance under this dreadful fire was Major Simmons of the 5th Fusiliers, with his orderly officer, Lieutenant Henry Delafosse, late 53rd B.N.I. Skinny, bearded, with sunken eyes and a somewhat wild air about him, Delafosse was a remarkable and true hero; the 22-year -old had been at Cawnpore through its awful siege and was one of only two officers to escape from the Satichura Ghat massacre on 27th June. By the time he reached safety "he was half-naked, badly sun-burned and temporarily deranged."[81] Now, 13 weeks later, he was fighting his way into Lucknow. The fire was ploughing up the ground, tearing down branches of trees, smashing through artillery wagons and causing some to explode. Simmons' horse, terrified, reared so much that the major was forced to dismount. Facing all the wrath that the Lucknow insurgents could throw at him, Delafosse alone sat on his horse at the head of the first two companies.

Finally Outram gave the order – "5th charge the guns!" Delafosse wrote:

About 100 yards ahead was a loopholed house inside a walled garden – the walls also loopholed – from which the enemy kept up a sharp fire of musketry. When we were approaching this, volley after volley were poured out; but before we could storm the place the enemy deserted it and moved on to meet us at some other defence. It was a marvel to me how I escaped, exposed as I was on horseback. A little higher up the road, another road crossed it diagonally. We turned down it to the right and were opposed by a tremendous fire of musketry from its further end, where the enemy was swarming. The Major gave the order: "Fire two volleys by sections into the middle of them!" This had the desired effect of driving back the enemy still further. We were then ordered to clear out a garden on our left. I was a little behind the Major, and had just turned my horse's head towards the gardens when a roundshot came and knocked the poor brute over and killed three men close by me. So now I too was dismounted! As we entered the garden, the enemy's artillery opened upon us ... killing and wounding many of us. But we rushed on through the garden, clearing it of rebels as we went.[82]

During this advance by the canal bank there were brief pauses and Lieutenant Danvers, with some others, broke off some stalks of sugar cane and refreshed themselves. But sharp-shooters were everywhere. Death lay hidden behind every wall, hedge and door. The 5th on one occasion surprised a body of enemy cavalry who bolted; on another they captured the embroidered regimental colours of the 6th Oudh Irregular Cavalry.

While the 5th cleared the gardens, HM 84th was ordered up to the front of the column. Led by Captains Willis and Pakenham they set off with a cheer driving the rebels out of side streets and houses near the canal. After 100 yards Pakenham was shot through the throat. The enemy kept up a brisk fire and stayed one step ahead of the British, often loading as they ran, "shoving the cartridges into the muzzles with their fingers and then banging the muskets on the ground to send the charges home".[83]

As the British pushed on forward they passed the bend in the road near the Yellow House. The bridge lay 100 yards further on. To delay their enemy the insurgents had dug a trench across the road just before the bridge, while on its far side could be seen a barricade, seven to ten feet high with loopholes and embrasures, supported by two heavy guns. If this was not bad enough for the British, the defenders had scores of men posted with muskets next to the stockade, behind more breastworks, with four more guns of lighter calibre.

Twisting impatiently in his saddle between the 1st and 2nd brigades was "Mad Billy" Olpherts with his horse battery. The men were caught in a crossfire from behind the British right rear. Tytler with Lt-Colonel Campbell of the 90th led a charge and Campbell's life was saved when a musket ball lodged in his prayer book The 90th captured the guns and were about to dismantle them when Olpherts shouted at them to hang on for a few minutes. In the words of his biographer:

> He galloped back to his own half battery, running the gauntlet of enemy fire from marksmen in the huts beside the road, to whom, exhilarated by the excitement of the moment, he raised his hat, shouting, "Salaam Baba Log" (Hullo children). Back at the battery he ordered a couple of spare limbers with reliable drivers to follow him. Together they all galloped hell for leather, limbers swaying, fired on from all sides, drivers spurring on their horses and drawing up with a clatter of wheels and the jangling of harness when they got to the enemy guns which they successfully limbered up, still under fire. Olpherts drew his sword and scratched on the figures "90" for the men who had been with him, before making yet another journey, carrying away not only the guns but also some of the British killed and wounded lying in the open.[84]

Then, infuriated by the fire coming from the hundreds of snipers lying in the fields beside the road, Olpherts rode back in a temper to Havelock and said, "If we don't clean out those snipers, sir, I'll need more men; but I'd rather take them into those fields, by God, than have them knocked over on the road!" The general agreed and ordered Colonel Campbell to clear the fields. Cantering across to where his men were, Campbell told them to root out the unseen marksmen, but the men held back. It was all too much for Billy Olpherts who shouted, "Listen men – we've got to make a move, one way or another! Either we allow ourselves to be potted by those rascals yonder, or we go in and clean them out! I say come on – let's clean them out!"[85] A bullet smashed into Olpherts' left shoulder.[86] He swayed in the saddle for a second, but waved his word and shouted, "Come on – follow me!" First one section of the 90th, and then another, and another rushed into the fields after Olpherts and Campbell, "like hunters driving bevies of quail".

Luckily, Olpherts wound was not life-threatening, so he rested for much of the day on the limbers of one gun and remarked, "I'd have welcomed a slug in the other shoulder as well by God, if that's what it would have taken to get those damned footdraggers to move!"[87]

Back at the Charbagh Bridge, Captain Fred Willis of the 84th had his horse shot from under him as he went forward. He hurried up some sharpshooters with their deadly Enfields to pick off the enemy gunners, then watched as Maude brought up his first two guns under a "murderous fire" at the very close range of 150 yards. Willis wrote:

The first discharge from one of the enemy's guns disabled one of Maude's guns, the greater portion of the detachment serving it being killed or wounded. It was then I offered to assist him, by calling for volunteers from my Regiment, many men of which, for some time, whilst lying inactive at Cawnpore, had, by order, been instructed in gun-drill. Private Jack Holmes was the first man of the Regiment to respond, and his example was followed by others... A portion of the Madras Fusiliers came up to the Char Bagh in support, and they, with the 84th, charged across the bridge.[88]

The leading Madras Fusilier officer was Lieutenant William Groom who we have met earlier; he had a foot blown away at the ankle (he died in the Residency hospital one month later). Willis was also wounded in the charge, hit in the left knee, but he managed to stand, found that no bones were broken, and hurried on with the others, all cheering like madmen.

Maude had lost 27 men in just 30 minutes at the bridge. He thought the number "comparatively few" considering the artillery duel was at point-blank range. His lead two guns were so close together that they recoiled past each other, "in a shower of sparks and smoke", setting fire to the loose gunpowder in the pouches of his "primers" (the men who primed the gunpowder into the vents of each gun barrel). Four or five men were injured that morning in this way. Gun bullocks were also hit or blown up by shellfire or exploding tumbrils. Maude was impressed by how well his team of gunners worked together:

> Lieutenant Eardley Maitland, my second in command and only remaining officer, set an example by his cool and steady bearing under fire. He himself served one of the guns. He had his nerves so well under control that he could let a shot pass close to him without even blinking. I confess I never arrived at that point, though I do not believe more than two or three men in our battery ever even bobbed their heads when shot came at them. That was considered "bad form" by Royal gunners … most soldiers eventually became too indifferent to any sort of fire to take much notice of it, and a kind of fatalism sets in. "If I am to be shot, I shall be shot," they say, "no matter what I do." And they're right… As the natives of India say, "No one dies before his time; and when the time comes, nothing can save him." Or as we say, "If you're born to hang, you'll never drown."[89]

Originally the Blue Caps had been spaced out on the left side of the road. It was Lt-Colonel Fraser Tytler, the D.A.Q.M.G., who had recoinnotred and decided that the bridge could be taken by a bayonet charge. Chafing at the bit was Harry Havelock:

> "Do something in the name of Heaven," called out Maude. Harry saw that the fire was destroying two of Maude's guns… There was nothing for it but a rush… Harry rode across through the fire to Neill who was sheltering in a bay of a garden wall waiting for Outram, and urged an assault by the Blue Caps. Neill replied, "I am not in command. I cannot take the responsibility. And Outram must turn up soon." In a rage Harry cantered back down the road as if to go to his father, turned, and after a suspiciously short interval rode up to Neill, saluted, and said, "You are to carry the Bridge at once, sir!" "Get the regiment together, then, and see it formed up," replied Neill. Without waiting for the regiment to form, Lieutenant Arnold of the Blue Caps with ten or a dozen of his men ran forward, with Harry and Tytler on their horses beside them. As they came on to the bridge the 24- pounder fired at point-blank range. Tytler crashed, his horse dead, but himself unwounded. Arnold fell hit in the legs.[90]

Harry Havelock sat on his horse miraculously unscathed, alongside his orderly, Corporal Jacques (called by everybody "Jakes" and later mortally wounded). From just 15 yards distance a sepoy took careful aim at Harry. The musket ball zipped through his cap, "grazing my head and cutting off a bit of hair". Then, in seconds, as the gun-teams were frantically reloading, Outram appeared higher up along the canal bank and it was at that moment the 84th and Blue Caps charged and carried the guns. "The thing was done," wrote Harry, "and we were in Lucknow!"

A number of officers and men subsequently received the Victoria Cross for their gallantry that morning. Francis Maude's astonishing bravery and excellence as a master gunner led to him being unanimously chosen – twice – by his own men. William Rennie of HM 90th had risen through the ranks, fighting in two Xhosa wars in South Africa, and at Mungulwar he had led a charge at the enemy guns where he used his fists on the rebel gunners, then did the same thing at the Charbagh Bridge, so that Havelock was forced to say, "To do once was bravery. To do it twice was madness." Private Jack Holmes of the 84th had been the first volunteer to man Maude's guns, while a comrade, Corporal Boulger, had shot dead a gunner on the far side of the bridge just as he was preparing to fire another round. Private Patrick Mylott, also of the 84th, was elected by the rank and file of his regiment. Recommended for the VC after several actions that day was Lieutenant Herbert Macpherson of the 78th. The regiment's surgeon, 38-year -old Joseph Jee, was rewarded for his "great exertion and devoted exposure" attending to the wounded at the Charbagh Bridge, along with his deputy, Assistant-Surgeon McMaster.[91]

One man who was a tower of strength all morning had been William Olpherts, who once called himself, "an old smooth-bore muzzle-loader hopelessly behind the times", yet his cheerful spirit as he dashed with his horse battery into action, his encouragement and exhortations to the troops, his total disregard for danger, made the fiery 35-year-old a favourite with officers and rankers alike. His actions on the 25th resulted in the award of the Victoria Cross.

As the troops crossed the bridge the 78th Highlanders were ordered to hold it and occupy adjacent houses until the rest of the army and the baggage had crossed over. The main column led by Outram and Havelock on horseback turned sharply to the right and advanced along the narrow lanes, ankle-deep in slush, skirting the canal. Eventually, this path led to more open country near the old barracks of HM 32nd. From here they marched totally unopposed to the Secundrabagh, turned sharp left and entered a narrow passage near a cluster of buildings known as the Moti Mahal ("pearl palace" due to the pearl shape of its roof).

Here the enemy hit them with grapeshot from four guns positioned in front of the Kaisarbagh, while sharpshooters opened fire from the *Khurshid Manzil* (palace of the sun), a few hundred yards to the north. The force halted to let the 78th catch up, but a party sent to look for them returned with bad news – they could not be found. It was as if the narrow streets of old Lucknow had swallowed them up.

At first there had been a lull in the fighting at the Charbagh Bridge, but the rebels had then launched a big attack from the Cawnpore Road that raged for four hours. For a time the insurgents made their headquarters in a small temple until it was rushed by Captain Hastings and a body of volunteers. The rebels fought bravely, several were bayoneted, others thrown out of the windows or over parapets. Ensign William Tweedie later recalled:

> After an hour's hard fighting, the enemy (failing to drive us from the temple) brought up three brass guns and swept the road with their fire to prevent us "petticoated devils" from leaving and reinforcements from arriving. Worst of all, for a time, our fellows had to keep in shelter and let the enemy blaze away, as the long-continued wet weather had so swelled our reserve cartridges that they would not go into the barrels of our rifles... Havelock, who was the staff officer superintending at the bridge, opportunely sent up a fresh supply and the time had come again for active measures. The stalwart Mr Webster stepped forward and thundered:"Who's for those infernal guns?" From a hundred throats came the answering shout:"I'm for the guns!" Far in advance of the rush of howling "devils" went Webster, vociferating violently as he ran... Armed with a heavy cavalry sabre – he despised the lighter and straight regulation sword – he made the weapon whistle round his head as he reached the guns and then brought it down hard on the head of a rebel gunner just as his portfire was at the touchhole. When the combat was finished, the gunner's corpse was examined. Webster's sabre had cut him down almost to the collarbone. The strong arm was soon to be powerless, however, for before nightfall, Webster was lying on his face near the guard-house gate of the Residency compound with a bullet through his brain... The guns were dragged in triumph to the canal and hurled into the waters.[92] By this time, the last supply wagon was across the bridge, and young Havelock declared that we were now free to bring up the rear. As he spoke, he fell with a bullet through his left elbow, which smashed the bones. The enemy had again come down, and had to be beaten back. Havelock was borne to safety on a litter.[93]

The 78th by this time had lost contact with the main body of the troops. In their haste to catch up they took a wrong turning and entered a narrow street called the Huzerutgunge. It was a dreadful mistake; the tall houses on either side were full of marksmen and the regiment had to pass through a vicious crossfire of musket balls. Ensign Kersey, carrying the Queen's Colour, was shot dead. As he fell a bandsman named Glen grabbed it. He also was struck, as was Sergeant Reid, the next soldier to hold the Colour. Assistant-Surgeon Valentine McMaster then took it and pushed on until the regiment halted and he could hand it over to Colour-Sergeant McPherson. Tweedie recalled how a wounded piper and three privates had fired their last ammunition and were cornered in a side street by a body of insurgents. The privates lowered their bayonets – 12 inch spikes nicknamed a "Cawnpore Dinner" – ready to fight to the last when the piper let out a wail on the bagpipes. The rebels, who must have thought it was some hellish machine, turned tail and ran.

Through the smoke and hell of it all the Highlanders pressed on and found themselves next in an open space not far from the Kaisarbagh. Ahead of them an entrenched battery was busily engaged in firing on the main British column. With pipers playing, the 78th lurched forward, stormed the battery and spiked the guns. Much to their surprise, the 78th were now at the head of the British column. With shouts and cheers they re-joined Outram and Havelock in the courtyard of the Chuttar Manzil Palace (known locally at the Fureed Baksh Palace), the large group of buildings which included the clocktower that had been used for weeks past by the rebels as a vantage from which to shoot at the Residency defenders.

It was now dusk and the sky was blood red. On his big mottled "waler" of a horse Outram sat calmly smoking a cheroot, his face dark and begrimed with smoke and a splash of blood. One arm was in a sling while he still gripped his Malacca cane with the other. Havelock was standing waiting for a replacement horse as he had just lost his – the seventh – killed by a roundshot. While pacing back and forth the old man got into a heated argument with Outram while staff and field officers huddled nervously nearby. Swelling into the space pressed soldiers, servants, guns, horses, elephants, bullocks and camels.

Havelock was all for pressing on to the Residency, which lay just 500 yards ahead up a rising street. Tweedie claims he heard the general say, "We have seen the worst. We shall be slated no matter what we do; but we can push through and get it over with before nightfall and before the enemy can surround us and cut us off."[94] Outram, much to the surprise of many, wanted to halt for the night; his view was that it would allow the baggage to catch up, along with stragglers, of whom there were quite a few; the Chuttar Manzil could be seized and a route to the Residency made through the intervening palaces, where the army had cover, a chance to rest, and hopefully fewer casualties. Most officers sided with Havelock, and finally his nephew, Charley, blurted out to Outram,

"For God's sake let us go on, sir!" Snatching a cigar from his mouth Sir James replied tersely, "Let us go on, then, in God's name!"

The rear guard were now in sight and Havelock ordered Lt-Colonel R. P. Campbell with 100 men of the 90th and two of Eyre's heavy battery under Lieutenant J. McK. Fraser to watch over the wounded and baggage carts at the Moti Mahal Palace. They would be brought in to the Residency later. Both from the Kaisarbagh and a nearby mosque the rebels kept up a heavy fire on the rearguard, but eventually they were driven from the latter and one gun was spiked.

Pride of place in the advance now lay with the 78th Highlanders who had Captain Brayser's Ferozepore Sikhs in immediate support. What happened next became a legend; as the columns entered the Khas Bazaar, a long curved street that meandered up to the Baillie Guard gate, the insurgents gave them a welcome that had been long in its planning and preparation. A constant stream of bullets whistled down from the upper windows, balconies and flat roofs of the houses. Projectiles – bricks, stones and pieces of furniture – tumbled down too. The British moved doggedly forward. In places they had to negotiate trenches across the road. There was little they could do to retaliate; to stop, or take aim, invited death. The lower parts of the buildings had been stoutly barricaded. The fury of the Lucknow rebels was extreme; some women even fired muskets as they moved along the housetops, sometimes with their skirts stretched out to cover the men as they crept from point to point. The British were spat on and, according to Tweedie, "One poor madwoman stood on a parapet with an infant in her arms, hissing and yelling curses until (unable to control her fury) she hurled the babe down upon the bayonet points of the 'petticoated devils.'"[95]

At ground level the troops trudged on and prayed they would survive. When a shot smashed into Private McGrath's back, he fell. Despite the trenches, he crawled forward on his hands and knees for over 200 yards before another bullet ended his life. Another ranker, Private McDonough, had his right leg shattered by a bullet. He fell but was picked up by his pal, Private Glandell, who lifted the wounded man on to his back; occasionally Glandell even stopped to fire a shot, propping McDonough up against a wall, before moving on.

Watching the advance was Brigadier Neill, who sat on his horse by an archway called the Lion Gateway (*Sher Derwaza*)) leading towards the Khas Bazaar. As Captain Willis of the 84th passed he smiled and shouted, "Hot work, this." According to Willis, "A black eunuch in a yellow robe leaned forward from a window above the arch, with his hunting-rifle out at arm's length, and almost touching Neill's head, which was turned aside. His bullet struck the side of Neill's head behind, and a little above the left ear, killing him instantly."[96] The brigadier's horse bolted in fright and the general fell from his saddle. His body was carried to a gun limber and the men reacted in fury, firing off several rounds at the houses nearby. He had been egotistical, cruel, active and brave, a man not without intelligence, a soldier's soldier who cared deeply for his troops. A paradoxical man, he had been the only senior officer to insist that supplies must include arrowroot for the besieged women and sugar plums for the children. Yet he forever smeared his country's name with dishonour.

On the Residency side of the Lion Gateway, Billy Olpherts set up a gun and tried to play bowls with the guns of the Kaisarbagh. It was, however, a brave but unequal duel. He later described it as an "anxious moment till the first round was fired and we were covered in smoke, for the houses and gateway were full of marksmen." Major North remembered the spot well; he had stopped for a moment to chat with Neill just before his death as bullets splattered around them; his horse was wounded in the hind leg by a bullet while another rattled down in one of his holsters.

The leading troops of the Highlanders were now fast approaching the Baillie Guard Gate. William Hargood, 1st Madras (European) Fusiliers, Havelock's adc, was the first to reach the Residency. "I was in front of everyone," he wrote home, "and how I escaped, I cannot tell, as I was a conspicuous mark being on horseback."[97] Another who claimed to be the first man in was Lieutenant George Barker of the 78th who explained that being on foot he got to the embrasure ahead of Outram who was on horseback and was bodily pulled over the barricade by "a great, unwashed, hairy creature". Outram's big old horse refused to leap over the parapet of sandbags; with much shouting and some heaving both horse and rider were hoisted bodily through a small wicket doorway on the right-hand side. General Havelock and his staff followed and after tumbled the "powder-grimed, muddy and bloody", yet joyful, Highlanders and Sikhs.

For many 25th September 1857 was packed with so many incidents that, in the words of one participant, it became a blur of "smoke and excitement". A typical adventurer was Lieutenant Hall who was galloping to reach the Madras Fusiliers at the start of the battle when his horse stopped in front of a stream and he was suddenly jettisoned into the water, soaking himself, his pistols and ammunition. By the time he got to the Charbagh Bridge it was strewn with dead Blue Caps and it was "impossible to avoid treading on them". Then, in the final advance on the Residency, Hall's horse once more baulked, this time at jumping a trench, and he was thrown off a second time. He scrambled along the ditch, bullets pinging around him, as he tried to use the animal as a shield. Finally he reached "a crowd in front of an archway with a gate behind which earth had been piled... This was the Bailey Gate... I clambered in with my horse, and at last found myself in the Residency."[98]

As their comrades plunged into the fiery gauntlet the main column, including the artillery, had been stopped by the trenches dug across the street. Thankfully, the staff included Lieutenant William Moorsom who had by a lucky chance been the engineer responsible for a scientific mapping survey of Lucknow back in 1856. No man knew the city better and Moorsom was able to lead the column by a different route, "a comparatively sheltered street, parallel to Outram's route".[99] All went fairly well, though the insurgents near the clock tower, taken in reverse, slung their battery around and managed to fire one volley of case-shot before running away.

It was now a pitch-black night. The ever exuberant Lieutenant Aitken decided to sally forth from the Residency with a party of his sepoys to help the column. Unfortunately, in the darkness the advancing British mistook the sepoys for rebels and bayoneted three of them. "It is all for the cause," gasped one of Aitken's loyal band as he sank to the ground.[100]

Inside the compound, cheers rent the air and tears flowed. The bearded Sikhs and Highlanders who had slogged, fought and watched many of their comrades die on the road from Allahabad to Lucknow were astonished as hands reached out to clasp theirs. Little children were picked up from their parents and held in a tight embrace as tears rolled down grimy cheeks. One Highlander embraced a defender with the words, "God bless you! Why, we expected to find only your bones!" A little girl saw tears running down Havelock's face. She asked her mother afterwards what he had been saying. The old general, dazed but otherwise unharmed, kept repeating the same words – "My brave soldiers! My brave soldiers!"

We have reunited our narrative.

6

Enter Sir Crawling Camel

Lucknow, Calcutta, The Ganges Valley &
Oudh, 25ᵗʰ September–10ᵗʰ November 1857

Joy at the long-dreamed of "relief" was to be short-lived. Yet, for a few short hours, everyone was happy. The sight of the Highlanders pouring into Dr Fayrer's compound was "the most exciting scene I ever witnessed", wrote Maria Germon. One piper dashed up to Captain Anderson's wife and asked her where she came from. When she replied Edinburgh, he answered with a whoop, "So do I, and from Castle Hill!" In her honour the pipes were unskirled. Elsewhere an ecstatic Leopold Ruitz Rees, the Swiss merchant, danced a wild hornpipe of delight. Under a bright moon it was 3am before he and many others fell into a contented sleep.

Havelock reluctantly agreed to dine with the Inglis's that night. The brigadier was, for once, in a happy mood, now that he could resign the strains of a supreme command. He hugged and kissed Julia, repeating, "Thank God for his mercies." Soon he would hear that he had been made a major-general and given a K.C.B. The party dined on mock turtle soup, beef cutlets and champagne.

Exhausted after the long day's toil, faint and weary from the heat, rankers of the various regiments stumbled into the Residency compound, a portion of the barricade having been torn down, only to collapse on the ground in many cases from exhaustion, dehydration or wounds. Sir James and his staff were given quarters in Dr Fayrer's house. Next morning the general was seen with his coat in his hand, "begging that some lady would kindly mend the holes in the sleeve".[1]

One of the first problems to be sorted was that many of the wounded had been left behind in the city. In the middle of the night Lieutenant W. T. Johnson of the Irregular Cavalry went out with his friend, Dr Greenhow (both had formerly served together in the 1ˢᵗ Oudh

Cavalry) and a few troopers to see if they could bring in some of the wounded on their horses. They managed to find about 20 injured men, "who would probably have died of their wounds before morning, or have fallen victims to the mutineers",[2] and brought them to safety.

The largest number of wounded had been left with Lt-Colonel Campbell and his small party of under 100 men of the 90th in the walled passage in front of the Moti Mahal Palace. Early on the morning of 26th September, a detachment of 250 men commanded by Major Simmons, 5th Fusiliers, assisted by some of Brayser's Sikhs, reinforced Lt-Col Campbell, the British moving across a nullah of waist-high water to occupy a large house and garden that had formerly belonged to an Englishman. Here the whole column was surrounded by insurgents. Colonel Robert Napier then set off from the Residency with a further 100 men of HM 78th and a body of sowars under Captain Hardinge, Oudh Irregulars. Napier wanted to take two of Olpherts' guns, but after a heated discussion "Billy" convinced him that it made more sense to leave the guns behind, "taking instead some spare bullocks with which to remove any disabled gun they could reach".[3] The column made its way "under a smart fire" along the river bank. A further reinforcement of men from HM 32nd under Captain Lowe, more Sikhs, and 50 men of the 78th also reached Campbell's position at the house. Lowe later recalled that the enemy fire was uncommonly hot, but what angered him most was "that the brutes fired at us out of our old mess-house and my quarters" in the city.[4]

The firing became too hot to think of moving the wounded during daylight, but after dark Olpherts, assisted by Private Thomas Duffy of the Blue Caps (one of the oldest men in the regiment aged 51 years), crept out unobserved by the rebels, successfully attached two drag ropes to a British 24-pounder that had been discarded on the previous day and recovered the gun using some yoked bullocks. Duffy was duly awarded the Victoria Cross.[5] That night, Napier led the whole force back towards the Residency via the Chuttar Manzil. Here there was a burst of fighting when a body of sepoys were found in an adjacent garden. Hardinge and his troopers made several trips bringing up fresh doolies and shepherding the camels laden with Enfield ammunition. Meantime the Captain's Bazaar area below the Residency was cleared of insurgents by three small columns; taken completely by surprise, the rebels fled downhill to the river, where a good many were shot or drowned. Two groups, led by Lieutenant Lawrence and Captain Hughes, 57th B.N.I., also led sorties towards the iron bridge over the Gumti. Hughes's men killed a great number of the enemy in the houses near the bridge and spiked two heavy guns before their gallant leader was shot and wounded forcing open a door. At the same time Corporal Samuel Cole and Private Michael Power of Lawrence's party succeeded in capturing a 9-pounder gun just before a second round of grape was fired at them. Lawrence took this gun back to the Residency, then returned to the Captain's Bazaar and captured an 18-pounder.

Not everything went to plan that day and the insurgents had their own victories over the British. In the morning, Mr Bensley Thornhill of the ICS had volunteered to lead a party to the rescue of his cousin, Lieutenant Havelock, along with a large body of wounded. All went well at first and the group began the return trek. Thornhill negotiated the river bank as far as the Moti Mahal Palace. There he lost his way and accidentally guided the doolie bearers into the same square near the Lion Gate where Neill had been killed. Immediately the rebels hit the British with sustained musketry fire. Assistant-Surgeon Bradshaw and Mr Hurst of the Surbordinate Medical Staff managed to turn around some of the doolies and got them to safety using the river frontage route.[6] But for most of the doolies in the square, as Surgeon Anthony Home later recalled, "the case was hopeless; the bearers were either killed or had saved themselves"[7] by running away. A screaming mass of rebels now ran into the square and began cutting the British wounded to pieces with their tulwars. Luckily for Harry Havelock his bearers had kept moving forward. "Private Henry Wood insisted on it," wrote George Forrest. "He remained by its side and vowed he would shoot the first man who abandoned the litter."[8]

Thornhill, aware of what had gone wrong, rushed back through the archway to try and rescue some of the doolies, but a musket ball shattered one of his arms, while another sliced his temple below the left eye. A small party of nine fit men, two wounded officers and three wounded soldiers took refuge in a small house and were swiftly cut off by the enemy. For 30 minutes Private Peter McManus stationed himself by the steps and killed so many of the insurgents, "that he had at last often only to raise his piece to cause all the enemy to stoop and leave their loopholes". One wounded officer still alive in the square was Lieutenant Arnold of the Madras Fusiliers. His distress so upset Private John Ryan that he asked for a volunteer to help him try and save the officer. McManus agreed to go and the two Irishmen rushed across to the doolie. Bullets whizzed everywhere but they found it impossible to lift the doolie, so the pair carried Arnold between them. He was shot and wounded again, but incredibly his helpers were not hit. The two volunteered to try another sortie and saved a further officer (who died in their arms) and four more privates.[9]

Within an hour, three of the nine fit men were wounded. By now Private Hollowell of the 78th had proved himself a skilled marksman and when the leader of the rebels, "an old man, dressed in white, with a red cummerbund, and armed with sword and shield" led a charge, Hollowell shot him dead.[10] The rebels were very tenacious; Dr Home, the senior officer, ordered three men to fire from the door and one from each window. "My post was at a window. I had only one revolver, with only five shots left. Sure enough, one of the game rebels came creeping up to fire as usual. When he got about three yards from me, I shot him dead, and another." The resourceful insurgents now wheeled a screen of heavy planks right up to the house. The rebels "rolled it against the door, and then proceeded to mount the roof, scrape through the plaster, and throw quantities of lighted straw into the room. It was quickly filled with volumes of stifling smoke and set ablaze."

Somehow the British group were able to get out via the back door of the house and took refuge in a shed on the north side of the square. During this rush Lieutenant Swanson, 78th Highlanders, was wounded a second time and died. Home was left with just six men capable of bearing arms and four wounded fit enough to act as sentries. Once again the rebels clambered on to the roof of the hut and tried to fire inside. Luckily, they grew wary after nightfall and the shooting died away. A false alarm at 2am left the party very despondent, but it was Private Ryan who, just after dawn, yelled that a far-off sound of firing was "our own chaps" – and he was right. To loud cheers from the little band, Lieutenant W.H. Moorsom of the General Staff arrived with a recovery column of 500 men.[11]

Other tragedies that day played out on a very personal level; for 15 lonely weeks Katherine Bartrum had dreamed of being reunited with her husband, Robert, after their parting at Secrora. He was known to be in the relieving force although no letters had arrived. A week earlier he had written to his mother saying his one desire would be "the pleasure of entering the city and relieving my beloved wife and child". Around 10am on the 26th he was one of those assisting Surgeon William Bradshaw with the wounded. "Bartrum, you are exposing yourself too much" chided the doctor. "Oh, there is no danger," replied Robert. Seconds later a sniper's bullet smashed into his skull. Bartrum spun around with the impact, choking in his blood, and said, "Bradshaw, it is all up with me!" For two whole minutes the doctor watched as his friend's lips tried to form words, but the message could not come down from his splintered brain. Then he died. Back at the Residency his wife paced up and down restlessly, but one officer said he had seen her husband earlier in the day, and that cheered her. "Not a thought of danger crossed my mind," she wrote later. Dusk was fading but still Katherine cradled little Bobbie and stood looking out across the city praying for her long dreamt-of reunion.

When finally, later that evening, Mrs Polehampton gently gave her the news of Robert's death, Katherine screamed and screamed again. "Oh God have mercy on me! Do not tell it me, I'll not believe it! Say he has been wounded but don't tell me he is dead … bring him to me, bring him to me – *then* I may believe it!" She ended her journal on that terrible day by contemplating how Robert had been "shot through his beautiful head, God bless you, my baby, and spare you to me, and I shall have something still to love."[12]

Forty-eight hours after the "relief" a cold reality had descended, like some miasma, upon the minds of all those in the Residency. The recriminations and whining were about to start. No one put it better than gunner Francis Maude:

It is difficult to resist the conclusion that the affair was a muddle, however gloriously conducted, from beginning to end. The battle was won, it is true. That is to say, nearly one-third of our little army, forced their way or ran the gauntlet of the enemy's fire and got into the Residency somehow that night. And more than a third came in in the course of the next day. But the remainder, who numbered nearly another third, were put *hors de combat*. We lost the whole of our baggage, and the ammunition of our heavy guns. The officers led their men right well that day; but of Generalship, *proprement dit*, that day there was little if any at all.[13]

The bleak truth was that Havelock and Outram's troops had increased the garrison by more than 1,000 men but were incapable of fighting their way out of the city. In his despatch of 30th September Havelock accepted that the killed, wounded or missing during the entry into Lucknow – "Some or all have fallen into the hands of a merciless foe" – amounted up to the evening of the 26th to 31 officers and 504 men (the rear guard alone had 61 killed and 74 missing presumed dead). A further 207 had been killed in the six days of continual fighting that followed the crossing of the Ganges and march through Oudh. Besides Neill, the death toll of officers included Major Cooper, commanding the artillery, and Lt-Col Campbell of the 90th who died under surgery.

Word soon spread among the original defenders that they were not relieved, simply reinforced, with more mouths to feed. Inglis told his wife that the situation was "most perilous". Mrs Harris noted on Saturday 26th:

Our propects today look gloomy enough… All at present is dire confusion and dismay, and faces in garrison longer than ever before.

Councils of war are sitting; as yet no line of action is decided on… J had nineteen funerals this evening. The hospital is so densely crowded that many have to lie outside in the open air, without bed or shelter. J says he never saw such a heart-rending scene. It is far worse than Chinhut – amputated arms and legs lying about in heaps all over the hospital.[14]

Next morning Adelaide Case wrote in her journal how "every one is depressed, and all feel that we are, in fact, not relieved."[15] Soon some people began using the term "blockade", although McLeod Innes, writing 40 years later, argued that "the relief" deserved the term since it was "succour in the direst straits [and] a rescue from a situation of the most imminent peril."[16]

Not every officer agreed with him; Lieutenant Inglis wrote this decription of his feelings and state of affairs on 26th September:

In fact, tho' the relief has come, we are worse off than ever … we eat up our provisions without either getting more or being able to displace the enemy… We shall either be all besieged again without having any new provisions or have to make a bolt of it to Cawnpore which, considering the numbers of women & children (about 300) and sick and wounded, together with our baggage, guns, mortars, shells, etc… Our want of carriages, too, is another difficulty. Uniform is completely out of the question. Generals Havelock & Outram with a few of their staffs are the only ones who wear it. I made my report to the General to-day dressed only in flannel shirt (without collar) and pantaloons. I have had only one flannel shirt for the last 3 months. I wash it myself every morning and then hang it out to dry and it is as good as ever.[17]

The first two or three days after the relief saw plundering on a large scale now that the area controlled by the defenders meant that the Chuttar Manzil, and its neighbour, the Tehree Kothi (residence of the ex-king's brother), along with their labyrinths of pavilions, inner gardens and courtyards, passages, outhouses and rotundas could now be explored. "Everywhere might be seen people helping themselves to whatever they pleased," wrote Rees. He listed what soldiers, sepoys and civilians were carrying away:

Jewels, shawls, dresses, pieces of satin, silk, broadcloths, coverings, rich embroidered velvet saddles for horses and elephants, the most magnificent divan carpets studded with pearls, dresses of cloth of gold, turbans of the most costly brocade, the finest muslins, the most valuable swords and poniards, thousands of flint guns, caps, muskets, ammunition, cash, books, pictures, European clocks, English clothes, full-dress officers' uniforms, epaulettes, aigulettes, manuscripts, charms; vehicles of the most grotesque forms; imaunns or representations of the prophet's hands, cups, saucers, cooking utensils, chinaware enough to set up fifty merchants in Lombard Street, scientific instruments, ivory, telescopes, pistols, and, what was better than all, tobacco, tea, rice, grain, spices, and vegetables – the provisions, however, unfortunately, in very small quantities.[18]

Captain George Blake of the 84th recalled that he got "eleven very fair pearls", but had to sell them to a native for £5, "in order to buy necessities". His soldiers felt sorry for him and kindly presented their officer with some precious goat's milk and "twenty yards of very fine silk".[19]

Not everyone took part in or approved of the looting; Assistant Surgeon Bradshaw told his parents in a letter home that if he had been caught stealing he would have had to forfeit his commission, while a private soldier merely got a ticking-off. He later went to the auctions organised by the prize agents, but came away with just "a sort of veil, two yards square", a few china and glass cups, saucers and dishes along with a coarse cotton sheet, costing three rupees, eight annas.[20]

Schoolboy Edward Hilton and some pals began exploring the Chuttar Manzil; he recalled rooms ransacked with the floors "covered a foot deep" with broken crockery embellished with the Royal coat of arms. The lads found a large store of fireworks so, naturally enough, they set off some of the rockets and before long the whole store caught fire. Within a few minutes the room was ablaze. "These buildings contained valuable property of some of the Begams which was all destroyed," wrote Hilton. "The place continued burning for some days, any efforts to put it out being impossible under the enemy's fire."[21]

One of the relieving force, Captain Edward Mason, 5th Northumberland Fusiliers, wrote despondently in his journal on 28th September: "We have only reinforced the old garrison, not actually relieved them... None of the officers brought anything but what they stood up in, except what could be carried in a haversack. We are now completely surrounded and cannot even communicate with the Alum Bagh... We are today placed on half rations."[22] Now rations were once again scaled down – 12 ounces of meat per day for a man, six for a woman including the bone. Loyal Indian troops were worse off than the ladies while camp followers now got just 1 lb of wheat, two ounces of grain and one quarter of an ounce of salt daily.

"Money had lost all meaning," wrote Richard Collier, one of the historians of the siege. Brandy had soared to £5 a bottle (about £500 in modern money), and hams fetched £7.10.0d each. Cheeroots were four shillings each. Without tobacco, smokers were having to make do with tea leaves dried after use as a beverage. Lieutenant Hall of the Blue Caps thought tea leaves "made not a bad substitute for tobacco" once one got used to them.

There were shafts of sunlight in the gloom; someone gave Mrs Harris seven pairs of stockings he had found in the palaces and during the first week of October it was realised that a commissariat officer had underestimated the amount of wheat and flour stored beneath the Residency by 160,000 lbs! Dr Fayrer one day saw a flock of sparrows and took aim with all four barrels of his sporting gun; he bagged about 150 and they made a nourishing sparrow curry for all at his house (save Maria Germon who pleaded lack of appetite).

Was a breakout worth trying? For several days Outram, Havelock, Napier and the other senior figures debated this tricky issue. On the evening of the 28th a body of cavalry was sent out at about 10pm to see if they could find a way through to the Alumbagh, but the venture was doomed from the start. William Swanston of the Irregulars explained why:

> It was a bright moonlight night: the enemy consequently could see our every movement. We were ordered to keep along the bank of the river for some way; but before we had gone far, we were met by such a heavy fire from the other side, and right in front, that our leaders deemed it prudent to pull up... Bugles blew, drums beat, and Sepoys howled. We had two horses wounded, and two men hit... One man was saved by having two biscuits in his pocket, which turned the ball. We returned – and how thankful we were.[23]

Outram concluded that a breakout was impossible simply because the insurgents were too strong. "The sick, wounded, women and children amount to upwards of 1,000," he wrote, "two additional Brigades with powerful field artillery will be required to withdraw."[24]

While Outram fretted and smoked his cigars, Havelock rose early every morning, put on his faded uniform and inspected on foot, with his staff, the whole perimeter. On his return he invariably went to Gubbins' House to see Harry, whose wound was slow to heal. Much of the old man's time was spent reading and he had the run of his host's library. Father and son were drawn to one another as never before. "Take God for your Father and Christ for your Counsellor and Friend," the general had frequently admonished his boy. Now the pair – at last – took time to pray together.

News that food stocks were not so low as previously thought was a relief. New estimates were made; grain and meat would last until 9th November, on reduced rations, but this date was later extended to 30th November. By 4th October, Outram had determined that they would all hold out until help came. His aim was to make the place an unbreachable fortress. By a series of dangerous forays he extended the defences to the south and east. This two-mile perimeter was commanded by Havelock while Inglis remained in charge of the old garrison. The area held by the British became three times as large as before. It included more than 1,400 feet of water front beside the Gumti, encompassing the entire Captain Bazaar district below the Residency and the colossal Chuttar Manzil palace complex. The old defences occupied the bottom west quarter of a rectangle. Eastern barricades and a heavy battery now met the rebels beyond the great palace by a place called the Steam Engine House (held by the rebels), not far from the square where Neill had died, which was just within British territory.

In a letter about this time Captain Spurgin of the Blue Caps, who had recovered Neill's body on 26th September, described what it was like living in the Chuttar Manzil Palace:

Such a scene of filth, mixed up with costly things, it is impossible to imagine. The finest china of the latest pattern from Bond Street used by the soldiers of the force, cookboys or anyone. Cookboys sitting on damask stools, cooking the men's dinners; shawls and ornaments all kicking about ... and all this mixed up with the dead bodies of sepoys, horses, camels, until the stench is so great we can hardly sit – and no one to move all the filth.[25]

During the forays conducted mainly during the first week of October the mutineers fought back bravely, even springing a mine on 3rd October. The saddest sortie had been on 28th September and Julia Inglis, now her ladyship, described it in her journal:

Very early in the morning a party of men assembled in our yard for a sortie to destroy guns. They were taken from the different regiments, the 32nd furnishing a good number. Mr M'Cabe was told off to lead. John protested against the selection saying he had already led three sorties, and it was not fair to take him again; but General Outram said he must have him. The affair was far from being successful; only seven guns were spiked and our loss was most severe. Poor Mr M'Cabe was carried past our door shot through the lungs. Mr Lucas, a gentleman volunteer, mortally wounded; Major Simmonds, 5th Fusiliers, killed;

Mr Edmonstone, 32nd, slightly wounded... Cuney and Smith of the 32nd were both killed; two braver men never lived; the former had no right to be out as he was on the sick-list, but he could not resist accompanying the party, as his comrade Smith and he had been together all through the siege.[26]

Gradually the efforts of the British paid off and, as historian George Forrest noted, "occupation of the palaces relieved the garrison of the entrenchment from all molestation on one-half of its *enceinte* – that is from the Cawnpore Road to the commencement of the river front."[27]

The detachment left at the Alambagh continued to hold its own. The situation there was well described by 26-year-old Sergeant Thomas McKenzie, 64th Foot: "

We had at this time sufficient eatables for the Europeans, but very little for our native followers (only a few, fortunately), and no forage. Therefore we were compelled to leave our little garrison and go in search of forage, and on each occasion were attacked by the enemy, and lost a few more men, but the enemy paid for it. At one of these attacks we took from them a gun and killed about forty men, seizing also all the forage they had in the small village they held close to the Alam-Bagh.[28]

On 7th October the garrison was strengthened by the arrival of 270 men and two heavy guns sent from Cawnpore under the command of Major Bingham, 64th Foot. Eighteen days later, 500 more men arrived with a convoy, thus making the force secure and also able to extend its foraging expeditions. Communication between the Residency and Alambagh was at first by runners and it functioned fairly well. This was later replaced by a flag semaphore system devised after a reading of "Telegraph" in the *Penny Cyclopaedia* in Mr Gubbins' library. Sir James was also able to arrange, via a native pensioner who had small farm, that he would arrive with carts near the Alambagh, and the garrison was instructed to fake a rush at them and pretend to plunder but, noted the general, the grain dealers would be with the convoy and expect payment in hard cash at five times the normal amount. "It is obviously necessary to manage it so that our friends must appear victims."[29]

For those families who had endured the siege from the start, the hard life grew harder. Mrs Huxham found the reduced rations very poor – "The rice had run out, and simple flour and salt, and a bone with about half a pound of meat on it, and often less, was all our fare."[30] Sometimes she was able to increase the victuals for her husband and young son (daughter Ellen Frances had died on 9th August), by buying a marrow bone for one rupee. Captain George Huxham, her husband, was wounded in one of the sorties on 27th September; he fell down a well in the tumult after getting shot in the thigh. Miraculously, he survived both the wound and the fall. Despite a loss of blood he somehow managed to climb out of the well, which had been dry at the bottom. Crawling out, he was shot again, this time in the ankle as he searched for his gun, a wound he concluded to be self-inflicted. By sheer luck and pluck George dragged himself towards the Cawnpore Battery and was finally spotted by the defenders. Mrs Huxham argued long and hard with the doctors, begging that she nurse her husband at home and, as his injuries were not life-threatening, the medics finally gave way.

Conditions at the hospitals had horrified many in the relieving force. Mortality was high at first, many of the wounds were gangrenous, pools of gore lay on the floors and surgeons worked hurriedly in blood-stained coats. Supplies of chloroform had long gone, antiseptic surgery was ten years away. Open wounds writhed with maggots as doctors probed with unwashed fingers and unsterilised knives. Up to 9th November, all amputations at Lucknow proved fatal. Outram and Havelock were among the first to make regular visits to the sick men. Women still made their way to the hospital every day to tend the sick; some cut their hair short lest their "light infantry" should fall down as they bent over the beds. "Each individual seems a heroine," declared one soldier.

Gradually, things improved, especially after the upper storey of the European Hospital was re-opened; it was given over to the sick of the original garrison while the relief force lay on the floor below. Men used to the semi-darkness and foul smells now enjoyed a view across the river and fresh air. Doors and windows no longer had to be shut all the time and the weather generally was getting cooler.

One of the chief instruments of improved health was Dr Ogilvie, the Sanitary Commissioner. He asked for, and got, as many men as he needed to clear away the filth of past weeks along with the rotting carcasses of dead animals. One huge benefit of all this was a dimunition in the numbers of flies and mosquitoes. Among other good works, the magazine was overhauled and all supplies of ammunition counted and graded. A factory was established by Major North to manufacture Enfield ammunition and it proved very useful; from this date until the end of the siege the defenders fired about 60,000 cartridges. Some old timers still swore by the old Brown Bess musket which, in truth, was quicker to load; in close fighting speed could make all the difference between life and death.

Outram was the heart of the defence and was hero-worshipped by his aides. One of them, Lieutenant Edward Chamier wrote of the general:

> He is fearless, bold and chivalrous, calm and collected under fire. He has given me the idea that he enters the field with a firm reliance on Providence, and a kind of dignified contempt for grape, round shot and musketry, from conviction which apparently never forsakes him in the dark hour of danger, that Almighty God directs the discharges of the enemy. There is a sublime bearing about him in the field that is indescribable, and fills me with amazement[31]

Francis Maude added:

> I never saw General Outram's equal for coolness. On one occasion, when the enemy had got our exact range, I saw him walk calmly up to one of our guns, and say to the "number" in charge of the portfire, "Oblige me with a light for my cigar," taking no notice of the roundshot that were whizzing past. And when the gun was fired, while others turned away and held their ears, he didn't move a muscle, but calmly walked away covered with smoke and powder.[32]

By early October spies were reporting to Outram that increasing numbers of taluqdars and their retainers were flooding into Lucknow making any thought of retreat impossible. On 30th September the general told one of his staff officers that "my hopes of a reaction in the city are disappointed. The insurgent sepoys have inspired such a terror among all classes and maintain so strict a watch beyond our pickets that we have not been able to communicate with one single inhabitant of Lucknow since we arrived."[33]

Among the insurgents their chief generals – Raja Nawab Ali Khan, Raja Jai Lal, Khan Ali Khan, Bande Hussain and Agha Habibi – still controlled their troops with confidence. There had been no rush to support the British, as optimists such as Outram had predicted would happen and, in fact, the reverse had been the case as landowners hitherto loyal to the East India Company were now preparing to change sides. One of these, Lal Madhao Singh of Amethi, marched into Lucknow at the head of 2,500 men in late October. In a letter to his British friend, Captain Barrow, Madhao Singh explained his dilemma and the logic behind his decision:

> Every soul likes to preserve his life and honour and just now the war is going on between the King's government and the British government.

Every one can see that the King's government army can probably overcome the British army, but all the people are getting ruined and destroyed while victory still remains undecided, for the King's army destroys all the friends of the British, and the servants of the English government destroy all who remain quiet, considering them enemies, in fact the people are ruined in every way.[34]

Above all, the young Begum, Hazrat Mahal, was proving to be quite brilliant at keeping her disparate and temperamental rebel alliance intact. She called a *durbar* (council) and spoke to her chiefs with more than an echo of Elizabeth I at Tilbury, though in the Begum's case her message was one of reproach:

Lucknow is endangered: what is to be done? The whole army is in Lucknow, but it is without courage. Why does it not attack the Alambagh? Is it waiting for the English to be reinforced and Lucknow to be surrounded? How much longer am I to pay the sepoys for doing nothing? Answer now, and if fight you wont't, I shall negotiate with the English to spare my life.[35]

The generals replied that they would fight or "be hanged one by one, we have this fear before our eyes". An historian commented: "A brave speech, a vainglorious reply."

Outram had feared that the Delhi rebels would reinforce their comrades at Lucknow. Numbers were indeed dribbling into the city and as a sign of the times, on 30th October a whole regiment of 300 sepoys arrived. They were given the task of constructing a bridge of boats across the river near the Chuttar Manzil and within range of the British guns at the Water Gate (the sepoys were later sent to harass the Alambagh's defenders). Indeed, some rebel generals constantly warned the Begum that unless the British were stopped they would reinforce the Alambagh and use it as a point from which to invest the city – which is exactly what happened. On 21st October, a party of some 25-30 women met with Hazrat Mahal and asked to form an Amazon troop. These women had formerly served as a special fighting force under Wajid Ali Shah. They became known as "the black cats". The Begum placed them on her payroll and they trained as guerrilla fighters.

Ferociously, tenaciously, the insurgents kept piling on the pressure. Their determination to oust the British led to some vicious encounters. On 6th October they sprang a mine by a mosque near the quarters of the 5th Fusiliers. The intense fighting that followed was described by Lieutenant Danvers:

The enemy swarmed everywhere, and you heard them yelling out defiance and abuse... We shot several men as they came rushing into the garden with drawn swords, muskets and matchlocks, hallooing out, "Maro, maro! chelo chelo!" ("Kill, kill! Come along!). They gave me very much the idea of men intoxicated with bhang, for they seemed to come on without any definite design, and rushed madly about, apparently unconscious where they were going to... After some time the enemy managed to get into the rooms above us... They fought from room to room, and from one corridor to another, and we made our way over the corpses of the killed. It was wretched fighting. In one room we shot and bayoneted no less than eight.[36]

By 13th October, the 5th Fusiliers had lost 110 killed and wounded at Lucknow and was now commanded by its senior lieutenant (O'Meara).

The rebel batteries were surrounded by huge piles of earth and the gunners worked in trenches 20 feet below. One result of the new British perimeter, bad news for the defenders, was that the rebel guns were now further away; the result was that their shots were hitting their targets rather than flying over them. On the south side of the entrenchments, the rebel fire remained severe. The Indian gunners had adopted new tactics, changing the positions of their guns frequently, so that their shots ranged all over the old Residency compound. On the night of 6th October they threw a roundshot into Mr Hale's bedroom at the Post Office that passed under his head and carried away half the pillow! By this stage "every single building seemed to be so riddled with balls you could scarcely put a pin's head between them,"[37] remarked the Reverend Harris. Maria Germon, on a rare visit to her husband's post, marvelled how he was still alive since the building trembled with every shot and was protected only by a bamboo stockade. As if to make this point Dr Willis had a nasty accident when he fell through a hole in the floor of the hospital and injured his ribs and legs.

Rebel miners remained hard at work and Captain Crommelin, Royal Bengal Engineers, had to supervise the digging of a wide system of countermines – a colossal 200 feet of shaft and 3, 921 feet of galleries. He was supported in all his duties by the famous engineer Colonel Napier, who was described by one volunteer as "a most dangerous fellow to be with [who] poked his nose into queer places and, whilst we stood shivering near him, would stare straight into the face of the enemy, as if powder and shot were nonexistent."[38] General Havelock's men, who feared nothing in the field, found the dangers of counter-mining very daunting. It was during this period that Lieutenant Innes, who had proved such a good engineer above ground, got his first taste of mining:

I may also tell of an amusing incident ... the enemy's miners were quite close to ours, and working very cautiously with trowels instead of picks... I had heard their voices, and at last became aware of a speck of light ... suddenly throwing myself against the film of earth that separated us, I broke into their gallery, and scrambled after the skedaddling enemy, and soon followed by my men with picks, reached the foot of their shaft ... the uproar and shouting was tremendous – soon followed by the pouring down of bucketfuls of water, evidently to drown us out![39]

Fate had the last laugh; next morning Innes was in agony, virulently attacked by scurvy and could not move, except on crutches, for several weeks.

Thomas Kavanagh, a volunteer who had guided some of the sorties, was promoted Assistant Field Engineer with several others. He discovered that "courage and resolution were even more at a premium below than above ground."[40] He had no previous experience at mining and his lanky frame seemed ill-suited to worming down narrow sandy passages. Decked out in a specially made suit of dungarees, Kavanagh attacked pistol in hand at any enemy miners he found. Once he argued through a wall with a group of them and the rebels almost surrendered. When Outram heard the news, he warned that under the Articles of War conferring with the enemy was a hanging offence.

One who found mining not to be his cup of tea was Lieutenant Hall of the Blue Caps who, besides disliking the "rat holes", wasn't happy with "the imminent risk of being buried alive". He recorded how, "when the small lamps by which the men would work could not burn we knew the air was too foul to remain in the mines, but after leaving the mines for a few hours the air was renewed and the work could be carried on." Hall much preferred soldiering above ground as a grenadier improvising with 9-lb shells, which he and his companions threw at the enemy. It seemed odd to lob shells, he admitted, but "after a bit we got used to it."[41]

On 9th October, news reached Outram and Havelock that the whole of Delhi was now in British hands and the old Mogul emperor had been captured. Better still, a column under Brigadier Greathed was marching towards Oudh. The same news reached the insurgents who greeted the tidings in stunned silence. Eight days later they sprang a mine under one of the outposts of the Chuttar Manzil, killing three men, blew up part of the garden wall and advanced into the breach, colours flying. When their leaders were shot dead the insurgents retreated leaving 12 men on the ground. Prisoners were not taken. "I told the guard that any man who wanted to let off his musket (in case of damp) might come and shoot a sepoy," wrote George Blake, "Several men at once came forward and I told them to march the prisoners down to the river bank to avoid having to carry the bodies there. Only one prisoner – a low caste man- fell at my feet and asked for mercy. I told him that the only mercy I'd give him was to have him shot first. All the rest died bravely and their bodies were hove into the river."[42]

On 20th October, a runner brought into the Residency a cossid from Captain Bruce in charge of intelligence at Cawnpore; he had received a letter from Raja Man Singh apologising for going over to the rebels. It turned out to be a classic case of fence-sitting as this leading taluqdar tried to imply he might still defect, though nothing came of it.

The defenders next found their rations further reduced. Private Henry Metcalfe decided that he could no longer feed himself and his faithful terrier but did not have the heart to kill it. So he took it back to Chaplain Harris "and told him that I thought I had fulfilled my part of the compact on account of the dog. I said I thought we had survived the siege and that I had much pleasure in returning the dog to Mrs Harris."[43]

Despite tensions and privations the situation was not all gloom and doom for Outram and the garrison; on 22nd October he got a message from the C-in-C, Sir Colin Campbell, saying that he was about to start for Cawnpore and sending his "best regards". Campbell was pressing into service "every available soldier" to his support. Greathed's column was on the road marching from Agra to Cawnpore. A mighty army would soon be ready to relieve Lucknow, perhaps by as early as 7th November, thought Outram.

"People are becoming more generous with brighter prospects before them,"[44] thought Mrs Soppitt, who was given a delicious glass of sherry, a special treat, by Mrs Ogilvie, the Sanitary Commissioner's wife. Another memsahib, Mrs Hamilton Forbes, cried one day when her husband's orderly appeared and smilingly presented her with two small glittering cubes of rock salt. Eggs were now a rarity and people dreamed of milk and butter. Yet one of the Martinière schoolmasters produced a plum cake on his birthday, saying he had saved it for just such an occasion; it was small but every boy got a slice.

On Wednesday 21st October Maria and Charlie Germon celebrated their wedding anniversary. Dinner that night was stewed meat, a little rice and dhal, a chupattie, some toast and water. Charlie had acquired a pint bottle of champagne for the occasion "and made me with his own hands some sugar cakes", wrote Maria. Her husband begged some milk and Maria had saved a little cocoa and two lumps of sugar. To her delight, Charlie pronounced the feast "capital".

The flurry of activity to save the Lucknow defenders had started in England. News had reached Whitehall on 11th July of General Anson's death from cholera 44 days earlier. Reports were also flooding in of outbreaks and outrages all along the Ganges plain and into Rohilkhand. Prime Minister Lord Palmerston refused to be ruffled even by his tremulous Queen. He told the War Minister that the news was "depressing" but "not really alarming as to our hold on India". "Old Pam" seemed to have got it into his head that 30,000 sepoys had simply deserted, a situation "better than their mutiny would have been". It was decided to send 14,000 troops to India.

It was clear that a new Commander-in-Chief, India, would need to be sent out without delay, a no-nonsense soldier who could restore control. That same afternoon, news reached Sir Colin Campbell at Horse Guards that Lord Panmure (Fox Maule-Ramsay, 11th Earl of Dalhousie) wished to see him in the War Office. Straightaway the 64-year-old soldier set off and when given the Indian appointment said he could leave that night if necessary. Panmure commended his zeal and said the next day would be fine. This was Sunday 12th July and Sir Colin met with the Duke of Cambridge, C-in-C of the British Army, and his superior's cousin, Queen Victoria, who had been a fan of the Scottish soldier since the Crimean War. Then, after dinner, he started for London Bridge station and the journey to India. "Never did a man proceed on a mission of duty with a lighter heart and a feeling of greater humility,"[45] he wrote in a letter.

Small and wiry, a grizzled old veteran of numerous fights and battles, with a shock of curly hair and a weathered face, Sir Colin had been born in Glasgow on 20th October 1792, son of a cabinet-maker who did not have his own business but worked for some fashionable retailers. Enough money was found to give the boy a grammar school education. After the death of his mother and one sister when Colin was just ten, he won the patronage of his wealthy mother's brother, Major John Campbell. He placed the boy in 1806 in a progressive school, the Royal Academy at Gosport. Two years later, aged 15 years, Colin was commissioned as an ensign in the 9th Foot.

Immediately, young Campbell was propelled into the cut and thrust of the Peninsular War, notably at San Sebastian where he led a desperate attack known as "a forlorn hope". He survived the awful Walcheren expedition of 1808 and fought the Americans at New Orleans in 1812. Decades followed of peacetime stagnation and Campbell thought his fighting days were over; 30 years later, now in the 98th Highlanders, he saw action in the 1st Anglo-Chinese War, then in India he led a brigade from the front at the disastrous Battle of Chillianwallah against the Sikhs and was censured for it. Knighted, he commanded expeditions against the Mohmands and the Afridis on the North-West Frontier in 1851, and the Ranizais and Utman Khel in the following year. A decade earlier he had written, "I am old and only fit for retirement," but he agreed to lead the Highland Brigade in the war against Russia. It was the first war followed closely by the new popular press and Campbell became a hero of theirs, especially after he led his Highlanders to immortality at the Alma and Balaclava. Always of a peppery nature, Sir Colin had felt his talents were being passed over; he resigned his command, was promoted and induced to stay on.

Campbell had his critics; his nickname among Indian troops was "Old Kaibadar" ("Old Careful") for his cautious ways. One Highland officer reckoned him to be "A brave man, undoubtedly, but too cautious for India, and too selfish for any place."[46] His namesake, the administrator Sir George Campbell (no relation), wrote that while Sir Colin was "pleasant, good-natured"he also "delayed everything for months, because he would do nothing till he chose."[47] Rankers forgave the old man his ways; they knew that he would not risk their lives under fire unnecessarily, yet was perfectly happy to bed down with them on a battlefield, seemingly oblivious to danger, and share their privations. He was, said one Tommy, "a regular, go-ahead, fire-eating old cock!"

The new commander's first opinions as he sailed East were "very unfavourable". The closer he got to Calcutta the worse seemed the situation. He landed on 13th August to find the inhabitants panic-stricken. Steamers were arriving each week with fugitives from the mofussil all recording a catalogue of horrors. Timid memsahibs slept each night in Fort William and some even carried poison about them in case of emergency. "Others went to bed with revolvers under their pillows, and practised with them daily."[48] "We had a very great surprise when the Mail Steamer telegraphed that Sir Colin Campbell was on board," wrote Lady Canning. "We had no idea that it was possible for the news of poor General Anson's death to have arrived so soon; he was here one month and a day after leaving England."[49]

Thirty-nine years old, attractive and vivacious, Lady Charlotte found herself drawn to the little general. On a drive together "Sir Colin talked all the way, telling no end of military stories. When he grows very indignant, he pulls off his little cap & scatches his head violently, leaving his hair standing bolt upright, exactly like his portrait in *Punch*."[50] She fretted that the new C-in-C could do very little until the 14,000 troops arrived from England.

Sir Colin's superior, Charles John, Viscount Canning, had been Governor-General for just 18 months. A diligent, overly serious man, handsome, yet prematurely balding at 44, he had been at his desk by 6am every day since the insurgency began, even on Sundays. Each morning a mountain of wine-coloured despatch boxes awaited his attention. Outside, green parakeets in the colonnade might squawk, guards – ramrods in scarlet slashed with white crossbelts – might mutter and snap to attention, the bells of the cathedral toil 10am for divine service, but nothing disturbed Canning as he read and digested the terrible news.

The son of a famous Foreign Secretary (who held the Premiership for four months), Charles had been educated at Eton and Christ Church, Oxford, gaining first class honours in classics and a second in mathematics. In 1835, he married the beautiful Charlotte Stuart, eldest daughter of Lord Stuart de Rothesay, an artistically inclined and intelligent girl who became a great favourite of the Queen after serving her as a Lady of the Bedchamber. She called her husband by his family nickname, "Carlo", and the pair honeymooned on a yacht for six months in the Mediterranean. One year later Canning entered Parliament as Conservative M.P. for Warwick. "Proud, reserved and sensitive" was how one of his secretaries remembered him. Another official described "a look about him of Hamlet distraction", while one of his biographers called him "An aloof, reserved man, cold on casual acquaintance, courtly, but not forthcoming".[51]

Canning's appointment as Governor-General came as something of a shock to everyone; the Queen was offended at not being consulted, and Charlotte feared that five years in India would seem "terribly long". Rumours in Whitehall suggested an old friend of Canning's – Lord Granville – had engineered the appointment to get Charles away from a mistress who was endangering the marriage. It is true that the move to India did much to to restore the Canning's relationship.

After the sepoys had risen at Meerut, the Governor-General found himself with little time for leisure. At first he thought that if Delhi, was cleared of the mutineers, "the neck of the Insurrection will be broken," but by 15th June he was writing to Vernon Smith at East India House that Upper Provinces were "not only in rebellion against us, but utterly lawless ... there are precious lives to be avenged, and I will never rest until the score is wiped out." After Sir Henry Lawrence's death he wrote that "of all men in India he is the one whose loss is least reparable at this moment... He would have been invaluable in the pacification of the troubled districts, hereafter both as a Soldier and Civilian."

Canning found Campbell to be an improvement on Sir Patrick Grant, the interim C-in-C. "Grant is admirable in the way of preparation and organisation. The two months I have had with him have been invaluable ... but as a leader in the field Sir Colin inspires me with more confidence."[52] His one complaint was that Campbell's staff did not speak Hindustani. Sir Colin, in contrast, was impressed by Canning who was, in his opinion, "Very clever and hard-working ... simple and gentlemanlike ... I cannot be too thankful of the good fortune that has put me under such a chief."[53]

Like a whirlwind, the old Scot roared into Fort William. He made no bones about the fact that he thought the East India Company was directly responsible for the insurrection and E.I.C. officers were in the firing line. "If anything goes wrong under your command, I will try you, sir, by court-martial," he told one nervous officer, "I will try everybody who is incapable."[54] Staff officers also suffered Sir Colin's hot temper if he thought them lazy or not doing their jobs properly. The only exception was his specially selected chief of staff, Major-General Sir William Mansfield, an efficient desk-soldier who had served in both Sikh Wars and in Campbell's own 1850 expedition against the Kohat Pass Afridis. The pair had continued their friendship in the Crimea and Campbell clearly saw Mansfield as a rising star. Not many people agreed with him; one officer decried Mansfield's "grand seigneur" manner; the war correspondent, William Russell, found him to be "dark, Machiavellian, very knowing ... an air of *hauteur*, some people say superciliousness".[55] One staff officer thought him "cold, calculating", adding bluntly, "no one really liked him."

Yet a cool, shrewd brain like Mansfield's would prove of great value in planning the re-conquest of much of northern India. On the ridge above Delhi the British were holding their own and troops were arriving for the big attack on the city, but Lucknow seemed doomed; one of Canning's Council, Mr J. P. Dorin, even proposed withdrawing all troops north of Allahabad until reinforcements arrived from Britain. "The question was not the will, but the means," wrote one of Campbell's biographers. He dare not strip the Madras and Bombay presidencies of British troops lest they become ungovernable. He had dared to request two battalions from Madras, one from Burma, and all that could be spared from Ceylon and the Punjab. Canning had written to Singapore requesting that 2,500 soldiers en route to China be diverted to India, but he knew that their arrival was weeks away. A similar request for help from the Cape of Good Hope did not reach there until the first week of August, and Campbell knew that it would be two months before any battalions arrived from South Africa. Just before his landing at Calcutta, the 37th Foot from Ceylon and the 5th Northumberland Fusiliers (diverted from China) had begun to trek up country. Sir Colin liked to advance and attack his enemy only when he felt totally ready and success was guaranteed. In the words of the historian, Sir John Fortescue, who castigated the misuse of military resources at Delhi and Lucknow, he believed the "one principle in warfare ... remains eternally true, namely, that to send forth a weak army and reinforce it by driblets is to ensure for it the greatest possible wastage and least possible power."[56]

Men were of little use without materials. "Owing to the state of the country – the people hanging back in all directions – we have the greatest difficulty in acquiring even an insufficient supply of carriage, food and camp followers,"[57] Campbell told the Duke of Cambridge. He, in turn. spoke bluntly to Panmure about the state of the Indian Army:

> It is clear from Sir Colin's letter that it is deficient of everything, not a spare set of harness in store, no shoes, no ammunition, no man able to make use of the beautiful machinery sent out to make Minie bullets. It is almost incredible, yet from the first I feared it and told you so.[58]

One small stroke of luck was that HMS *Shannon* from the China flotilla with 20 32-pounder guns, 30 8in guns and a massive 68-pounder complemented by 300 Royal Marines had docked at Calcutta on 8th August. It was supposed to take Lord Elgin, Ambassador Extraordinary, to China. He placed the entire crew and arsenal at Canning's disposal and ordered another ship, HMS *Pearl,* to do the same. Five days after Campbell's arrival, a Naval Brigade of sailors and marines left by steamer for Allahabad – 408 officers and men under the energetic command of Captain William Peel VC, a son of the famous Prime Minister – henceforth known as the *Shannon's* Brigade. The unit was primarily a heavy artillery force, though it had its own quota of small arms men. It was to take part in numerous actions and see much close quarters action.

From Ranegunge where the main railway line ended, Campbell instituted a relay of bullock carts. These were fragile, had no springs and frequently broke down, "travelling at the brisk pace of two to two and a half miles an hour",[59] but it was much less tiresome than marching. Soon these bullock trains were conveying 200 men a day northwards; the animals and drivers were changed every eight miles and plodded on day and night, but drivers who "persisted in going to sleep, and falling off the seats, were frequently killed by the wagons going over their heads!"[60] Campbell insisted that the large retinues of servants and impedimenta normally kept in India by officers must be kept to a minimum (he slept on campaign in a small bell tent).

The distance from Calcutta to Lucknow was twice as far as Wellington had marched across Spain. Sir Colin remembered the bad experiences of his youth and wanted "a solid supply chain in place before starting on the offensive". Despite those who grumbled about his delays, he stuck to his plan of pushing men and materials forward first so that the actual campaigning could be done in the cold weather season. He did not want small columns chasing rebels hither and thither; these measures led to no real pacification and the columns could be ambushed, besieged or cut off. As biographer Adrian Greenwood wrote: "Unfortunately for Campbell, the Lucknow garrison was setting the timetable." For a time he tried to reinforce Havelock on his march to Lucknow, but as soon as he despatched troops the men were commandeered by local administrators along the way. At one point his military secretary, Major Archibald Alison, complained that he had 2,400 men proceeding to Allahabad and 1,800 of them were "on one pretence or another laid hold of by the civil power".[61] Canning did not help matters by diverting troops to Patna, where he feared an insurrection.

During the summer months of 1857, with revenge in the hearts of all Europeans in India, Campbell had to tread a careful course. "Sir Colin is utterly opposed to such extreme and reckless severity," wrote Russell. "He seems for every vigorous measure, and for fairness and justice," confirmed Lady Canning, "there is nothing bloodthirsty about him."[62] The C-in-C had seen enough blood-letting in his lifetime to make him heartily sick of wasting lives or of seeking violent revenge in anything like a sadistic manner. "I well remember how emphatically I once heard him express his disgust when ... he entered a mango-tope full of rotting corpses, where one of the special commissioners had passed through with a movable column a few days before,"[63] wrote Corporal William Forbes-Mitchell of the 93rd.

On 31st July, Canning was bold enough to clarify his feelings in a private circular sent to senior officers. The burning of villages was now to be a last resort. Only rebels guilty of violence were to be executed. Those who surrendered unarmed or sepoys who had simply deserted were to be imprisoned.The Anglo-Indian newspapers had a field day along with the press back home. *The Times* scorned the "Clemency of Canning", another British newspaper frothed at his "namby-pamby proclamations in favour of leniency and soft dealing". Locals in Calcutta started a petition to have him recalled. To some extent the reaction in India was not surprising – newspapers across the sub-continent hated him ever since he introduced a "Gagging Act" in June aimed at toning down their "incendiary tone". Personally he did not care "two straws for the abuse of the papers" and told the E.I.C. directors that "To this phrenzy we must not yield" because he needed the support of Indians to govern India. A contemporary historian later wrote: "His crying sin was this, that he took little or no pleasure in the extermination of the people whom he had been commissioned by his Sovereign to govern and protect."[64] A later historian, Sir Penderel Moon, commented that "His unpopularity was partly his own fault. His studied air of composure ... gave the impression that he was blind to the gravity of the situation ... soon gossips made it notorious that he was slow in the despatch of public business, poring over files late into the night, and immersing himself in superfluous details."[65]

On 20th September – much to Campbell's joy – his favourite regiment, the 93rd Highlanders, landed at Calcutta. They had formed his "thin red line tipped with steel" at Balaclava and he went to the quayside before his *gogra-wallahs* (petticoated ones) disembarked. Then came more news; Havelock and Outram had got blockaded at Lucknow and "effectively neutralised" the one significant army in the country. Their act took "almost all the available field-artillery, leaving Campbell with none." On the heels of this disaster came the news of Delhi's capture. "Sir Colin came from the cantonments in the highest spirits," wrote Lady Canning, "having given the news to be spread everywhere."[66] Calcutta rejoiced. Officials declared that "India is saved!" British newspapers such as *The Times* blurted out, "It may indeed be said that the Indian mutiny is at an end." The truth was actually mixed; the fall of Delhi meant that many rebels headed towards Oudh and Lucknow, partly since their homes lay there and partly as the two places offered further resistance to the hated British and also a chance for more plunder and pay. Yet the end of the rebellion in the old Mogul capital also meant that British soldiers from there could be sent south towards Cawnpore and Lucknow.

The pressure was piling on Campbell to make a move; Panmure in Whitehall impatiently urged that the general's divisions should "sweep India from one end to the other". Still Sir Colin refused to budge. "What is consistently overlooked in the assessments of Campbell's Indian Mutiny performance – which was adequate to the task but hardly spectacular – is that he had just come from the Crimean War," writes historian, Bruce Watson, "in which incompetence, indifference and inept leadership ruled the day."[67] He chose to remain in Calcutta but permitted a relief column from Delhi to set forth.

The 2,790 Delhi column marched off before dawn on 24th September. It consisted of two troops of horse artillery with four guns each and a further battery of six commanded by George Bourchier, a mutton-chop whiskered veteran of the Bengal Artillery who had first seen action 14 years earlier at Punniar in the Gwalior campaign. There were also

200 sappers, 300 officers and men of HM 9th Lancers, 450 more drawn from HM 8th and 75th regiments, both decimated at Delhi, (Lieutenant Barter, adjutant of the 75th, thought his regiment should not have been selected at all, since it only had 250 men left in total out of 928), along with detachments of the 1st, 4th and 5th Punjab Cavalry and Hodson's Horse – a further 400 sabres – together with the 1,200 officers and men of the 1st and 4th Punjab Native Infantry. In command of the column was Colonel Edward Greathed, 8th Foot, an officer some thought "a fool" or a "funk-stick". Travelling with them in a civil capacity was George Campbell, an acerbic but intelligent commissioner who had served in India for 15 years. He concluded that Greathed was a moderate man, "but he had not a very good control over his officers."

Barter of the 75th never forgot the morning they left Delhi, where the fighting had been so intense that people called it "the city of the dead":

> The march through the city was simply awful; our advanced guard, consisting of Cavalry and Artillery, had burst and smashed the dead bodies, which lay swelled to an enormous size, in the Chandni Choke, and the stench was fearful. Men and officers were sick all round, and I thought we were never to get through the city; anticipating something of this kind I had stowed away in my holster pipes a bottle of eau-de-Cologne, which I had looted out of a shop in the city, and this I have to thank for not having suffered as much as the rest; all the same it was a ride I don't care ever to take again, and the horse felt it as much as I did for he snorted and shook as he slid rather than walked over the abominations with which the street was covered.[68]

Captain Fred Roberts, the force's DAQMG, agreed and wrote afterwards:

> Here a dog gnawed at an uncovered limb; there a vulture disturbed by our approach from its loathsome meal, but too completely gorged to fly, fluttered away to a safer distance. In many instances the positions of the bodies were appalingly lifelike. Some lay with their arms uplifted as if beckoning, and, indeed, the whole scene was wierd and terrible beyond description... It is impossible to describe the joy of breathing the pure air of the open country after such a horrible experience.[69]

Early on the 28th Roberts was riding ahead of the column and in the company of Henry Norman (shortly to become the Indian Army's D.A.G.), and Alfred Lyall, an old schoolfriend who was due to take up a post as assistant magistrate at Bulandshahr, a town a couple of miles up the road. At a crossroads where one track led to the town and another to a fort at Malagarh, the trio halted, put out pickets and waited for the dawn. The dozing officers were awakened suddenly by shots being fired by their pickets and some rebels. It soon became apparent that insurgents from Jhansi and Nowgong, supported by locals, occupied Bulandshahr.

As the British advanced around 7am the rebel cavalry fell back and as the column came in range of enemy cannon the horse artillery under Captain Remington galloped forwards. The column collected itself, a small attack on the baggage train was beaten off, and the infantry formed up while Bourchier's guns took up a position on the left side of the road and blazed away. Sitting on his horse, Greathed, according to Barter, "smoothed his moustache and seemed inclined to sit there for ever". The artillery on both sides contentedly played "long bowls" and the cavalry and infantry grew impatient. It was all too much for an Irish private who, like many of his comrades, was growing weary. "Arrah, are we going to sit here all day? Let's go and take the bloody battery," he shouted. "The effect was magical," wrote Barter, "with a cheer the men and officers jumped to their feet and over the bank they tore."[70]

Small and slim, riding a hot-tempered Waziri horse that had belonged to his great friend, Brigadier John Nicolson (who had died at Delhi), young Roberts seemed to be everywhere. He raced up to the 75th and pointed at some guns they had captured. "If you fellows won't mark the guns, I will for the Artillery!" This prompted Captain Barter to scratch "75" on them. In the middle of the fighting a rebel sepoy took deliberate aim at Roberts who tried to ride hard at the man, "but the crowd between him and me prevented my reaching him. He fired; my frightened animal reared and received in his head the bullet intended for me."[71] The wound was "right between the eyes – luckily his head was in the way or I should have caught it."[72]

A second column consisting of the greater portion of the cavalry, along with two horse artillery guns under Lieutenant Cracklow, galloped into the town and met with sharp resistance in a tangled maze of narrow streets.[73] Four officers of the 9th Lancers were wounded along with six troopers and 20 horses killed and wounded. The action was over by 11am. Some 300 insurgents had been killed and a large amount of baggage and ammunition captured. Total British losses were 6 men killed and 41 officers and men wounded.

Several Victoria Crosses were won at Bulandshahr; Captain the Honourable Augustus Anson, "an indifferent horseman and a bad swordsman", nevertheless was courageous enough to lead a charge and when insurgents tried to block his men in a narrow street with some carts he grabbed a lance and knocked over the drivers.[74] Trooper James Roberts was with Anson and went to the rescue of Farrier Stillman who had been shot out of the saddle.[75] In another act of rescue both the victim, Lieutenant Robert Blair, whose arm was nearly hacked off at the shoulder, and his rescuer, Private Patrick Donohoe, won the VC for fighting off some 60 of the enemy.[76] Lance-Corporal Robert Kells had been a boy-soldier and had seen his first battle in the 2nd Sikh War. He was orderly officer to Captain Drysdale. He went to his assistance when the officer's horse fell, trapping him and fracturing his collar bone.[77] Two horse artillery gunners, Richard Fitzgerald and Bernard Diamond, both Irishmen, also won the coveted medal for the manner in which they stuck to their guns.[78]

After a couple of days rest the column marched on, surprising and killing two Rajput chiefs at Akhrabad, 14 miles from Aligarh on the road to Cawnpore. While some writers (Bourcher and Roberts) record that the local villagers were happy to see the British back after they had been at the mercy of local brigands for weeks, it appears that the cavalry harboured grudges. Major Henry Ouvry wrote of taking a "severe revenge" against locals who, in the words of one officer, "befriended the enemy and kept them in supplies". Sir George Campbell, writing 36 years later, recalled the march as "quite a pleasant one … there were no cold-blooded executions of any kind … most villages seemed quite friendly."[79] Perhaps so, but we must assume he did not follow the cavalry troopers to outlying places off the main road. Two days later, after reaching Aligarh, one of the more religious officers, Major Octavius Anson of the 9th Lancers, wrote:

Fathers are shot with all their womenkind clinging to them, and begging for their lives … there was a sowar with three women on the top of him, trying to conceal him. One woman got shot in the arm by accident; the sowar got up and ran away, twelve pistols being fired at him without effect (this was the time when my horse was wounded); he was finally, but with much difficulty, lanced. Unarmed cowherds were mercilessly pistolled together with about twenty armed men. What the poor women and childen in this place are to do without their men, who are being killed in every house, I cannot say.[80]

Greathed now faced a dilemma – letters had come from Agra "beseeching, commanding him to hasten at the utmost speed to succour that place".[81] The colonel read the letters with "a mixture of amusement and contempt", well aware that the Europeans in that city were seemingly safe behind the walls of its mighty fortress beside the Yamuna river, protected within by a garrison, but it was also known that large bands of rebels from Gwalior and Delhi were roaming the district. To check that

Agra was secure Greathed turned aside from the Cawnpore road and headed by forced marches – 44 miles in 28 hours – to arrive beneath the walls of the fort at sunrise on 10th October.

The weary soldiers were disgusted; the 6,000 or so people crammed into the famous fort seemed to be in no danger. "Ladies were riding and driving about in all directions," wrote Bourchier, "yeomanry cavalry were careering in full equestrian pride, while from every hole and corner loomed the muzzle of an iron monster ready to annihilate any amount of Pandies."[82] Roberts remembered: "We presented, I am afraid, but a sorry appearance, as compared to the neatly-dressed ladies and the spic-and-span troops who greeted us, for one of the fair sex was overheard to remark, 'Was ever such a dirty-looking lot seen?'[83] Our clothes were, indeed, worn and soiled, and our faces so bronzed that the White soldiers were hardly to be distinguished from their Native comrades." One lady was heard to comment as HM 8th Foot tramped by, "Those dreadful looking men must be Afghans!" Her companion wrote: "I did not discover they were Englishmen until I saw a short clay pipe in the mouth of nearly the last man. My heart bled to to see these jaded miserable objects, and to think of all they must have suffered since May last, to reduce such fine Englishmen to such worn, sun-dried skeletons."[84]

The Dehli column's newly appointed intelligence officer, 25-year-old Fred Roberts, son of a Bengal Army general, was notably energetic and intelligent, but even the sharpest man can make mistakes. He marked out a camping ground and accepted news from locals "that the Pandies had fled, hearing of our approach and re-crossed a stream about 10 miles off."[85] He decided to leave reconnoitring until the evening, which turned out to be a bad error. Greathed began bivouacking his soldiers, neglected to post pickets and went off with Norman, Roberts and several senior officers to enjoy breakfast inside the fort. On the parade ground below its walls, "Crowds of natives from the town were flocking round the camp, and among them were four jugglers who walked up, tossing their balls into the air and catching them towards the tents," wrote Thomas Rice Holmes. "Suddenly flinging away their balls, they drew swords and rushed in, striking out right and left. Simultaneously, two troops of cavalry emerged from the crops and a number of round-shot crashed into the camp."[86] Contrary to Roberts' intelligence assessment, the insurgents had returned, "bag and baggage, with all their material and many guns", taking clever advantage of a field of millet 10 to 12 feet high so that, in the words of George Campbell, they could reach the parade ground "quite unobserved". All was confusion as the heavy baggage of the column on its way into camp met the stampede. "Seldom was there seen such confusion," wrote George Forrest, "instantly elephants, camels, led horses, doolie-bearers carrying the sick and wounded, bullocks yoked to heavily laden carts, were swept into this immense torrent."[87]

The British were caught completely unawares – but reacted quickly. Inside the fort, Henry Norman heard the firing and screams and rushed off to help, as he recorded in his journal:

> I started for camp, but before I could get out of the gate heard guns and met people flying in, the whole of the Agra volunteer horse scuttling like mad, and declaring our camp was taken and everyone cut up… On coming to the parade ground I certainly saw a queer scene. Not a dozen tents had been pitched, and little baggage was up; men and horses were very tired, when suddenly from cultivation in front of them a sharp fire of heavy and field artillery was opened with a dropping fire of musketry, and bodies of cavalry advanced on both flanks. Our men rushed to their arms. Blunt advanced with his troop, but a gun was disabled, the horses being killed by round shot, and six out of seven Europeans being cut down. Their sowars began to carry it off when a squadron of the 9th (not sixty men) led by French and Jones charged the enemy's horse full five times their own numbers. They rode over the enemy, but French was killed and Jones desperately wounded. On reaching the parade ground I … killed three men, two with Sir Colin's sword, and one I shot. For about three miles the rebels made successive stands at villages, but on each occasion we opened fire with artillery, then pushed forward and took the guns they had been firing. At three miles we came on a camp where they made a short stand. From this it became a simple pursuit – our blood was fairly up, and the chase was delightful – till we reached the Kari river across which we drove them. At last we returned to camp, having marched sixty-six miles, and fought an action in forty hours.[88]

Every British officer tried to be in on the chase, even the elderly local commander, Colonel Cotton, who had the splendid nickname, "Gun Cotton". "Peafowl, partridges and Pandies all rose together," commented one officer, "the latter gave the best sport."[89] The civilian commissioner, George Campbell, rode with the 9th Lancers and even captured some guns. Another rider, Lieutenant Arthur Lang, Royal Bengal Engineers, wrote in his journal:

> Along the road (choked with camels, gharis, bundles etc.) and through the fields on either hand, were the flying enemy in hundreds – sepoys of the 22nd, 23rd and 47th, 1st Cavalry, red-coated Irregulars, and men armed with matchlocks and tulwar; they were so panic-struck that they

let a few officers and (I suppose) Agra volunteers ride through them like sheep. It was absurd; excited as we were, we rode through them, slashing and thrusting, and leaving them behind. I knocked over lots, and killed 12 outright.

During the melee several officers had close encounters: Roberts was almost killed in a single combat when his revolver misfired; Lang rode up against two sowars:

> I gathered my horse for a rush and, as it were, threw myself on the nearest. Before he thought I could be on him, I cut him down, and instantly turning on another saw him about ten paces off, firm as a rock, his carbine barrel steady and straight on me. I gave myself up for dead, but ducking my head instinctively, with my spurs in, I spun my horse round and round like a teetotum, the fiend still steady waiting for a sure shot. My horse stumbled and fell forward, and I too. The sowar fired simultaneously, missed me and was off again.[90]

A Victoria Cross was awarded to Private John Freeman,[91] a Kentish lad, for saving the life of wounded Lieutenant Alfred Jones. Another went to one of the Indian Army's bravest cavalry officers, Captain Dighton Probyn, the dashing 24 year old commander of the 2nd Punjab Cavalry: he charged ahead of his men into a party of rebels, cutting down two before his troopers reached him; he was then bayoneted in the chest but killed his opponent before he charged again, this time at a rebel standard bearer and a group of sowars and sepoys. It was in this encounter that Probyn's orderly had his arm sliced off while defending him (he died two days later), but the 2nd Cavalry captured the standard.[92]

During the pursuit to the river, Lieutenant George Younghusband commanding the 5th Punjab Cavalry was riding hard when he and his mount fell down a well. To make matters worse, two more horses and their riders fell in on top of them! Luckily for Younghusband, he had fallen in a sitting position and his horse fell standing and across him so that it took the full weight of the other two horses and their riders, who were all killed. Younghusband[93] got out of the well with just bruises.

The British lost 11 killed and 56 wounded in the battle at Agra. After a few days rest the column set off again for Cawnpore. They marched in on 26th October with bands playing. Along the way, at Ferozebad on 16th October, Colonel Hope Grant of the 9th Lancers joined the column and took over its command. In the first few days at Cawnpore, every officer and man visited the scenes of the massacres and vowed vengeance.

"I was no longer a Christian and all I wanted was revenge" was a typical remark. "In the Crimea I never wished to kill a Russian," wrote Lt-Colonel John Ewart of the 93rd, "but now my one idea was to kill every rebel I would come across."[94] Arthur Lang also visited the entrenchment where General Wheeler and the garrison had tried to hold out. "Never did I see buildings so thoroughly riddled," he wrote, "not a foot unscarred by round shot; you would wonder how any hardy soldiers could have held them for two days, much less that delicate women and children could have lived through 22 days of siege." The devil is in the detail:

> The floors are still covered with mementoes of the defenders; a sock, a child's shoe, letters, leaves of books, pieces of music, papers, etc. One officer picked up Wheeler's last pay certificate; another a few leaves of a book bearing the name of a Lady whom he well knew; another letters of a great friend of his, and so on; it was very sad work looking at all this, and more than sad. I felt that I could vow my life to revenge, to take blood from that race every day, to tear all pity from one's heart. I would not go there again for anything.[95]

While Grant's troops rested at Cawnpore events were tending to drag in Lucknow. Writing a letter on 28th October, Lieutenant David Hay spelled out the situation:

> I have been seedy for the last week – in fact done up *completely,* like all the others who have been shut up since 1st July... General Outram was very happy to give me the Adjutancy of the 12th Irregular Cavalry... We are as closely besieged as ever and they fire their guns and shell all day long, but the palaces where the men are located are difficult to get at, and they don't do much harm. Our provisions are very scanty; they are to be spun out to 1st December. The Cavalry horses get no grain, and grass is not to be had, so they are likely to be all dead before we get out. It is a common thing to see them eating old rope or any little thing of that sort.[96]

In late October, word reached Outram that the well-trained army of the Maharaja Sindhia of Gwalior, known as "the Gwalior Contingent", had mutinied, had accepted the offer of Tantia Tope to lead them and was marching west to join hands with the Nana Sahib and a large band of mutineers from Dinapore. The general wrote to the C-in-C urging him to treat the Gwalior Contingent as his first threat and worry about Lucknow only as a "secondary consideration" when this threat to his Cawnpore base had been nullified.

Above left: 1. Opinionated and with a whirlwind of ideas for India, James Broun-Ramsay, Marquess of Dalhousie and Governor-General 1848-55.

Above right: 2. The man with the uprising on his shoulders: Charles John Viscount Canning, Governor-General of India 1856-62.

Above left: 3. Loved by all who knew him, kindly and wise Sir Henry Lawrence, Chief Commissioner of Oudh, killed by a cannon ball on 4th July 1857.

Above right: 4. Considered a fool and martinet by his critics, yet unquestionably brave, Lt-Colonel John Inglis led the defence of the Residency after Lawrence's death.

Above left: 5. Not a man to be rushed but a remarkably effective general – Colin Campbell, Lord Clyde.

Above right: 6. Major-General Charles Windham's reckless behaviour at Cawnpore almost cost the British the war. Some of his unexpurgated letters are included in the text.

Left: 7. A sketch of the best of the Indian generals, Tatya Tope, who was complicit in the Cawnpore Massacre and almost defeated Windham at Cawnpore.

8. Bahadur Shah, the sick old Mogul emperor who became a figurehead for the insurgents.

Above: 9. The 32nd Foot messhouse photographed by Felice Beato.

Below: 10. The entrance to the Residency after the final battle in March 1858, an area of total ruins.

Above: 11. An interesting photo that shows the rebel earthworks in front of the Begum Kothi Palace. By the time of the final British assault, much of the city had been turned into a defensive network that proved difficult to assault.

Below: 12. Inside the ruins of one of the palaces.

Above: 13. A river view at Lucknow, the famous fish pleasure boat of the last Nawab in the foreground.

Below: 14. The Residency immediately after the capture of the city.

Above: 15. Interesting view of the old Machi Bhowan fortress (see chapters one and two) that shows the earthworks thrown up by the rebels to make its capture difficult for the British.

Below: 16. The famous Beato photograph of the Sikanderbagh, scene of some of the heaviest fighting during Sir Colin Campbell's attempt to relieve the garrison in 1857. Note the unblocked doorway. It appears that Beato had skeletons pulled out of the ruins and strewn across the foreground to make a more dramatic picture.

Above left: 17. Sir James Outram, Lawrence's predecessor as Chief Commissioner; he had many sympathies with the local people, yet managed a spirited defence of the Alambagh after Campbell got away with the Residency garrison.

Above right: 18. From obscurity to national hero in one summer; Major-General Sir Henry Havelock led a small army to relieve Lucknow but then became trapped inside with his troops.

Left: 19. Volunteer cavalry charging insurgents at Chinhat (see Prologue).

20. The Residency a few weeks into the siege. The image does not show the Union Jack that always flew from the turret.

21. Dr Joseph Fayrer, one of several doctors besieged in Lucknow.

22. Fayrer's house before the siege left it a heap on ruins.

23. Highlanders, part of Havelock's tiny army of "lambs", fighting their way towards Lucknow.

Above left: 24. Rare 1840s photograph by John MacCosh of ruthless, hot-headed and mentally unstable Brigadier-General James Neill.

Above right: 25. Expert gunner for both Havelock and Clyde, Captain Francis Maude V.C. had to battle twice into the besieged city.

Above left: 26. Kavanagh V.C. in the costume he used to escape out of Cawnpore and reach Campbell's army.

Above right: 27. Lieutenant Robert Danvers, 70th B.N.I., whose letters give us one of the best insights into Havelock's famous march. Danvers was killed in China in 1858.

28. Stiff fighting by Havelock's army on the road to Lucknow.

Above: 29. The Alambagh on the outskirts of Lucknow where Outram made camp and kept a British presence between Campbell's relief of the Residency and his return to re-capture the city in March 1858.

Left: 30. The courtyard in which Neill was shot and killed as Havelock and Outram's men advanced on the Residency. The marksman apparently leaned out of the window seen just to the left of the gateway.

Below left: 31. The road leading up towards the Residency by which Havelock's men had to endure a bombardment from armed insurgents and local people.

Above left: 32. The irrepressible Rutz Rees, a besieged civilian, who was so happy to see Campbell's soldiers that he danced a jig on the spot.

Above right: 33. Handsome little Lieutenant Fred Roberts V.C. soon to be a rising star in in the Indian Army and a later Field-Marshal.

Right: 34. Reclining nonchalantly in a chair while an aide stands by, Robert Napier, Campbell's brilliant chief engineer. He was also responsible for reconstructing Lucknow after the British capture.

35. Loyal sepoys.

Above left: 36. A rare photo of Misr Kanauji Lal, the Indian who bravely accompanied T. H. Kavanagh in his exciting escape through rebel lines to the tent of General Campbell.

Above right: 37. A photo in old age of Lt-General John Ewart, 93rd Highlanders. His arm was blown off by a cannon ball on 1st December 1857.

38. The looting of the Kaisarbagh Palace during the final British assault on Lucknow in March 1858.

39. The officer on horseback is actually a naval man, Captain Oliver Jones R.N. and the fighting took place during Campbell's winter campaign in Oudh before the final assault on Lucknow.

40. Captain William Peel V.C., son of the famous Victorian Prime Minister, led his Naval Brigade bravely until mortally wounded in the last assault.

Above: 41. Some aspects of the Uprising became part of national myth and legend for both sides. "Jessie's Dream", the famous painting of a Scots lass who heard the sound of the Highlanders' pipes the day before Lucknow was relieved. The story turned up in several newspapers at the time and was endlessly reproduced in prose, drama, verse and sheet music.

Left: 42. It was suggested that a pack of monkeys should be let loose in the Residency grounds to propitiate the gods. Lawrence led his visitor over to a an 18-pounder gun. "See here," he said, "Here is one of my monkeys; that is his food," indicating a pile of cannon balls "There! Go and tell your friends of my monkeys!" The exchange was deemed worthy of illustration by the children's magazine *Look and Learn.*

Most of the garrison were suffering from ennui; "I am getting tired of this kind of work," said one officer who spent his time dreaming of eating Devonshire cream! Havelock was starting to look pale and thinner than normal on the scanty diet, though Mrs Bartrum's boy was growing stronger and Katherine thought how happy he would have made his father. Danger and death still stalked the unwary; on 20th October an 18-pounder cannon ball came into the Harris's room again (it was not the first) and smashed Mrs Harris's dressing table to smithereens. On 4th November, Ensign Charles Dashwood, 48th B.N.I., was sketching in a part of the grounds where he had been warned of the dangers when a roundshot carried away both his lower legs and feet. A few weeks earlier he had been wounded while cleaning his gun but the injury was not fatal and he had returned to his duties. He was, all agreed, "such a nice boy, a great favourite with everyone and such a tall, handsome fellow".[97]

The Irregular Cavalry, so vital to Havelock on its march towards Lucknow, were now of no real use and were assigned to Innes's Post. Lieutenant Swanston recalled: "We had several men shot there ... one day while we were sitting at breakfast, bang came a 24-pound shot right through the roof, and very nearly fell on one of the men, who was lying down, covering us with dust at the same time. We jumped up, and found out that it was one of our own 24-pounders, but through the bad practice of the officer firing it had hit us by mistake; so we sent him up the ball with our compliments, and a request to fire a little higher next time."[98] During a lull one day, the officers at the Brigade Mess climbed onto their roof and collected the enemy's cannon balls lying there – a staggering 435 of them.

In the royal camp the great excitement during late October was the arrival of a party of British captives: these sad folk were Captain Patrick Orr and his wife and daughter; Sir Mountstuart Jackson and sister, Madeleine; a three year old orphan, Sophie Christian, whose father had been in the ICS; Lieutenant G. Burnes and Sergeant-Major A. Morton. Orr had been Deputy Commissioner at Mohamdie in Oudh. Jackson also was a newly appointed ICS official from Sitapur. The men were heavily fettered and the group had been made to march to Lucknow under a fierce sun with an escort of 300 gloating sepoys for six long days. The only food they had eaten was what was thrown at them and they got precious little water. In each village they had been treated with contempt and loaded down with indignities and humiliation. At Lucknow they were put in a small room of an outhouse attached to the stables of the Kaisarbagh Palace. All the captives were exhausted and Jackson, "nothing but skin and bone", was sick with fever. The Begum and her lover clearly intended that these feringhees should suffer but, thankfully for them, an educated man called Meer Wajid, described by P. J. O. Taylor as "in charge of the financial arrangements of the Durbar", took pity on them; he arranged a larger cell and did them many small kindnesses. The Begum grew suspicious and at one point Meer Wajid had to hide from her for a few days.

The Orr party were not the only British captives in Lucknow; Amelia – "Amy" – Horne was a girl in her mid teens, daughter of the late Captain Frederick Horne R.N. and his Eurasian wife who somehow survived the appalling conditions of the siege at Cawnpore and was saved during the Satichura Ghat massacre at the riverside by an Indian sowar, Mohammed Ismail Khan. He "protected" her and duly raped her. After various travails, Amy and Mohammed arrived in Lucknow. Inflamed by drink and opium, many of the rebels in the houses where they stayed said the infidel girl should die. Finally, to save Amy's life, Mohammed took her to see the populist leader, the Maulvi Ahmaddulah Shah. A bright girl, Amy claimed to be a Moslem and carried off this pretence so well that it convinced the Maulvi. She was allowed to become one of his followers and in return was given a room to herself and two meals a day.

The Maulvi's full name was Sayyid Ahmad Ali Khan and he belonged to a rich family from Madras. He is described as a "tall, lean, muscular man, with thin jaws, long thin lips, high aquiline nose, deep-set, large dark eyes, beetle brows, long beard and coarse black hair falling in masses to his shoulders".[99] As a deeply religious "ghazi warrior" he tried and to some degree was successful in turning the revolt at Lucknow into a religious crusade. He claimed to have visited Europe and even had an audience with Queen Victoria (some Indian historians, such as Smita Pandey, accept this as a fact, while others such as Ansari and Qureshi, think it was a figment of his imagination). Certainly, the Maulvi spoke some English and told Amy how all her countrymen were bad (the only good one had been Sir Henry Lawrence), and he would take his jihad to Britain and make the Queen one of his bond-slaves. Amy listened poilitely but in truth hated all her captors, the long incarceration, her charade and degradation. Five times a day she knelt and prayed loudly (so all might hear), "Allahu akbar! Allahu akbar! Allahu akbar!" Within her heart she repeated a different prayer – "O, God, please God, have mercy and let me die!"[100]

Sir Colin finally left Calcutta with his headquarters staff on 27th October. "Dispensing with his dress uniform, Campbell changed into simple white trousers, a blue frock-coat, pith helmet and puggaree with his old Peninsular War cavalry sabre by his side."[101] Just below Benares, he narrowly avoided capture or death from a body of mutineers about 500 yards away. These were detachments of the 32nd B.N.I. who had mutinied earlier that month. Luckily, "they kept on their own course without molesting us," wrote one of the C-in-C's staff. At Allahabad Sir Colin read a letter from Outram saying he could hold out until the end of November on reduced rations. As Campbell pressed on towards Cawnpore he got the news that a sizable body of British troops, aided by 103 men of Peel's Naval Brigade, had defeated a rebel army of 4000 – half of them ex-sepoys wearing their uniforms – at Khujwa, some 20 miles to his left. The fight had been a touch and go affair and ended at sundown; it left 95 British killed and wounded and Sir Colin was scathing about the dispositions, but they had triumphed, securing two enemy guns.

On the morning of 3rd November, Sir Colin arrived at Cawnpore. Two days earlier all the troops gathered there had crossed into Oudh under Hope Grant's command. "A splendid force" is how Captain Barter described them; besides the Delhi column it now included the 93rd Highlanders and fresh troops from Britain armed with the Enfield.

Destined to be one of the most important officers in the re-conquest of Oudh, Grant was 49 years old, brother of one of the country's most famous portrait painters. He was a remarkable cavalryman who had seen action in three campaigns already and made friends with Campbell when they served in China. Since 1826, when he joined as a cornet, Grant had served with the 9th Lancers. Besides his horsemanship and courage, he was famous for his integrity and on one famous occasion had tried to arrest his colonel for drunkenness on the battlefield. A staff officer, Garnet Wolseley, described Grant as "a tall man of muscle and bone and no unnecessary flesh about him... His faith in an all-seeing God, who watched over his soldiers, was as the very life within him."[102] A stickler for spit and polish, Grant was also as tough as he was brave; on one occasion he had 25 mutineers executed, followed by 50 of his own men flogged for looting. For relaxation he played the violincello – he called it "my big fiddle" – like an angel.

Camp was made at Bunthera, six miles before the Alambagh. Here the army awaited the arrival of the C-in-C. While marking out the camp Captain Frederick Roberts was attacked by infantry and cavalry from a neighbouring village. He had a hair's breadth escape from death when his horse rolled over in a waterlogged gully. "In the fall my hand was slightly cut by my sword," he later wrote, "the blood flowed freely, and made the reins so slippery when I tried to remount that it was with considerable difficulty I got into the saddle." Hope Grant had heard the commotion and when Roberts and his fellow subaltern, Augustus Mayne, galloped into camp he kept shaking their hands and repeating "Well my boys. Well my boys, very glad to have you back! Never thought to see you again!"[103] In response, Grant ordered the troops to attack the village and two others with fire and sword. Major Ouvry with a party of cavalry was nearly surrounded and had to send back for reinforcements, but he eventually extricated himself.

Meanwhile at Cawnpore the magistrate, John Walter Sherer, paid a courtesy call on Sir Colin and found him, at first, to be "elaborately polite", before he launched into sarcasm; he was angry with George Campbell over some expression he had used about one of the regiments and furious over the Battle of Khujwa; he needed all the men he could get and did not approve of officers like Colonel Powell of the 53rd Foot fighting unnecessary battles, against general orders – and getting killed into the bargain.

Sir Colin's immediate concern was for the defence of Cawnpore. Lucknow was, he knew, 53 miles away, but even closer was Calpee at 40 miles, and there the 5,000-strong Gwalior Contingent was assembling with its 16 heavy guns, 24 field guns and a huge store of ammunition. Once the Nana Sahib joined forces with them, their numbers would swell to more than 10,000 men. After thinking over the situation, Campbell decided, rightly or wrongly, to advance on Lucknow; critics might later damn him for failing to secure his base at Cawnpore and line of operations first, yet even the Iron Duke had declared it was "the duty of a wise man to chose the lesser of any two difficulties which beset him",[104] and the C-in-C thought Lucknow the lesser peril. On 4th November Major-General Charles Windham, a Queen's officer of impeccable Crimean War credentials, was told to hold Cawnpore with just 500 soldiers. All other reinforcements passing through were to be hurried up the line except for 500 men of the Madras Native Infantry and six guns of the Madras Artillery expected to arrive shortly. Campbell was hoping to be back at Cawnpore before the Gwalior rebels arrived. It was a huge risk, but he had confidence in Windham who was told to strengthen his admittedly weak defences, keep within them, be wary of any sign of attack and not take any provocative action unless under actual bombardment. Sir Colin's measures ignored the advice of Outram, but Campbell was not a great fan of India's "bayard": he did not like army officers who had spent much of their career in the political service of the E.I.C. and during Outram's spat with Sir Charles Napier in the 1840s he had sided with the latter man. Above all, as he told his sister in a letter, "Our friends in Lucknow have food for for only five or six days. The effort must be made to save them at any cost."[105]

At Bunthera the soldiers were itching to get at the enemy; soon the men were calling Campbell "Old Crawling Camel". On the 5th a column of 1,500 men with six guns conveyed ammunition and provisions to the Alumbagh, fighting their own peculiar battle along the way; they were attacked by an angry swarm of bees and several officers and men were stung severely, especially the Highlanders who, in their kilts, felt uniquely exposed. The incident was blamed on a foolish cavalry officer, Lieutenant Evans, who had poked a nest with his lance.

Escorted by a couple of horse guns and two squadrons of cavalry, Sir Colin left Cawnpore at 3am on 9th November. He arrived at Bunthera at 4pm the same day looking "worn and anxious". About 5am the next morning, he stepped outside his tent to be greeted by a curious sight – an Indian, no, a white man on a Burmese pony dressed partly in Indian clothes, his face now white where lamp-black had been washed away. "I am Sir Colin Campbell, and who are you?" he asked the stranger. Whipping off his turban, the man dismounted and handed him a note of introduction from Sir James Outram. Campbell read it and said, dumbfounded, "Is it true?" The stranger was none other than the wild Irishman, Thomas Kavanagh, survivor of the Lucknow siege. He had come through the rebel lines in disguise the previous night. He was ready to guide Campbell's army into Lucknow; but first he had a story of high adventure to tell.

7

One Corner of Hell
Lucknow, 10th–17th November, 1857

There was nothing in Thomas Kavanagh's demeanour to suggest that he was any more the hero than the hundreds of other men who had endured the terrible siege. He was, in fact, a "ludicrously vain" Irishman of 36 years, disgruntled with his life as an impoverished junior clerk who had "narrowly escaped dismissal on landing himself in debt to various money lenders".[1] He was tall and bushy-bearded with a persuasive Hibernian tongue in his head, yet during the early part of the siege Kavanagh had been delirious with fever and not present at Chinhat. He had a bevy of small children and a long-suffering wife of 13 years.

He came to the fore as an expert tunneler and men started to talk of this human mole who delighted in provoking the enemy below ground. On 7th November James May, an engineer draughtsman, had shown Kavanagh plans he was producing to aid the relieving force. At once Thomas saw a flaw in the plan: it offered only one route into the city and even that would present innumerable obstacles to a general ignorant of the terrain. Ifs started to float in Kavanagh's brain – what if the resistance by the insurgents was stiffer than that faced by Havelock in September? What if, in fact, the rebels suddenly retreated and offered an easier route? What was needed, he concluded, was someone who knew the city well and could guide the army, someone in fact like himself.

Two days later, his mind fully made up, Thomas had the lucky fortune to run into "bantam-sized" Kanauji Lal, a former baliff at the Oudh royal court who, during the previous night, had bravely crossed the rebel lines and brought to Outram the latest news of Campbell's army. Like a flash, Kavanagh asked if he could accompany the messenger if, as he supposed, a fresh missive had to be taken to Sir Colin? Though the lanky Irishman offered to don a disguise, Kanauji thought he was crazy and it took two hours before Kavanagh, using all the blarney he could muster, got the spy to agree based on "an unusually large reward". At 2pm he went to see first Napier and then Outram with his idea. Both men were astonished. After listening in silence Sir James begged Kavanagh to forget the whole thing; he saw before him a brawny man of 5 feet 11 inches with freckled hands, red gold hair, beard and moustaches and "blue blazing eyes". As historian Richard Collier wrote: "Of the 2,396 Europeans within the Residency, few less resembled an Indian peasant."[2] Undeterred and using every ounce of his Gaelic charm, Kavanagh spoke back and eventually Outram agreed that he would allow the scheme if a perfect disguise was devised.

Seeking out camp followers and servants, but not revealing his true intentions, Kavanagh flitted around the Residency that afternoon and acquired a short jacket of orange silk, a two-handled dagger and tight silk native trousers; to these he added a cream-coloured turban and muslin shirt, an embossed shield, a curved tulwar, a white waistband, a yellow chintz cloth for his shoulders and soft Persian slippers. This new wardrobe he kept hidden.

About 6pm he set off for duty in the mines as usual, not even letting his wife, Agnes, know what he was up to. She, poor woman, was in a highly nervous state and only a few days earlier had been wounded by a roundshot glancing off one of her legs. Thomas made sure to kiss her and his four children. His costume was all tied up in a bundle at an outhouse near the Slaughterhouse Post. Here he stopped to change his clothes helped by Anglo-Indian Francis Quieros, who helped him dress and held up a small mirror as Kavanagh coated all his exposed skin in lamp black. Oil was applied in an attempt to make the blacking adhere better, while Quieros snipped away at the Irishman's red-gold curls. Cheekily he then walked into Outram's headquarters and plumped himself in a chair. There was consternation from officers – how dare an Indian stroll in wearing slippers and take a seat uninvited! No one recognised the lanky Irishman save Kanauji Lal, who started to chuckle. Once the charade was exposed everyone wanted in on the joke; helpful hands readjusted the turban, a pair of baggy, purple-striped pyjama trousers were found as a finishing touch and Sir James, who could see the funny side of things, shook with laughter when more lamp black had to be applied. Finally Captain Sitwell, Outram's adc, presented the new spy with a loaded double-barrelled revolver so that if it came to the worst he could die fighting – or blow his brains out.

About 8.30pm the laughter died away. Both Napier and Outram shook Kavanagh's hand and wished him luck and godspeed. Guided by Captain George Hardinge, Oudh Irregular Cavalry, the two spies trod noiselessly through the compound to the Water Gate. Hardinge squeezed Thomas's hands and whispered, rather unreassuringly, "Noble fellow! You will never be forgotten!" Then he was gone in the darkness. Kavanagh takes up the story:

> The night was dark – the sky without a cloud – and there was nothing to guide us but the bright mysterious stars, and a few lights flickering across the river. On our right lay the lines of the enemy, extending past the palaces to the bridge of boats, and on the left they crowded towards the elegant iron bridge, and the old stone bridge beyond, over which we were to recross the river that flowed calmly and silently before us, and divided the two armies.[3]

Stepping out of his clothes and holding them in a bundle on his head the naked Kavanagh plunged into the Gumti. "The cold water chilled my courage immensely, and if the guide had been within reach I should, perhaps, have pulled him back, and given up the enterprise." On the opposite bank Kanauji and Thomas got dressed under a grove of low trees. Both hid when a man came down to the river's edge to wash, but he went away without seeing them. Passing by some native huts, they met a matchlockman. Boldly, and with growing confidence, Kavanagh said it was a cold night. The fellow agreed, and "I passed on, observing that it would be colder, by-and-bye."

Some six or seven hundred yards further on, by the iron bridge, the pair were hailed by a native officer who seemed to be in command of a cavalry picquet. Kavanagh kept to the shadows while the couple said they had come from Mandaon and were going into the city "to our homes". The ruse worked and a further 800 yards walking led to the stone bridge. Here they turned and entered Lucknow. The streets were fairly busy with people, despite the late hour, and to Kavanagh's relief the main street (*chowk*) "was not illuminated so much as it used to be." Armed men jostled them on every side but they saw only one guard of seven sepoys who were dallying with some prostitutes. Kanauji Lal tried to enter some of the narrow side streets, but Kavanagh felt safety lay within the crowds. Finally, as they trudged along, the muddy lanes gradually fell behind them and eventually "the stars glittered above silent fields." Thomas was excited after so many weeks cooped up in the Residency to see once more green things. "Every plant was fragrant," he wrote, "I greedily sniffed it all as I devoured a delicious fresh carrot."[4]

Four or five miles walking in the dark past fruit trees and flowering bushes led the two spies to the conclusion that they were on a wrong road and somewhere near the Dilkusha park occupied by rebel sepoys. They asked an old man for directions but he pleaded infirmity. A second villager ran off shouting and Kavanagh and Kanauji fled and hid in the canal. Now followed a nightmarish hour or two. "We entered another village for a guide," wrote Thomas, "The whole ground was so cut up by ravines and barred by garden walls, that we made no progress through it; and there was reason to fear that we might awkwardly stumble on one of the many parties of troops in the neighbourhood."[5] Taking a huge risk, Kavanagh entered a "wretched" native hovel and in the darkness his hand brushed against the thigh of a young woman. This "good-natured creature" woke her mother and the two women not only put the spies on the right path, but "blabbed all they knew of the proceedings of the enemy".

Despite this piece of luck, Thomas was finding the going increasingly painful – his feet were now raw and weeks of malnuitrition were sapping his strength. About 2am the two men stumbled into an enemy picquet but after a few words of conversation were on their way again. Kanauji, who was getting increasingly nervous, begged Kavanagh not to approach the Alambagh, which, he said, was surrounded by the mutineers, honeycombed with trenches and a place he had never visited. He wanted the Irishman to head towards Campbell's old camp 18 miles from Lucknow.

An hour later, stumbling along on blistered feet, Kavanagh startled a singer surrounded by a bunch of about 25 ex-sepoys in a mango grove. Terrified, Kanauji now threw away his despatch from Outram, fearful that he would be searched. Kavanagh refused to do the same and kept his cossid hidden in his turban. The couple said they were poor travellers making for a village in the country to tell a friend about his brother's death in Lucknow. This plausible lie worked effectively and the sepoys showed them on their way, but the pair next found themselves stuck in a swamp. It seemed to be everywhere, mud sucked at their heels and at one point the water was so deep that Kavanagh had to help raise Kanauji Lal, while the reeds seemed almost razor-edged. Kanauji swore at every step – he blasted the rebels, the swamp, the mud, the reeds, his old and lovely land of Oudh, he even laughed at his own obscenities. Soon both men were laughing together and feeling better. Unfortunately for Kavanagh, the dye had now come off his hands and he could see in the first streaks of dawn light that they were pink and freckled.

It was approaching 4am as the pair skirted several fires and groups of insurgents. Villagers were also now seen on the main road fleeing with bullocks and chattels. One of them said the British were nearby, murdering and plundering all around them, but the frightened fellow refused to stop and answer more questions. Kavanagh slumped to the ground. He was exhausted and despite Kanauji's objections demanded a rest. A moment later he heard a sepoy's voice – "Hoo cum dar?" Rushing forward the tall Irishman found Kanauji trying circumspectly to ask questions of a sentry. Thankfully he turned out to be part of a British picquet and Kavanagh, to his great joy, was able to convince a Sikh officer that he really had come from the Residency with a message from Outram for Sir Colin Campbell. Along the way he was intercepted by Lieutenant Goldie, HM 9th Lancers, who led him to his tent, gave Kavanagh a glass of brandy, some dry stockings and a pair of trousers. Captain Dick, HM 29th Foot, commanding the advance guard of the British army, found a little Burmese pony for Kavanagh and walked by his side for the quarter of a mile into camp as word started to spread like wildfire that a Briton had got through from the besieged lines. The sun was now rising majestically into a clear blue sky and Thomas Kavanagh felt he was living some strange dream.

After meeting Sir Colin and briefly telling him some news the Irishman begged that he might be permitted to sleep before a full discussion. The C-in-C acquiesced willingly and Kavanagh was given a bed in a staff officer's tent that was darkened for his comfort. Five or six hours later he was up to enjoy a hearty breakfast with the general and his "laughing staff of young scamps". They all listened attentively to his tale of the previous night's adventures as Thomas enjoyed, for the first time in many months, eggs and bacon, Scotch marmalade and coffee with milk and sugar.

Details of the situation within the Residency were kept for Campbell's ears only. The despatch carried by Kavanagh along with a map sent by Outram helped the general decide finally on his plan of operations. This plan had been taking shape in his mind ever since he left Calcutta. Sir Colin wanted to avoid the narrow and twisting streets of Lucknow and the heavy loss of life suffered by Havelock's troops. Instead, he was pinning his hopes on a flank march across open country to the Dilkusha Palace and its park, from where he intended to advance upon the Martinière School and the line of the canal, moving gradually closer to the river. His right flank would thus be free of any direct attacks (though not of enemy artillery fire). He would next seize the old barracks of HM 32nd and the Sikanderbagh, enabling him to get his gun batteries in nice range of the insurgents holed up in the Kaisarbagh – key to the enemy position – carry any buildings in between (but not assault the Kaisarbagh), reach the Residency and withdraw the garrison.

The early part of this plan agreed with Outram's suggestions, but Sir Colin departed from Sir James's intentions on the approach to the Sikanderbagh; after doing his own reconnaissance on the 15th, the general found the route via the canal bridge and suburbs to be strongly held by the enemy, so he decided to keep to the more open ground near the Gumti. He hoped that as he headed along the river near the Moti Mahal Palace that Outram might sortie to meet him. The difficulties cannot be underestimated. The Victorian military historian George Forrest summed up the problems in the style of that era:

> No more difficult and delicate an operation was ever planned by a commander. With a force of 4500 men of all arms he had to rescue Outram from the grasp of 60,000 trained soldiers occupying strong positions. He had to carry and hold these positions until he reached the post held by Outram's force. He had to do it, on account of the want of provisions, within a limited period. He had also to hold a succession of posts on the left so as to keep a clear road from the Residency to the open country. He had to bring away the sick and wounded, women and children, evacuate the Residency, and withdraw his troops, first to the Dilkoosha, and then to the Alum Bagh. He had to leave here a small body of men to threaten the enemy, and then proceed with all haste to Cawnpore to save Windham and his garrison. The chances were against him, the risk was immense. But the risk had to be run to save women and children, to rescue an Empire.[6]

Grandiloquent perhaps, but none the less true. To do all this Campbell had a force of a little more than 4,000 men: Forrest put their number at 4,200 sabres and bayonets; Thomas Rice Holmes calculated 3,400 and the Residency engineer, Innes, opted for 3,800; Lord Roberts plumped for about 600 cavalry and 3,500 infantry with about 42 guns, while another participant, George Bourchier, calculated 3,200 infantry, 900 cavalry, 400 naval brigade and artillery and 200 sappers – 4,700 men. Since he was an artillery officer Bourchier is probably correct when he estimated 12 heavy guns, 10 mortars and 27 light field guns.

In the same way that we cannot be sure how many British troops were about to march into harm's way, there is no accurate account of precisely the size of the rebel force within the city. A contemporary intelligence report came to a figure of 53,350 armed men awaiting the British attack (see Appendix A). Rudrangshu Mukherjee analysed this data:

> This breakdown clearly shows that the rebellion in Awadh had transcended a purely sepoy base. For one thing the fighting force was quite large and for another more than sixty per cent was drawn from the general rural populace... Of the thirty-two talukdars (or their men) in the list, the places of origin of twenty-one talukdars are readily

identifiable ... the districts in which the talukdars' control was the strongest and where they had lost heavily in the Summary Settlement supplied the bulk of the rebel forces.[7]

Ex British sepoys and their regiments were also strongly represented; the Sikanderbagh in particular was held by some 2,000 of them including 400 men of a newly constituted Nadiri regiment. The Begum's new bodyguard – the all-female "Black Cats" – were also waiting to fight and die there.

The ex-sepoys had their old Brown Bess muskets, their officers carried swords, but the Indian combatants incorporated many other traditional weapons; some fought with maces (*gadas*), or carried one or more fearsome daggers such as the *bhuj* or axe-knife, or the better-known *katar* with its H-shaped hand-grip and V shaped blade. A number of peasants were armed with simple but deadly bows and arrows. Swords included not just the curved tulwar but also straight swords like the double-edged *khanda*. The rebel gunners from the Bengal Artillery throughout the Lucknow campaigns had fought with ability, courage and perfect discipline. Many times, their former British officers had been impressed by these men who were now fighting in some cases their own relatives on the other side.

While Sir Colin's plan largely avoided fighting in narrow streets it is worth remembering that his small army was expected to capture "a series of isolated strongposts, each one a fortress in itself".[8] His long line of communications from the Residency to the Alambagh was going to require one quarter of his force – 1,000 men – to cover what would become 4½ miles of retreat. A participant – and later Commander-in-Chief – Garnet Wolseley, wrote: "I do not know of any instance in military history where a general was called upon to face a more difficult, a more dangerous problem than that which Sir Colin Campbell had before him."[9] Already, Campbell had spelled out his weaknesses to Outram in a letter: "I have not ammunition for more than three days firing... My communications are threatened from Calpee, where the Gwalior Contingent, with forty guns, sixteen of which are heavy, are swelled by remnants of many regiments to about ten thousand men... You must make your arrangements for getting everyone clear of the Residency when I am able to give the order, abandoning guns, but saving the treasure."[10]

On the afternoon of 11th November the British troops were drawn up to be reviewed by the grizzled old soldier who would lead them into battle. Thomas Kavanagh had also been invited, but someone gave him a highly spirited horse who refused to go anywhere it was told, and to its rider's humiliation it finally galloped back to the tents. The army was spread out in quarter-distance columns on a large plain surrounded by trees. Riding down the lines the old Chief spoke kindly to each Corps as he passed by.

HM 9th Lancers looked resplendent as always, their polished swords, harnesses and lances gleaming in the sunshine, the men sitting upright in their saddles in blue uniforms with white turbans twisted around their forage caps and each horse neatly groomed. Next to them were detachments from three Punjab cavalry regiments and Hodson's Horse – all hardy frontier warriors, Sikhs and Pathans, riding "every variety of horse with every variety of bit, bridle and saddle".[11] Sir Colin knew that they were excellent light cavalry and stopped to say "what good service we had done at Delhi," wrote an officer, "and in the march down country, and [he] complimented the native officers and men." The Sikhs had carefully combed their silky beards and fine whiskers, "their silver-mounted firearms and gleaming scimitars resting easily against the clean cloth of their loose, fawn-coloured robes".[12]

Next to the native cavalry were standing the tough sepoys of the 2nd and 4th Punjab Native Infantry alongside HM 8th and 75th regiments. All four Corps had been weakened by the fighting at Delhi. The strain of long weeks campaigning showed on the mens' faces and they were clad in a jumble of costumes, basically the new dun-coloured cloth called "khaki", but in varying hues of brown. "Dirty Gordon", described by one of his captains as "a queer and eccentric fellow, perfectly useless as a parade-ground officer but a most gallant soldier", commanded the 75th and sat on "a reddish-brown brute of a native horse". His men's uniforms, originally white, but now dyed khaki, were patched and worn, and their commanding officer was dressed in an outfit that would have given a Sandhurst colonel apoplexy:

First then, his head dress was a kind of thing shaped like a basin, and made he told me out of an old shako with a brass ventilator at the top made in a bazaar, and held on his head by an old regulation chin strap with brass scale rings, the strap being much too long hung under his chin and mixed up with a ragged beard which adorned the lower part of a most peculiar countenance. His jacket was khaki in colour, but was not according to the regulation of our Regiment which had a turn-down collar. Gordon's was hooked round his throat and decorated by a row of small Regimental brass buttons while his shoulders displayed a pair of faded gold cords of the shabbiest description. He had on his nether man a pair of khaki trousers thrust into jackboots *a la* native trooper of Irregular Cavalry, the heels of which were armed with a pair of huge brass hunting spurs, which as well as the rest of his accoutrements were guiltless of any attempt at being clean. A Cawnpore leather sling belt sustained an enormous light Cavalry sabre to which by way of sword knot was attached a pyjama string of green, yellow and pink silk, the finishing touch being given to this martial costume by a pair of old, what had once been white gloves, but were now all colours from filth and age.[13]

HM 53rd Foot looked smart enough, but the Madras Fusiliers alongside them had patched their uniforms with "curtains and other draperies", while some of the men wore pyjamas of coloured silks and jackets of green baize. A lieutenant in HM 8th who had lost his jacket was kitted out in "a grey flannel coat and trousers and a sowar's belt and pouch that [he] had picked up."

The Punjabis listened to Campbell's words in solemn silence, save one sepoy of the 4th PNI who fell down crying that he could not go into battle due to stomach pains. His regimental surgeon, James Fairweather, was embarrassed and rushed the sepoy off to his sick tent convinced that he was malingering. The man died next day (probably of a burst spleen or appendix).

After passing the Bengal Artillery the C-in-C reached the ranks of his beloved 93rd Highlanders, the famous "thin red line" and equally famously his pet regiment. Here he was welcomed with loud cheers that rolled across the plain. This "solid mass of brawny-limbed men", half of them wearing their Crimean War decorations, were a Bible-fearing, tough, Gaelic-speaking regiment that included such legends as caber-tossing George Bell, six feet four inches tall and reckoned to be the most powerful man in the British Army, Sergeant Daniel White who, in battle, liked to recite Sir Walter Scott, Captain "Wee Frenchie" Burroughs who checked to see that his men had washed behind their ears, and Adjutant "Willie" MacBean, Inverness plough boy who rose to become a general. The 93rd did not have on scarlet tunics, but light brown blouses, faced with scarlet (and intended originally for boat work in China where the regiment had been heading), rolled greatcoats slung across their shoulders and Sutherland kilts. Every fifth man carried a three-gallon copper camp kettle and a billhook. Each soldier had with him 60 rounds of ammunition held in his pouch with 100 rounds in reserve, a water-bottle, and a linen haversack with three days rations, plus his Enfield rifle and bayonet. All the officers and sergeants were wearing their sashes. Each officer had a claymore, some also dirks and revolvers. Their greatcoats weighed twice as much as the ordinary soldiers' (and turned out to be useful bullet stoppers).

Most of the British infantry officers were using the 1845 sword worn in a black leather scabbard. Chief killing weapon of the infantry was the new Enfield rifle with its 39-inch barrel, .577 calibre, weighing 8lb 14½ ounces, sighted to 1,200 yards. The socket bayonet was 17 inches (sergeants and rifle regiments had a 6 inches shorter and 10 ounces lighter version sighted to 1,000 yards with a 22½-inch sword bayonet). A few reactionaries still clung however to the "man stopping" Minié rifle. Many officers carried revolvers of various kinds, though the most popular was the .44 Adams.

Sir Colin was not normally given over to Havelock-style long orations, but on this special day and in front of his special regiment he was moved to make a speech:

> I must tell you, my lads, there is a work of difficulty and danger before us – harder work and greater dangers than any we encountered in the Crimea. But I trust you to overcome the difficulties... The eyes of the people at home, I must say the eyes of Europe and the whole of Christendom are upon us, and we must relieve our countrymen, women and children, now shut up in the Residency of Lucknow. When you meet with the enemy you must remember that he is well armed and well provided with ammunition... So that when we make an attack you must come to closer quarters as quickly as possible; keep well together and use the bayonet... Ninety-third! You are my own lads and I rely on you to do the work![14]

To loud hurrahs the old general and his staff cantered off the field.

At break of day on 12th November 1857 the army began its move towards Lucknow. Everyone was excited and many awed by the colour and verve of it all – the 9th Lancers in their neat blue uniforms and smart horses, the sailors of the Naval Brigade in smocks and straw boaters, khaki-clad infantry, kilted Highlanders, camp followers in every imaginable oriental costume, swift horses, patient elephants, slow and snorting bullocks heaving heavy guns, light field guns, hackeries and carts of every description, and mile after mile of undulating camels laden with supplies all moving in long lines.

The advance guard had only gone a short distance through some woods in the general direction of the Alambagh, the band playing a merry tune, "Castles In The Air", when it found the insurgents, with a breathtaking display of impudence, drawn up with 2,000 infantry and two heavy guns protected by an earthwork blocking the path. Hope Grant cantered over to 24-year-old Hugh Gough, commanding Hodson's Irregular Horse, and ordered him to take his squadron and capture the guns or spike them. Gough saluted and rode off hoping that the surprise of a flank attack might give him the element of success. "I made a considerable detour," he wrote in his memoirs, "and managed under cover of some fields of growing corn or sugar-cane, to arrive on the left flank of the enemy perfectly unseen:"

> Between us and them lay a marshy *jheel,* with long, reedy grass – an unpleasant obstacle, but which served admirably to cover our movements. I then advanced my men through this *jheel* and long grass at a trot and so concealed our movements till we got clear, when I gave the word, "Form line" and "Charge." My men gave a ringing cheer and we were into the masses... My horse, "Tearaway"carried me like a bird, and I found myself well ahead. It seemed like cutting one's way through a field of corn, and I had to make a lane for myself as I rode along. The men followed me splendidly, and in a very short time the affair was over – the guns were captured, the enemy scattered, and the fight became a pursuit.[15]

Gough's description of the fight omits that although he was unhurt, "Tearaway" suffered two sabre slashes. Luckily for Gough, the thick folds of his puggaree wound around his forage cap saved him as it was slashed to the last fold by a rebel tulwar. Several staff officers and then Sir Colin rode up to congratulate the young man after his return to the column and he was duly awarded the Victoria Cross.[16]

That night the camp was pitched a short distance from the Alambagh and out of range of enemy artillery fire. Kavanagh had brought a code of signals from Outram, so a semaphore was erected on the roof of the Alambagh. Sir Colin's first test message to the Residency confused the defenders, since in their excitement the senders had reversed the symbols by mistake. Then the bizarre word "Goon" was made out. Slowly more letters appeared and the garrison understood – "Go on we are ready."

Commanding at the Alambagh immediately prior to Sir Colin's arrival had been another Scotsman, Major McIntyre of the Gordon Highlanders. This feeble-minded old officer, who had done nothing to prevent the insurgents shelling his position, had also refused to give up despatches from Outram, even when cavalry had arrived to collect for the C-in-C. McIntyre insisted he would part with the despatches only when he saw Campbell in person. Now this officer was the recipient of his general's wrath as Sir Colin did "a sort of war dance", shaking his fists, while the major stood "with hands behind him and with his eyes on the ground like a naughty schoolboy".[17] This scene greatly amused Captain Garnet Wolseley of HM 90th who had been holed up within the Alambagh for several days and was thirsting for action. He almost did his own war whoop of joy when told that his three companies of the 90th would join Adrian Hope's infantry brigade.

Next morning, Hope was ordered to seize little Jellalabad Fort where the enemy had proved troublesome sniping away at the Alambagh. On arrival Hope found the place deserted – the insurgents had scuttled away at dawn – so he blew a few holes in the walls with gunpowder to make it less defensible. Sir Colin used that day to make his final preparations; all the tents were moved to the Alambagh and a new garrison composed of HM 75th who had suffered heavily at Delhi, along with 50 men of Brayser's Sikhs, now took charge.

When he next moved forward, Campbell intended to take with him all his baggage and provisions for 14 days – food not just for his men but also the people within the Residency. Carts also had to be taken along ready to convey women, children and the wounded. The rear guard was to be under the command of Lt-Colonel John Ewart of the 93rd with three squadrons of cavalry under Captain Octavius Anson of the 9th Lancers, Blunt's troop of Bengal horse artillery and about 500 infantry drawn from HM 84th and 90th regiments as well as a few Madras Fusiliers.

To deceive the enemy, a strong reconnaissance was made towards the Charbagh Bridge led pluckily by Campbell himself. While jogging along the C-in-C told Lieutenant Fred Roberts, AQMG, to the young officer's intense delight and pride, that he had been chosen to guide the army on its first march to the Dilkusha. More troop reinforcements arrived that day from Cawnpore numbering about 700 men composed of more sappers and artillery, with two guns of the Madras Artillery, the headquarters of HM 23rd Foot, a detachment of HM 82nd Foot and 200 men of the Military Train (a version of the commissariat), now given horses and laughingly called by the men of the 93rd "dumpies" as "they looked exactly like a very rural corps of Yeomanry Cavalry on the first day of assembly for the annual training."[18]

On 13th November, Sir Colin issued his last orders. His little army consisted of just three infantry brigades, the strongest being that commanded by the Honourable Adrian Hope, a popular officer of the 93rd Highlanders. He had 934 bayonets and 48 officers of all ranks from the 93rd along with a wing of HM 53rd Foot, "hardy old soldiers, well acquainted with Indian battle", and the 4th PNI, weak in numbers but men of undoubted courage from the fighting at Delhi. A second brigade was commanded by Brigadier Greathed and composed of HM 8th Foot and the 2nd PNI, and a battalion of detachments. The third was led by Brigadier Russell with a wing of the 23rd Royal Welsh Fusiliers, a regiment new to fighting in India and consisting mainly of recruits (due to its losses in the Crimea), and two companies of HM 82nd Foot.

The artillery commanded by Brigadier Crawford, a Royal officer, was augmented by the Naval Brigade of 250 seamen and marines from HMS *Shannon* who manned six 24-pounders and two rocket tubes. The cavalry under Brigadier Little was composed of two squadrons of the 9th Lancers, detachments of the 1st, 2nd and 5th Punjab Cavalry and Hodson's Horse commanded respectively by four energetic lieutenants – Watson, Probyn, Younghusband and Gough. Assisting the cavalry were the "dumpies" of the Military Train organised as two squadrons of cavalry. Lastly was a small brigade of engineers under Lieutenant Lennox R.E. with both Madras and Bengal sappers.

Late that night, Campbell wrote a few lines to his sister: "My force is high and powerful in spirit and courage, but our numbers are not so many as may be desirable. Our friends in Lucknow have food only for five or six days, and the effort must be made to save them at any cost."[19]

On 14th November, after a breakfast of tea and biscuit, the army pushed off about 9am. Sitting on his white steed at the front of his army, Campbell looked through his ivory spy-glass at the way ahead and then said, with a wide wave of his arms, "There is your bed – take and lie on it!" It was over open country, cultivated in places by corn and cane, dotted with clumps of large trees, bordered in the north by the canal and flanked in the north-east by the Gumti river, which wound and twisted its way like an English stream. Sitting on a plateau was the Dilkusha ("Heart's Delight") Palace, built for Nawab Saadat Ali Khan in 1805 as a hunting lodge amid a parkland well stocked with deer and antelope. The place was a "green-shuttered summer palace like a French chateau" and "almost an exact replica of Seaton Delavel, an English building built by Sir John Vanburgh in Northumberland,"[20] four-storied with corner towers. Nearby was a large, shallow lake populated by ducks, where the profligate Nasir-ud-Din Haider used to sit in a hide by the water's edge and regularly massacre the birds.

Below the plateau, half a mile further on, lay the Martinière, formerly the home of its creator, the French adventurer, Claude Martin, but by 1857 he was long dead, buried in its crypt, and the building was a school, its teachers and some pupils having been fighting courageously for weeks at the Residency. Sir Colin had decided that the Dilkusha and Martinière should form the basis of his relief operations.

For three miles the army marched in almost festive mood, some of the soldiers stopping at one point to dig up and eat some carrots. British gun carriages jolted along towards the park's south east corner, the colourful uniforms of the troops contrasting with the rich green of the grass and trees while herds of spotted deer and black buck bounded away terrified, or lazy, short-horned antelope (*nilgai*) shambled off disgusted at being disturbed. "It was such a pretty scene, a very picturesque sight for a battle," thought Lieutenant Arthur Lang, Bengal Engineers. He was also amused when some of the soldiers started firing at the "Pandies" in the trees, but, guffawed Lang, "they turned out to be monkeys!"[21]

It was not until they reached the park wall that the insurgents hit the British advanced guard with a long line of musketry and shells from a masked battery of six guns. Well out in front a roundshot passed over Lieutenant Roberts guiding the army. The ball sailed between the right of No 7 Company of the 93rd and the line, but a second shot was better aimed and seemed to strike Roberts' horse. "Plucky wee Bobs is done for!" exclaimed one of the Highlanders scanning forward. But it was not the lieutenant's horse that had been hit but a trooper riding alongside him. Then a 9-pounder ricocheted at a right angle and took off the head of young Private Kenneth Mackenzie, "just level with his ears". His distressed colour-sergeant stared down at the smashed skull and brains and said, "Poor lad, how can I tell his mother? He was her favourite laddie!" The shots now started bounding towards the regiment and old Colonel Leith-Hay ordered the men to close ranks, but wise MacBean, the adjutant said in an undertone, "Don't mind the Colonel lads, open out and let them through, keep plenty of room and watch the shot."[22]

Surgeon Fairweather of the 4th PNI was uncomfortable. "This was nasty kind of work, "he wrote, "for the regiments were so divided and lost to each other among the fields and woods that we ran a great risk of being hit by our own men."[23] As the British advanced past the Dilkusha and towards the Martinière, the rebels melted away. Pushing on, the cavalry and artillery reached the brow of the slope. Hardy of the Royal Artillery, having brought up a heavy howitzer, Remington's troop of Bengal horse artillery and Bourchier's guns, gave the retreating insurgents a shelling. "One more broadside, if you please, gentlemen," exhorted Captain Peel V.C. to his naval gunners. Yellow-white smoke rolled over the trees as his 24-pounders boomed out. Shell splinters and bullets flew about from the enemy, but Peel refused to lose his cool. "Nonsense, nonsense, it is only dust and dirt," he reproved the rationally nervous. His actions gave heart to some of the camp followers who began washing their clothes in the lake. "Rebel fire drenched them with vast geysers of water," wrote Richard Collier, "unperturbed, they scrubbed on."[24] Even shell fragments bursting all about them, as Surgeon Collins of the 5th Fusiliers noted, "did not seem to disturb them in the least."

The cavalry chased the rebels right to the canal where a dam had caused the water to rise to an infantryman's shoulders. Here, by the water's edge, in the hand-to-hand fighting Lieutenant John Watson, 1st Punjab Cavalry, slew the native cavalry leader, a strapping officer of the 15th Irregulars. He was then set upon by six native troopers but held them off, swords slashing left and right, until Dighton Probyn galloped forwards with two squadrons to save his comrade.[25] Arthur Lang watched this fight from a vantage point high up on the Martinière and wrote that "Watson fought like a 'lion' as his men said: his steel gauntlet was cut through at the knuckles, he was nearly stunned by a cut on the head, which his puggaree saved from being fatal; his arm and leg were both hit and bruised, and how he escaped the crowd of enemy he was amongst seemed a miracle."[26]

Back at the Alambagh the rear guard did not leave until about 1pm. "It was scarcely possible to breathe, "wrote Surgeon James Wise, due to the huge clouds of dust thrown up by the advancing army. Lt-Colonel Ewart was almost the last man to set out for the Dilkusha and, as he expected, the rebels were waiting to pounce just as soon as the last cart passed the road that led towards the Charbagh bridge (the route taken by Havelock). "The rebels shouted and made some noise," he recalled in his memoirs, but "had not the pluck to attack."[27] When they got pluckier, he returned with some artillery and a few rounds sent them off.

Much to Ewart's surprise a short time later some British troops appeared in his rear. These turned out to be the final reinforcements from Cawnpore consisting of the 23rd Royal Welsh Fusiliers, a detachment of HM 82nd, some Royal Engineers, Military Train and artillerymen with two heavy guns – about 700 men in all.

In the advance to the Martinière the insurgents had again hit the British with rifle fire and shells, a few soldiers being wounded and a man of the 93rd losing his head, but a howitzer and 11 field guns soon silenced them. The building was not to everyone's taste; an "eccentric array of statues, the huge lions' heads, the incongruous columns, arches, pillars, windows and flights of stairs leading to nothing".[28]. It was true that in this vast wedding cake of a building its creator had blended Tuscan and Corinthian influences in a series of yellow rooms some people found stuffy, with a *zenana* for the ladies tacked on. British officers were of varying opinions: Lieutenant Herford of the 90th thought it "a handsome building with its statues ornamenting the roof, its marble court, its ball-room and orchestra gallery".[29] John Ewart concurred, but Garnet Wolseley thought the place "a very large, ugly and un-Indian looking edifice".

During the afternoon Russell's brigade seized two villages on the banks of the canal that were of strategic importance. The insurgents retreated into the city after their artillery shelling and the British cavalry trotted back to the Martinière where they were ordered to bivouac for the night. No sooner had the horses been untraced when the Indians made a second attack close to the canal. Remington quickly limbered his guns, riders desperately tried to clamber into their saddles, while HM 53rd and HM 93rd supported by the 4th PNI went into attack. By now a remarkable camaraderie had developed between the Highlanders and the Punjabis, all hillmen of proud lineage, and they ran together cheering as fast as they could. At the water's edge many of the rebels threw down their weapons and tried to swim to the other side but not before at least 30 of them were bayoneted. Now well in advance of the rest, the 4th PNI took one end of a village on the far side of the canal. The insurgents refused to budge from the other end and the men of the 4th were "rather disgusted" on not being relieved the next morning, having to hold their forward position throughout the 14th and 15th under an "incessant crossfire", though only one man was hit, sleeping on the cold earth.

During that afternoon's fighting, two promising careers were cut short: Fred Roberts friend, Lieutenant Augustus Mayne, Bengal Horse Artillery, was shot through the breast, and Captain Wheatcroft, Carabineers, doing duty with the 9th Lancers, was ripped apart by a shell. Only a few hours earlier Wheatcroft had cradled a baby bullock in his arms and when friends suggested the animal would make a Christmas feast he had replied, "I wonder how many of us will be alive?"

That evening Thomas Kavanagh built a bonfire on the roof of the Martinière, another sign to the Residency defenders that their relief was on its way. He had earlier helped in the erection of a semaphore on the topmost pinnacle of the building and from this vantage point showed Sir Colin the city spread out before him, including Outram's defences at the Chuttar Manzil and the enemy's at the Kaisarbagh.

The men lay on the hard ground that night. Late in the evening Campbell visited his field hospital, spoke separately with every wounded man and ordered that "if necessary their wants should be supplied from his own private stores." Then he, too, despite his age, curled up and slept next to his troops. Kavanagh did the same and was proud to lay so close to so great a general.

It had originally been the C-in-C's intention to make his main attack on the 15th, but he was still waiting for more provisions and ammunition, so his army stayed up on the plateau. An attack on some picquets near the river on the extreme right British flank, along with a reconaissance on the left, were the only military actions. During this latter operation a 12-pounder struck a trooper's saddle in Watson's squadron with strange results, as reported by Frederick Roberts:

It must have lifted the man partly out of it, for it passed between his thigh and the horse, tearing the saddle to shreds, and sending one piece of it high into the air. The horse was knocked down, but not hurt; the man's thigh was badly bruised, and he was able to ride again in a few days. One of Watson's officers, Captain Cosserat, having examined the man and horse, came up and reported their condition to Watson, who, of course, was expecting to be told they were both dead, and added: "I think we had better not tell this story in England, for no one would believe it."[30]

Most soldiers kept their heads down all day. "Luckily the enemy shots were high and did us little damage," wrote Jones-Parry of the Blue Caps, "the small branches of the mango-trees suffered most, and they came tumbling down upon us. Had we remained there long enough we should have been buried in leaves like the Babes in the Wood."[31]

Perhaps the biggest excitement in camp was afforded by an encounter between a Bengal Artillery gunner and a ghazi fanatic. The burly gunner wandered towards the woods for a morning stroll or perhaps intending to have a pee. He was outside the line of sentries and the grass was high. He failed to see a ghazi, clad in just a loin cloth, with a robe thrown over one shoulder, creeping up to him with a tulwar. Officers in camp, however, saw the rebel and started shouting warnings. The gunner, a big Irishman, then drew his sabre and waited for the attack which came in traditional style, the ghazi holding his sword over his head as he charged screaming insults, swinging his robe in the other hand. The two men parried blows for a full 10 minutes while British officers and men watched in awe and started to take bets on the outcome. Eventually the gunner saw his chance and drove his sword up to its hilt through his opponent's stomach, literally disembowelling him, but the Indian showed no sign of stopping; he kept dancing around the gunner until a "dumpie" spoiled the show by riding up, knocking the ghazi to the ground. This was too much for some of the crowd, who did not like "dumpies", and thought the ghazi had fought well. Shouts of "fair play" rang out. In this spirit of "sportsmanship" the Bengal gunner refused to kill his opponent and returned to the cheering ranks.

That evening another gunner reported that the ghazi, despite his fearful wound, was still alive. So some Highland officers went to investigate; Captain George Balfour Traill, Bengal Artillery, spoke softly to the fanatic lying on the ground in a pool of blood who said he dreamed of killing a feringhee and entering Paradise. The officers returned and Traill ordered the gunner with whom the man had fought to "put a bullet in his head and end his pain."

That night a huge bonfire was set alight by the troops to let the Residency defenders know their relief was imminent. "We advance tomorrow" was relayed by semaphore. Balloon shells lit up the sky and Peel's sailors had fun firing streams of rockets into the city. Arthur Lang watched it from the battlements of La Martinière, marvelling at "forests of domes, minarets and gilded pinnacles, stretching away as far as the eye could see, that wonderful river, the Gomti, appearing everywhere in the most impossible twisting manner, but *the* sight was the glorious British Union Jack floating at the Chattar Manzil."[32]

Sir Colin's plan was to continue to move north-east, then veer in a circular movement through the outer suburbs of Lucknow in the general direction of the Residency. He knew that on the morrow his stiffest fight might be at the next large building to be taken and won; this was the Sikanderbagh ("Alexander's Garden"), a handsome Grecian style two-storied building with a high walled enclosure of about 120 acres, originally built as a retreat for the last King of Oudh and a favourite wife. The focal point of the Sikanderbagh was not the building itself but the magnificent garden designed for pleasure and relaxation, with a central pavilion set amongst flowering trees and shrubs. The storming of the Sikanderbagh, as it turned out, was to be especially violent and horrific – no single building fought over during the Great Uprising came to symbolise the ferocity of this war like the events of that November day, for within the space of a couple of hours over 2,000 men would lose their lives – shot, stabbed, hacked and burnt to death. No Indian rebel would ask for quarter, nor any man – or woman – receive it. The British themselves would admit that its capture spoke little of glory, but a great deal about the savagery and futility of war.

Early risers remembered the dawn of that 16th November – a classically chilly sunrise, the fields "warm with the vivid yellow of flowering mustard, the soft blue of flax"[33]. There seemed to be no warmth in that early breeze. Surgeon Munro of the 93rd, attending to his early morning tasks, later recalled a colleague looking wistfully at the soldiers as they ate their breakfasts, who said, "This is the last sunrise many will see." A chaplain years later would rememberthe oaths of soldiers as they awoke, "men's breath foggy and nauseous with the sweet stink of rum". Savoury smells soon mingled in the air as cooks set to work; for some men it was just biscuit washed down with syrupy tea, but at the Dilkusha, others, who had done a little poaching on the 15th, breakfasted on peacock or parrot roasted with strips of bacon and succulent venison steaks. Richard Collier set the scene: "Anxiously, like actors in the wings, Highlanders pressed their bonnets firmly on their heads, checked the tension of bayonet-springs, loosened their ammunition. Those who could trap fire-flies inserted them down their rifle barrels, to illumine the least speck of rust between muzzle and breech."[34] Besides their morning tea the men were given three days rations: three pounds of salt beef each and a dozen hard biscuits.

One of the earliest up that morning was Campbell himself. He had sent Lieutenant Roberts off to the Alambagh the previous night to bring up the reserve rifle ammunition. His column got lost in some ravines, so the sun was high in the sky before the task was completed. Roberts never forgot how, as he rode up to the Martinière, "I could see old Sir Colin only partially dressed standing on the steps in evident anxiety at my non-arrival."[35]

Also marching in at first light were the tough sepoys of the 4th PNI, at last relieved from their outpost duty by the 2nd PNI. The men "snatched a hasty breakfast consisting of cold meat, without bread, washed down by strong draughts of tea, without sugar or milk. Some men endeavoured to wash and dress but that was a difficult proceeding under the circumstances."[36] They were "astonished" to learn that there would be no rest for the regiment – it was to fall in behind its comrades of HM 93rd for the general assault.

A squadron of Hodson's Horse led the way at 8am with Blunt's troop of horse artillery and a company of the 53rd Foot and the 93rd under Colonel Leith-Hay. Hope and Russell's brigades followed. The ammunition and engineers came next while Greathed's brigade brought up the rear (save HM 8th Foot who were left to garrison the Dilkusha and La Martinière). The staff were in their blue coats and forage caps, the cavalry with white muslin turbans wound over theirs, the British infantry in pith helmets and dust-coloured cotton jackets and trousers, while HM 93rd wore brown China Expedition jackets.

By damming the canal the insurgents had made a mistake because this left a portion further east that was now completely dry. Even the British heavy guns had no difficulty crossing and climbing its banks. Clinging to the river the army then had to negotiate some narrow lanes and an area of low plantations enclosed by mud walls until it struck a cart track. Bending sharply to the left, the track led into a village with gardens and here the advance guard met a heavy musketry fire. At the end of this street lay the Sikanderbagh. To make matters worse, the place's southern entrance was shielded by a traverse of earth and masonry while on the north side a wicket-gate was stoutly defended. Some 250 yards from the south side the insurgents had occupied and loopholed a burnt-brick caravanserai.

The British, it seemed, had marched into a box; from front, left and right, in houses and gardens, the insurgents kept up a stiff fire.

The British cavalry could not advance and were soon bottled up, while the road behind was quickly choked with infantry and artillery. Surgeon Wise recalled: "The confusion in the narrow streets was awful, bullets whistling about, officers hurrying to the rear to bring up the heavy guns and infantry, and native grooms blocking up the road with led horses."[37] A colleague, Surgeon Fairweather of the 4th PNI, recalled how there would have been a lot more casualties had not some protection been provided by a wall that ran along the right side of the road. "When we got to the end of the wall we were told to lay down under its shelter till Peel's guns had effected a breach in the nearest bastion. Thus we got mixed up with the Highlanders."[38] Campbell ordered the 53rd to lie down in a shallow trench to avoid the enemy fire. Bullets whipped through the feather bonnets of the Highlanders. "Lie down, 93rd, lie down!" spluttered Sir Colin, "Every man of you is worth his weight in gold in England today!"[39]

Hugh Gough and his troopers got the sharp end of the old general's tongue for seemingly blocking up the road, though it was hardly the cavalry's fault. Then the 53rd, cheering, seemed ready to try a charge, a move that infuriated Campbell who roared out, "Steady 53rd! Keep steady! Damn all that eagerness!" When young Lord St Mawr, a son of the Duke of Somerset, waved his sword aloft and seemed ready to lead the men it was all too much for the general, who called the young officer over. Mawr cantered up, shame-faced, but Campbell always respected bravery above all else and now tempered his annoyance with a kindly word: "I witnessed your gallantry with great pleasure," he told the young officer, "but the 53rd have no need of it. Consider yourself, my Lord, as attached to my staff for the present. I admire your noble spirit and must take care of you."[40]

Gradually, order emerged from confusion: a gun was run out and opened fire on the Sikanderbagh; a company of the 53rd lined the enclosures on the right and the cavalry managed to get themselves into some side lanes. The Chief ordered Captain Blunt to go into action. With a dash the "Red Men" galloped forward through a deadly crossfire, rode their guns up "a seemingly impracticable bank", swung right and after much struggling gained an open space between the serai and the Sikanderbagh. Shouting out orders to his men, Blunt supervised as the guns opened fire. Sir Colin also had to face that steep bank of earth but with two or three strides his horse brought him alongside Blunt. To try and keep the enemy at bay Blunt had to keep turning his guns – to the right to keep down the fire from the Sikanderbagh, to the left to check a deadly fusillade from nearby huts and to his front where the rebels at the Kaisarbagh had now started a cannonade. Several gunners were struck down and even Sir Colin was hit in the thigh by a spent bullet that had just killed a gunner.

The men's blood was up. Surgeon Collins, 5th Fusiliers, knocked up the rifles of three soldiers who took aim at a harmless old native squatting on the ground some 30 yards away, but a fourth man shot and killed him.

Not to be outdone by the artillery, the men of the 53rd and 93rd started clearing the enclosure, some of them running down a lane to the left, hoping to get into the huts, but they were stopped by a dead end. Seeing this problem Campbell yelled, "In at the roof! Tear off tiles and go in through the roof!"[41] Once this hot work was completed, supported by two of Blunt's guns, men of the 53rd and three companies of the 93rd under Colonel Leith-Hay ran some distance across the open plain to seize two enemy guns at the bayonet's point, driving the rebels out of the serai and capturing the huge, cross-shaped old building that had once been HM 32nd barracks. Regiments were getting increasingly mixed up. In this melee some men of the 90th led by Lieutenant Herford got separated from Captain Wolseley, who was busily engaged across the serai in some ruined huts. Herford then had the run of his life:

> The only way I saw was to go across in front of the guns, but here they would not let me pass. I dodged through – was told in which direction to go – and ran! Never had I run so fast! The faster I ran, the more did the shower of balls seem to come around me... After a run of about 300 yards, when ready to drop, I reached the remains of walls, not breast-high. There I found Wolseley, but was so choked, that the only thing on arriving was to point to my mouth for water, before I could speak, and apologise to Wolseley for not having come with his company.[42]

While all this was going on the sappers had managed to cut down part of the high bank so that two 18-pounders could be dragged closer to the Sikanderbagh. The men hauled on ropes as bullets landed all around them from shooters at the south-east corner of the building just 60 yards away. Luckily for the British infantry, a small copse with a low mud wall in front gave them some protection. Enfields out, the British responded, and in the ensuing duel Captain W. Hardy R.A. was killed, his senior subaltern wounded, Blunt's beautiful grey Arab was shot, "and of the few men under his command 14 Europeans and 6 Gun Lascars were killed or wounded: 20 of the troop-horses were also knocked over."[43]

Uncovering his grey hairs, Sir Colin waved his forage cap and gave a sign to advance. Blunt's 9-pounders and two 18-pounders under Travers R.A. had taken, in the opinion of an observer, "more than one hour to hammer" a small hole in the wall of the Sikanderbagh. Stepping forward, Lt-Colonel Ewart waved his sword as a signal and the whole British line rose to their feet from the trench with a cheer. About 200 men made for the small hole in the wall, about three feet square and about three feet off the ground. They were a mix of HM 93rd and sepoys of the 4th PNI. Roberts, who witnessed this charge, wrote: "It was a magnificent sight, a sight never to be forgotten – that glorious struggle to be first to enter the deadly breach, the prize to the winner of the race being certain death! Highlanders and Sikhs, Punjabi, Mahommedans, Dogras and Pathans all vied with each other in the generous competition."[44]

Who was first through the hole was one of those arcane military topics still being hotly debated half a century later by old officers in their clubs, or in the columns of *The Times*. It hardly matters if, as Lord Roberts wrote in 1897:"A Highlander was the first to reach the goal, and was shot dead as he jumped into the enclosure; a man of the 4th Punjab Infantry came next, and met the same fate. Then followed Lieutenant Cooper of the 93rd, and immediately behind him his Colonel (Ewart), Captain Lumsden of the 30th Bengal Native Infantry, and a number of Sikhs and Highlanders as fast as they could scramble through the opening."[45] The simple truth is once the charge was launched, it became a scrum, a living hell of smoke, gunfire, screams and bloody fighting It was impossible to see more than a few yards ahead and to add to the confusion the 93rd were wearing brown jackets not so very different from the khaki uniforms of the 4th PNI.

The majority of the 4th PNI avoided the breach and charged at the main gate encouraged by the shouts of Dogra Subardar Gokal Singh.[46] With bullets whistling everywhere, they and others rushed the traverse, drove the rebels from the earthworks and went at the gate. Just as it was shutting Subedar Mukarram Khan[47] pushed his left arm and shield through the narrow opening preventing it from being closed. In an amazing display of courage, when the rebels hacked off his arm, he quickly pulled it out and thrust in his other one. Fred Roberts, a few steps behind, watched in awe as the gallant native officer refused to budge until his hand was all but severed. But it was too late for the insurgents now trapped inside; the 4th PNI pushed back the doors and rushed forwards while men of HM 53rd entered through a window on the right.

Highlanders, British regulars, swarthy Pathans and others now dashed and slashed their way into the garden where four paths led to a central pavilion. Historian Christopher Hibbert described the action vividly:

The slaughter inside was appalling. Colonel Ewart, his feather bonnet blown off his head, shot six rebels with six successive shots of his revolver. A taciturn, well-educated Highlander, known in the regiment as "Quaker", Wallace was believed to have killed twenty, driving his bayonet through their bodies as he chanted verses from the 116th Psalm. Other soldiers shouted "Cawnpore! You bloody murderers!" as they lunged towards the mutineers who "fought back like devils"... And, having fired their last shots, some of them hurled the muskets at the *Firinghis*' bayonets like javelins; then, shouting "Deen! Deen!" they actually threw themselves under the bayonets, slashing with their tulwars at their enemies' legs.[48]

Once Captain Paul of the 4th PNI had rushed ahead waving his sword, the British sappers dropped their gun ropes and joined in the fray. Lieutenant Lang took part and wrote in his journal:

> Such a distracting row of thousands of rifles firing without intermission I never heard, and such a sight of slaughter I never saw. In the open rooms right and left of the archway Pandies were shot down and bayoneted in heaps, three or four deep ... at each corner tower a few desperate men were holding out, and lives were being thrown away in attempting to force little narrow winding staircases.[49]

One rebel kept the British at bay on a staircase for two hours and "when his ammunition was done, appeared on the rooftop, and with fury, hurled his tulwar down amongst us, and fell amongst a volley of bullets."

The killing became, as Richard Collier described it, "one nightmare symphony" of death. The sights were extreme and never to be forgotten, nor were the sounds. Quaker Wallace shouting at the top of his voice, "I'll of salvation take the cup. On God's name will I call. I'll pay my vows now to the Lord. Before his people call." Rebels screaming "*Chalo, bahadur!*" ("Come on, my brave one!"). The Sikhs yelling their war cry, "*Jai Khalsa Jee*" and the British infantry cries of "Cawnpore!"

Surgeon Collins, 5th Fusiliers, saw the sepoys of the 4th PNI spitting in the faces of the rebels as they placed the muzzles of their rifles against chests and fired away. Beyond the garden and pavilion the fight blundered from room to room in the surrounding houses.

Norfolkman Lieutenant Cubitt, 5th Fusiliers:

> There were hundreds of sepoys, dead and dying, many on fire. Piled around the entrance and in every court and garden of the place, they lay in heaps, three or four deep, a suffocating, burning, smouldering mass, while many a Highlander, Sikh, 50th and a few of ours lay among them. Now and then a stray shot came from some wretch yet able to

pull his trigger. While there I saw 64 collected, drawn up and bayoneted with yells of "Cawnpore". God forgive us.[50]

Surgeon James Fairweather watched as his men of the 4th PNI ascended the spiral staircases of the gateway towers, Sikhs and Highlanders vying in ferocity, while another storming party drove the rebels back through the garden until they won possession of the central pavilion. Gradually the insurgents were made to bunch up at the end of the garden in a long, double-storied building with verandahs both below and above. During the shooting duel across the garden, Captain Lumsden, the 93rd's interpreter, was killed. "While all this was going on the bastions and other places on the walls and the houses round the garden were being cleared of the enemy until a final assault was made on their final position at the far end of the garden," wrote Fairweather. "They had barricaded the door on the left of the double-storied house but our men forced their way through the one on the right and the carnage began."[51]

Outside, in the garden, the ground was covered with the wounded and the dead. Piles of rebels, five feet high in places, were so densely entangled that the living could not extricate themselves, but lay there, struggling and cursing the British who, in derision, pulled off the petals of flowers and threw them over their foes. Writing home a few days later, Lieutenant Roberts told his mother that the insurgents were "literally in heaps ... a heaving mass, some dead, but most wounded and unable to get up by the crush... You had to *walk over them* to cross the court." He was impressed by the way the dying cursed him and said, "If we could only stand, we would kill you!"[52]

Corporal William Forbes Mitchell of the 93rd saw Quaker Wallace shoot down a woman "in a tight fitting red jacket and tight-fitting rose coloured trousers", clearly one of the Begum's regiment of Amazons. She had been armed with a pair of old cavalry pistols and been perched in a tree. When Wallace saw that he had shot a woman he started to cry, exclaiming: "If I had known it was a woman, I would rather have died a thousand deaths than have harmed her."[53] Fairweather saw the body of a dead woman "lying with a cross-belt upon her, and by her side a dead baby also shot with two bullet wounds in it (through the child's thigh)". Lieutenant John MacQueen of the 4th PNI saw a Highlander bayonet another woman and when he upbraided the man he "turned upon him like a madman", but the next moment a bullet "sent the man to Kingdom Come".[54]

One tragic incident took place when Anson, Hope Grant's aide, went inside the Sikanderbagh to reconnoitre for his chief. He saw an old woman trapped beneath some bodies. After helping her get free he told the woman to follow him out of the place, but in terror she scrambled up a low tree where a Highlander, some distance away, mistook her for a sepoy, shot and killed her.

It was pure slaughter, a smoky hell of death. Appalled by the horror of it all, Ewart, now severely wounded in his right arm and carrying a colour he had captured from two rebel officers, staggered out of the inferno to where Campbell outside was sitting rigidly on his charger. "I have killed the last two of the enemy with my own hand and here is one of their colours," he gasped. "Damn your colours, sir," shouted an irate Campbell, furious at what he perceived as irregular behaviour, "It's not your place to be taking colours! Go back to your regiment this instant, sir!"[55]

"Very much upset" by his general's harsh tone, Ewart returned inside the Sikanderbagh to find that the 93rd had lost 9 officers and 84 men killed or wounded. The butcher's bill also included 72 casualties in the decimated 4th PNI, including all three of its British officers.

The killing at the Sikanderbagh went on until sunset, individual dramas played out in different parts of the garden. It was late with a blood-red sun falling when ex-sepoys on the flat roof of the north-east tower were located. A rope was thrown up and they were told to surrender. Escape was impossible and so they did so, "like lambs coming to be slaughtered" noted Surgeon Collins, 5th Fusiliers; the scowling men agreed to line up against a wall and were then shot.

A brief rest was ordered for the troops as the rebels' bodies blackened and hissed and crackled in the Sikanderbagh's flames. In front of the army lay a plain, "not unlike Woolwich Common", on the opposite side of which was a large mosque, the Shah Najeef, with a row of grass-thatched low mud huts running along its side. To the British left were some strongly fortified houses and to their right the mound of a small mosque, the Kuddun Russool, containing a stone brought from Arabia bearing an impression of a foot said to be that of the Prophet.

The Shah Najeef had been built between 1814 and 1827 as the last resting place of Nawab Ghazi-ud-din-Haider, and his silver tomb lay in the centre of the building, flanked by the even larger and more imposing silver and gold tomb of his favourite wife, Mubarek Mahal ("the blessed one"). Tombs of two other wives lay close by. The building had a double tier of low white walls loopholed for musketry, an imposing entrance, wide cloisters at its centre, a paved courtyard and a rose garden.

It was well after 2pm before Adrian Hope led his brigade down the road. As they got closer to the Shah Najeef, men began to fall. One of them was Midshipman Daniel who was killed by a roundshot that tore off the right side of his head. Peel had just asked him to fire his howitzer and Daniel had time to reply, "Aye, aye" when his life was cut short.

Major Roger Barnston's battalion of the 90th were now ordered to drive the enemy out of the enclosures, but he fell, wounded by the premature bursting of a British shell. The soldiers began to waiver. Instantly a staff officer, Captain Henry Norman, spurring on his horse, galloped up to the middle of the 90th and asked them if they were going to retire before a pack of rebellious sepoys. This kind of language had the desired effect. More infantry came forward to support them. It was tough, but the assault moved onwards. From the Shah Najeef, the Kaisarbagh and the former mess-house of HM 32nd the insurgents kept up a heavy fire on the British. Far from accepting any kind of defeat, the rebels even opened up with a heavy gun from across the river at 4pm; its first shot blew one of Peel's tumbrils to smithereens. The Shah Najeef was now wreathed in columns of smoke from buildings burning in its front. Through this haze, as the British cautiously advanced, came the flashes of hundreds of popping muskets like bright sparks.

For three hours, Peel's Naval Brigade and the British artillery hammered away at the giant tomb, but the impression they made upon its stout walls was "negligible". Campbell realised what he must do. He rode over to the 93rd and said: "I had no intention of employing you again today, but the Shah Nuijeef must be taken. The artillery cannot drive the enemy out, so you must with the bayonet."[56]

To give the infantry their utmost support a battery of artillery passed Peel's guns and tried to get as close to the Shah Najeef as possible. "To loud cheers, the drivers waving their whips, the gunners their caps, they galloped forward through the deadly fire, unlimbered and poured round after round of grape upon the parapets of the enclosure."[57] Peel, in support, redoubled his efforts and used all his guns, too.

Then, marching at the head of his men, Colonel Alex Leith Hay led the 93rd forward. In support came Barnston's men of the 90th Light Infantry. With a colossal disregard for his own safety, Sir Colin now rode forward with drawn sword. His staff followed and within minutes Colonel Sir Archibald Alison's left arm was shattered by three bullets; his brother, Captain F. M. Alison, was wounded; Adrian Hope fell as his horse and most others of the staff were hit. Unhurt, Hope, regardless of his brigadier rank, set to work with the sailors to drag on the gun ropes. William Forbes-Mitchell recalled "A poor sailor lad, just in front of me, had his leg carried clean off above the knee by a round shot, and, although knocked head over heels by the force of the shot, he sat bolt upright on the grass, with the blood spouting from the stump of his limb like water from the hose of a fire-engine, and shouted, 'Here goes a shilling a day, a shilling a day! Pitch into them, boys, pitch into them! Remember Cawnpore Ninety-Third, remember Cawnpore! Go at them, my hearties!' and he fell back in a dead faint, and on we went."[58]

When Captain Peel commented that one rebel marksmen on the parapet of the Shah Najeef was a particular nuisance, Lieutenant Nowell Salmon R.N. climbed a tree with the help of a black seaman nicknamed "Snowball", Leading Seaman John Harrison and Lieutenant Southwell R.N. and tried to pot the rebel. Southwell was shot and killed and Salmon severely wounded. It was Victoria Cross style bravery;[59] two others were won by Lieutenant T. J. Young and William Hall, "captain of the foretop", a black sailor of Afro-Caribbean descent. [60] Hall's father was an escaped slave from Virginia. William had been born at Horton's Bluff, Nova Scotia, in 1827 but became a boy sailor at the age of twelve. For a time he had served in the American Navy, but enlisted in HMS *Rodney* while at Liverpool in 1852. Now, in the thick of an Indian battle, Hall wrote how they ran a gun right up to the mausoleum, where "my gun's crew were actually in danger of being hit by splinters of brick and stone mortar from the walls we were bombarding."[61] From above the rebels hurled down grenades in fury.

The defenders of the building fought resolutely, all the time "yelling like demons". A favourite shout was "*Jai Kali maki!*" ("Victory to Mother Kali"). In addition to bullets they were firing steel-tipped arrows; several British were hit by them and the arrows were very difficult to extract. Grenades hurled from above set light to several thatched huts but otherwise did little damage. Peel impressed everyone by the way he coolly worked his guns, "as if he had been laying the *Shannon* alongside an enemy frigate," as Campbell remarked. "The poor fellows were shot down round the guns like sheep,"[62] wrote Midshipman Lord Walter Kerr.

The 93rd Highlanders had also run into difficulties; the walls of the Shah Najeef were more than 20 feet high and the British had no scaling ladders. Despite all the shelling, the walls still looked solid so Campbell ordered that the big guns be withdrawn. During this operation Peel was told to fire his rockets with the hope that these hissing and unpredictable fiery serpents might terrify the rebels.

Sir Colin called off the attack and ordered Brigadier Hope to collect all the dead and wounded. For once the British seemed to be in retreat, when Sergeant John Paton of the 93rd turned up at HQ to report he had found a small indentation in the Shah Najeef's wall at its north-west corner, a hole covered by some bushes. Adrian Hope, with his schoolboy chum, staff officer Lieutenant George Allgood, stealthily crept through the brushwood near the walls to check out this piece of astounding news.

A soldier was able to scramble through the narrow opening and reported back to say he could see no one about. A company of sappers were ordered up to enlarge the hole. Then, stealthily, Hope with Allgood and a few men entered just in time to see insurgents exiting the rear of the building. Fearful that Peel's rockets would ignite 5,000 lbs of gunpowder stored inside, the rebels thought it best to slip away by the river gate on the northern wall. As one historian wrote: "The rocket had inadvertently won the day when all else had failed!" Hope and Allgood opened the main gateway and the latter officer reported to the Chief that the Shah Najeef was in British hands. When told of the news Peel exclaimed: "Well, you know rockets are rockets. If the enemy are only half as much afraid of them as we are who fire them, they are doing good service."[63]

Officers and men swarmed inside. Some went to the top of the building and it was while he was there that Fred Roberts saw a sepoy saunter up to the water gate, "evidently in happy ignorance of what had happened". Realising at the last moment that all his comrades had departed the man dropped his musket, ran to the river and started swimming to the other side. For Roberts this incident provided a little light relief on a day of dreadful violence.

Shortly after its capture Sir Colin ordered the Highland pipers to march around the Shah Najeef playing "The Campbells Are Coming". The wail of the pipes and the familiar tune carried on the air to the Residency where the defenders had been far from idle. From an upper storey of the Chuttar Manzil, Havelock and Outram had anxiously watched the progress of Campbell's army. When the Sikanderbagh was stormed the Residency fired two mines, both feeble attempts, while guns aimed at the Kaisarbagh passed through a wall, "as it would through a sheet of paper". Despite these setbacks Vincent Eyre and Billy Olpherts continued to batter away. In the courtyard of the Chuttar Manzil, Francis Maude also opened fire with his artillery. At 3.15pm two mines at the Hirun Khana exploded to good effect and 30 minutes later the bugles sounded "Advance".

"It is impossible to describe the enthusiasm with which this signal was received by the troops," wrote Havelock, "Pent-up in inaction for upwards of six weeks, and subjected to constant attacks, they felt that the hour of retribution and glorious exertion had returned." The rebels fled as the Residency troops rushed forward. Adjutant Gordon of the Ferozepore Sikhs recounted the violence:

> Immediately on jumping down into the enclosure, I had the satisfaction of seeing three men rushing at me with a yell. The first – a big and tall fellow, evidently excited almost to delirium by bhang – raised his sword

and made a backhanded slash that must have sliced my head off had I not been able to parry the blow just in time... I now had my turn and immediately gave him a chop on the head that cracked his skull... Anyway, at the same moment, one of our Sikhs bayoneted him in the back; and Captain Brayser, our commander, ran him through the left side and finished him off. I must say Brayser seemed to be everywhere at once, laying about him with his scimitar; and wherever there was action, his big red turban and flowing white beard and flashing sword were always conspicuous... It was then that I got two more slight sword cuts ... made by a sword glancing off a Sikh's rifle barrel. The fellow who did it was immediately bayoneted in the throat.[64]

Men of the 84th came to the aid of Brayser's Sikhs and the last dozen or so rebels fought like tigers when cornered in a gardenhouse. The "scuffle", as Gordon called it, was now over, save for two of the Begum's female bodyguard on some ramparts, who kept firing pieces of telegraph wire, "which inflicted nasty wounds ... defying us to come and get them." The Europeans were not keen to kill women, but the Sikh soldiers "shot them down, then they cut them up with their scimitars."[65]

As night fell, the artillery from the Residency was pushed forward until it was within good range of the Kaisarbagh. After dark, the scene still resembled Dante's *Inferno*; the panorama was a blaze of light from numerous fires while shots and shells still whizzed about and the rattle of musketry never ceased. Lieutenant Paul, who had valiantly led the 4th PNI all day, was blown up in an explosion of gunpowder in one of the bastions of the Sikanderbagh along with two native officers and two sepoys; he was terribly burnt before his flaming *meerzai* (padded native coat) could be torn off him.

As the men tried to get some rest, so ended 16th November 1857, a day such as British India had never seen, nor would again; the assault on the Sikanderbagh holds the record for the most Victoria Crosses won in a single action – 16 – while the day saw more VCs awarded than any other in British military history including the two World Wars – 24.[66]

The British troops slept on the open ground that night in a large semi-circle and the C-in-C joined them. Staff officer Henry Norman recalled, "A nice cold night we had of it, with a soaking dew." Some of the men chopped up dead gun bullocks and made a delicious stew for supper, especially good since the insurgents had left curry and dhal boiling on camp fires. Others mixed the meat and juices with some meal to make a thick potage. Midshipman Lord Walter Kerr went to visit injured sailors before feasting on some hard ship's biscuit in his haversack. When he got back to his guns he could not procure a blanket, so went and took a sack cloth off one of the gun bullocks, "and laid down in the road to sleep as jolly as possible".[67]

William Forbes-Mitchell had a hair-raising adventure when he went for a late stroll into the main vault of the Shah Najeef where, as he raised his lamp, he realised he was standing ankle-deep in loose gunpowder. "I felt the skin of my head lifting my feather bonnet off my scalp," he wrote later, "my knees knocked together, and despite the chilly night air the cold perspiration burst out all over me and ran down my face and legs. I had neither cloth nor handkerchief in my pocket, and there was not a moment to be lost, as already the overhanging wick of the *chirag* was threatening to shed its smouldering red tip into the live magazine."[68] Warning his superiors, the work of removal began at first light; nearly 5000 lbs of loose gunpowder, 20 more barrels and 150 loaded 8-inch shells were got away just before enemy batteries across the Gumti began a dawn barrage.

As the early morning sun began warming the ground, Captain Garnet Wolseley had a surprise:

> I had a cold bivouac that night in a thin silk jacket without a greatcoat. When I sat up the next morning, I smelt something burning, and upon looking at the high wall of the Sekunder Bagh immediately above me I saw the dead body of a sepoy lying across it, and partly hanging over its edge. He was dressed in a cotton-padded sort of greatcoat, which had caught fire and was slowly burning; the smell of his frizzling flesh was not very refreshing in that early morning hour.[69]

Within minutes Wolseley also saw some Sikh soldiers telling three rebels still holed up in a corner tower to come out and surrender. They did so meekly, "for I presume they had had no food or water for many hours." The Sikhs made the men kneel and, after questioning them, sliced off their heads with their tulwars.

Taking a last look around the Shah Najeef in the early morning light, Henry Norman saw that all the glass ornaments around the tombs in the mausoleum had been smashed and even the marble floor broken up. "I could not understand it," he wrote in a letter to his wife, but then he met a sailor outside with a 24 pounder shot who confessed to damaging the tomb, as "he did not intend to stand any of their idolatry."[70]

The morning promised more fighting to secure Campbell's last two objectives between his troops and the Residency. HM 32nd Mess House was more properly called the Khurshid Manzil ("House of the Sun"), completed in 1818, a two-storied building with a large central dome and eight towers topped by battlements. The place resembled a Gothic castle of sorts with a revetted moat and four entrances, all of which originally had drawbridges. For a time it had been the home of the royal astronomer. Even larger was the Moti Mahal ("Pearl") Palace built by Nawab Saadat Ali Khan over 16 years; its dome resembled a pearl and the place stood in the middle of gardens filled with orange and lemon trees enclosed by an unbaked brick wall in dilapidated condition, although the place was held in force by the enemy. An extra wall had been built near the main entrance, which was loopholed by the insurgents. All other entrances had been bricked up.

From the roof of the Shah Najeef, bullets whistled past their ears as Lieutenant MacBean, assisted by Sergeant Hutchinson, hoisted the regimental colour of the 93rd. It was soon answered by a colour on the roof of the Chuttar Manzil. A 12-year-old boy of the 93rd played on his bugle "Yankee Doodle Dandy", which he thought would amuse his relatives in North America if the incident got reported in the press.

After a three-hour bombardment from Peel's guns the Mess House was attacked. The storming party was led by Captain Wolseley of the 90th who headed across a drawbridge for the main entrance. "My bugler sounded the 90th call and the advance as we crossed the drawbridge, and I soon found my 'pal', Captain Irby, with his company beside me; with them also came a number of the 53rd Regiment... The enemy opened a heavy fire upon the house as soon as we got into it." Surprisingly, it had not been defended. "I had no orders as to what we should do if we succeeded in taking the place," continued Wolseley, "so pointing to a very large and fine building to our left front I said to my good cheery comrade, Captain Irby – who laughed at everything – "You go and take it, whilst I take the place to our right."[71] Irby set off and took the "House of the Stars" where the astronomer royal had his telescopes. Wolseley, though he did not then know the name of his objective, led men towards the Moti Mahal.

One of Wolseley's biographers, Joseph Lehman, takes up the story:

Wolseley's men tumbled over the garden wall and rushed down a broad street in the direction of the Residency, speeded on their way by bullets whizzing out of the Kaisar Bagh (king's palace) and other nearby buildings. Before the wall of the Motee Mahul they found shelter in an arcade-like structure. Pausing for a moment, Wolseley sized up the loopholed entrance to the palace. Happily the sepoys had failed to dig a ditch before their position. So, after the enemy fired a volley, he rushed his men up to the wall to gain control of the loopholes... The mutineers were first to abandon the struggle, though frequently one of them would crawl along the wall, pop up and fire a quick shot.[72]

Thomas Kavanagh helped bring up sappers to help. He then went to Sir Colin to say that Captain Wolseley of the 90th had secured the Moti Mahal but could not get inside the place. Campbell was furious, his cheeks went red with anger, and he exclaimed, "What do you mean, sir? You first say you have captured the place, and then say that you have not got into it? What am I to think of this contradiction! You have told an untruth, sir! I have lost confidence and will never believe you again!"[73] Back at the wall of the palace Wolseley's soldier-servant, Private Andrews, took two bullets trying to direct the digging operations. Ensign Haig wriggled on his belly through a small opening. Others soon followed, "and pursued the sepoys from one lavishly-decorated room to another". When the insurgents ran into the river, Wolseley and his men "had capital practice" firing at them in the water. This action was interrupted by a loud explosion near the west wall of the courtyard. Through the dust stepped Captain Tingling of the Lucknow garrison, who had just detonated a mine. Hands were clasped and Wolseley "had won the distinction of being the first of Sir Colin's army to reach the beleaguered garrison".[74]

Only open ground between the Engine House and the Moti Mahal Palace now separated the two British forces, but bullets spat everywhere from muskets in the Kaisarbagh and the big rebel guns situated at the Badshahbagh across the river still roared out death.

The first man over from the Residency side was the intrepid Captain Moorsom. He returned with two officers and with the enemy fire slackening, Outram, Havelock and their respective staff reached the Moti Mahal. The relieving soldiers flocked around Havelock and gave him three cheers. "This was too much for the fine old General," wrote an eye-witness, "his breast heaved with emotion and his eyes filled with tears." He turned to the men and said, "Soldiers, I am happy to see you; soldiers, I am happy to think you have got into this place with a smaller loss than I had." A little taken aback, "tall and gaunt" Hope Grant asked Havelock what he thought their loss amounted to. He estimated 80 dead and wounded, "and was much surprised and grieved when I told him we had lost 43 officers and 450 men killed and wounded."[75]

The group of officers threaded their way to the Mess House to meet Sir Colin Campbell. During this short trek a shell bounced off a wall and burst near Havelock. He was thrown down by the concussion but otherwise unhurt. The distance was only 75 feet, but four staff officers including Colonel Napier and Harry Havelock, Brigadier Russell and Lieutenant Sitwell were all wounded running this gauntlet of fire.

Yet the meeting on the sloping ground just outside the Mess House was a happy affair. Everyone shook hands enthusiastically and there were smiles all around. Raising his cap, Campbell said, "How do you do, Sir James?" Then he turned to Havelock with the words, "And how do you do, *Sir* Henry?" This was the astonishing news for Havelock that a grateful Parliament and people had made him a baronet in September. A faint smile fell over the old man's face. An enfilade of cheering now began and was taken up in succession all along the line, "until it sounded like a faint echo."[76]

The worst of the fighting seemed over – or was it? Sir Colin knew that besides a grisly butcher's bill he had over 1,000 sick and wounded as well as around 500 women and children now in his care in a city full of revengeful and active rebels who were not even cowed. Getting his army and the civilians out of Lucknow could prove a nightmare and every minute counted if they were all to be got to Cawnpore. Ominously, he had gotten precious little news from General Windham, and did not know if the Gwalior rebels had fallen on that city. If the bridge across the Ganges had been destroyed or taken by rebels, then the whole operation could still end in the biggest defeat in the Empire's history.

8

Windham Takes a Gamble

Lucknow and Cawnpore,
17ᵗʰ November–6ᵗʰ December 1857

Sir Colin Campbell was desperate to evacuate the Lucknow garrison. Immediately. If not at once, then within 24 hours. Inglis, Outram and others had to convince him that the malnourished, unkempt and lice-ridden men, women and children needed one more day to prepare themselves for departure, while the insurgents had to be cowed and hoodwinked. When Thomas Kavanagh introduced him to Outram the old soldier dismounted, shook the bayard's hand and then said, "Are you prepared, Sir James, to quit the Residency in two hours? Time is precious." A startled Outram replied, "It is impossible, Sir Colin." "Nothing is impossible, sir!" snapped Campbell. "If you will permit me to explain the reasons for considering it impracticable," replied Outram, " you will, Sir Colin, be well satisfied that it cannot be done."[1]

One week earlier the C-in-C had written to Outram stating bluntly that on arrival, "I shall blow up the Residency." He continued:

> My communications are threatened from Calpee, where the Gwalior Contingent, with forty guns must be dealt with. You must make your arrangements for getting every one clear of the Residency when I am able to give the order, abandoning baggage, destroying guns, but saving the treasure. Until the wounded and women are in my camp, the real business of the contest cannot go on, and all the efforts of Government are paralysed.[2]

On the 18ᵗʰ Outram now suggested that the Kaisarbagh should be stormed and taken, after which "two strong brigades of 600 men" would be enough to hold the city. Campbell would have none of it; he argued that he needed the same number of men just to hold open his line of communications with the Alambagh, and that really Outram's plan required four brigades. Sir Colin had from the start been critical of the whole military position at Lucknow, which he thought a false one; he felt that Sir Henry Lawrence should never have tried to hold the Residency in the first place, "and after becoming acquainted with the ground, and working my troops upon it to relieve the garrison, that opinion is confirmed." He held that a "strong moveable division outside the town, with heavy and field artillery in a good military position, is the real manner of holding Lucknow in check."[3] He also fretted about the poor communications in the North-West Provinces, since he needed to be able to communicate with different places and various officials if he was to fall back on Cawnpore, "the key of all future operations".

Outram did not give up easily; he argued that such a major withdrawal – even allowing for a good-sized token garrison retained at the Alambagh – would send a bad signal to the wavering taluqdars of Oudh. Many of these landowners, now in despair, would throw in their forces with the rebels. Most of the staff agreed with Outram who was, after all, the senior political officer, a man with considerable knowledge of Oudh, but Sir Colin would not be budged. He decided to leave the final decision to Lord Canning in Calcutta. The Governor-General on 20th November fell in with his C-in-C's wishes: "The one step to be avoided is the total withdrawal of the British forces from Oudh. Your proposal to leave a strong moveable division with heavy artillery outside the city, and so to hold the city in check, will answer every purpose of policy."[4]

So the die was cast; withdrawal it would be, though as things turned out, Outram's worst fears about the taluqdars proved true. Yet Campbell was faced with a difficult task and the decision had to be his alone. Only many years later could a participant, Frederick Roberts, write: "The Chief was right … every man was on duty night and day; there was no reserve to fall back upon… The wisdom of his decision was fully proved by subsequent events, and unreserverdly acknowledged by Hope Grant and others who at the time differed from him in their ideas."[5]

In those first hours of Campbell's arrival there were reunions, happiness and surprises for many. The *Shannon's* Naval Brigade men were a curiosity to most of the garrison, women tending to pet them like exotic creatures in a zoo. Captain Garnet Wolseley took a keg of rum to his old comrades of the 90th. He found some fellows sitting in a summer house but recognised no one and was just on the point of leaving when someone shouted, "Why, it's Wolseley!" Then he realised that the unshaven, gaunt and bedraggled soldiers were his old friends. A different kind of surprise awaited army surgeon Frederick Dalziel, who ran into a

Mr Mackay among the garrison; he had last seen him 17 years earlier in Edinburgh where Mackay had been his Latin master at school.

The state of the half-starved garrison shocked many of the relieving force; when someone offered Mr Rees a small orange he danced a jig in delight and brought tears to the eyes of some of the watching Highlanders. Now the children's faces could glow to see real comforts – bread, butter and some fruit, while their parents could enjoy tea with milk, a tot of rum or read a newspaper from home – the first news of the outside world for many of them in almost six months. Mr Rees, besides his orange, was delighted to get a letter of credit from his bank in the mail and find that he was no longer penniless. One little girl, eyes gleaming, rushed up to her mother after seeing a trestle table laden with food and cried, "Mama, there is a loaf of bread on the table, I'm certain of it!"[6]

Despite his problems Sir Colin was charm personified to the women, tender as a father to his sick, and joked with and chafed his officers, even making up with Wolseley over his attack on the Moti Mahal Palace and promising him promotion. The man who suffered his stern ire was Martin Gubbins, at whose house he was invited to dine on the first night. The C-in-C's eyes flashed when he saw the table laden with "meat, vegetables, truffled sausages and champagne". Curtly and clearly he told Gubbins in front of the guests, "How is it, Mr Gubbins, these things were not given to the starving garrison?" Then, arms folded, he sulked and "sat grimly throughout the meal, refusing so much as a crumb".[7]

Lieutenant Robert Inglis heard the news that an evacuation was planned and found it to be "incredible". It seemed strange that "after holding the place so long and after so much blood has been spilt, we have to leave it. It seems a tacit acknowledgement that we are licked." He was on duty on 18th November at the Baillie Guard Gate to prevent members of the old garrison wandering into the new camp. Few ordinary soldiers came the other way, "just a few individuals, orderlies & a few seamen", though several officers rode over to see the see the ruined Residency and defences. He thought it delightful to see new faces "and the sight of an officer of the 93rd Highlanders in kilts, and of a naval officer is quite refreshing... It reminded me of old times to see officers ruffed out in full tog lumbering about ... and horses, how different from the miserable half-starved animals we have in here, hardly able to carry themselves."[8]

Throughout the night of the 17th the rebels did not cease their artillery fire. Shells rained down especially hard on the barracks occupied by the Highlanders. Brigadier Russell sent word to Sir Colin that he needed heavy guns to silence the enemy and so next day, while stunned men, women and children took in the news of their evacuation, the fighting continued. It was a day not without its tragedies for the British and success for the rebels. A 9-pounder shot wounded Russell. Colonel G. Biddulph, D.Q.M.G., took over and was preparing a storming party when a bullet passed through the hat of Colonel E. B. Hale, 82nd Foot, smashed into Biddulph's brain and killed him stone dead. Hale now took over and bravely led an attack on the hospital, which was carried after some stiff fighting, but the thatched roof had been set alight, and the fire forced the British to withdraw to their original position. Emboldened by their success, the insurgents made an attack on the centre line of British pickets, but this time Sir Colin decided to personally take charge of the operations; he successfully sent forward men of HM 23rd and 53rd Foot as Captain Remington's troop of horse artillery dashed forward and fired on the rebels at point-blank range.

These attacks convinced the C-in-C that a retreat via the main road leading from the Sikanderbagh to the Dilkusha was out of the question; an early reconnaissance on the 19th showed that the country roads leading towards the canal from the back of the bungalows on his left rear were good enough for the transit of heavy guns and wagons. He decided to use these paths for the main withdrawal while Ewart's 93rd Highlanders held the barracks and Colonels Hale and Wells the bungalows until the women and children were away. A protected walkway known as a "flying sap" had been constructed by the engineers to screen the women and children from the fire of the Kaisarbagh as they crossed the open ground between the Engine House and Moti Mahal Palace. Midshipman Lord Arthur Clinton was given a naval gun by Captain Peel and told to position himself on the road between the Sikanderbagh and Moti Mahal in order to return fire if the rebels tried a bombardment.

Many of the women had been "thunderstruck" when word came that the evacuation would start on the night of the 18th and that no one could take more than a small bundle. Departure was delayed one more day to the 19th and Maria Germon prepared for it like many other women:

I dressed in all the clothes I could, fearing I might not be able to get the others carried on from the Secundarbagh. I put on four flannel waistcoats, three pairs of stockings, three chemises, three drawers, one flannel and four white petticoats, my pink flannel dressing-gown skirt, plaid jacket and over all my cloth dress and jacket ... then tied my Cashmere shawl sash-fashion round my waist and also Charlie's silver mug and put on a worsted cap and hat... I forgot to say that I had sewed dear Mother's fish-knife and fork in my pink skirt and I had a lot of things in the pocket of it. I had also two under-pockets, one filled with jewellery and cardcase, the other with my journal and valuable papers. I then filled my cloth skirt pocket with pencil, knife, pin-cushion, handkerchief etc... At half past ten Charlie and Captain Weston, with great difficulty, got me up on my pony which was no joke dressed and laden as I was, and were in fits of laughter.[9]

In those last hours everyone had things to do; Mrs Polehampton had a headstone carved for her husband's grave by a stonecutter she found in the ranks of the 90th and Mrs Barbor made a little sketch of the churchyard as a keepsake. The chaplain's wife filled her pockets with Henry's sermons and sewed his gown, hood and stole, together with her dead baby's clothes, into a pillow.

Soldiers had less to carry or think about; Lieutenant Inglis found his old knapsack and inside his toothbrush, knife, fork and spoon. "This in case of moving I was determined to carry on my back,"[10] he wrote in a letter to his mother. It became apparent late on the 18th that more baggage could be taken after all. Mrs Polehampton now decided to transport the harmonium that had been presented to her husband by men of the 32nd. The creaking carts also conveyed jewels and valuables belonging to the ex-royal family, 25 lakhs of treasure, stores of all kinds including grain and a large number of obsolete guns.

When the exodus began at 10am on the 19th, some women and children rode in hackeries, others on ponies, the less able in doolies or on foot with a camel provided for each family's belongings. Mrs Boileau was one of the first to set out to cries of "God bless you mum!" from soldiers. The women looked forlorn and gaunt, the children much cheerier. The kindness of the soldiers was surprising to many, even overwhelming; Mrs Brydon was met at the Sikanderbagh by a ranker who offered her a biscuit while another proffered some fresh bread. Mrs Case, wife of the dead colonel of the 32nd, filled her carriage with gleeful children while she and Lady Inglis walked escorted by the major-general's aide, Lieutenant F. W. Birch. Chaplain Harris and his wife rode in a carriage drawn by a pair of half-starved ponies who were so unused to walking that they stopped every five minutes, usually in exposed places, forcing the couple to get out and take cover. Sir Colin watched all the "dear creatures" arrive at the Sikanderbagh where he and his staff handed out wine, tea, biscuits and bread and butter. Some of the ladies noticed that the place had a bad smell from the hundreds of bloated corpses that had been collected and walled up inside the building.

Sir Colin seemed that day in remarkable spirits. When a Highlander of HM 93rd asked him if he could help an English nanny with a child, Sir Colin said, "Is she pretty, man?" When the soldier gave an evasive answer, Campbell repeated the question, "For I thought if she were pretty you would be all the better pleased to help," he said with a grin.

The Highlander, a stern Bible-reading Scot, shook his head and replied, "There you are, Sir Colin, at your old nonsense again!"[11]

Surgeon Collins of HM 5th Fusiliers thought some of the women such as Mrs Germon, now rotund and puffing under the weight of layers of clothes, looked silly. He much preferred the children who were enjoying their first taste of freedom in months. The exodus was, he noted, ""a chaotic and struggling mess".

Harry Havelock, who had been wounded again, looked in on his father before departing. The old general smiled, laid down a copy of Macaulay he was reading in the dim light, and said softly, "My poor boy!" The general's aide, William Hargood, walked by Harry's horse all the way, "against all my protestations", sleeping on the cold ground until daybreak, and then riding back to tell the general that his son was safe.

From the Sikanderbagh and under cover of darkness the column made its way towards the Dilkusha park. This was a nightmare journey for many; people and animals wandered all over the place, firing could be heard in the distance, all was confusion. Katherine Bartrum, now a widow in black after her husband's death two months previously, set off in a doolie about 11pm with her son Bobbie. After some time she became aware that she could hear no other sounds but the tramping feet of her bearers. Looking out from the litter's curtains she saw that they were on an open plain. When questioned, her bearers simply shrugged their shoulders and one said they were lost. Terror gripped Katherine. Then she heard voices. These turned out to be some lost British soldiers, one of whom cried hysterically, "Oh God! It's all up with us! We're done for now!" Somehow at 3am they reached the Dilkusha by accident. Katherine wanted to sit down and cry, but an officer took her a large tent full of others, gave her a cup of tea, some milk for Bobbie, and told them to try and sleep.

Maria Germon remembered the journey as "miles and hours of confusion that night and all in pitch darkness, for even when Mrs Barwell had a candle lighted thinking her baby was dying (its breath having been caught by the cold air) it was ordered to be put out immediately on account of the number of ammunition waggons."[12] Mrs Case and Lady Inglis had more luck than most; Major Ouvry, 9th Lancers, got them a bullock cart into which they squeezed for the bumpy journey with two other ladies and four children. Lieutenant Huxham who, earlier in the siege, had been badly injured, tried to go the distance on his crutches. At the Dilkusha a friendly commissariat officer gave him and his wife a tent, but soon others were begging admittance. "We could not refuse," wrote Mrs Huxham, "so poor George had to lie down between the two walls of canvas and the exposure, owing to the delicate state of his health, affected his lungs, and was the cause of serious illness."[13]

After that awful night dawn offered a chance to relax, chat with friends and strangers – and eat! HM 9th Lancers gave the ladies and children a breakfast such as they had not had in ages – cold beef and mutton, tea with milk and sugar, biscuits and jam, freshly baked bread with butter. The camp was a sprawling jumble but, as they munched away, the Lucknow defenders hardly cared.

Campbell's next step was to cow the insurgents. On 20th November Peel's naval guns opened up on the Kaisarbagh. Relentlessly they pounded the palace's walls, and by the 22nd it was clear that there were now three breaches. With the rebels preparing for an onslaught, Sir Colin sent Outram instructions to evacuate the Residency at midnight. Remaining enemy shot was dropped down the wells. Engineers began bursting the large arsenal of captured native guns. Many of the defenders were unhappy to be leaving and "unutterably disquieted" by the way in which Campbell had behaved, "treating us all in the most unfeeling way".[14]

Just after 11pm the 14 garrisons around the Residency were withdrawn from their outposts. Captain Peel kept up his cannonade until the last minute. In the darkness the sight was impressive, "shells perpetually flying through the air", wrote Lieutenant Hall, Madras Fusiliers. As the clock struck twelve the "illustrious garrison" marched out as silently as possible through the Baillie Guard Gate under the watchful eyes of Inglis and Outram. The brigadier was not by nature an emotional man, but he knew the moment was historic; he had commanded through the most perilous days of the siege, seen many friends die, fought in countless actions and, indeed, been connected with the defence of the Lucknow Residency since before the Great Uprising had even begun. To his credit, John Inglis had even asked Campbell if he might be permitted to remain with one regiment and keep the flag flying, but Sir Colin turned the offer down as absurd. An aide now saluted. "All have passed, sir." Outram waved his hand for Inglis to proceed him, but the brigadier stood as rigid as Cornish rock. "You will allow me, Sir James, to be the last and to shut the gates of my old garrison?" Outram nodded and Inglis closed the gates. The two officers shook hands and walked off down the incline together.

Staff officers then jostled one another in a schoolboy-type scuffle to see who would be the last. This game ended up with Captain Wilson rolling down the hill and Lieutenant Birch having the honour of being the last to leave – or so he thought – but that night an exhausted Captain Waterman, 13th B.N.I., had fallen asleep somewhere and not been woken by his busy comrades. At about 2am he snapped awake with the awful realisation that he was left behind. He ran to the posts but no one was there and quite alone set off through the dark streets to try and catch up. It must have been a harrowing experience and, as Birch wrote, Waterman eventually found the British army but "the fright sent him off his head for a time."[15] According to Forbes-Mitchell, another dawdler was Sergeant Alex Macpherson of HM 93rd who also woke up late in the barracks and had to catch up with the rest. He was forever after known as "Sleepy Sandy".

Silently, the soldiers filed along, "so bedraggled and strangely dressed". Dr Gilbert Hadow, formerly surgeon of the 5th Oudh Irregular Cavalry, was wearing his hair "in elf locks" and "thirty yards of muslin in the shape of a turban for a hat, a dark flannel shirt with red spots, a shooting coat several sizes too large, a pair of private's regimental trousers, and a great pair of ammunition boots".[16]

Commissioner Martin Gubbins recalled his journey to safety:

> We have now left our defences, and glance up to the right towards the Kaisar Bagh, to see if the enemy is visible. No, all is still, and not a shot is fired. The high road is reached – now the Sekunder Bagh is passed, and we halted for some time in the sandy lane. Again, we move on, and emerge into the open country. It is bitterly cold, and we are again halted for half an hour, without being able to discover why. And now we move in the Martinière Park, and halt again; we know our way, why longer tarry with the military, who seem to be taking up their positions for to-morrow? Come along – we strike off to the left and soon hit the direct road to the Dilkoosha, and turn down it. Who comes there? Friends! Has the garrison left? It has and we are part of it. Good night! We pass on, and in a few minutes reach the camp.[17]

A soldier's experiences were recorded by Lieutenant Hall, 1st Madras Fusiliers:

> We were all bitterly disappointed at having to evacuate Lucknow, but there was no help for it & we were the last to go. At 12'o'clock the order to turn out was given in a whisper & the men fell in, in deep silence. Not a round shot was heard, not a bayonet clashed & we filed out without a word of command. We found the rest of our force (Outram) covering the rear & marched along in the dark. We passed the Secundra Bagh as we knew of the smell which was something fearful & then past the 9th Lancers. There they sat like statues. It is impossible to believe horses could be so still, not a sound was heard, not a movement to be seen. I never was more struck with the perfection in which drill, discipline and training can be carried out than I was on that night.[18]

At last Hall reached the Martinière and was grateful to sleep on some straw in the cold open air. Next morning, while chatting with some comrades, he saw a cloud of smoke and ran over to discover the charred remains of three private soldiers. It turned out that one of them had knocked out the ashes of his pipe on some sacks of gunpowder. That day Hall moved on to the Dilkusha and enjoyed his first beer in months.

One of the those on guard was Lieutenant George Cracklow, Bengal Artillery: "I think the most unpleasant night I have spent since the whole affair commenced was this one – waiting, waiting, waiting for the guns to come out... Old Sir Colin was walking up and down the road by the guns in a dreadful fidgety state." At last, around 2am, the artillery began to pass. Cracklow had been waiting patiently since sunset and was very tired. Then he had to wait another hour, "to give them a good start on the road... All luckily went well and about half past 4 I got the order to retire my guns."[19]

Once the Residency compound seemed empty, Colonel Hale's troops, holding buildings to the left of the line of retreat, peeled back towards the Dilkusha. "Each exterior line came gradually retiring through its supports, till at length nothing remained but the last line of infantry and guns," reported Sir Colin, "with which I was myself to rush the enemy if they had dared to follow up the picquets."[20] The honour of rearguard was given by Outram to HM 78th Highlanders because they had led the advance into Lucknow under Havelock. Campbell remained on his horse near the Sikanderbagh with 15 guns pointed up the road to cover the retreat. Once he was satisfied all was well, he set off towards the Martinière. "Well, young man, what's your opinion of the move?" Sir Colin asked Lieutenant Gordon-Alexander as they prepared to bivouac for the night. "I don't understand it, sir," said the always outspoken officer, "It looks as we are running away." "Of course we are!" the C-in-C replied, "But *il faut reculer pour mieux sauter* (you have to step back to jump further)."[21]

On 23rd November the C-in-C issued a General Order thanking his soldiers for all they had done. He congratulated them on their endurance and patience, reminded them of their achievements during the previous six days of fighting and declared that he had never seen men fight better. The rescue of the garrison had been "a model of discipline and exactness" that had fooled a city packed with foes.

Before the troops could feel a glow of self-congratulation came a note of sadness. General Havelock, his body worn out by toil and sickness, went to meet his Maker. On the 20th the old man had suffered some diarrhoea. Dr Collinson, his staff surgeon, administered medicine that seemed to alleviate the trouble, but that night Havelock began passing blood. Next day, as Peel's guns boomed out, he grew weaker. It was decided to move him where the air was better, but this entailed a jolting journey in a doolie that swayed over the four miles of rough ground. Here Harry met his father by the light of flaming torches, "faint and moving with difficulty, but still able to stand with assistance".

An ordinary soldier's tent was all that could be found for Sir Henry. Harry and William Hargood sat nearby in case he needed anything. On the morning of 22nd November he seemed quite cheery, but upset Harry by saying that he knew he was dying. Mail arrived that day and Havelock was delighted to hear all the news from his devoted Hannah, and relatives in England. Hope Grant, another God-fearing man, visited him and found the old soldier on "a miserable doolie under some trees" where Sir Henry said: "The hand of death is upon me. God Almighty has seen fit to afflict me for some good purpose."[22]

That night he could not sleep. Harry and Hargood continued their vigil. Next morning Dr Collinson in consultation with Dr Fayrer agreed that Havelock was close to death. His acute dysentery worsened. Various friends stopped by the tent including his old staff. He was heard to repeat the words, "I die contented." The most poignant meeting happened on the early evening of the 23rd when Outram came. Sir James later wrote that his old comrade met him with a "tenderness like that of a brother. He told me he was dying ... looked back to our past intercourse and service together, which had never been on a single occasion marred by a disagreement of any kind, nor embittered by a single word."[23] Sir Henry told Outram that for 40 years he had ruled his life so that "when death came I might meet it without fear." Next dawn, and in a weak voice, Sir Henry called out for his son. Harry ran to the bedside and saw his father smiling at him. "Harry, see how a Christian can die,"[24] he said. They were his last words. As the troops outside bustled and ate breakfast, and the parakeets in the trees began their daily chattering, Havelock went to his God, cradled gently in his son's arms while he and Hargood wept. "His end was so peaceful," wrote Harry, "that I hardly knew when life was extinct."[25] It was 9.30am, 24th November, 1857.

The frail little body that had seen action in countless battles was buried in the garden of the Alambagh while every member of the army and every civilian felt "sorrow and consternation". It was a short no-frills ceremony, the kind Havelock himself liked (it was pleasing to think of him looking down from Heaven and making one of his sermon-speeches), the Last Post was played, then the grave levelled by Baggage Master Hall to prevent it being desecrated by rebels. It was difficult for Harry Havelock to move on; he said his own private farewell by the grave, then carved into the fleshy trunk of a mango tree nearby the letter "H".

On the 24th and with everyone now gathered in a higgledy-piggledy mess at the Dilkusha, Campbell sent on his civilians and most of the wounded to the Alambagh. Trying to make order out of chaos that day was Lieutenant Fred Roberts:

> My time was chiefly occupied in assisting in the distribution of transport, and in carrying out Hope Grant's directions as to the order in which the troops were to march. Round the Dilkusha the scene of confusion was bewildering in the extreme; women, children, sick and wounded men, elephants, camels, bullocks and bullock carts, grasscutters' ponies and doolies with their innumerable bearers, all crowded together. To marshal these incongruous elements and get them started seemed at first to be a hopeless task. At last the families got off in two bodies, each under a married officer whose wife was one of the party, and through whom all possible arrangements for their comfort were to be made, and their place on the line of march, position in camp, etc., determined.[26]

"Never, I believe, was such a scene," recalled Mrs Germon, "the whole army marched excepting a few to keep the Dil Koosha for a short time. One thousand sick were taken in doolies and 467 women and children in any kind of conveyance that could be got for them."[27] The women grumbled yet insisted on trying to convey their heavy loads: Mrs Brydon took her large harp, while Mrs Polehampton had indeed found a conveyance for her late husband's beloved harmonium. Georgina Harris felt inclined to "lie down and die" from exhaustion and fatigue, "only it seemed ungrateful and wrong to grumble now at any hardships after our merciful preservation."[28] Despite having no bedding and losing her ponies, she slept very soundly that first night at the Alambagh on the ground.

On the 26th, the C-in-C spelled out to the Governor-General the current situation: he would march on the morrow for Cawnpore taking with him most of the old Residency defenders, most especially the women and children. Outram was to be left in command at the Alambagh with 4,000 men and 22 guns, "of which four were heavy, besides ten mortars," with one month's supplies and plenty of ammunition. He thought Sir James's position "a good one".

Sir Colin Campbell, the "Crawling Camel" who hated to see men's lives wasted and refused ever to rush his plans, had achieved a victory forgotten by most but none the less remarkable. One of the few survivors of the disastrous British retreat from Kabul in 1842, Major Vincent Eyre, wrote: "The removal of some 600 women and children and 1000 wounded and sick, without a single accident or loss, in the face of a besieging enemy four times his own in numerical strength, and their safe transfer to Cawnpore, was a feat far more difficult in warfare than the defeat of an enemy in the field."[29] Garnet Wolseley, not a soldier to bestow praise lightly, later called it "the best piece of staff work I have ever seen."[30]

With the British now evacuated, there was much talk among all ranks about whether Havelock and Outram had mishandled their so-called "relief". Frederick Roberts wrote to his mother that Outram "is no soldier, and I should say no politician. The whole business from Cawnpore to Lucknow, for which he and poor Havelock got so much praise, was simply disgraceful. Nearly all their wounded were left in the streets and cut up ... they brought no provisions, were but an encumbrance to the garrison."[31] It was a debate that would rumble on among old campaigners for many years.

At 11am on the 27th the troops set out for Cawnpore. The men had rested in the preceding few days and busy officers like Roberts had been able to have their first bath in weeks and a change of clothes. He recalled the odd procession:

> Everything in the shape of wheeled carriage and laden animals had to keep to the road, which was narrow and for the greater part of the way raised, for the country at that time of the year was partly under water... Delays were constant and unavoidable ... country carts innocent of springs must have been most trying to delicate women and wounded men. Fortunately there was no rain; but the sun was still hot in the daytime, causing greater sensitiveness to the bitter cold at night.[32]

The narrow road was described by one officer as "like a railway embankment" with the cavalry, their horses, the marching infantry, snorting elephants and langorous camels "making their way as best they could" on either side, sometimes encountering ponds and swampy ground. On the road itself the dust rose high in clouds. ""We moved along at a foot's pace and had several stoppages,"[33] recalled Julia Inglis. Dr Fayrer thought they were very lucky not to be attacked and nervously saw enemy cavalry "hovering about in the distance".

They made a first camp two miles beyond Bunnee Bridge where the road crossed the Sye River. Then, as Campbell reported, "We were surprised to hear very heavy firing in the direction of Cawnpore. No news had reached me from that place for several days."[34] It was now apparent that the C-in-C's worst fears had been realised; the Gwalior Contingent had reached Cawnpore and battle had commenced. If the rebels had the luck or foresight to destroy the bridge of boats over the Ganges then the exodus was most likely doomed. If the insurgents defeated the small garrison stationed at Cawnpore, then besides their deaths and the shock of such a defeat, Sir Colin would face a huge rebel army and a pitched battle. As he rode along to the distant sound of a cannonade the C-in-C must have pondered on the qualities of the man he had left in command at Cawnpore, an officer of whom he was not overly fond, a man with a reputation for disobeying orders.

Charles Ash Windham was 47 years old, a short man with a round, cheery face and a full bushy black beard. He was not, in fact, a Windham at all, being the fifth son of Vice-Admiral William Lukin, but had changed his name in 1824 when his father inherited the Windham estates, principally Felbrigg Hall in North Norfolk where Charles had been born. He had been a soldier for most of his life, being packed off to the Royal Military College, Sandhurst, at the tender age of thirteen. His army progress had been slow, hampered for some years by lack of money, but a successful marriage to a wealthy young woman allowed him, in 1854, to purchase a lieutenant-colonelcy. Then when war with Russia broke out, he was lucky enough to be made A.Q.M.G. of the 4th Division. The Crimea was his first taste of war. He displayed great courage and tenacity in the battles at Sebastopol, so much so that by 1857 he was known throughout the army as "Redan Windham".

Charles had many good qualities: he was loyal to his friends; a loving husband and an over-indulgent father who adored his children. He was undoubtedly brave and never blamed his troops, believing implicitly that officers should lead from the front. Most people found him charming, "never hard upon others, in word or deed, and always inclined to make allowances for human feelings."[35]

Windham was also too enamoured of his own talents. He might have stayed in England since he had just been elected Liberal M.P. for East Norfolk, but he responded to the call of duty when asked to go out to India that summer. On board ship, Charles was heard declaring that "he was going to take Delhi in 10 days, put the army on a new footing and ignite India in six weeks."[36] Bar room talk probably, but the press having vaunted his talents, Windham was conceited enough to believe the hype and his mistake in underestimating his rival native general would sully his reputation ever after.

When Major-General Windham arrived at Calcutta in August, he assumed he was to command the Sirhind Division. Two weeks later he was still in the capital and was telling anyone who would listen that the mutineers would flee before the British reached Lucknow. Both Canning and Campbell were cordial to him and it was with some surprise that he received instructions in late October to proceed to Cawnpore. "I arrived here quite safely last night, "he wrote to his wife on 4th November, "having escaped without even seeing a single mutineer until this morning." With his usual optimism he declared: "Upon the whole things are looking much up – the Enemy have been beaten in every encounter and from the number that have surrendered, they are evidently giving up the cause as lost."[37]

Five days later, Windham wrote again to say that Sir Colin had decided to leave him at Cawnpore with 500 men and nine guns while he marched to Lucknow. He was intelligent enough to realise the seriousness of his situation – the Gwalior rebels were led by Tantia Tope, the best Indian general, and believed to number 10,000 men with seven batteries, a large siege train and plenty of ammunition. For a few miles in the direction of Lucknow the two generals rode together chatting things over. Campbell had given Windham little freedom of movement; he was ordered to place his troops in the new entrenchments and small fort by the river and not to attack the enemy unless by doing so he could prevent a bombardment of his trenches. He was further ordered to forward with all haste detachments of infantry marching up country and not to detain those troops even if threatened without first getting new instructions from the C-in-C.

With his usual energy, Windham set to work; he was in fine spirits (prickly heat that had dogged him earlier had abated) and he wrote to his wife seven days after Campbell's departure:

> I am working very hard in improving the fortifications of the town and in two days they will be so strong as to defy any of the sepoy armies of the neighbourhood... Sir Colin has sent me a great complimentary letter regarding my manner of hurrying forward troops to the front. I am in excellent health – work always suits me. I am up every morning at or before 5 writing and working all day and to bed about 10.[38]

Cawnpore was Windham's first independent command. He was determined to make a success of it, but he also did not like his independence being circumscribed. Orders were, however, orders, even when irksome. He began demolishing houses within a broad parameter of the entrenchments. Groves of nearby banyan and mango trees were slashed back to the stumps. On 15th November came fresh orders from Sir William Mansfield, Campbell's Chief of Staff, allowing him to "halt at Cawnpore until further orders" all new detachments of troops. Day by day, Windham's little force thus grew; he had a Madras Brigade commanded by Brigadier Carthew with a wing of the 27th, four

9-pounders manned by natives and two more manned by Europeans; driblets of companies arrived composed of HM 34th, 82nd and 84th regiments, a few men of the Rifle Brigade and the entire 27th Madras Native Infantry. By 27th November, his original 500 men had swollen to 1,700 officers and men.

Facing Windham was Tantia Tope, "a stout, audacious and impatient man with a flat nose, pockmarked face, and a commanding gaze that burned beneath the smoky gray arches of his bristling eyebrows."[39] Spies kept him well informed of events at Cawnpore and Lucknow while his cavalry tracked Campbell's movements. Once the British commander entered Oudh, Tantia intelligently crossed the Jumna with thousands of men and soon occupied every town from Akbarpur to Sheorajpur, some 20 miles northwest of Cawnpore. Here the insurgents waited until news came that the British were fighting in the streets of Lucknow.

The Gwalior Contingent that formed the backbone of Tantia Tope's army had been created in 1844 following a treaty between Maharajah Scindia of Gwalior and the East India Company. Its expenses were met by Scindia, but its command was entirely in the hands of British officers. Over the years it expanded until in 1857 its cavalry numbered 1,658 sowars and the infantry 6,412 sepoys. The corps had 16 professionally trained native gunners and the whole body was effectively managed by Brigadier Ramsay. Everything changed on 15th June when the Gwalior troops mutinied. Some British officers and their families died, the rest fled to the safety of Agra Fort. The rebels begged Scindia to lead them, but he politely refused and, fearful of British repercussions (he did not want to lose his state like the rulers of Oudh or Jhansi), he did some desperate diplomatic fence-sitting. So it was that the insurgents threw away the maharajah's royal standard and decided to fight under new green and white flags. They gave their support to Tantia Tope who had helped destroy the cursed feringhees at Cawnpore.

It was not certain that the insurgents would attack Cawnpore; Sir Colin had held to the opinion it was more likely Tantia's army would cross over into Oudh, encouraging more and more local people to support them, until he faced a massive army. Yet it was also obvious that Windham's position was precarious, not helped by the fact that his fortification was really nothing more than "a mere *tete-du-pont* ... an enemy could easily approach it under cover, even with artillery, to within musket-range."[40]

When Windham heard a rumour on the 22nd that insurgents had seized the Bunnee bridge, he sent a wing of the 27th MNI to recover it. That day a letter arrived from Campbell requesting that ten days' provisions be sent on at once to Lucknow. This suggested to Windham that things might be going badly; in the previous three days he had gotten no despatches from Lucknow. Some historians have suggested that he was itching to put his troops into action, but we cannot be sure. What is certain is that after some thought he decided to disobey his orders and, as one of his biographers wrote, "throw instructions to the winds".

By 17th November, Windham had formulated a plan; he would take his troops along the canal and pounce at night on one or two villages held by the insurgents, then return to Cawnpore to repel any counter-attack. That day he forwarded his scheme to Campbell for approval, but due to a breakdown in communications, no answer was received and the plan fizzled out. While he was getting no response from the C-in-C, Windham kept up a stream of telegraphic messages to the Governor-General in Calcutta. At noon on the 21st he cabled: "The Gwalior force has certainly begun to cross the Jumna at Calpee, and preparations for further crossings are going on; six guns are said to be on this bank... No news this morning from Lucknow. Mr Devere of the Electric Telegraph Department, and two followers, murdered on the road between Alumbagh and Bunnee."[41] By the 25th he was writing: "Three thousand men from the Gwalior Contingent are at Sechunder, about six miles from my camp on the canal... I should think it quite possible that I may have to fight to-morrow or the next day... Not a word from Lucknow since the 19th."[42]

Exactly one week later, no word having been received from Lucknow, General Windham decided he must take the offensive. That morning he broke up his camp, leaving just four companies of HM 64th and a small force of artillery behind, and boldly marched six miles in a south-westerly direction close to a bridge where the Calpee road crossed the canal. Like a warrior accepting a thrown gauntlet, Tantia Tope immediately marched with a detachment from Akbarpur and halted on the right bank of the Pandu Naddi river three miles south-west of the British troops. Tope's 2,500 infantry and 500 cavalry poured some volleys at the British before being driven away. It was a short, sharp fight and at one point the rebel cavalry had charged the British line but been defeated by HM 34th Foot, who formed squares and hit the troopers with sustained volleys. Windham's action had resulted in the capture of three guns and some ammunition at a rather heavy cost of one officer and 13 men killed and 78 wounded. Back at camp the day was crowned with the good news at last from Lucknow that all had gone well there, and the army was about to set off for Cawnpore. Windham knew that all he had to do was hold out for two or so more days and his anxieties would be at an end.

Tempering his happiness was the realisation that the enemies he had beaten were just an advance guard of a far larger rebel army. Windham now went far beyond Campbell's instructions and moved most of his soldiers to a new camp near some brick kilns on the Calpee road, a spot he thought more defensible than the old one. There were several topes of tall trees nearby, but it was a reasonably wide and open space. He had written to General Mansfield about the matter and had received a reply by him (and *not* Sir Colin), in the Chief of Staff's vague kind of way: "I am not able to give an opinion on the military position."

Spies had alerted Tantia Tope to Campbell's departure from Lucknow and the rebel leader realised that it was time to strike hard. He suspected rightly that Windham was nervous and that the British had little or no information as to the actual size of his army, which amounted to about 14,000 soldiers including the Gwalior Contingent, another 11,000 irregulars and over 60 guns – fifteen times the number of British troops and ten times the number of artillery. Windham's intelligence on the rebels was almost non-existent. "The spies feared to venture out," wrote one of his staff, "several during the previous days had returned horribly maimed, with their arms, ears and noses cut off."[43]

About 10am on the 27th a cannonade began on the British right flank. Hurriedly, Windham sent Brigadier M. Carthew to supervise operations. Under him were HM 34th Foot under Lt-Colonel Kelly, a Madras battery under Lieutenant S.H. Chamier, and a portion of HM 82nd. Almost simultaneously a similar artillery fire began directly on the British centre front at the junction of the Delhi and Calpee roads, where it was met by some companies of the Rifle Brigade under Colonel Walpole, HM 88th Foot and four guns under Captain Greene R.A., along with two naval 24-pounders manned by *Shannon* sailors under Lieutenant Hay R.N. Two distinct battles were being fought with about 600 men apiece on the British side. The flank attack was met and well-resisted. "We knew they were coming and were prepared for them,"[44] wrote Chamier. For a time Windham watched these proceedings as he feared the flank attack was the easiest way for the rebels to reach the entrenchments. Satisfied all was going well, he then galloped over to his centre.

"Undisciplined" was how Captain John Oliver R.A. thought matters were:

> By some mistake the infantry never advanced until we had fired off half our ammunition, and the native drivers bolted with the rest... By this time we were attacked again on all sides by a very superior artillery force, and were completely outflanked – in fact, nearly

surrounded. We only had thirty cavalry, the Sepoys 600, who drove back our skirmishers, and the result was, we were obliged to retreat through Cawnpore to the entrenchment leaving our camp to be plundered. I believe that a message was brought to Wyndham that the entrenchment had been captured, and that he ordered a retreat. The mistake was found out five minutes after, but too late, as the infantry had already given way.[45]

What seems to have happened is that the rebel guns, superior in calibre and firepower, were blasting holes in the British centre ranks. As the soldiers ran out of ammunition, they started to retreat and the bullock-drivers followed them. Windham issued orders for his men to fall back on the brick kilns and sent HM 34th to reinforce the camp. He also ordered Carthew on the right to fall back on the kilns. It seems the brigadier thought this a false step and he did not immediately obey. Only after he was ordered a second time to fall back did he do so. "The order was a grave error," admitted Captain Drury, Carthew's brigade-major, "General Windham says he sent a countermand afterwards. That never came."[46]

Exploiting an enemy's weaknesses is a major task for a general; seeing the British in retreat, Tantia Tope ordered his sepoys forward, firing all the way. The British soldiers now became nervous, excited and confused. The village of Sesamhow on the the immediate right flank needed to be held to cover the withdrawal, but Lt-Colonel Robertson, HM 82nd Foot, "actually gave orders for the retreat of his own regiment and a portion of another in the very face of the orders of the General." (as Sir Colin later told the Duke of Cambridge), an action that was "pusillanimous and imbecile to the last degree".[47] By the time Carthew got to the brick kilns he found the tents had been removed, "while the heavy baggage lay strewn on the ground, the camels and elephants having been allowed to run away."[48]

Things went from bad to worse; after telling General Dupuis R.A. to hold the brick kilns, Windham galloped back towards the old entrenchment. Along the way he was stopped by a staff officer who told him that the insurgents now held the lower part of the city. Suddenly, up the Delhi-Allahabad road, as if summoned by the clarion of St Peter himself, marched a detachment of the 2nd battalion the Rifle Brigade. With unquestionable pluck, Windham took personal command of the new troops and drove the rebels out of a portion of the lower city.

Carthew was now ordered to return to the right – one suspects he must have thought Windham a fool to have ordered him away in the first place – with two companies of the 88th and four six pounders.

His objective was to hold the Cawnpore Theatre, about a quarter of a mile from the entrenchment, full of stores and clothing for the troops. At the point of the bayonet the brigadier gained the Birthur road, only to be met by rebel gunners who at once unlimbered and opened fire. They were silenced by Lieutenant Chamier's six-pounders.

By this time, the retreat of Windham's army had turned into a rout. Many of the soldiers were raw recruits who "disgraced their colours by rushing in panic to the entrenchment; broke open the stores; drank the wine intended for the sick; and smashed their officers' boxes in drunken fury."[49] Many men were cut to pieces, stores lost and, as darkness came on, the insurgents set fire to 500 British tents. The retreat threw into panic the whole neighbourhood, as one officer observed:

> From the native city came merchants with their families and treasure, seeking the protection of the fort; from the field, helter-skelter, in dire confusion, broken companies of English regiments, guns, sailors, soldiers, camels, elephants, bullock-hackeries with officers' baggage, all crowding at the gate for entrance. Ponderous and uncivil elephants bumped their unwieldy sides at the gate-posts; and good-humoured tars joked and chaffed freely upon the *status quo*.[50]

Chaplain Moore, whose brother, a captain in HM 32nd, had died at the Satichura Ghat massacre, wrote: "In the outside hospital, poor fellows whose legs were only amputated the night before sprang out of bed in agony of fear." Of the drunkenness, he concluded that "If the enemy had come on that night, I fancy that few men were sober enough to fight. The only exception I know was the 64th."[51]

Next morning the rebels launched a blistering attack on both sides of the city. "The rain of balls was thick enough to intercept sight," recalled an eye-witness, "and the thundering noise of the cannon did not rest even for a moment."[52] On the left Colonel Walpole and Brigadier Wilson had some success, but poor Carthew was in the thick of things on the right, which went badly. Tantia Tope had realised that the right was Windham's weak spot and he now exploited it. In the city streets insurgents scoured houses for any stragglers from Windham's army, and it was reported that two officers of HM 64th, possibly Lieutenants Gibbon and Mackinnon, were captured and with grim irony hanged from a banyan tree that Neill had once used as a gibbet. It was a day of constant fighting – Captain McCrea Q.M.G. fell dead defending the Bithur road, Major Stirling of the 64th died fighting hand-to-hand and old Brigadier Wilson pushed on his horse shouting, "Now, boys, you have them!" before a bullet burst open his lungs.

Carthew did his best to advance using Chamier's guns. The young lieutenant knew he was outgunned, his six-pounders little match for the enemy's 18-pounders. Carthew told him to limber and advance with 200 infantry in support. He did so but after 200 yards was hit by a withering fire. Once again Chamier seemed to silence his opponents, despite "some warm showers of grape". He then tried to get the infantry to charge, but they refused to do so. Retiring back to the bridge on the Allahabad road he held it all the rest of the day until night fell. "That evening, on the bridge," he wrote, "I had ten men wounded out of fifteen. The fire was terrific. Men who had been all through the Crimea said they were never in, nor even heard of such showers of bullets and grape. We had twelve or thirteen officers wounded out of our small party."[53]

"Please, Goodness, I hope never to see such a hailstorm of bullets again," wrote a gunner, "I saw men fall on every side of me … splinters hit me, pieces of earth from bullets etc., while a hurricane of balls passed through us."[54] Carthew was wounded. "The noise of the firing, the shouts and cries, were terrible," wrote Lieutenant Lewin of HM 34th, "I shall never forget that Bridge at Cawnpore as long as I live. The bullets whizzed past us as if the air was alive with them."[55]

Sitting upright on his horse, a brave and conspicuous target, Carthew was finally and reluctantly forced to pull back his troops, fearful that his whole brigade might be outflanked and cut off. There was little else he could have done except fight to the last man, but his action gave the insurgents command of the riverside, put the bridge of boats in jeopardy and enabled them to grab all the British stores at the theatre.

By this stage, men were talking openly of "Windham's mess". His generalship "had failed". The Victorian historian, Thomas Rice Holmes, castigated him: "He had already sent supports to Walpole, whose task was comparatively an unimportant one, and whose original force had proved amply sufficient. But to Carthew, who was sustaining the chief burden of the fight, with whose fortunes the fortunes of the entire army were bound up, he did not send a single man."[56] His initiative had resulted in the the deaths of 13 British officers with another 29 wounded and his total losses in killed and wounded amounted to some 350 soldiers. Windham openly admitted that his refusal earlier to move his baggage and stores to safety was a mistake of his own making. He also must be blamed for an overextended position, since "I thought it was my duty to hold as much of the town as I could."[57] Morale had fallen away. Windham had shown great personal courage but precious little generalship. A head cold had also taken away his voice, so that "when he desired to be especially empathetic, a wheezy earnestness was all that could be produced."[58]

The general may well have wondered when Sir Colin would show up. Once the C-in-C had heard the booming of the guns he rode in what he later described as "an agony of suspense". Horse artillery and cavalry rode with him. At some point a native ran out from under a hedge and handed him a letter dated 26th November from Windham saying Cawnpore was under attack. Sir Colin quickened his pace and at Mungulwar the ride became a gallop. Just before dark on the 28th he reached the Ganges and saw, to his great relief, that the bridge of boats was intact and still in British hands. For all Tantia Tope's acuity, his failure to destroy the bridge would now be his undoing.

Campbell looked across and saw Cawnpore in flames. A subaltern commanding a British picket on the Oudh bank got the shock of his life when the C-in-C galloped up with a small escort. Recognising the general, the lieutenant saluted and shouted out, "We are at our last gasp!" This melodramatic statement was all Sir Colin needed to release his frustrations; the officer got a furious tongue-lashing as the general pointed out in no uncertain terms that HM troops were *never* at their *last gasp*. Spurring on his horse over the creaking bridge he galloped into the fort and was immediately recognised by men of the Rifle Brigade. Quickly the word spread – the C-in-C is back!

Campbell quickly held a meeting with Windham and learned the true state of affairs. "I will not state the few words that I heard Sir Colin say to General Windham when they met," wrote bugler Thomas McKenzie, "but may say that he was very angry."[59] Campbell saw straightaway that an immediate British offensive was out of the question. Besides the low morale of Windham's frightened troops, his own army from Lucknow was full of weak and exhausted men who needed a few days rest. "Scarcely 300 out of 800 men were with the colours," wrote Surgeon Munro. The destruction of their kits left them very dejected and no chance to change their filthy threadbare clothes or even get a new pair of socks. Campbell wired Lord Canning that he needed greatcoats as fast as possible (and 3,000 of them were indeed sent from Allahabad by 6th December). Sir Colin's first priority had to be the women and children; his ten mile column had to be got into Cawnpore fort and also sent on down country as fast as possible.

Dawn on the 29th revealed the white tents of the British on the Oudh side of the river. Tantia Tope now brought his guns to bear on the bridge of boats, but Peel's heavy guns and all the British field batteries replied in unison. Both banks of the Ganges were wreathed in clouds of smoke as the artillery duel played out. It was the British who won. Then the advanced guard of Campbell's army marched across the bridge followed by the civilians. "The round-shot hissed with a vicious sound overhead and plunged sullenly into the river,"[60] recalled Surgeon Munro. "Until I am disencumbered of the women and wounded, 2,000 in number of helpless creatures," wrote Campbell, "I can hardly do anything more than stand still."[61]

"Several of them were dissatisfied at not being provided with better conveyances than covered carts," wrote Hope Grant, "but we had done our very best for them, and told them that they should be more satisfied – they should be thankful."[62]

A watching army chaplain named Mackay thought it a wondrous sight when he looked across the river at 5.30pm:

A procession of human beings, cattle and vehicles, six miles long, is coming up to the bridge of boats below the intrenched fort. It is about sunset. The variety of colour in the sky and on the plain, the bright costumes and black faces of the native servants, the long train of cavalry, infantry, women, children, sick, wounded, bearers, camp-followers, horses, oxen, camels, elephants, waggons, carts, palanquins, doolies, advancing along the road; and here, within the intrenchment, the crowds of camels and horses, the rows of cannon, heaps of shot, piles of furniture etc in the foreground, all seen between the pillars of this verandah, which is raised eight or ten feet from the ground, produce a very picturesque effect. But the groans of the poor fellows on charpoys (native beds), and on the floor behind and around me, dissolve the fascination of the scene.[63]

The gradual passage of all these people, animals and baggage took that night and until 6pm on 30th November. "We were several hours in crossing the wretched bridge," wrote Dr Fayrer, "more or less under fire the whole time and amidst the greatest confusion."[64] Reaching the fort was also far from pleasant; Julia Inglis wrote:"My feelings upon entering Cawnpore were indeed most painful. The moon was bright, and revealed to us the sad spectacle of ruined houses, trees cut down, or branches stripped off, everything reminding us of the horrors that had been enacted in the place and making us thoroughly miserable."[65]

A young subaltern, Thomas Lewin of the 34th, went to the hospital that evening to visit a friend who was dying with a ball in his liver. From another bed a man yelled, "For God's sake ask the doctor to do something for me! This is hell torment!" Lewin spoke to a busy surgeon who replied: "He'll be dead in half an hour. I can do nothing for him." Nearby lay another soldier shot through the chest. "As I stood beside him," wrote Lewin, "he said to the comrade who supported him, 'Give my love to my dear wife, Jack, and say' – here he raised his arm – 'say that I died for old England, and I'd do the same again.'"[66] In a gruesome letter to the London *Times* one young assistant surgeon told how on the "first day I amputated eight limbs, dressed more than 80 wounded men, scarcely knowing night from day... Three round shots passed through my hospital roof... All my clothes are spoilt with blood, my hair was matted with blood; my arms and hands covered. Blood spurted from arteries into my mouth and eyes... In one week I saw more surgery than many surgeons see in a lifetime."[67]

To relieve the pain a lucky doctor might have opium, laudanum, belladonna or chloroform at his disposal (Sir Henry Lawrence had been given chloroform at Lucknow), but most likely a man with a gunshot wound got a tot of brandy before surgery done without antiseptics. "During all my service in India, I never knew or heard of a case when a patient survived the amputation of a leg,"[68] wrote Lieutenant Gordon-Alexander.

It was a huge relief to Campbell when he was at last able to get the women, children and many of the sick off in a convoy to Allahabad. They left on the evening of 3rd December. Julia Inglis felt "wretched" having to say farewell to John, who walked a little way with her before she joined Mrs Case, her sister and the Inglis's children in a bullock cart and mule carriage. The civilians were escorted by "a wing of the 34th regiment, four guns and a few native cavalry", a token escort, but as Lady Inglis recorded, "the number of troops constantly passing up country made the road pretty safe."[69] The convoy reached Allahabad without incident on the afternoon of 7th December. Some days later, steamers took them down river to Calcutta where they were greeted by a royal salute and every ship in the river was decorated in bunting to welcome them – "15 poor widows, 20 wounded officers and 130 men," wrote Lady Canning. "The first widow walking on shore with her four little children was loudly cheered & so were they all."[70] In the capital some of the women at last found rest, feted as heroines before the inevitable sea voyage home to England; others still had personal tragedies to come, the loss of soldier husbands or children. But it seemed by the time they got to Calcutta that the worst was over; they had lived through an epic siege, stared death daily in the face for months, and somehow survived.

Within rebel-held parts of Cawnpore the insurgents grew more aggressive. Tantia Tope ordered that all Sikh women should be massacred. This act was quite deliberate, a provocation towards the Sikh soldiers fighting alongside the British – and more than a hundred innocents had their throats cut. Needless to say, perhaps, but it was another reason why during the rest of the war Sikhs fighting for the

British were especially ruthless and cruel to Hindu rebels, whom they called "poorbeah dogs".

Sir Colin was well aware that his inactivity would encourage Tantia Tope to grow bolder. It was a risk but a calculated one in the general's eyes, since he wanted the women and children away before he went on the offensive. "However disagreeable this may be, and although it may give confidence to the enemy, it is precisely one of those cases in which no risk may be run,"[71] he told his staff. The rebel attacks were wearying and continuous; on the 4th Tope even sent fireboats to burn down the bridge of boats, but the attack failed. Nor could he prevent more fresh troops arriving from Allahabad. During the shooting, one officer made *hors de combat* was Lt-Colonel Ewart of the 93rd; he was field officer of the day on 1st December and out visiting his pickets when a cannonball suddenly struck him on the left elbow, completely carrying away his arm:

> I was aware that I had been struck violently on the left side, but did not know what had actually taken place, until I looked down and saw the bleeding stump. The ball had also broken the handle of my revolver and smashed my field-glasses... The blow did not knock me down, nor did I feel any inclination to fall; but a soldier of the 93rd named Peter McKay ran up at once and tied his handkerchief tightly round the stump. I was placed in a doolie, and carried off to a bungalow which had been converted into a field hospital. Here I was immediately attended to by Dr Munro, the Surgeon of my regiment, who, after looking at the wound, cut (I think with a pair of scissors) the thin piece of skin by which the arm had been left hanging. He then said a further amputation would be necessary, but that I must keep quiet, as it would not be safe to perform the operation until I had recovered from the shock which my system had received. I begged him to go on then; but he said No... My entreaties at last prevailed, and in accordance with my wish I was carried off to the amputating table... Some chloroform was then administered... when I came to myself again, another piece of the arm was gone, and the wound had been nicely bandaged up.[72]

With men continuing to get injured like Ewart, there can be little surprise at Lieutenant Arthur Lang's words that "Sir Colin seems to have no dash and we are all grumbling at his want of pluck."[73]

By 6th December, however, Campbell at last felt the time was right to attack his enemy. He had amassed 5,000 infantry, 600 cavalry and 35 cannon. Against him Tantia Tope commanded about 25,000 men:

the Gwalior rebels along with mutinous levies, regular and irregular, serving Nana Sahib, with about 45 heavy guns. The insurgents held an area of great strength: their left flank was protected by the Ganges; their centre occupied most of Cawnpore where they had erected barricades in the narrow streets and lined the rooftops with marksmen. Their weak spot lay on the right where, on an open plain beyond the brick kilns, the Gwalior Contingent had their camp.

The groan of the bagpipes and a trumpet sounding reveille woke the soldiers next morning. At 7am the tents were struck and Campbell conferred with his leading officers: Greathed was given a brigade of HM 8th Foot and 2nd Punjab Native Infantry (PNI) and told to attack the enemy centre; Walpole had the 2nd and 3rd battalions of the Rifle Brigade, a detachment of the 38th and a battery of Royal Artillery, all tasked with preventing the rebels escaping via the city gates and helping their friends on the right; Brigadier the Hon. Adrian Hope was given the main task of driving the rebels back towards Calpee and to this end had HM 53rd Foot, the 42nd and 93rd Highlanders and 4th PNI. Supporting him was Inglis's brigade of HM 23rd Fusiliers, 32nd and 82nd Foot.

It was a Sunday, clear and cool, with a cloudless sky. Every soldier was rested, well-fed and anxious to inflict a defeat on the rebels. Officers knew what had to be done: a feint on the enemy's left and centre, a staunch attack on his right. At 9am General Windham who, rather pointedly, had not been given a brigade but was left in command of the entrenchment and fort, opened up with every gun he had. Sir Colin rode down the lines to inspire confidence and told the men that the women and children had safely reached Allahabad. Then Walpole and Greathed's brigades moved on the rebel centre, musketry rattling all along the canal. At 11pm Hope and Inglis's brigades moved forward. At the brick kilns the 4th PNI and HM 53rd charged with bayonets gleaming and drove the insurgents across the canal. When some rebels tried to make a stand Captain Peel silenced them with round after round from his 24-pounders. Soldiers cheered as Peel and his sailors moved forward, enjoying the rare sight of 24-pounders advancing with the first line of skirmishers.

Peel's guns were drawn usually by thirteen pairs of oxen. Elephants quite wisely objected to being under fire, but the bullocks, as Captain Oliver Jones noted, "will advance under the heaviest volleys of musketry and cannon, with the utmost unconcern, and even if they are hit, take it in the most praiseworthy and philosophical manner."[74] On this occasion, as the 93rd Highlanders reached the canal, Peel's sailors were shouting out, "Damn these cow-horses! They're too slow. Come on you 93rd, give us a hand with the drag-ropes as you did at Lucknow!"[75] So a company of Highlanders dashed forward to help while the pipers struck up "The Battle of Alma". Naval cadet Edward Watson stuck close to Peel throughout the battle:

> On we went up a road where they had two guns in position and they gave us a tremendous fire, and a good many stood their ground and gave us volley after volley of musketry... On we went, the brutes saw us still advancing and off they took their guns. On came our Infantry and we fairly set them running. Captain Peel now dismounted and I went with him, and we came over a bridge on the road which went through a field crowded with sepoys. I can't tell you how jolly it was seeing the brutes run. I could hardly believe my eyes. I felt perfectly mad, and our men got on top of the guns, waving their hats and cheering and yelling like fun. It was most awfully exciting.[76]

From all fronts the Tommies cheered and hooted as they rushed the Gwalior Contingent's camp. So complete and unexpected was the attack that chupattis were found grilling for lunch on the camp fires, and Indian doctors ran for their lives from the camp hospital.

With the rebels in retreat, Sir Colin now made one of his rare bad moves; he gave a field command to his leggy Chief of Staff, Major General Sir William Mansfield, telling him to cut off the retreat of the Nana's troops to the north of the city. Mansfield was an excellent chief of staff, though his *hauteur* offended many, but he had not, as Thomas Rice Holmes wrote, "the eye of a general" (a deliberate choice of words as Sir William was notoriously short-sighted). He had the rebels on the run, but despite the remonstrances of his staff, refused to advance beyond the spot that he had been told to seize. This was typical of a man who did things carefully, slowly and precisely. As it was, he allowed the rebels to escape, "and returned to camp having accomplished absolutely nothing".[77] Mansfield was rather pleased with himself and Sir Colin admired the general too much to criticise his actions. "What is the use of intercepting a desperate soldiery whose only wish is to escape?"[78] declared Mansfield. Most soldiers, however, agreed with Lieutenant Lang who complained: "I don't think we are half-satisfied allowing the enemy to escape, without good corporal punishment."[79] The general mood was summed up by Lieutenant Gordon-Alexander who said: "Major-General Mansfield had mistaken his profession: he should have been a lawyer, a politician, or perhaps a permanent official at the Treasury, but never a soldier."[80]

To crown the day, Campbell himself took part in a cavalry pursuit. A Bengal gunner, Lieutenant George Cracklow, was impressed:

He galloped up to our battery ... to know if we did not want the Infantry to advance, and then it quite did one's heart good to see the old fellow take off his hat and cheer on the Sikhs, "*Chulo Sikh log Chulo*" ("Come on, Sikhs, come on") and away he went at their heels with the shells bursting over his head and the round shot whistling round him. With such a jolly old fellow, who wouldn't join?[81]

The cavalry spread like lightning across the plain. Lieutenant Roberts was in the vanguard:

What a chase we had! We went at a gallop, only pulling up occasionally for the battery to come into action, "to clear our front and flanks". We came up with a goodly number of stragglers, and captured several guns and carts laden with ammunition. But we were by this time overtaking large bodies of the rebels, and they were becoming too numerous for a single battery and a few staff officers to cope with. We had outstripped the Commander-in-Chief, and Hope Grant decided to halt, hoping that the mssing Cavalry and Horse Artillery might soon turn up. We had not to wait long... Sir Colin had also come up, so off we started again, and never drew rein until we reached the Pandu Naddi, fourteen miles from Cawnpore.[82]

Private Frederick Potiphar, HM 9th Lancers, recalled that Sir Colin told the troopers, "We should make good fox hunters as we bagged the game so well, meaning, I suppose, the 16 guns we had captured ... also about 170 carts laden with ammunition and stores."[83]

After the three days' humiliation at the hands of the rebels, it was to be expected that revenge was bloody and sweet to the British, who administered it ruthlessly. "We made short work of the stragglers and dying," wrote Sergeant Walter Robertson of the Black Watch, "fires being lighted, their bodies were thrown on them in hundreds, as they prefer to die in the fire, we gave them their wish for once."[84]

The British returned to Cawnpore in a fine mood. Sergeant Taylor of the 93rd thought the pursuit of the rebels was "one of the smartest affairs that I have seen during the Mutiny."[85] Everyone was in agreement. British losses had also been not too severe: 13 officers and men killed and 85 wounded.

In the aftermath of the Windham debacle Carthew was censured by the C-in-C for retreating the way he did, but several officers came forward to defend the brigadier's actions and, after hearing what they had to say, Sir Colin was fair-minded enough to offer an apology and retraction of his comments. The events of 26th-28th November became gossip in the camp; Chaplain Moore wrote in his diary how Tantia Tope had inflicted a "jolly good licking" on Windham:

> They came down in fine style and commenced the favourite game of long bowls which I regret to say General Windham answered with small guns... An order was then given to spike guns and return, no enemy being up to then in sight ... no three men were to be found together when our Infantry advanced to retake the guns. The 88th who charged the day before refused to advance ... it was a case of save who can. The troops bolted in through the city any way they could and our whole camp fell back into the hands of the enemy, and only if they had followed it up they could have taken the entrenchment, I believe, for we had hardly a man fit for duty.[86]

And what of the general himself? Windham held to the view that everyone was to blame except himself, though his especial ire was reserved for Major-General Mansfield who, he felt, had not passed on letters he sent asking Campbell for instructions. In a letter to his wife Windham told her that the fighting had been "very sharp and my position owing to want of numbers was very difficult to hold. For my part, altho' always on horseback & therefore very visible, I was not hit, one musket ball brushed my gray hair just above my left ear when I was abusing the men for their slackness in not advancing... In plain English I have had to thank God, for having.shown me mercy."[87]

His rage at Mansfield and Campbell did not find its way into the books of his two biographers, who censored what he wrote. The general actually told his wife on 12th December:

> I am by no means comfortable with this Army. Sir Colin does not like me – is jealous of me in vitality and yet is ashamed at once to say so. I have had words with his chief of the staff and also with him... I spoke to Mansfield the strongest ... he is a low Jesuitical imposter – no soldier at all. Old Sir Colin, on the contrary, is a soldier, but no General – between the two they have divided the army into factions and I think it would be very wise to withdraw them both.[88]

Campbell did not like arguing with his subordinates and Windham's insolent remarks were reported to him. In a letter on 9th January Windham told his wife that "When I told Mansfield that I had written to him repeatedly (every day, sometimes twice a day, from 18th to 20th November without receiving one word in reply, he did nothing)." Sir William insisted that Windham's letters had never arrived and he referred the matter to Campbell. At a meeting between the generals, "Sir Colin at one time began to come the sergt-major, but I simply said, 'You did not allow me to finish, my sentence, sir.' ... it had been my firm belief that he had received my letters and did not choose to answer them." Windham felt bitter that he had tried to say that the Gwalior Contingent were on their way, and got "not the slightest" reply in return. He had to face the rebels with insufficient artillery, no cavalry support, "one colonel that by cowardice would have ruined anything, and another whose wrongheaded stupidity (Brigadier Wilson) I had been left expressly to control." So the skulking of the former and imbecility of the latter prevented the town being defended properly. Windham concluded this appalling letter by disparaging all that the C-in-C had done at Lucknow, with a prediction that, "in the open the enemy won't fight," and declared, "The only real fighting there has been during the war was at Delhi & Havelock's entry into Lucknow & after that their attack on our men at Cawnpore."[89] His blasts of annoyance had by this time so infuriated the C-in-C that he had decided to send Windham off to a quiet posting in Lahore.

That night after the rebels ran from Cawnpore, the soldiers could relax for the first time in weeks. Well almost all – the tough and hard-working sepoys of the 4th Punjab Infantry did not get into camp until the middle of the night and could not find their allotted camping ground: "We spent a miserable night lying on the cold ground with no covering and nothing to eat,"[90] recalled Surgeon Fairweather.

Others were much luckier; Brigadier Hope, handsome, young and well-liked, made his headquarters in the house of a British civilian that had somehow escaped destruction, "and such large quantities of native-made rose-water were discovered that the officers quartered there for the night were enabled to refresh themselves with rose-water baths,"[91] recollected Gordon-Alexander. Some of the men of his regiment roasted a few of the Gwalior Contingent's fat bullocks and calves, there was plenty of boiled rice and chupattis in the enemy camp, and two companies of the 93rd added pigeons to a stew. No. 6 Company dug up some good asparagus to add to the repast, the feast served to officers and men on beautiful French china found in an abandoned villa. The great luxury of the evening, however, were beautiful soft beds for the whole regiment, since the enemy camp contained quantities of handsome wadded Indian silk quilts. The men slept feeling for once that they were, if not kings, at least princes. Even the Punjabis awoke to find that they had slept close to a grocer's wagon; they quickly chopped up fresh onions, mixed with flour and ghee, and breakfasted on hot chupattis and strong mugs of tea.

9

Potting Ducks and Hanging Rebels

Cawnpore, Allahabad,
Ganges Valley and Oudh
7th December 1857–27th February 1858

History abhors a vacuum. So it was that as the British soldiers and civilians exited Lucknow, so Sir James Outram's prophecy rang true and thousands of rebels flooded into the city, plundering anything their foes had left at the Residency, reducing the buildings to even worse ruination. The influx from the countryside is quite understandable; many of the Oudh landowners had sat on the sidelines for months, but now, with the feringhees seemingly on the run, it looked as if the Kingdom of Oudh was truly restored to its old rulers.

To verify this, the Queen-Regent issued a royal proclamation that the British had abandoned Lucknow. Figures can be unreliable, but it is generally assumed around 50,000 armed men in November soon swelled by year's end to over 100,000 armed insurgents in the city. To these numbers must be added the civic population of some 300,000, many of whom had already fought the British, or had by now lost a family member or relative in the struggle, and so had good cause to hate them. Soon, thousands of these troops and citizens were toiling to build a massive series of earthworks. "Every street and lane has been barricaded," spies reported, "and all the houses are loopholed." These three lines of defences were developed on the Begum's instructions at a cost to the royal treasury of 500,000 rupees.

Politically, the already delicate situation between the rebel leaders was fragile. Sadly, we have few administrative documents from this period since most were destroyed in the sacking of the city. Most of what we do know comes from the reports of British spies collated by Major Carnegie of the Intelligence Department. In early January 1858, he still reported "levies daily being raised". In the villages, rumours abounded that "the Nana is the Master of Cawnpore, that he has driven out the British, that he will shortly march on the capital." Yet it seems that Begum Hazrat Mahal her lover, Mammu Khan, and Raja Jai Lal Singh who led the court faction of the boy-king, Birjis-Qadr, "had to guard themselves not only against an eventual British counter-offensive, but also against the mounting hostility of an army demoralised by failure and riven with jealousies about unequal pay."[1] The Maulvi, Ahmadullah Shah, rose in popularity, especially with the newly arrived regiments from Delhi. Seven more of these reached the city on 20th December and the pay grumbles got louder: old soldiers got 12 rupees a month and new recruits just 7 rupees. An ugly squabble was settled by agreeing to pay all of them 12 rupees.

The British garrison at the Alambagh refused to be subdued and remained a constant thorn in the flesh of the Oudh nationalists – for the idea of ejecting the British from India was waning, if it had ever really existed in more than a few minds, but determination to oust them from Oudh was stronger than ever. "The War is now fully believed throughout Lucknow to be a religious crusade," wrote Carnegie as Sir Colin led the soldiers and civilians towards Cawnpore, "and crowds of people are flocking into the capital,"which was soon "swarming with fighting men."

While the situation within Lucknow remained volatile, the British in December 1857 were finding things moving in their direction at last. Having secured Cawnpore and driven off Tantia Tope's army, Sir Colin sent Hope Grant with 2,797 officers and men and 11 guns to pursue the rebels in the direction of Bithur. Hearing that his enemy was trying to cross the Ganges, Grant changed direction and proceeded 25 miles to the Serai Ghat ferry. Seeing the insurgents trying to embark some guns, Grant ordered up his artillery. After half an hour of British gunnery the rebels were in full retreat, but not before their cavalry valiantly tried to take the guns. They were met in a fine clash of steel by the 9th Lancers under Major Ouvry, the 5th Punjab Cavalry under Lieutenant Younghusband and Hodson's Horse under Lieutenant Gough. Fifteen enemy guns were captured and while the rebel grapeshot "was most severe and well-placed, falling amongst the artillery like hail", the only person injured was Hope Grant, hit in the foot by a spent ball. One lone Indian rebel gunner continued to load and fire his piece until he was alone and then met his end bravely.

Campbell's operations at Cawnpore had been a remarkable feat of arms: he had captured 34 enemy guns and at a cost of just 99 casualties.

Now he ordered Hope Grant to complete his mission to Bithur and destroy the Nana Sahib's palace. Sappers set charges to bring down the walls and the soldiers enjoyed wrecking the building. Rumours abounded that a deep well hid countless treasures beneath its 42 feet of foul-looking water. Heavy beams and other junk had been thrown in, but the general declared that the well should be drained. Next day some pewter pots were dredged up. They were ancient but hardly the kind of loot that the soldiers wanted. Hope Grant wrote in his journal that the well gave up "a number of gold and silver articles, which to judge from their shape, must have been of great antiquity". But Lieutenant Gordon-Alexander was present and recorded:

> A great quantity of silver plate – solid silver, be it understood – was brought to light, which, owing to the action of the water, came up jet-black. Among these silver articles, the State howdah of the ex-Peshwa, in solid silver, was fished up, besides quantities of gold plate and other valuables. Below the plate, which was merely deposited loose in the water, as in in a hurry, the sappers came upon an immense store of ammunition boxes tightly packed with native rupees and gold mohurs ... the value of the coin alone being reported in camp on December 27 to be over £200,000, in addition to the value of the gold and silver plate and the ornamental jewellery.[2]

Back in England some newspapers crowed that with the relief of the Lucknow garrison, the "Mutiny" would soon be at an end. But one Calcutta observer wrote how the energy and resistance shown by the rebels at Cawnpore against Windham and Campbell "ought to satisfy the British people that the task of 'stamping out' the rebellion is a more formidable one than many were willing to imagine or believe."[3] Queen Victoria, as usual, saw things with simple clarity. She wrote on 10th December to her cousin, George, Duke of Cambridge, C-in-C of the British Army, to say that she put her faith in Sir Colin Campbell: "Pray say everything kind and flattering to him in our name, and express the hope that he won't expose himself unnecessarily. On him depends *everything* there now."[4]

Sir Colin was forced for a time to remain inactive while he waited for the return of the carts that had transported the women, children and sick to Allahabad. It was clear to him that before he considered re-conquering Oudh, or neighbouring Rohilkhand, he had first to open communications with Delhi and the Punjab. This meant establishing control over the Doab – the large tract of land between the rivers Jumna and Ganges, running from Delhi to Allahabad. British authority here would put an end to insurgents threatening his supply line along the Grand Trunk Road and, critically, its telegraph communications. To retake the Doab, the general had decided upon three columns: he would march north-east from Cawnpore; Brigadier Walpole would head south before sweeping north-east; a third column under Colonel Thomas Seaton was already proceeding south-east from Delhi. All three columns would rendezvous at Fatehgarh. With Seaton on his way, Walpole set off on 18th December and the day after his carts returned Sir Colin did the same on Christmas Eve.

The C-in-C's first objective was the suspension bridge at Kala Nudee ("little river"), a stream close to the Ganges, five miles short of Fatehgarh. He reached it on New Year's Day 1858 to discover that the insurgents had burnt a 30-foot section of the bridge before making camp at the village of Khudaganj close to the opposite bank. Hope Grant was sent forward with his brigade reinforced by a squadron of cavalry, four light field guns and a company of engineers. Inspection showed that the pier and main chains were undamaged and the sappers worked all through that night on the bridge to put it in some state of repair.

Next morning Sir Colin rode down to see how the work was progressing. He spotted a number of men clad in white assembling near Khudaganj. He thought they were villagers and "desired someone to go and tell them not to be afraid, as they would not be hurt, when all of a sudden off came a round-shot from amongst them which killed four men of the 53rd."[5] Sailors washing their garments by the water's edge left "their soap-suds and clothes, never to see them again" and rushed to their guns. Case-shot and bullets were fizzing about; on the far side of the river a British picquet was reinforced by HM 53rd Foot. Campbell quickly ordered up support from his headquarters camp, four miles away, while the Royal Navy and Royal Artillery guns opened fire. Brigadier Greathed arrived with his brigade about 11am and HM 8th and 64th regiments were sent across the bridge, soon followed by Captain Peel, who somehow managed to trundle over three of his guns and took shelter with them behind a small yellow bungalow.

The insurgents had clearly decided to make a major stand. Mid-afternoon they brought up a large gun, which killed five British soldiers and mortally wounded two others with its first shot. Clearly, the ex-sepoys had some first-rate artillerymen in their ranks.

Commanding one of the naval 24-pounders was Lieutenant J. W Vaughan of HMS *Shannon* who was, in fact, short-sighted and always wore a monocle, but was "a capital shot and as cool when under a shower of bullets, as if there was no such thing as gunpowder and lead."[6]

His first shot struck the roof of a house, the second struck the wall, and the third dismounted the big gun and blew up its carriage. Captain Peel, who was standing by, then said in his usual laconic way, "Thank you, Mr Vaughan; perhaps you will now be so good as to blow up the tumbril." A fourth shot missed its mark, but a fifth destroyed the tumbril and killed several of the enemy. Peel had watched the proceedings with his cool, deep-set, blue eyes, "intelligent, sharp as a needle", as one friend wrote, his brown wavy hair carefully brushed back off his clean-shaven, oval face. "Thank you," said Peel in his blandest and most courteous tone, "I will now go and report to Sir Colin."[7]

The weak state of the bridge meant that it took time to get the cavalry and artillery across it. Then along came the 93rd Highlanders and it was clear that Sir Colin intended to use his favourite soldiers in the attack. No sooner had the Scots appeared on the bridge than a drummer boy of the 53rd sounded the advance. The C-in-C was furious, his temper not helped by a spent bullet that had just winded him in the stomach (the boy soldier later explained that he sounded the advance without orders because "I was afraid the men would lick me if I didn't")[8]. Campbell rode up and tried to stop the action, but the men of the 53rd, a largely Irish regiment, just laughed and cheered him until even he was grinning.

Very quickly the rebels now began retreating in good order towards Fatehgarh. It was now Hope Grant's chance to shine; this brilliant cavalry commander took his troopers in a wide detour to the left, trotting parallel to the enemy's line of retreat, but hidden from them by groves of trees and high-growing crops. Then, as the distance narrowed to under 300 yards, he wheeled his horse to the right, trumpets sounded the charge and the fleeing rebels found themselves facing the dreaded 9th Lancers. Major Octavius Anson described the charge in a letter home: "Then commenced the work of cutting and pointing, and sights the most bloody that you can conceive. I knocked over three, young Anson seven, Martin some three or four, Fawcett the same, and even that young, gentle lad Sitwell pistolled one. Some 200 or more were sabred."[9] The swarthy Punjabi hillmen of Probyn and Younghusband's cavalry regiments also took part and the latter officer was mortally wounded by a rebel hidden in a ditch who shot him through the lungs.[10] Hope Grant was almost killed himself, and he was impressed by the bravery of his enemies:

My 9th Lancer orderly, Corporal Caine, who was carrying a bamboo lance for me – a fine rider, and a plucky young fellow – saw a rebel a little ahead of us with his musket cocked and levelled, defying anyone to approach him. Caine putting his lance in rest rode at him. When, within 5 yards of his antagonist the latter pulled the trigger, but providentially the cap snapped, Caine ran him through the body. At another time, as a squadron of the 9th Lancers were advancing at a trot, a dismounted rebel sowar, wearing a red coat, and armed with a splendid long gilded lance, turned round, and, with a defiant gesture ... hurled the lance into the ranks with all his might, striking a horse to the ground. The sowar was instantly killed.[11]

It was after Lieutenant George Younghusband, 5th Punjab Cavalry, fell from his horse that Lieutenant Frederick Roberts saw a Sikh sowar being bested by a rebel sepoy armed with a musket. He rode straight for the sepoy and killed him with one stroke of his sword. Then, seeing two other sepoys making off with a standard, he overtook them. "While wrenching the staff out of the hands of one of them, whom I cut down, the other put his musket close to my body and fired: fortunately for me it misfired, and I carried off the standard."[12] With captured flags at their head the cavalry rode back to camp. A delighted Sir Colin doffed his hat to them as they passed by his tent. The captured flags caught the breeze, as Highlanders tossed their feather bonnets in the air, and a romantically inclined officer thought it "reminded one of the old days of chivalry" (an odd remark coming after the ugly butchery of the cavalry chase). Losses that day had been just 10 soldiers killed, with 30 men and two officers wounded, along with one officer and two men of the Naval Brigade wounded.

The Naval Brigade reached camp at about 9.30pm and parked their guns in a ploughed field. No baggage or provisions had arrived except a cask of spirits. "We were each glad to drink our day's double allowance," wrote Edmund Verney, "and even Captain Peel, who rarely drinks spirits, tossed off with gusto the abominable arrack that is served out in lieu of rum." Verney managed to buy a chuppatie for a rupee and shared it with a tent-mate, though the actual tents did not arrive on elephants until midnight and the camp was pitched in total darkness. The baggage showed up on hackeries at 4am. "Every tent was then illuminated, and roaring fires blazed in rear of the camp; and at about five, as the first streaks of dawn hove in sight, we sat down to a *late* dinner."[13]

With the bridge secure, Campbell took Fatehgarh and nearby Furruckabad without a fight that day, "gaining a valuable gun-carriage factory in the process".[14] Verney noticed that the road into town "and the fields on each side of it were strewn with dead bodies, some of old men, some of young, and some of even boys, covered with ghastly wounds... Some of the wells we passed were choked with corpses."[15] On 4th January the young officer saw a sight that disturbed him. The rebel commander at the Kala Nuddee battle, Madir Khan, a cavalry commander, had been captured and a crowd were tormenting him:

> When I saw him there was a crowd round him, some pulling his hair, and others throwing dirt in his face as he lay tied to some boards. He was a very handsome, strong-looking man, with black beard and moustaches, and richly dressed. I can hardly think it right or brave to torment a bound prisoner, however heinous his crimes may be. He lay there quite dignified and indifferent to the taunts, &tc of the crowd round him: it is said he was a chief mover in the atrocities at Cawnpore.[16]

Tied to a native bedstead and carried to the gallows tree, Madir Khan was stripped and flogged before the noose was placed around his neck. Both Captains Peel and Jones of the Royal Navy were present and, like Verney, found the carnival atmosphere of the proceedings distinctly unpleasant. The soldiers tried to stuff their prisoner with pork. At a first attempt the rope broke and Khan fell down and broke his nose. "The man behaved with great firmness," wrote Jones. "While the rope was being adjusted, a soldier struck him on the face, upon which he turned round with great fierceness and said – 'Had I had a sword in my hand, you dared not have struck that blow.' His last words before he was launched into eternity."[17]

On the 6th, Seaton's and Walpole's columns arrived. Both had seen some tough fighting. Seaton confessed in his memoirs that he was "so knocked up that I was compelled to remain on my back the whole of the next day."[18] With him came a new irregular cavalry regiment that had made its mark at Delhi and was named after the man who led it; the force was called Hodson's Horse and its commander, Lieutenant William Stephen Raikes Hodson, remains one of the most controversial soldiers who fought in the Uprising, so notorious that historian E. Jaiwant Paul singles him out as one of the "villains" of 1857.

Hodson, third son of a bishop's chaplain, was born near Gloucester in 1821. He was educated at Rugby and Trinity College, Cambridge, before enlisting in the H.E.I.C. Army at the age of 23, serving first in the 2nd Bengal Grenadiers and then the 1st European Bengal Fusiliers. A contemporary described him as "a tall man with yellow hair, a pale smooth face, heavy moustache, and large, restless, rather unforgiving eyes ... a perfect swordsman, nerves like iron, and a quick intelligent eye". In fact, Hodson was one of those brave young men who make perfect warriors; he got a reputation as "the finest swordsman in the army", a brilliant rider, and also an expert with his favourite weapon – the hog spear. He was also, without question, energetic, courageous, irrepressible and quite ruthless, besides being a poor desk soldier.

After the Sikh Wars he joined the newly formed Corps of Guides whose job it was to police the turbulent north-west frontier districts. Here his troubles began; in 1855 he was removed from his civil functions by Lord Dalhousie because of a "lack of judgement and gross negligence" in the matter of an imprisoned Pathan chieftain and his son. To make matters worse, that same year Hodson was accused of misappropriating some of his regiment's funds. Eventually, after an exhaustive inquiry, Hodson was cleared of the charges, but the mud stuck. Later, during a tour of Kashmir with Sir Henry Lawrence, he was dilatory with the accounts and then accused of embezzling the funds of the Lawrence Asylum at Kasauli. John Lawrence, formidable head of the Punjab administration, concluded that Hodson had many fine gifts but was untrustworthy. These and other matters of financial impropriety dogged him off and on. Within the Indian Army he soon had many admirers, especially those who worked with him closely, but there were also critics.

At the outbreak of the Great Uprising he rode 152 miles in 72 hours carrying the C-in-C's despatches through a hostile countryside. It led to him being allowed to form a new irregular cavalry regiment composed of hardy Sikhs and frontier tribesmen, who became a popular sight in their khaki uniforms and red turbans. As a cavalry leader and Head of Intelligence, Hodson was a major player in the fighting at Delhi. Here, however, he committed an act that made him controversial throughout the entire army. On 22nd September 1857 he met just outside the city with three of the sons of the old Mogul Emperor, Bahadur Shah, demanding their unconditional surrender. Taking them as his prisoners he headed back towards Delhi with his small escort, but was met by a large crowd near a city gate. The mob was an ugly one and Hodson's subaltern later said, "Our lives were not worth a moment's purchase."[19] Hodson knew what he must do. He had intended to hang the princes (*shahzadas*) but, "Seizing a carbine from one of my men I deliberately shot them one after another," he said, an act that awed the onlookers so much that they just melted away. Army officers generally supported Hodson's measure, but there were some, like Frederick Roberts, who thought it was a "blot" on a good career. Others went further and gossiped that to kill in hot blood was acceptable but to kill in cold blood was murder. Thus Hodson's reputation as he rode into Fatehgarh was, as the Victorian historian T. R. Holmes wrote, that of "a splendid leader of irregular horse, but a most unscrupulous man".[20]

Seaton brought with him 4,000 camels and something missing until that time – a large number of Indians who were willing to work as servants. Edmund Verney described the camp and its servants, presenting us with a good picture of what such a camp was like on campaign:

A walk through the camp in the morning is very amusing; everybody breakfasts at about nine, and hence at half-past eight all the world is dressing etc; in front of every tent door are one or two officers enjoying their morning's bath, which ceremony is performed in this wise: the devotee, attired in the lightest conceivable dress, squats on his marrow-bones on a small board at the tent door, and his bheestie then proceeds to torture him by first letting the chilly water trickle slowly over him ... gradually, however the stream increases, and at length the very last drops are emptied over the now shivering wretch ... young ladies, with brass and and silver bangles on their ankles and bracelets on their wrists, contrasting with their polished black skins, and dressed in white robes with bright-coloured shawls round their heads supply the camp with milk, and their jetty, sparkling eyes, and tall, graceful figures, surmounted by the shining brass chatty, form no unattractive addition to camp scenery. And now while their masters are breakfasting, the syce grooms and caparisons the horse of the field officer, and the bearer of the captain or subaltern gives his sword an extra rub up for the coming parade; the little cooking-pots in rear of the officers quarters send up grateful odours of curries and omelettes, and little pots hiss and bubble, slyly lifting their lids, and daring you to guess their contents ... and while burning green twigs crackle, subs and captains prattle, plates and dishes rattle, the bugles for parade summon all to duty.[21]

The next objective on Campbell's agenda was the invasion and conquest of Rohilkhand. He particularly wanted to capture Bareilly and subdue the enemy in several districts before the hot weather season. After consulting with Mansfield, he drew up a memorandum for the Governor-General that showed how Lucknow could not be attacked with fewer than 30,000 troops. Once completed, 10,000 of these would be needed to occupy the city and hold it "until the whole province shall have been conquered and the rebels driven out of their last stronghold." Priorities during the coming hot weather season meant that "it's absolutely necessary to economise the forces of which we are now possessed."[22] This document reached Canning after he had already sent a letter on 20th December telling his C-in-C:

So long as Oude is not dealt with, there will be no real quiet on this side of India. Every eye in India is upon Oude as it was upon Delhi: Oude is not only the rallying place of the sepoys, to which they all look, and by their doings, in which their own hopes and prospects rise and fall, but it represents a dynasty; there is a king of Oude "seeking his own"... Oude and our dealings with it have been in every native's mind for the last two years.[23]

A spat now began in earnest. In a letter that crossed again with one from Canning, the C-in-C argued that if his forces held off from conquering Rohilkhand there was a danger of losing what had been gained, and that other garrisons might end up being besieged. Canning was an intelligent man but also an obstinate one. On 8th January he told Sir Colin that "I am obliged to say that I still think these operations should be directed against Lucknow at no long interval." He pointed out that the Nana Sahib was now fomenting rebellion in the Saugor territories and intriguing with the Mahratta princes of Western India. News from Pegu also made Canning jittery about the situation in newly acquired British Burma. "Then there is the most formidable of all lurking places of danger and revolt – Hyderabad – especially Mahometan, and deeply sympathising with Oude, because fearing, however unreasonably, the same fate. The recovery of Oude would be of the greatest value to us there; whilst the penetrating into Rohilkhand, leaving Oude untouched, would be little thought of."[24]

"The Great Blow", as Canning termed it, could not be deferred to another cold season. On reaching his decision the Governor-General had also been influenced by Outram, who wrote frequently of the precariousness of his position at the Alambagh, while Campbell argued that Sir James could "hold his own against any thing". Back in Britain the Duke of Cambridge supported Campbell, but it was Canning who had the last word.

For several weeks, Campbell's army stayed at Fatehgarh while units scoured the countryside and punished rebel chieftains. At the forefront of these operations was Mr Power, the local civil commissioner, known by the nickname, "Hanging Power" due to his fondness for the rope. "At each halting-place Mr Power held a court of summary jurisdiction,"[25] wrote Gordon-Alexander. At Mhow, 127 mutineers caught hiding in the town and surrounding fields were hanged from a great peepul tree in the square. One wonders if any knew the species name, *Ficus religiosa*, sacred fig... One of the officers involved, Lieutenant Robert Biddulph R.A., admitted that executions were performed "in a summary and somewhat brigand-like manner". This meant, as Major Anson declared, that they were either hanged "or tortured to death". Villages were burned, ordinary natives flogged, captured sepoys shot or hanged. "I cannot consider these sepoys as human beings," wrote one officer of HM 90th, while Lieutenant C. R. Nicholl, Rifle Brigade, told his sister in a letter: "Nobody means to leave a sepoy *alive,* much less *wounded.*" A youth fresh out of Eton, Nicholl had read the atrocity stories in the newspapers on his way out East and wanted to punish the wretches who had killed innocent women and children. He found Fatehgarh "a nice place [with] a splendid view of Oude" from the Ganges, where he enjoyed "a stunning bathe". Life in camp meant reading novels, shooting snipe and pigeons, losing at card games and stoning the townspeople for sport before church service at 4pm. Everyone still talked of the massares at Cawnpore; while out shooting deer and peacock Nicholl and his fellow officers tried to bag "runaway sepoys", he told his mother in a letter, then hanged them "on the trees for to dry".[26]

It was while stationed at Fatehgarh that Surgeon James Fairweather, 4th Punjab Native Infantry, attended an auction:

> I fancied that a man behind me was pressing rather rudely against me. I dug him with my elbow without looking round but he seemed to return the dig. I then turned rather angrily round towards the man and found that it was the body of a man that had been hanged on a tree close to where I was standing… It gave me a bit of a shock, but such scenes were so common at those times that the fact of a swinging corpse forming part of a crowd round an auction seemed to affect no one.[27]

Soldiers were soon swearing about the enforced delay. The newspapers rounded on Campbell and called him a tortoise. Besides wanting to increase his army, the C-in-C had political problems; Lord Canning wished him to work in concert with an ally – Jung Bahadur, the all-powerful and wily chief minister of Nepal. He had offered 3000 of his Gurkhas in July 1857, who had done good work. Now they were formed into a brigade under Brigadier-General Franks, a tough martinet of the old school, more feared than loved by his men, but also a soldier of great personal courage. On 21st December Jung Bahadur's complete army of 10,000 Gurkhas composed of 14 infantry regiments with four batteries of artillery, each with four guns, reached the British frontier. Taking command of them was Brigadier-General George Macgregor, who found to his surprise that the Nepalis "marched as steadily as any troops I ever saw". Many of them seemed giants compared to Gurkhas in British battalions. On 25th January, this new Gurkha force reached the Gogra river and crossed over into Oudh.

Five weeks ahead of these Nepalis was Thomas Harte Franks, whose field force consisted of HM 10th, 20th and 97th regiments and six battalions of Nepalese, together with two field batteries and an irregular cavalry unit drawn largely from Franks's own regiment, the 10th Foot. On 19th February this army of 5,710 officers and men collided with a rebel force of about 10,000 ex-sepoys under Mehndee Hussan, supported by more than 8,000 irregular insurgents under Bunda Hassan, at Chanda, a large village with a mud fort. Franks's troops soon took the position but at sunset the rebels returned. It took a charge at bayonet's point to rout them. While waiting for his baggage to arrive next morning, Franks heard that Mehndee Hussan, far from being cowed, intended to bar his progress at a steep ravine guarded by a mountain fortress at Budhayan, six miles to his front. The brigadier set off at dawn on 21st February and after arraying his troops in battle order he cunningly captured the hill fort by a flanking movement.

To his great credit, Mehndee Hussan still refused to give up and next tried to stop Franks at Sultanpur. He now had with him 25,000 insurgents, of whom 5,000 were ex H.E.I.C. sepoys, along with 1,100 cavalry and 25 heavy guns under one Mirza Gaffoor Bey, who had been a General of Artllery in the ex-King of Oudh's's army. To make matters worse for the British, the rebel line extended for a mile and a half, from the Sultanpur bazaar to a range of low hills. Franks proved more than a match for his enemy; he realised on a reconnaissance that the rebel line might be turned on its right and so, concealed by mango groves, he marched his men around the enemy's right flank. Riding with the leading skirmishers was Lieutenant James Macleod Innes of Lucknow Residency fame. He was the first to secure a gun. He then rode on, shot a gunner in the act of applying his match to a gun and then kept the rebels at bay until help arrived. Cap in hand, Franks charged with his beloved 10th Foot, just as he had in the Sikh Wars, and his men captured 21 guns.[28] The battle was at an end and the enemy fled in all directions. Lieutenant S. H. Chamier was "in the thick of it ... very exciting and enjoyable work silencing one battery after another and tearing full gallop at these fellows." He fully expected his gun carriage to break apart, "for I never saw such ground for guns, replete with obstacles of every description, in the shape of ditches, mud-walls etc."[29]

Throughout the months of December, January and part of February, while the Doab was re-conquered by Campbell's columns and Eastern Oudh cleansed of rebels by the Nepalese and Franks's armies, Outram and his soldiers held on at the Alambagh which, in a sense, became another "siege of Lucknow". He had under his command 3,395 European and 1,047 Indian troops. The infantry was formed into two brigades under

Colonels Hamilton and Stisted, Vincent Eyre handled the cavalry and artillery ably assisted by the legendary Victoria Cross winners Captain "Hellfire Jack" Olpherts and Captain Francis Maude.

The Alambagh itself was too small to accommodate all the troops and the main force camped about a mile in the rear on an open plain crossing the road to Cawnpore, though protected by abattis and batteries, covering a circuit of about 11 miles. The dilapidated fort of Jellalabad had also been re-garrisoned and fortnightly convoys marched to and returned from Cawnpore. After discounting the garrisons, men on convoy duty and outposts such as the important picquet of 4,000 holding the Bunnee bridge on the Cawnpore road, Outram had about 1,600 troops to put into the field against the many thousands of insurgents in Lucknow. The rebels had set up batteries and a series of trenches facing their enemies.

Sir James made no bones about the fact that he disliked his position; the Alambagh was too cramped and too close to Lucknow, enabling the rebels to "attack him when they thought fit, and to make good their retreat when defeated", as historian George Forrest wrote.[30] Outram himself had argued to his superiors that "It is immaterial what particular spot in Oude is held as proof that we have not deserted it, so long as a footing is retained in the province; for no civil government can be exercised so long as we are not in possession of the capital itself."[31] He urged Canning to make a proclamation that "our withdrawal from the capital is merely temporary."

At first the general had great difficulties in getting supplies for his troops from the nearby villages – Mukherjee and some other historians see this as proof that the whole kingdom had turned against the British – but it appears that the insurgents in the city had requisitioned everything locally for a time. Grain was particularly scarce. Villagers may well have been scared at first of helping the feringhees. How long would they stay? On 14th December, Outram reported that the nearest place which would help with supplies was 11 miles away. He also felt that his troops were badly equipped; for a time the only regiment he had fully supplied with the new Enfield rifle were the Madras Fusiliers. Sir James also complained of his want of cavalry and commented that the volunteers who formed his Military Train irregulars could only mount 140 horses as the poor horses suffered from want of food, the cold at night and sore backs. Campbell remained adamant that "he cannot coincide in the reasoning of Sir James Outram and he does not think it possible for him to be threatened by real danger,"[32] though Colonel Berkeley, chief of staff at the Alambagh, had pointed out to Mansfield on 11th December that it was necessary to protect the land between the Alambagh and Fort Jellalabad, vitally needed as grazing land; thus the garrison had to police a front altogether of nearly four miles with limited numbers of troops.

Luckily for the British, it was a few weeks before the insurgents made their first attack. Meanwhile the garrison found the Alambagh dull. "There is nothing going on here," wrote Hugh Pearson of the 84th on 20th December. He had bought himself a smart brace of pistols and took his shotgun out for sport but couldn't get close to geese or teal, and when he managed to hit a snipe he couldn't find its body. Lieutenant Herford, 90th regiment, enjoyed being stationed in little Fort Jellalabad with its high mud walls and rounded bastions, "a picturesque object situated among trees covered with moss and creepers."[33] When he first got there the place was inhabited by large numbers of monkeys.

The rebels finally felt ready to launch an attack on 21st December. Outram's spies told him the insurgents intended to cut his supply line by seizing the village of Guilee, three miles from camp. By that evening 4,000 rebel infantry with 400 cavalry and four field guns were in position. Outram moved out at 5am next day with 1,227 infantry under 40-year-old Henry William Stisted, a Queen's officer and veteran of the Ist Afghan War. He had with him 190 irregular cavalry (made up of men from the Military Train and Barrow's Volunteers) plus six 9-pounders commanded by Olpherts and Maude. A spirited British attack caused the rebels to flee back towards Lucknow leaving over 50 dead, and, in Outram's words, "hardly a casualty on our side".

Gradually, Outram's little army got used to its situation. On Christmas Day Surgeon Home noted that the officers' mess menu included soup, tinned salmon, roast leg of mutton (cooked in a copper pot in a pit surrounded by hot ashes), served with new potatoes and peas, a dish of chickens, plum pudding, lots of fruit, coffee and spirits. By early New Year, according to Captain Jones-Parry of the Blue Caps, villagers were bringing in supplies of fruit and vegetables. There was a Sports Day for the garrison on 1st January, which went off without mishap; there were sack and egg and spoon races, while the Sikhs proved themselves to be excellent quoit-throwers and wrestlers.

Eleven days later, the insurgents made a second attack on 12th January. It was a more than unusually cold day with classic weather for Northern India, the season of violent north-westerly winds carrying clouds of dust, bleak and biting. This time a commander called Mansoob Ali led more than 20,000 insurgents, who spread out around the front and flanks of the British positions. British officers watched fascinated as the rebel troops "still stuck to the colours we had given them" noted Herford, "and used the bugle calls learnt in our service."[34]

"At 8am we heard the assembly sound and shortly afterwards ours followed suit," wrote Surgeon Collins, 5th Fusiliers, as across a wide plain "we could see the Pandies marching in thousands."[35] Sir James had carefully prepared his forces and outposts to meet the Indians. On the left flank Billy Olpherts moved at a gallop completely driving off a large body of enemy cavalry and infantry as he unlimbered and fired his guns at 500 yards range. Garnet Wolseley described the scene:

> First came dear old Billy himself, clad in garments he had used in the Crimean War, a fez cap and a Turkish grego, the latter tied round his waist with a piece of rope. About fifty yards behind came his well-known battery sergeant-major in a sort of shooting-coat made from the green baize of a billiard-table; then a gun, every driver flogging as hard as he could; then another at long distance in rear. One broke drown, to the unpractised eye hopelessly, immediately in front of my company. Some of the spokes had gone: they all rattled.[36]

On the right flank the insurgents brought up three of their own horse artillery guns, supported by thousands of infantry, to attack the picquet connecting the British right with Jellalabad. Outram adroitly moved Brayser's Ferozepore Sikhs and the HM 5th Fusiliers, with two guns led by a bullock battery, away from his front to handle this latest threat, took the enemy in flank and drove them back. Maude's guns at the Alambagh completed the rout and later in the day, when the insurgents audaciouslyy returned and attacked the Alambagh itself, Maude's battery silenced their hopes as expert riflemen picked off rebel by rebel. The enemy, noted Surgeon Collins, were running out of shells and mainly firing grapeshot,t which made a "howling or screeching or cooing or whistling through the air, so there is very little difficulty in recognising it at a distance."[37] He also noted how the insurgents were picking up the fallen British roundshot and hurrying back to their lines with it.

Five days later, the rebels were back again. This time they were led by a man painted and dressed to resemble Hanuman the monkey god. A few of his disciples were also wearing monkey caps and tails. Their goal was Fort Jellalabad, but they were met by a fierce fire and driven back leaving their leader on the ground (historian Roshan Taqui says he was a "Hindi fanatic" called Barhke Das Alais Hanuman). Accounts vary as to this man's fate. G. W. Forrest and some other historians say he was killed, but he seems to have survived because a witness as impeccable as Surgeon Home insists that he treated the man's wounds. The patient was "quite collected" and defiantly answering questions. He had lost his monkey tail and most of his make-up. The poor fellow had three tulwar cuts across his forehead, blinding him, also opening up his brain, while a fourth cut had severed part of his chin, which hung by a strand of skin to his neck. The surgeons did what they could for the man and put a piece of glass over the exposed part of the brain. Some accounts say that the Sikh soldiers made a pet of the man and treated him quite well. Surgeon Home adds a postscript: 27 years later he was again in Lucknow and related the monkey-god incident, only to be told that the man was still alive and even enjoyed a small government pension because of his injury! If so, he was one very lucky rebel.

That night the insurgents were back again and attacked the villages on the extreme British left. Major Gordon of the 75th cunningly allowed them to approach to within 80 yards, then raked them with a withering fire of grape and musketry. Olpherts once more rode out to do wonders with his four horse artillery guns. In the darkness, the rebels returned to carry off their wounded, something they invariably did at night. Lieutenant Herford recalled "a few dead bodies, some pools of blood, and heaps of shoes which had been kicked off, lying everywhere."[38]

These attacks, despite their losses, were teaching the rebels much about the strengths and weaknesses of Outram's defences. For almost one month after the night attack, the British were left in relative peace. Small parties of officers went in to the nearby swamps to shoot ducks and on 12th February there was even a steeple chase in the camp.

Three days later, during a violent dust storm, rebel cavalry supported by infantry tried to launch an attack just as a convoy from Cawnpore was approaching the British camp. The Maulvi, no less, led his troops, though he kept within his palanquin. Olpherts was fast into the saddle with two guns, and with a troop of the Military Train "galloped to the front, and opened on them with grape, killing and wounding several and dispersing the remainder,"[39] wrote Outram. He claimed the Maulvi was wounded. He certainly did not return to lead his soldiers.

Next day, as if in anger at the Maulvi's humiliation, the rebels returned in the morning but kept their distance. Regimental calls and bugles sounded all day and the British had concluded just as dusk was falling that no attack would materialise when suddenly, screaming war cries, the insurgents issued from their lines of trenches and hurled themselves towards the British left and centre. Yelling "*Chalo bhai!*" ("Come on brothers!"), there was a determined assault on the left front village. Here they were repulsed by a picquet of 200 men commanded by Lt-Colonel Smith, 90th Light Infantry. Night soon fell and for two hours the rebels kept up a heavy musket duel with the Alambagh garrison.

Time was running out for the Oudh nationalists and they knew it. Every day brought fresh news of the two columns marching on the capital from Eastern Oudh and of Campbell's own preparations for his advance. By now reinforcements were arriving in Outram's camp; he had HM 7th Hussars, Hodson's Horse, the 1st European Bengal Fusiliers and an extra battery of horse artillery. On 21st February the insurgents launched a fresh attack. It was a Sunday and spies had reported that many of the British would attend church parade that morning. As the first speck of red appeared in the dawn sky, 20,000 Indians with good artillery support crept towards the British lines. But Outram also had spies. He had been warned on the Saturday night and so, as the rebels trod softly through the long grass, Sir James detached 250 cavalry with two guns to surprise them near the rear of Fort Jellalabad. Ten thousand insurgents, supported by 500 cavalry, threw themselves on the British left flank only to be met by five field guns and a squadron of the Military Train. Stuck inside the fort, Richard Harrison R.E. recalled, "All sorts of missiles, jingall balls, smooth bore bullets, round shot and shells, seemed coming from every direction."[40] Dispirited, the rebels drew back towards Lucknow.

His enemies, as Outram noted, were becoming desperate. Four days later they returned, this time equipped with scaling ladders, in what would be their seventh and final assault. To inspire her army the Queen-Regent with the boy-king, accompanied by royal officials, all mounted on state elephants wearing costly trappings, joined the soldiers "to witness her triumph". About 9am large bodies of enemy infantry and cavalry with four heavy guns began to menace the British left. At the same time around 30 regiments of infantry with an impressive 1,000 cavalry and eight guns moved towards the British right. Sir James first despatched some of his cavalry to disperse rebels trying to sneak around Jellalabad. Then, in person, he accompanied his 1st Brigade and cavalry. Olpherts "wheeled his four guns to the left, and advancing a little distance, unlimbered and opened fire. The royal pomp quickly left the field."[41] Remington's troop of Bengal Horse Artillery, in advance of Olpherts, blasted away with the Ferozepore Sikhs and 7th Hussars in support. As they moved forwards the rebel retreat became a rout. The British firepower was overwhelming as they had improved case and grapeshot, each one containing 537 small but deadly lead balls.

Following up this retreat, there was a problem for a few minutes with the troopers of Hodson's Horse who, after an initial charge, "lost all formation and scattered".[42] A rebel sowar tried to spear Hugh Gough, the regiment's adjutant, but Hodson galloped up and cut the man down. The insurgents then ran, rallied for a few minutes, then lost control and fled the field when the Military Train went to the aid of Hodson's men. To Gough and Hodson's chagrin, the regiment had been lucky to lose only three men and five horses killed, and one officer, six men and 23 horses wounded. Some rebels had hidden themselves in trees and shot at the British riders. A round or two of grape failed to dislodge them. Finally infantry were called up, "who soon put an end to their fun," wrote Hugh Pearson, "and brought them out of the trees with a"squelch"... like so many rooks."[43]

The commissariat volunteers who composed the Military Train – laughed and jeered at in their early days – were now an accepted corps. It was the proudest moment in the life of Major James Robertson, commanding the 2nd battalion, as he led his men back to camp, and everywhere soldiers were shouting, "Bravo! Bravo Military Train!" as they clapped hands and patted the horses' heads.

Three hours later the rebels made one last desperate attempt to take the British left flank. Bravely they advanced before the massed fire of the British guns and Enfield marksmen, who drove them back. Private Charles Wickins, 90th Light Infantry, returned to camp with some of his pals and two captured guns, which they said Sir James could have after they had "drunk his health in an extra dram of grog". On hearing this news Outram laughed and obligingly allowed the soldiers to keep the guns for 24 hours – and sent them their extra grog.

For weeks, the Alambagh troops had beaten off huge numbers of the enemy. A British artillery officer during ten days of duty had counted 2,017 cannon shots fired by the Indians, 360 of which had either hit the Alambagh or fallen into the enclosure. It is worth remembering that most of the rebels had been well-trained and officered ex H.E.I.C. regiments. Their opponent, James Outram, had shown great skill as a commander, but it was his human qualities that pleased his men, proud of their general's "all-enduring fortitude, his unflagging cheerfulness, and all-embracing sympathy as a man". One officer who accompanied him wrote:

Sir James had a cheery word for officers and men at each post, generally some small compliment – such as a regret the enemy would not come on, "because you are so well prepared". I was told that when he did "let out" at any one, especially a youngster, he was not comfortable till he had made it up by some kind word or deed, and that as often as not a "wig" ended by the offer of a cheroot – a valuable gift at the Alambagh. His holster was stuffed with these luxuries, instead of a revolver, and he dispensed them right liberally.[44]

Outram's way of handling his men was recalled by Major Robertson, Military Train: "He never harassed them out a moment before he wanted to repel the repeated attacks of the rebels, and he dismissed them as soon as he could dispense with their services, generally ordering a dram of rum, or half a dram, to be issued, if he had it to give."[45] The men hero-worshipped him, especially those closest, such as his aide, Lieutenant Edward Chamier: The poorest camp follower in the Force has a place in his thoughts before any Officer! He knows the latter take good care of themselves: but he visits with severe displeasure any want of care on the part of the Medical Department on their treatment of the sick or wounded dooly bearer etc."[46]

By mid-February the C-in-C was ready to initiate his own move on Lucknow. Earlier in the month Sir Colin had made a flying visit to Allahabad where Lord Canning had moved his headquarters to be closer to the front. Campbell found a Governor-General who was tired and fearfully overworked. The two men discussed strategy and a pardon for the rebels. At first, Canning seemed agreeable to an olive branch of sorts; nine or ten regiments would "never" receive a pardon, but the rest might be allowed to return to their homes with full pardon after laying down their arms. After some reflection, the Governor-General decided that the regiments might flee, and anyway it was a mistake to let the Lucknow rebels go unpunished. "We shall come to shame and contempt if we offer a compromise to Traitors who are still unbeaten and insolent before us," he told Campbell, "No power on earth will induce me to speak of terms until they have been driven from the city or crushed within it."[47] Senior officers, especially East India Company soldiers, were not happy with Canning's decision. "He is acting against the advice and opinion of Sir John Lawrence, Outram and the Com'r in Chief, and all wise people among whom I include myself," wrote Major-General Sir Archdale Wilson, hero of Delhi, "I think he is acting very foolishly and is badly advised by those about him ... a war of extermination is risking the safety ... of the whole of India. Without some pardon the whole of Oude will band against us, and be supported by Rohilkhand and Bundelkund... Lord Canning has now, in my opinion, entailed upon the army work they will never be able to carry out."[48]

A disappointed Campbell returned to Cawnpore. Here on 12th February he met with a unique individual he had first met in the Crimea. This was 39-year-old William Howard Russell, special correspondent of the London *Times* newspaper, the world's first war reporter. Reports of the Uprising had started appearing in British journals in July beginning with the *Illustrated London News*. John Delane, smart editor of *The Times*, had sent Russell to the Crimea, where his incisive and witty reporting had exposed the errors of the high command and shocked and moved the British people, including the Queen, although he had met with open hostility from some officers. "That blackguard, Mr Russell, ought to be hung" wrote an officer of Fusiliers. The country had been gripped by the writer's descriptive pen as he related such disasters as the Charge of the Light Brigade, the sufferings of ordinary soldiers in the harsh winter conditions, and the pen portraits of leading generals – including Campbell. A thick-set, bearded man who first started writing sketches for the *Dublin Penny Journal* when only 16, Russell was described neatly but cruelly by one VC-winning officer in the Crimea:

> A vulgar low Irishman ... but he has the gift of the gab, uses his pen as well as his tongue, sings a good song, drinks anyone's brandy and water, and smokes as many cigars as foolish young officers will let him, and he is looked upon by the men in camp as a Jolly Good Fellow. He is just the sort to get information, particularly out of youngsters. And I assure you more than one "Nob" has thought best to give him a shake of the hand rather than the cold shoulder *en passant* ... rather an awkward gentleman to be on bad terms with.[49]

Now Russell was in India and intended to follow Campbell's army. Sir Colin was affable and dealt with the journalist in his usual brisk manner: "Now Mr Russell, I'll be candid with you. We shall make a compact. You shall know everything that is going on. You shall see all my reports, and get every information that I have myself, on the condition that you do not mention it in camp, or let it be known in any way, except in your letters to England."

"I accept the condition, sir," beamed Russell, "and I promise you it shall be faithfully observed."[50]

On 10th February in a General Order the C-in-C had announced the formation of the Army of Oudh: Major-General Sir Archdale Wilson, who had commanded the army that re-took Delhi, was given the Artillery Division; Brigadier Robert Napier would command the engineers and Brigadier Hope Grant the cavalry; the infantry was to be divided into three brigades with the 1st under Major-General Sir James Outram; the 2nd under Brigadier Sir Edward Lugard, a soldier who had fought in the 1st Afghan War, Sikh Wars and Persia; the 3rd under Brigadier Robert Walpole, a favourite of Campbell's, though a rather poor general. These appointments caused disquiet among officers newly arrived from England but, as Sir Colin told the Duke of Cambridge, it was impossible for a newcomer to "weigh the value of intelligence ... he cannot judge what are the resources of the country, and is totally unable to make an estimate for himself of the resistance the enemy opposed to him is likely to offer."[51] In other words, there was no room for more Windhams making a mess of things.

Campbell told Canning that the Nepali and Franks's columns would increase his army by 12,000 men, but the earliest they could arrive would be 27th February. Tired of waiting, he told the Governor-General that everything was ready for an advance without Jung Bahadur and that "we are able to take the strongest positions of the city without him."[52] Canning quickly replied with a salient observation:

> I wish the pause in the operations before Lucknow could have been avoided; but I am sure that, as matters stand, we do better to accept the necessity, and wait for Jung Bahadoor. It would drive him wild to find himself jockeyed out of all share in the great campaign... I am convinced that he would break with us and go back to the hills within a week. The loss of this help would be very inconvenient, but to find ourselves on bad terms with him would be much more so.[53]

The Governor-General added: "It will be a good thing if the intervening time be turned to account against the Nana."

Sir Colin chafed at this imposed delay and telegraphed Macgregor for news of Jung Bahadur's movements. Meanwhile he had Cawnpore's defences improved, just in case the Gwalior rebels returned, then sent Hope Grant in search of Nana Sahib. This expedition did not find the Raj's No 1 public enemy and involved a stiff fight with insurgents at the town of Meeanjung in Oudh on 23rd February. Five hundred of the enemy were killed and 400 taken prisoner. But as the captives were mainly townspeople, Hope Grant insisted they should be set free, "to their inexpressible surprise and delight", one of the few conciliatory gestures in the whole of the Uprising. Grant was, if anything, tougher on his own troops than he was on the rebels. He was his own provost marshal and a stickler for obedience to the rules; when he found 25 Irish soldiers of HM 53rd robbing some native houses he had 12 of the men flogged on the spot and two of the regiment's officers placed under arrest.

10

The Last Battle

Oudh and Lucknow,
28ᵗʰ February–21ˢᵗ March 1858

With no sign of the Nepalis, a disconcerted Campbell led his army out
of Cawnpore in the early hours of 28ᵗʰ February 1858. He stopped,
as before, at Bunthera. "Here such a force was collected as must have
paled the cheek of Pandy's spies," wrote an artillery officer, Lieutenant
Vivian Majendie, "Magnificent it was to see this vast assemblage of white
tents stretching out for miles."[1] Jogging along on a sedate horse (he had
given his frisky mare to Thomas Kavanagh), rode Russell of *The Times*.
He described the march:

> As soon as we had advanced a few miles from the Ganges, not only
> the broad road, but the broad track at each side of it, was thronged by
> an immense and apparently illimitable procession of oxen, hackeries,
> horses, ponies, camels, camp followers on foot or riding, trains of
> stores, elephants, all plodding steadily along in the burning sun under
> the umberella of dense clouds of white dust... All these men, women
> and children, with high delight, were pouring to Lucknow to aid the
> Feringhee to overcome their brethren... Their houses were their tents;
> their streets the camp-bazaar; their ruler the bazaar kotwal; their
> politics the rise and fall of rice ... whole regiments of sinewy hollow-
> thighed, lanky coolies, shuffle along under loads of chairs, tables,
> hampers of beer and wine, bazaar stores or boxes slung from bamboo
> poles across their shoulders.[2]

Russell also noted the squawking turkeys, screaming parrots, snorting
camels loaded with beer, pickles, potted meats and soda-water, monkeys
on the backs of camels, panting tame deer and, at the back, the pariah
dogs always looking for a free meal.

313

One of the oddest sights were the sailors in their straw hats pushing and pulling their huge guns. The entire Naval Brigade from HMS *Shannon* set out for Lucknow, over 430 officers and men, with eight 24-pounder and six massive 68-pounder guns, two 8-inch siege howitzers and eight rocket tubes. The ammunition for the 68-pounders alone took up 20 carts. These were the largest guns that had ever been taken on a field campaign (the ones used in the Crimea had been static).

At the Alambagh the wait for Campbell's army to arrive was starting to tell. "If Sir Colin gets up here soon, and we are followed with a fortnight's moderate weather, I believe Lucknow will be ours," wrote John Chalmers, one of the garrison, "but if not, I think we must sit here through the hot weather and rains as in Delhi and lose at least half our men and *possibly* have to begin again to reconquer India."[3] Also having doubts was an artillery officer who wrote: "There are, I believe about 100,000 men in the city. What a slaughter-house it will be whenever we take it."[4]

The epic siege of the Lucknow Residency, with all its heroism and suffering, Havelock's epic attempt to relieve the city with his tiny army, Campbell's epic battle in November 1857 that had seen the largest number of VCs ever won in a single day and finally, Outram's equally epic defence of the hunting lodge known as the Alambagh for over three months, were now all to be eclipsed in a battle of vast proportions. While it cannot be compared with the millions thrown into battle in the world wars, the scale of what was about to take place at Lucknow in March 1858 has been forgotten. Detailed intelligence reports suggested that the insurgents numbered 37 regiments of ex-sepoys, 14 new levies, 106 corps of militia, 26 regiments of regular and irregular cavalry and a camel corps – approximately 98,500 men. These trained troops are exclusive of the armed retainers sent by various landowners and believed to number not fewer than 20,000 men. By late February, there had been some desertions by a few of the taluqdars and their retainers, notably Man Singh, who rightly guessed that the British would prevail. In Man Singh's case, he sidled off to his fort at Shahganj to await events. But there were probably more than 100,000 insurgents in total awaiting the British and they had 127 big guns.

Sir Colin Campbell was putting in harm's way 1,613 artillery, 2,002 engineers, 3,613 cavalry (with 3,587 horses), and 12,543 infantry – a total of 19,771 officers and men. Brigadier-General Franks' column joined the C-in-C on 5th March with a further 5,893 men. Unprecedented was the massive cavalry proportion. There were 16 battalions of British infantry. Jung Bahadaur's 8,000 Gurkhas expected in a few days brought the British forces to at least 33,000 troops armed with no fewer than 165 heavy guns.

Thus on the plains around Lucknow and in the city streets some 135,000–140,000 combatants were about to collide, fight, live or die. These numbers dwarf, for instance, the 108,000 men who fought at Blenheim under Marlborough, and it would be the largest battle ever fought by the British in India (and possibly in Indian history), and certainly the greatest confrontation in British colonial history.

Many British regiments of fresh-faced soldiers now joined Campbell's tough older regulars. They included HM 93rd Highlanders – the general's pets – and their special comrades, the Punjabi hillmen of the 4th Punjab Native Infantry. Many of these men had faced death a score of times. Now they wanted to finish the job with one last battle. They were facing, in many cases, good regiments that had originally been officered and trained by the British as part of the East India Company's army, including many ex-British sepoys who had fought bravely at Delhi and knew exactly who they were up against. Some had faced Havelock's men in September and Campbell's in November. It was a third clash for them and they were willing to die, for the shirkers and cowards had long gone. The Indians the British faced were mostly battle-hardened and would sell their lives with immense courage buoyed in the belief that, after Tantia Tope's victory over Windham at Cawnpore, it *was* possible to beat the British.

While Sir Colin's troops had been away, their foes in Lucknow had not been idle. The city had been divided into four sectors. Because the British had attacked twice from the south-east, a "wet ditch" had been constructed, fed by the Gumti. Behind this was a massive earthwork structure, a first line of defence, built with proper loopholes and embrasures for the big guns. There were trenches dug for the defenders and sunken rifle-pits for sharpshooters:

> The first great wall ran from the Hosseinabad Bridge, east of the Charbagh, to the river, a distance of two and a half miles. Further west, and crossing the new Cawnpore road, which General Havelock had marched along in September, was an even longer mud wall and dry ditch, running from the fortified village of Para, through Jalalpur, to the Yellow House, north of the British-held Alambagh.[5]

Besides these two lines of defences, a third had been created by strengthening the Kaisarbagh and the Moti Mahal palaces, as well as the rebels' military headquarters at the Khurshid Manzil. Earth embankments, stockades, entrenchments and parapets had been thrown up in many streets. A moat had been dug around the 400-square-yards enclosure of the Kaisarbagh, a new parapet now surmounted the gateway of the Sikanderbagh, and the strategic Tripodi Gateway that led into the Great Imambara mosque had earth walls up to its second floor. The bridges, especially the Stone Bridge, had been fortified with gun batteries. The old Macchi Bhawan fortress was now surrounded by ditches and embankments of earth studded with giant timbers. As Rosie Llewellyn-Jones observed, "Lucknow was as impregnable as could be." Taking a tour of the streets after the fall of the city, a British officer was impressed: 'The preparations for resistance were made with a skill and perseverance which no words can adequately describe: there is not a corner, an angle, a street or a building without its defence, either a buttress looped with holes, or an abattis of timber and mud; batteries and trenches intersecting each other; not a garden in the vicinity on which labour has not been spent."[6]

Politically, the situation in the city remained tense; the Maulvi and the Queen-Regent distrusted one another completely. In December Ahmaddullah Shah had moved out of the city and began to build his own bridge of boats. Hazrat Mahal sent her lover, Mammu Khan, to stop him. A reconciliation of sorts took place in late December and the Maulvi agreed to send some of his troops to try and delay the Nepalese in eastern Oudh. This column got under way and then a rumour reached it that it was all a ruse to get them out of the city while the Begam could hand the place over to the British. Returning to Lucknow, the Maulvi's followers then got into a brawl outside the north-west entrance to the Kaisarbagh on 7th January with supporters of Hazrat Mahal, and over 100 men were killed.

On 24th January, Outram had sent the Queen-Regent an offer of one lakh of rupees as a pension if she agreed to surrender. The deal agitated Mammu Khan and it appears that Hazrat Mahal actually considered it briefly before she told one of her generals to destroy the letter. When, in early February, she heard about the deal offered by the British to Jung Bahadur, she sent a counter-offer that included giving away the city of Benares, but her two "ambassadors" were caught and hanged by the British.

Campbell was well aware that Lucknow was more strongly defended than ever before. "I could not hope to invest a city having a circumference of twenty miles,"[7] he told Lord Canning, even with the troops at his disposal. He had decided, instead, to force a break in the earthworks and storm the Kaisarbagh. Knowing that the rebels expected an attack from the south-east, Outram had urged an assault from the north-west. Robert Napier, chief engineer, warned "the west side presents a great breadth of dense and almost impenetrable city." He favoured an attack from the east:

First [it was] the smallest front, and was therefore more easily enveloped by our attack; secondly, ground for planting our artillery, which was wanting on the west side; and thirdly, it gave also the shortest approach to the Kaisarbagh ... across the canal in the first instance at Banks's house under cover of our artillery – and to place guns to bear on the mass of buildings which flank the European Infantry barracks – the Hospital – the Begum's House and the Hurzat Gunge [Huzerutgunge] ... and to take that mass of buildings ... which extend to the walls of the Kaisarbagh.

After occupying the Dilkusha overlooking the city, Napier was thus advising Campbell to push through the earthworks by Banks's House, then bring his cannons to bear on the long line of imposing buildings leading towards the Kaisarbagh, while at the same time sending cavalry and artillery around the city, north-east of the Gumti, to assemble opposite the Residency and "cut off the enemy's supplies, and to deter them from bringing guns on the North Side of the river to annoy us."[8]

Sir Colin weighed all these strategies and decided to expand on Napier's plan with a two-pronged attack. Outram would be given an infantry division and storm Lucknow from the north, approaching the enemy in their rear, "to take their works in flank and reverse, whilst our attack is pressed with vigour from this side ... as soon as the Martinière is taken."[9] Tactically, it was a hazardous plan, a bold one that flew in the face of accepted military logic, which said generals should not divide their forces.

The general advance on Lucknow began on the morning of 2nd March 1858. As the army spread out across the plain heading towards the Dilkusha, they saw reminders of the last time that had been this way. "Here and there, with bits of red cloth still fluttering on the bones, lay the sun-dried skeletons of rebels who had fallen in attacking Outram's gallant band"[10] and Campbell's November assault. The insurgents gave way as the giant column approached the Dilkusha, "its once opulent grounds dilapidated and forlorn", as the rebels had cut down many of the park's tallest trees. Enemy artillery at the Martinière soon found their range and peppered the British lines; two of the Naval Brigade were killed and Brigadier Little of the Cavalry Brigade badly wounded when a ball went through his left elbow. Bullets struck a tree close by Sir Colin. As a result of these and similar instances, he moved his main camp to behind the Dilkusha. One officer described the taking of this position:

The Pandays were regularly taken by surprise on our arrival on this ground. They had only a small picquet and some three guns in advance;

but our Cavalry and Horse Artillery were so sharp down upon them, that they could not take away two of their guns, which were captured. There is great rivalry between the Royal and Bengal Artillery. Major Tombs rather opened the eyes of the former by taking his troops at full gallop over a 3-foot wall with a ditch on each side. The same place rather puzzled the 9th Lancers, who were with him, and some of them got thrown at the same jump, but nothing can stop the Bengal Horse Artillery.[11]

The view of Lucknow from the heights astonished Russell:

A vision of palaces, minarets, domes, azure and golden, cupolas, colonnades, long facades of fair perspective in pillar and column, terraced roofs – all rising amid a calm, still ocean of the brightest verdure. Look for miles and miles away, and still the ocean spreads, and the towers of the fairy-city gleam in its midst. Spires of gold glitter in the sun. Turrets and gilded spheres shine like constellations. There is nothing mean and squalid to be seen… Not Rome, not Athens, not Constantinople, nor any city I have ever seen, appears to me so striking and beautiful as this.[12]

Brigadier Franks arrived on the 5th and despite having marched 130 miles in 13 days, beaten superior numbers of rebels in four major actions and captured 35 guns, the notorious martinet now endured a tongue-lashing of his own from the C-in-C. Just eight miles short of Lucknow, Franks had decided to disregard his chief's strict instructions to proceed as quickly as possible, and attacked a small fort at Dhowara, two miles off his track. His reasoning was that these insurgents might attack his baggage train. Refusing to listen to the advice of Harry Havelock (who had re-joined the 10th Foot, his old regiment) and some other officers, the brigadier sent his men into action without using his 24-pounder guns. The insurgents managed to beat off the assault, wounding Macleod Innes in the process. Campbell was furious that Franks had wasted valuable time; he had been planning to give him the role that he now assigned to Outram. Franks and his troops would fight well in the coming days as a 4th Brigade, relieving Lugard's 2nd Brigade, but after the battle Campbell refused to give Thomas Harte Franks another field command.

Now with his army enlarged by Franks's column including 3,019 Gurkhas, the C-in-C decided that he was not prepared to wait any longer for Jung Bahadur's soldiers to join him. Two makeshift bridges made from wooden casks covered in boards, each 135 feet long, were placed over the Gumti and shortly before dawn on 6th March Outram's troops started for the river. He had with him large numbers of British and Bengal sappers; three troops of horse artillery; 2nd Dragoon Guards, 9th Lancers and 2nd Punjab Cavalry with detachments of the 1st and 5th Punjab Cavalry; the 5th Infantry Brigade consisting of the 23rd Royal Welsh Fusiliers, 79th Highlanders and 1st Bengal Fusiliers; the 6th Brigade made up of two battalions of the Rifle Brigade and 2nd Punjab Infantry.

The sun rose, dispelling a thick mist that had hung about over the river all night. It shone on the glittering lances and bayonets. It was, an observer wrote, "a magnificent sight, the Rifles in green, the gallant 23rd Fusiliers in their admirable dress, looking so ready for work, the old 1st in their blue caps and tunics and clean white belts, the 79th with waving plumes and tartans, the well-tried Sikhs, the gorgeous Bays."[13] Watching the advance, W. H. Russell enthused:

Will the column never cease? Hour after hour it has been passing us… What swarms of camp-followers! What a mighty *impedimentum* of baggage, all pouring along towards the river, and then following in parallel lines the folds of the serpent-like column which is winding away through the corn- fields till it disappears in the woods on the horizon. The column and its dependencies were four hours crossing over; as to the baggage, it was not clear of the bridge even at night.[14]

Outram led his soldiers in a long circuit around and outside the city to the north. They had not gone too far when 400 enemy cavalry appeared. The 2nd Dragoon Guards, known as the Bays, full of fresh-faced young men all new to India, galloped after the enemy. It was a moment of high excitement. The regiment was on its first campaign in 40 years. Their glorious charge was also a rash one. The Bays had a severe mauling and had to leave Major Percy Smith, a "gentlemanly, good-looking & kind-hearted young fellow", dead on the field. Next day his body was recovered, severely mutilated and with his head cut off. Campbell was furious when he heard about the charge; he could ill afford to lose good horses and saddles. Some officers, such as John Chalmers, newly appointed adjutant of the 24th PNI, were not impressed with Outram's generalship:

All I can say from what I saw and know is that with a force far superior to any we ever had at Delhi, he attacked an enclosure and *did not take* it, and that he had a Major of the 2nd D.Gds. killed and *did not* bring away his body. I cannot call this a victory, although the papers, I suppose, may try and do so. To-day Gen. O. again commenced to advance. The enemy came out and met him and they had a fight.

The enemy certainly went back into the city, and Gen. O. certainly did not go forward. Neither do I call this a victory. The honest truth is that as yet we are overmatched, and the odds are rather increasing against us than improving.[15]

Rushing headlong into the city was no part of Campbell's plan, so his apparent slowness infuriated some officers, especially the junior ones. "The great mistake all the swells *now* in command out here make, is that of treating the Pandies as if they were European troops," complained Lieutenant Charles Macgregor, 1st Bengal Fusiliers. "There is too much caution."[16] The general deliberately wanted his artillery to first pound the city before he risked men's lives in the kind of street fighting that had cost Havelock dearly at the first Relief and also hindered his own Relief in November. "The roar of artillery and musketry, with the yells of the rebels was continued the whole night,"[17] wrote Trooper T. S. Palmer, B troop, 7th Hussars, in his diary.

Heavy guns reached Outram on the 8th and he began advancing towards the city on the 9th. Christopher Hibbert left us a vivid description of the British advance:

For many of his men this was their first battle, and they remembered it afterwards in vivid detail: the still hour before the action began when – surrounded by horses with heads deep in nose-bags and officers handing round cigar-cases and brandy flasks – the men ate what for many of them would be their last meal, carving out hunks of bread and lumps of meat with pocket-knives which, being used also for cutting tobacco, imparted to the meat a particularly racy flavour. Then came the enemy's opening shots, whirring and rattling through the mango trees, bringing down showers of green leaves and shattered branches, or whooshing and bounding across open ground, tearing up turf and stones, then bounding up, perhaps, to pass overhead with a sort of scream or land with a thud in a bank.[18]

Outram's first objective was "the Yellow House" (*Chakar Kothi*), a "glaring shell of brick and stucco", grandstand of the royal race course. Here the fighting took a terrible turn. A small group of defenders refused to give in and eventually the British had to use artillery, lobbing 20 or so rounds at the building. During the delay, an officer was killed and his Sikh troops were the first to enter the smoke-filled interior. They dragged out one dazed rebel, trying to pull him apart and stabbed the man repeatedly with bayonets. Then the Sikhs laid him on an improvised griddle and roasted the fellow alive. "The horrible smell of his burning flesh, as it cracked and blackened in the flames, rising up and poisoning the air," wrote Lieutenant Majendie, who watched the proceedings in horror. Englishmen, he noted, "looked calmly on".[19]

Next Sir James pushed the enemy back through the old irregular cavalry lines and suburbs to the Badshahbagh ("Garden of the King"), a high-walled garden built by King Nasir-ud-din-Haider, where "gaily hued flowers bordered shallow marble lakes filled with sweet-scented rose water in which the favourites of the harem were wont to disport themselves."[20]

"The fortified gates were blown open and the garden occupied, and two guns found by our troops,"[21] wrote the general. While the place had a number of small summer-palaces "with prettily laid-out walks radiating in every direction, shaded by splendid orange trees", it was still a dangerous spot. "Round shot came bounding through the garden at frequent intervals," wrote Lieutenant Edward Vibart, "thus rendering our stay there anything but pleasant."[22] Soon, Outram held the ground all the way down to the river nearby and could start firing into the heart of the city.

Young Ensign Jervis rushed to the top of the Yellow House and planted the colours of the 1st Bengal Fusiliers. Seeing Outram's flag flying at about 2pm, Sir Colin ordered Lugard's 2nd Division to attack the Martinière, instead of following Napier's plan to push the rebels north-west of the Dilkusha. The reason for the change was the intense shelling coming from some expert rebel gunners at the Martinière barely 600 yards away. Napier pointed out a wall he wanted breached and Captain Peel, with his usual indifference to danger, was standing on a small mound directing the fire when he was hit in the right thigh. He was carried off to the surgeons in a litter and though he looked deathly pale was expected to recover, but his injury cast a gloom over the Naval Brigade.

Having tried to bombard La Martinière with his heavy guns, Campbell now launched his 4th Brigade, supported by the 3rd, at the building. An order that morning had stated: "The men employed in the attack will use nothing but the bayonet."[23] Watching with his telescope from the top of the Dilkusha, and seeing his men inside La Martinière, Campbell galloped over with his staff. The enemy roundshot still whizzed in their direction but no horse or rider was hit. Soon the old general was on the highest balcony watching his horse artillery unlimbering by the sandy bank of the Gumti to pound away at the rebels behind the canal works, while Adrian Hope's soldiers supported them with musketry fire. As Campbell and his staff watched events, they spied a lone figure in blue trousers with red stripes emerge from the river on their side and wave up at them. This was Lieutenant Thomas Adair Butler, 1st Bengal European

Fusiliers. He had swum across the river to alert the Highlanders to the fact that three entrenchments nearby appeared to be deserted (as viewed from the opposite bank), and should be seized. Wet, cold and dripping, Butler made a perfect enemy target until he finally caught Sir Colin's attention. Having reported to a Highland officer, Butler saluted and plunged back into the river again. He had 60 yards to cross and it was running swiftly.[24]

It was assumed that the attack on La Martinière would result in a heavy loss of life, "but we dashed into them with little loss," wrote Fairweather of the 4th PNI. His commandant, Alfred Wilde, then decided to advance further without orders from above when he saw that the earth wall and deep ditch in front of it were badly manned. He managed to get close to the great wall and that night, helped by the 42nd, held some gardens nearby.

Early on the 10th, a battery started shelling Banks's House. This two storied building had been used 50 years earlier as a powder magazine, but was named after Major Banks, the Commissioner killed during the Residency siege, who had made the place his home. A breach was made through the great earth wall, and to the sound of the bagpipes Scots bonnets were soon waving from the ramparts. "Very fine ramparts they are," wrote engineer, Arthur Lang, "I was at work till past midnight, cutting through this rampart and throwing a causeway across the canal, so as to make a nice road for the guns."[25] Campbell now converted Banks's House into a strongpost and placed four guns and eight mortars near it to breach the Begam Kothi ("Queen's Palace"). Another battery of two guns and six mortars to the west of the building also hammered away at the palace.

That day, Sir James strengthened his position near the river bank, but Major Sandford, 5th Punjab Irregular Cavalry, was shot and killed in a melee at a nearby village. Led by the gallant Dighton Probyn, 2nd Punjab Cavalry, men returned later to search for and recover Sandford's body. All night the guns near Banks's House lobbed their shells at the Begum Kothi "like showers of falling stars".

"On every front," wrote Adrian Greenwood, "the gunners and sappers led the assault." Next morning Outram continued westwards as far as the Stone Bridge where strongly entrenched rebels forced him to pull back to the Badshahbagh, leaving a detachment guarding the north end of the Iron Bridge and the mosque on the old cantonment road. Lieutenant Moorsom who was guiding the troops, just as he had guided Havelock's 2nd column, was shot through the head, a sad end to a promising career. Captain Thynne of the Rifle Brigade was also killed when roundshot pulverised his arms and thighs. Amputation was tried but he died of shock an hour later.

The British pincers were moving ever westwards. After seizing Banks's House, the C-in-C was starting to approach the Begum Kothi along the line of palatial houses that ran down the Hazratgange (then, as now, Lucknow's main street). On the 12th the Sikanderbagh fell, this time with minimal casualties. Arthur Lang described Campbell's advance:

Medley, Carnegie and I, being with 100 sappers at the Sikander Bagh, and having a strong objection to the dreadful odour of the 1,840 Pandies buried there, and pretty sure that the Kadam Rasul was deserted, took three sappers and stole into it and found it empty. From the top of it we saw the Shah Najaf seemingly also deserted. While Medley galloped to get General Lugard's permission to occupy it, I rode across the bridge of boats and warned the Artillery and Rifle posts across the river not to fire on us... So we moved into the Shah Najaf and fortified it. Pandy had done most of this for us. One of Outram's rear batteries kept up very nice practice *just* over our heads into the Mess House and Moti Mahal, and, at last, a little powder being short, in came a huge 8 inch shell and cut off the arm of a 53rd man, as if a razor had done it.[26]

It was at this critical moment that Jung Bahadur and his Nepali troops finally arrived. The Gurkhas seemed "a rum-looking little lot" to one officer, "few of them are over 5ft 2, but are said to fight well. Although the officers are very bad. They will be of use in preventing the escape of the mutineers, but I fear not much else."[27] Lieutenant Herford was even less impressed, describing them as "extremely dirty". He wrote: "They introduced themselves to us, as searching for plunder; in fact, the whole time they were with the force, and until they were *escorted* with their 'loot' to their own country, they did nothing else."[28] The troops were kitted out in loose blue trousers, green jackets and red turbans with a brass crescent in the front. The Nepalese first minister was "magnificently dressed, his turban ornamented with a splendid tiara of diamonds and emeralds."[29] After "a good deal of bowing and salaaming", Jung Bahadur demanded a royal salute for himself and his brothers. Sir Colin's temper was soon up: "Salutes are never fired at sieges!" The 4pm grand durbar saw him decked out in gold lace and cocked hat, replacing his regular dress of tartan waistcoat with cotton sleeves and moleskin trousers. By 4.25pm the royal party had still not turned up and the general was pacing the floor to and fro in a bad mood. At about half past four, just as Campbell had scheduled the big attack on the Begum Kothi, in walked the Nepalese. While the durbar was taking place a staff officer reported that the Begum Kothi was taken. There had been little loss on the British side and about 500 of the enemy killed. "The effect was magical," wrote an observer, "the unfinished programme of solemn nonsense was cast to the winds."[30]Sir Colin could not conceal his delight. "I knew it! I knew it!" he said, clapping his hands and jumping up and down, "I knew my Highlanders would take it!"[31]

The Begum Kothi (not to be confused with a much smaller building in the Residency enclosure with the same name), had been built by King Amjad Ali Shah in 1844 as a place for his Queen, Malka Ahad Begum, possibly on the site of a similar earlier building. It was yet another of Lucknow's pseudo-classical palaces built, as one critic said, "in the worst possible taste", though many found it pleasing.

First into the palace had been Adrian Hope's 93rd Highlanders, 4th PNI, some sappers and miners carrying powder bags, and 500 of Franks's Gurkhas in support. Inside, the building was crammed with 5,000 insurgents and just like the fight at the Sikanderbagh in November, they were prepared to sell their lives dearly. First, the British had to mount a huge parapet of earth with two ditches on the far side, one 10 feet deep and 18 feet wide, the second nearest the building much smaller. Luckily, two breaches had been left undefended and the men climbed out of the ditch and heaved themselves up to one of these holes. Once inside, however, a destructive fire came down on them. "Every room-door, gallery, or gateway was barricaded. At every window or coign of vantage was a rebel marksman. In threading their way through the narrow dark passages many a man fell shot down by an unseen foe."[32]

To the sound of wailing bagpipes the troops had moved forward, struggling past doorways half blocked with earth, each darkened small room a potential death trap. "The 93rd lost two officers killed and were very savage," wrote Lieutenant Lang, "dragging out bodies, heaping them up, and making assurance doubly sure with the bayonet."[33] Small bags of gunpowder were thrown into each room to clear it of rebels. This set light to clothing and to whatever furniture was in the rooms. Soon hundreds of bodies all round were burning, or others half-burnt, "and the stench was sickening." William Forbes-Mitchell wrote later how "... one barrier after another was forced, and men in small parties, headed by their officers, got possession of the inner square, where the enemy in large numbers stood ready for the struggle... The command was given: 'Keep well together, men, and use the bayonet; give them the Sikanderbagh and the sixteenth of November again.' I need not describe the fight. It raged for two hours from court to court, and from room to room; the pipe-major, John

M'Leod, playing the pipes as calmly as if he had been walking round the officers' mess-tent."[34]

No quarter was given or asked. "Only one prisoner was taken,"[35] noted Captain "Wee Frenchie" Traill-Burroughs. British losses were 31 dead and 86 wounded in the taking of the Begum Kothi, and 518 native corpses were counted and buried next day. Lieutenant and adjutant Willie McBean of the 93rd had cut down 11 men with his heavy cavalry sword, saying afterwards, "I didna mean tae hurt 'em."

The most famous British fatality was the arch-adventurer, William Hodson. He had actually been in camp when the attack started, but on hearing the news, had galloped off impulsively to join the attack as a volunteer.It was late afternoon, about 5.30pm. Hodson entered one of the small rooms with the same impulsiveness, despite warnings to wait, and was shot through the chest. He managed to say "Oh, my wife!" but was immediately choked by blood. Dr Anderson, Hodson's Horse regimental surgeon wrote:

> He was hit by a musket ball which had passed thro' the liver and came out in the back and that there had been profuse bleeding... When the soldiers were searching for concealed sepoys in the courtyard and buildings adjoining it, he said to his orderly, "I wonder if there is anyone in this house," and pulling down a doorway, looked into a dark room, when a sepoy inside fired and hit him. He staggered back some paces and then fell. Some Highlanders came up and bayoneted the men in the dark room. His orderly, a powerful Sikh (Nihal Singh) carried him in his arms, got a doolie and brought him to Banks's House.[36]

Anderson held his patient's hand all night. Hodson was in great pain but drifted into sleep for a couple of hours. Daybreak saw him rally and Anderson thought he might recover if the bleeding would only cease. He drank two cups of tea. But at 10am the bleeding began again. He sent for Colonel Napier, settled his business affairs and dictated a message to his wife. He died at 1.25pm on 12th March.

Hodson's death shocked many in the army, not least Sir Colin, who wrote to his widow that he had been "the most brilliant under my command and one I was proud to call a friend."[37] Surgeon Frederick Dalzell heard the general lose his temper with his chief engineer, saying: "Napier, you're a fine officer, but you haven't sufficient of the Devil in you. Why did you not place Hodson under arrest? I have lost in him one of the finest officers in the army."[38] At the funeral held behind the Martinière, the general was actually seen to weep. "A more daring, fearless, brave man never existed," wrote Montagu Hall. "The finest

Cavalry and Intelligence officer in the army," echoed Lieutenant Lang. There were other eulogies, though none more touching than one sent to Mrs Hodson by Lt-Colonel Thomas Seaton:

> He was everyone's Hodson, but he was *our* Willie. I say *our*, for I was his comrade and then his commander ... during the whole of the terrible siege of Delhi, we lived together in the same tent... It was there that I saw in all their splendour his noble and soldierly qualities, never fatigued, never downcast, always cool and calm, with a cheerful countenance and a word of encouragement for everyone ... the brave and stern soldier had also the tenderness of a woman... He was perfectly indefatigable.[39]

Soon there were rumours that Hodson had ridden to the Begum Kothi in search of loot. Events there seem to discount this myth, but besides the many who mourned him were others who, like Major-General Sir Archdale Wilson, said: "He had no right to be at the Begum Kothi. He should have been 5 miles off with his Horse."[40] Ashton Warner, General Walpole's aide, said much the same thing, adding, "He had no business to be where he was, this is often the case with volunteers."[41]

About 20 or more royal women were found hiding in the Begum Kothi and a kindly staff officer, Robert Biddulph (he had a special fondness for elephants), was told to take the princesses to safety. The women were terrified, "talking and cackling like geese", noted Biddulph, apart from one who fainted and had to be carried. "They seemed to think they were going to be shot at once," he wrote, "chiefly they bewailed the loss of their jewellery."[42] When W. H. Russell interviewed them, the princesses seem to have recovered some composure and told him that their menfolk would win in the end.

These were not the only women rescued; the three English females who had been hidden and cared for in the city for months – Madeleine Jackson, Mrs Annie Orr and infant daughter, Louisa, were also saved. Their benefactor, Wajid Ali, got word at last to the British. The child was carried to the British lines "like a bundle of old clothes" on the back of a native woman. The other two were in a room when they heard gunshots and footsteps on the stairs. "I flew out to see what was happening and there was a tall Englishman!" said Madeleine. 'We are saved,' I called out to Mrs Orr. He came in and another Englishman ran up – Captain MacNeill and Mr Bogle. They said, 'Are you Miss Jackson and Mrs Orr?' – Come at once.'" Then little Gurkhas carried them up and down ravines "like cats" and presently they arrived at the British camp. "It seemed such an impossible thing! English soldiers rushed up to greet us. Sir Colin Campbell and the Ghoorkha Chief and a lot of officers came and shook hands with us. Telegrams were sent to England at once and to Calcutta. They asked me who I wanted to send one to in India, and I burst into tears, and said all mine were killed."[43]

On the 12th and 13th, Campbell one again halted his advance so that Napier could use his guns against a building called the Small Imambara. Back at the Alambagh the garrison had been straining their eyes through telescopes to understand was was going on each day. But that night "the effect from the roof of the Alambagh was glorious and could truly be compared to a magnificent display of fireworks," wrote Frank Ashley Cubitt, "as the heavens were lit up by the fiery rush of the rockets, the perpetual circling of stars of shells and then the explosion with thousands of sparks, while huge fires in the city made it almost as visible & light as day."[44] Jung Bahadur was requested to move his Gurkhas closer to the canal and the troops at the Begam Kothi were relieved, General Lugard's place being taken by General Franks. Napier constructed new batteries, Outram was reinforced with artillery and the Naval Brigade rockets started behaving unpredictably; the sticks and explosives had gotten too dry so they shot off all over the place, or fell short of their proper range.

By dawn on 14th March two breaches in the walls of the Small Imambara, though more correctly termed the Maqbara of Amjad Ali Shah, made an assault possible. This Nawab or king had reigned from 1842 until an ulcer (or poison) finished him off in 1847. He was buried there in a large rectangular chamber, approached through a gateway and a fine flight of steps. The room was full of priceless art treasures, silken carpets and wonderful chandeliers. Beneath a trapdoor in the centre of the floor was a cobwebbed vault and the king's tomb. The storming party consisted of two companies of HM 10th Foot and 60 men of Brayser's Sikhs led by the long-bearded old warrior himself. From nearby rooftops, the tops of walls and the Maqbara itself, rebels kept up a fire of musketry. While soldiers got ready, young Lieutenant Beaumont R.E. blasted a hole through the mud walls of a house connected by a trench to the holy building. He next blew a gap in one of its walls and Brayser's Sikhs rushed in. Julius Medley, one of the engineers, recalled a room "full of chandeliers, mirrors and an extraordinary assortment of ornaments, most of which were smashed by our men out of sheer mischief."[45] Watchers soon saw a Sikh and then the commandant himself on the parapet. More troops followed and the building was secured with minimal loss of life.

This method of working along the south side of the Hazratganj by sapping was remarked upon by Edward Vibart in a letter to his brother: "Fancy getting into a house in Park Lane, only twice the size, with gardens and courtyards, and knocking a hole in the next with 68-pounders, then bringing up the gun, and knocking a hole in the next, and rushing in, and so on. The rebels did not understand it, they had prepared the streets with batteries, loopholes etc, while we went into the houses themselves and broke through from house to house."[46]

Tough warriors who had fought alongside Havelock, Brayser's men were jubilant and they scented even greater success; they pursued the retreating rebels into an outlying court of the great Kaisarbagh Palace. From nearby rooftops, Harry Havelock (now Franks' Adjutant-General), Brayser and men of the 90th fired so heavily on the insurgents that they abandoned three bastions of the Kaisarbagh. In the street, several troops were killed or wounded as they reached the Cheenee Bazaar that skirted the huge building. By now, Havelock and the Sikhs had breached the enemy's second line of defences.

Brigadier Franks and Colonel Napier decided it was time to consult with the C-in-C. During this intermission Lieutenant Medley was told to fortify the gateway of the Kaisarbagh. While talking to Captain Wall of the 87th with bullets splattering all around, Medley watched in horror as his comrade fell on his face, shot through the spine by a sepoy in a nearby house.

Shortly after 11am an orderly rode up to headquarters and told Sir Colin his troops were in the Kaisarbagh. The news spread quickly. "What is it Norman?" asked Russell as the D.A.G. sped by on his horse, "Have we got the Imambara?" Henry Norman reined his animal to a halt and grinned. "The Imambara! Why man, we're in the Kaisarbagh!"[47] Campbell had assumed his day's operations would end with a long fight for the Imambara. Now he hastened there and as he walked up its steps, both Franks and Napier assured him that the Kaisarbagh could be in British hands before the end of the day.

Back in 1847, the Nawab Wajid Ali Shah, last king of Oudh, had begun work on his Kaisarbagh with the intention that it should be the eighth wonder of the world. It had been completed three years later at a colossal cost of eight million rupees. All the buildings, including two major palace complexes within the grounds and one main courtyard, were designed in an 18th-century baroque style. Constructed over an area larger than the Tuileries and the Louvre put together, it was by day an Arabian Nights fantasy of scented fountains and lush gardens fit for the king, his harem of nearly 400 and his entourage of dancers and musicians. At night it was blaze of light, as magnificent chandeliers reflected in a thousand mirrors, bathing rooms full of costly antiques that jostled alongside Victorian bric-a-brac.

From the bazaar, 150 of Brayser's Sikhs had entered a courtyard at the back of the palace, driven the enemy from their guns in the courtyard of a mosque and were in the palace's central enclosure. Fighting here was desperate and hand-to-hand, but the rebels were forced back towards the Badshah Munzil, the special enclosure of the king. George Forrest related what happened next:

> Here a large body of the enemy was ready to oppose them. Brayser was vastly outnumbered, but he plunged his handful of men into them with the bayonet, and they bore them onward till they forced them to the Badshah Munzil ... the rebels now began to collect in their rear, while from the windows of the palace came gusts of bullets. Slowly, the small band fell back till they reached the bronze gate on the north-west side of the Kaisarbagh ... outside the gateway in their rear was a second gateway, and in front of it the enemy had a gun protected by a loopholed wall. The gun opened fire... From the palace buildings on their right the enemy plied them with musketry. A supreme moment. Then Brayser and Lieutenant Cary, 37th Native Infantry, burst open a window in front of the gun, and jumping down were soon followed by several Sikhs. The gun was captured and the enemy driven to the second gateway. They were kept there in check till reinforcements arrived.[48]

The storming regiments flooded in, all mixed together – turbanned Sikhs and green-jacketed Gurkhas, swiftly followed by British soldiers and bluejackets – all pushing the rebels back through courtyards filled with marble statues and splashing fountains until every palace became a fortress. Behind green jalousies and venetian blinds the rebels poured a stream of death until their attackers were slipping in blood on the marble floors.

The palace was a remarkable building. "If the Tuileries, the Louvre, Versailles, Scutari, the Winter Palace, were blended together, with an entourage of hovels worthy of Gallipoli, and an interior of gardens worthy of Kew, they would represent the size, at all events, of the palaces of the Kaisarbagh,"[49] wrote W. H. Russell. Now the attackers burst open the strong boxes of the Oudh royal family in a crazy lust for silver, gold and jewels, rough hands tore down brocades and silks, gems were prised out with bayonets or knives, silver plates torn off the royal throne, rare paintings slashed or trampled upon, china broken, crystal glass smashed – all in an orgy of destruction that soon turned into a massive hunt for loot. By nightfall, the Kaisarbagh resembled "a ruined charnel-house".

Arthur Lang had fought his way in with some Sikhs and so was one of the first to see the plunder. "I was knee-deep in valuables":

> Seeing that I did not help myself, a man held up a bag full of jewels – a bag as big as his head – and said, "Take a share, sir. Take this." Like a fool

I came the magnamimous and rejected everything!... One officer in the tent next to mine has upwards of 500,000 rupees worth of diamonds, pearls and rubies. I never saw such precious stones as I have here."[50]

Surgeon Collins watched aghast as soldiers in one room jumped into crates of china simply to destroy it. He noticed much of the china bore the name "Spode". The men also amused themselves firing musket balls at mirrors to create a star effect. Rifles butts were used to smash up furniture or handsome doors on cabinets. All pictures, "without exception" were ripped up and anything of glass "smashed to pieces". Lieutenant Herford was amused and shocked by the sights. "Nothing seemed to come amiss to our men," he wrote, "there was one trying to hurry off with a ponderous silver punch-bowl so heavy indeed that he left it by my side at the gateway ... another came out of a house with an armful of Cashmere shawls!... People seemed to change into clothes dealers and pedlars, there was such buying and selling of wearables, furniture and ornaments."[51] The looting lasted the rest of the day and into the next. Edmund Verney could not believe the opulence, from a royal coach panelled in sheets of silver – "perfectly dazzling" – to "priceless silks, cashmeres, pictures, gilding, glass and china to an extent I hardly believed to have existed, and room after room was fitted up in a style of lavish magnificence devoid of taste."[52] He saw a tawdry crown lying on the ground, made of cardboard, red satin and rusty iron wire, and sewn all over with dull white beads. He kept it as a keepsake and later found the dull beads were actually pearls and the crown was worth £2000 (£200,000 today). One officer of the 8th B.N.I. took rings and a diamond bracelet worth over £400, while an officer called Lance acquired one of the largest emeralds in the world, "which the king of Oudh used on state occasions," wrote Lieutenant H. H. Stansfield in a letter home. He bought a "handsome tulwar set with precious stones"[53] for 40 rupees as well as cashmere shawls and royal china.

Russell could not decide which was worse – the violent sights in the streets or the plundering:

Oh the toil of that day... It was horrid enough to have to stumble through endless courts which were like vapour baths, amid dead bodies, through sights worthy of the Inferno, by blazing walls which might be pregnant with mines, over breaches, in and out of smouldering embrasures, across frail ladders, suffocated by deadly smells of rotting corpses, of rotten ghee or ... the seething crowd of camp followers ... like the birds of prey they resembled, waiting till the fight was done to prey on their plunder.[54]

Of the Kaisarbagh he wrote:

> Laying amid the orange-groves are dead and dying sepoys; and the white statues are reddened with blood. Leaning against a smiling Venus is a British soldier shot through the neck, gasping, and at every gasp bleeding to death! Here and there are officers running to and fro after their men, persuading or threatening in vain. From the broken portals issue soldiers laden with loot... Court after court is the same.[55]

He watched with horror in one court as the soldiers lit a fire in its centre and pitched the contents of several rooms into it:

> Embroidered clothes, gold and silver brocade, silver vessels, arms, banners, drums, shawls, scarfs, musical instruments, mirrors, pictures, books, accounts, medicine bottles, gorgeous standards, shields, spears and a heap of things... They smashed the fowling-pieces and pistols to get at the gold mountings and the stones set in the stocks... One fellow, having burst open a leaden-looking lid, which was in reality of sold silver, drew out an armlet of emeralds and diamonds, and pearls so large that I really believed they were not real stones.[56]

Later, Russell heard that the stones had been sold to a dealer for £7,500 (about £750,000 today). The oddest item taken from the Kaisarbagh, however, was a "a very old tame rhinoceros" seized by soldiers of the 53rd Foot. They got it all the way to their camp and fussed over the animal, which was blind, like an exotic pet.

Pockets of resistance at the Kaisarbagh were extinguished on the morrow, especially in buildings along its north side. Sappers had to work hard putting out the fires and explosions of gunpowder were frequent. Campbell ordered the looting to stop. Passing the Kaisarbagh that morning was Surgeon Henry Kelsall, HM 20th Foot: "I saw Geraghty, our adjutant, with a firing party & 2 or 3 sailors about to shoot some prisoners: they made them stand on the parapet & shooting each, stuck their bayonets into them & pitched them into the moat, the sailors giving a few finishing strokes with swords; the ditch being already nearly full of them."[57]

During that momentous afternoon at the Kaisarbagh, events had also been taking place across the river. At the Iron Bridge the insurgents had kept up a brisk fire on Outram's troops on the other side. Two brave men, Lieutenant Wynne and Sergeant Paul of the 4th Company, Royal Engineers, began removing the bags of a barricade that blocked the advance. Slowly, these bags were passed down a line of waiting men.

Lower and lower dropped the barricade until Wynne and Paul were crouching by the floor and finally lying on the ground as bullets whistled overhead. Eventually all was ready for the crossing. Troops lined up ready to advance when Outram rode up and explained that Sir Colin had just sent an order saying he should not advance "if he saw the chance of losing a single man."[58]

This order is generally considered to be a huge error on Campbell's part and the most controversial aspect of his generalship during the campaign. By not crossing over, hundreds of rebels were able to escape the city. Already many were leaving for Bareilly or simply going to their homes. "We are so destitute that it is difficult to describe," complained one rebel, "there is no ammunition left." So, instead of a killer blow as the two British pincers came together, Campbell's error saw, in the words of one British civil servant, "the province swarming with armed rebels still capable of resistance."[59] It was an "absurd order" wrote the historian, Sir Penderel Moon, while Colonel Julian Jocelyn in his artillery history said: "Surely the most astounding order ever sent to a British general... Another year of desultory fighting was quite needlessly imposed upon the British Army."[60] George Malleson, one of the most famous Victorian writers on the Uprising said bluntly that Campbell's Iron Bridge order relegated him to the second rank of great commanders.

Why did Sir Colin send this order? Generally it has been assumed, as Field Marshal Sir Evelyn Wood wrote, that he wished to save the lives of his men, but by doing so, "he expended many more lives, and much more marching, than he would have done had he accorded General Outram a free hand."[61] Campbell's most recent biographer, Adrian Greenwood, suggested the general wanted to save Indian lives, too, and a second Sikanderbagh, this time in the streets of Lucknow, was thus averted. Even Malleson admitted that had Outram's men gotten into the central streets, "the slain would have been counted in thousands." Yet to this argument Sir John Fortescue, historian of the British Army, and one of Campbell's fiercest critics, replied it was the general's "imperative duty to inflict the greatest possible punishment". Sir Colin was known to be a conciliatory man who hated bloodshed if it could be avoided, and had asked Canning to grant clemency to the rebels; he was hopeful that leniency would achieve more to end the Uprising than fighting.

I propose an alternative and simple reason; Campbell was much influenced by his chief of staff, the bookish Sir William Mansfield, and together they had a plan. That plan required the slow, unhurried, co-ordinated capture of the city, wearing down the enemy resistance and conserving the lives of British troops. Already that day the plan had been altered by the speedy capture of the Little Imambara and the rushed assault on the Kaisarbagh, which had turned into a looting frenzy. Sir Colin felt enough had been done that day and, as historian Peter Collister has noted, he "wished to preserve Outram's division intact as a longstop to the north until the main body had fully consolidated."[62] Campbell knew that rebels were leaving the city and he seemed to agree with his chief of staff's words after the Battle of Cawnpore: "What is the use of intercepting a desperate soldiery whose wish is to escape?" It so happened that the fighting in the centre of the city was a furious affair. "Little knobs of desperate rebels, here and there, shut themselves up in houses, where they fought fiercely, necessitating an infinity of small sieges on our part to drive them out,"[63] wrote Vivian Majendie.

Outram that day had suffered his severest fight in the campaign. This took place at the Engine House, a large building surrounded by smaller ones and several outhouses. Two companies of HM 20th Foot under Major Radcliffe were ordered to seize it with some of HM 38th in reserve. The units somehow became split up, while at the same time detachments of other regiments (Majendie said they were from "every native regiment in the service"), all armed with a mixture of Enfields, matchlocks, muskets, old cavalry sabres, tulwars and pistols, followed them. Finally, they reached the defenders in a narrow inner room – a howling mass hacking and hewing at one another until the floor was slippery with blood. The insurgents retreated into the main engine room full of pipes, furnaces and boilers. Corpses started to pile up in the doorways, bullets whizzed about the room, ricocheting off metal surfaces and flashing around. Soon the place was on fire, "a sickening, smouldering mass of disfigured corpses". Three hundred rebels died in the Engine House and 50 more fell outside while attempting to escape.

That the British behaved brutally in Lucknow is without question. "British soldiers ran in search of hiding sepoys who were dragged from cellars and cupboards and lined up against walls to be shot, bayoneted or have their throats cut," wrote Christopher Hibbert, "Unarmed men suffered with the rest."[64] Even the native servants of officers were often badly treated and had to run a gauntlet of stones hurled at their feet in imitation of grapeshot. The more a servant howled, the more a British officer laughed. Vivian Majendie recalled two men hiding in a house who were shot by an officer "in a cold-blooded, deliberate way which was most repulsive",[65] though he avoided the details. He was also appalled when a decrepit old man near the Iron Bridge, severely wounded in the thigh, was brought in for questioning. "Have his nut off" yelled someone. "Hang the brute," said another. "Give him a Cawnpore dinner" said a third. The prisoner appeared unmoved, stoic, betraying no emotion, though he probably guessed his fate. Two soldiers took him outside. The rest returned to their cards. When the pair returned someone asked, "Well, Bill, what did yer do to him?" "Oh," said the man as he wiped the blood off an old tulwar, "Oh, sliced his 'ed off!", resuming the game, "and dropping the subject, much as a man might have drowned a litter of puppies, but it was disgusting to see."[66]

Yet even these kinds of atrocities look trivial in comparison with some described in oral testimony still handed down to this day; the Indian historian, Roshan Taqui, spoke with an old inhabitant of Lucknow two decades ago who had been told by his father that Outram's troops had butchered 350 people near the Fyzabad Road. One of the dead had been an eight-year-old girl while 50 other females had been raped, the clothes stripped off them and their nude bodies thrown down a well. This atrocity story went unreported and, on the surface of it, seems highly unlikely, though it may be true in essence but with inflated numbers. Generally, Indian men were fair game, especially if suspected of being rebels. The British thought of them as little more than "brutes" and there was Cawnpore to be avenged. But while the killing did run amok, the British Army at Lucknow included men with a conscience such as Octavius Anson, and Hope Grant, who wrote: "It really sickens one to think of slaughtering any more of the poor wretched creatures of whom three-fourths were forced into the Mutiny."[67] And while rapes no doubt occurred, many soldiers, such as the Bible-carrying Highlanders of the 93rd, would have taken a very dim view of molesting and killing women. Still, the story persists, and surely haas its foundations in some foul deed.

Some British, of course, had their own dark agendas. Sadism or general blood lust did not enter into it. They simply had scores to settle. One such was Lieutenant George Hale, 57th B.N.I., who arrived at Lucknow with the Gurkhas only to find that his wife, Fanny, and eldest daughter, Kate, had both died of typhoid fever during the siege of the Residency, and their eight-month-old baby, Henrietta, had died of starvation. All three were buried in the grounds. Hale swore a blood oath on the rebels: "We cut up a lot, took a lot of prisoners," he wrote, "What followed, never mind, you can picture to yourself the treatment shown to n*****s by our men. I prayed I had not been uncharitable to the enemy."[68]

But not every man became a monster; doing good work as a guide for Outram's troops was Thomas Kavanagh. He was still a civilian and had extemporised an odd uniform of his own – "a red tunic, stitched by a lady of the garrison, French-grey breeches, once worn by a noble fellow lying in the ruined churchyard; a felt hat belonging to the Commander-in-Chief; and coarse jack boots".[69] Proceeding down streets with the soldiers, they often caught terrified citizens and noticed how some people committed suicide jumping into wells. Major Carnegie, the magistrate, and Kavanagh "had the gratification of drawing up three females and a man from one which we reached in time to save them."[70]

On the 15th, Outram's army crossed the Gumti not by the stone or iron bridges, but the wooden one of boards laid over casks now in position near the Sikanderbagh. The soldiers passed through the Kaisarbagh by an improvised road made by the sappers and miners and headed towards the Residency. "I thought I should have expired at the charge uphill to the Residency from the pace and the heat," wrote Surgeon Frederick Dalzell, "Bullets were whizzing all around us, and many poor fellows, Highlanders and others, falling wounded and killed from the bullets from the rooftops."[71] At the top of the slope, Outram, out in front on his big horse, yelled "Charge!" and led the 23rd Fusiliers through the gateway and into the grounds where bayonet work finished off the rebels. The sun was fierce and Outram told officers to let their men rest in the shade of the Residency's cellars.

After an interval, the soldiers swept on. At a wooden barricade near the river, the insurgents let loose a volley. Before they had a chance to reload, the Fusiliers were upon them and captured the brass gun that had dominated the Iron Bridge from that side. "In all directions the rattling of musketry was heard," wrote Russell, "and the bullets, fired at great elevations from distant houses, whistled overhead right and left" as the the general advance continued. The 79th's bonnets, "like a waving black sea",[72] surged forward as the Sikhs, ever hungry for loot, smashed open the doors of shops and houses, pitching the contents out of the casements. It was during this advance as HM 23rd, the Bengal Fusiliers and the Ferozepore Sikhs negotiated a warren of narrow streets that a bullet mortally wounded Jeremiah Brayser. He had served 25 years in India, beginning as a humble gunner in the Company's service and once said of himself and his straggly beard, "Everyone thought I was a burly Seikh." The Macchi Bhawan was found undefended and the British pressed on towards the Great Imambara mosque.

Built in 1784, the Great Imambara was dedicated to the three Imams and lavishly decorated in their honour. It was famed for its gigantic chandeliers, "hung with immense lustres of silver and gold, prismatic crystals and coloured glass ... temples of filigree, eight or ten feet high, and studded with precious stones ... ancient banners of the Nawabs of Oudh, swords of Khorassan steel, lances and halberds."[73] The tomb of Nawab Asaf-ud-Doulah was covered in silver, as was his mother's. The building was also said to contain a remarkable pair of life-size green glass tigers (though they seem to have been smashed during the Uprising). The British troops rushed into the courtyard at the front of the building, its floor decorated with richly tessellated paving, then climbed its grand flight of steps and seized the mosque's central hall where over one million pounds sterling of glittering chandeliers and sparkling mirrors reflected the grimy and blood-stained faces of the invaders. Outside, the rush went on and Captain Salusbury and some Bengal Fusiliers even seized the Constantinople Gate (Rum Darwazi) of the city.

Russell huffed and puffed his way to the top of the Great Imambara:

Lucknow, in its broad expanse of palaces, its groves and gardens, its courts and squares, its mosques and temples, its wide-spreading squalid quarters of mean, close houses, amid which are kiosks and mansions of rich citizens, surrounded by trees, all lay at our feet, with the Dilkoosha, and Martinière, and distant Alambagh plainly visible, and the umbrageous plains clothed in the richest vegetation and covered with woodland, which encompasses the city. In the midst winds the Goomtee, placid and silvery, though its waters are heavy with the dead. Across the Stone bridge, in wild confusion, are pouring the rebels, budmashes, matchlockmen and inhabitants of the place, and from the Iron bridge guns are opening on them incessantly, and the showers of our Enfield bullets cut the surface of the waters like rain.[74]

While Walpole's troops were engaged near the Stone Bridge, masses of fugitives crossed the river higher up and escaped via the Fyzabad road into the countryside. That day, Campbell had made another series of errors, sending Hope Grant on a wild goose chase to intercept fugitives heading towards Sitapur, while Brigadier Campbell of the Bays did similar duty on the other side of Lucknow in the Sundeela direction. During this expedition, Lieutenant A. R. Mackenzie was impressed by the bravery of two village matchlockmen who decided to sell their lives dearly. This pair, "two tall peasants, clad in their usual white cotton working clothes, each of them carrying a matchlock," took up positions on the other side of a steep nullah from 2,000 British cavalry and began picking off the riders. "They knew that their puny effort to stop us was hopeless," wrote Mackenzie, "but yet they did all they could, and devoted themselves to death in defence of the brown mud walls which held their household gods. In vain we shouted to them that we did not intend to harm their village – that we were going past it and would not enter it. They evidently did not believe us, and continued to load and fire with as much expedition as their long, clumsy, tinder-locks allowed them."[75] Eventually, some British troopers got across the nullah and the two men were killed.

"Vast numbers, both of armed and unarmed men, are evacuating the city," Sir Colin admitted to the Governor-General. "Everybody wonders how the rebels have been allowed to escape," wrote Chaplain Mackay. "Another hot weather campaign is inevitable." The Queen-Regent had told her followers that she would die sword in hand rather than surrender to the British but, urged to flee, she left late on the afternoon of Tuesday, 16th March, with her son, the boy-king. They fled in the direction of the Nepalese border country, Hazrat Mahal continuing to issue defiant proclamations that she would return and oust the British from her land.

That same day Lieutenant Thomas Bland Strange R.A. was instrumental in emptying into a well at the Kaisarbagh a quantity of gunpowder found in a lower level room while the building was in flames. The next day, under the central enclosure, he located a 50-foot-square vault "filled with sacks sufficient to shake half the city to its foundations", he wrote in his memoirs. "I shall not survive this job,"[76] he gloomily predicted, but before attempting to move the gunpowder he showed his "treasure" to a senior officer. Equally shocked, the major agreed that the explosives were best destroyed in situ – and quickly – before a disgruntled Indian put a match to them, so a trench was dug and the vault flooded.

While Strange was investigating the Kaisarbagh's gunpowder, the rebels made a final attack on the Alambagh. Unluckily for them, Billy Olpherts was still there with his horse artillery. The camp was held by two weak regiments and many later praised Olpherts' quick actions. Surgeon Collins, who was present, was disgusted that the C-in-C did not order the Nepalese, camped only half a mile away, to help. "Our supposed friends had no intention of coming to the front," he wrote, "Had it not been for the sudden appearance of Olpherts with his supports nothing could have saved our camp." One of the "supports" – the Military Train – was led by Major Robertson, who claimed in his memoirs that it was his troopers who saved the camp (though in his despatch at the time he did praise Olpherts). This debacle, noted Collins, was not mentioned in the despatches. He had words of praise for the insurgents:

It really was a fine sight to see the Rebels marching out of Lucknow to the attack, in columns of Regiments ... bearing the Colours under which they had been so frequently led by their Officers to victory. They came along with a jaunty, self-satisfied air, as if they meant to swallow us up, and this they might easily have done... We estimated the Cavalry at 3,000. The Sepoy Regiments over 16,000... The troops attacking the Alambagh were led by a man bearing a large Banner which they, no doubt, intended to hoist on the building.[77]

After the fight the rebels retired in a westerly direction out of the city, "in perfect order and unmolested", noted a disgusted Collins.

Next day it was the Nepalis' turn to be attacked near their postion on the Cawnpore road. Maharaja Jung Bahadur in person led his soldiers around the enemy flank and captured 10 guns.

Expelled from the city, the rebels made a stand at the Musabagh, an old brick building overlooking Lucknow. It had been designed by General Claud Martin (of Martinière fame) on the lines of an English country manor house. Its fields sloped gently towards the Gumti and effigies of Nawab Nasur-ud-din-Haider adorned some of its walls It was here that 7th Oudh Irregular Cavalry had been stationed in 1857 and refused to bite the new cartridges, so it was perhaps fitting that the city's great rebellion should now end here on 19th March.

Outram was ordered with a large force to capture the Musabagh and Brigadier William Campbell was told to make sure that his cavalry prevented any rebels escaping. On the opposite side of the river waited Hope Grant to make doubly sure the C-in-C's instructions were carried out. At 6.30 am the attack began, led by the 79th. It went well at first and the 9th Lancers did good work capturing six guns and killing about 100 of the enemy. Once the building had been taken, thousands more of the rebels fled into the surrounding country, a tricky place of broken ground and deep nullahs. Brigadier Campbell, however, was caught napping and masses got away before he realised it. The brigadier later claimed that he had lost his way, but one officer commented that "his error appears to be partaken of wilfulness. He moved his force in utter disregard of the statement of his guides, in opposition to the protestations and explanations of all to whose information and advice he was bound to listen."[78] One anonymous officer, in a long letter to his brother, spelled out the frustrations of the cavalry:

As I told you in my last, Lucknow fell with very little loss on our side and I fear not sufficient loss on that of the enemy. I cannot help thinking that a loophole was left for them to escape with the idea perhaps that it would be easier to lick them in the open than in the streets of Lucknow, but then if such was the idea why was not the pursuit followed up sharp?... In a day or two they began to leave the city in earnest ... they would have been polished off in thousands, but one old muff by the name of Campbell ... was not at his point at the time indicated and the enemy escaped the punishment intended for them... Campbell was to have cut them into very small pieces as they bolted, but as he did not make his appearance during the day the plan of course failed and the chief rebels escaped. Our Genl., Hope Grant, was to have polished them off if they attempted to cross the Goomtee by the numerous fords thereabouts existing and was ready and willing to do so. Outram, as he always does, did his work well – and pushed them out sharp... After all this there seemed to be a gloom upon all the good folk in Lucknow, everybody in our camp who went into the city noticed it.[79]

During the latter part of the day Captain the Hon. Hugh Chichester, supported by Lieutenants Sandeman and Mackenzie with two troops of the 1st Sikh Irregulars, were galloping along and had just decided to give up what seemed a fruitless chase when from the far side of a ravine a rebel fired his musket at bearded Captain Wale, the 1st Sikhs commandant, who reeled in the saddle, hit in the mouth, before another slug tore through his throat and he dropped dead. He was "instantly avenged for, as the rebel sepoy turned to fly, he also fell dead, hit in the spine by a bullet from the revolver of Captain Chichester."[80] Much loved by his Sikhs, Wale was buried under a spreading mango tree in the walled garden behind the Musabagh with a tombstone that noted he had "lived and died a Christian Soldier".

The Begam had fled but the Maulvi had decided to face the British with two heavy guns and his most fanatical supporters at a fortified shrine in the western part of the old city. On 21st March, Sir Edward Lugard, with two of the toughest and most expert sets of fighters – the 93rd Highlanders and their friends, the 4th Punjabis – were sent to dislodge these last Lucknow rebels. Captain Cockburn-Hood of the 4th PNI was hit in the face by a round of grape that carried away his cheek bone, making a ghastly wound (he survived). Then, advancing up another street, the C.O., Alfred Wilde, was wounded in the groin (he also survived). It was a tough assault on the shrine and the 4th lost 17 killed and wounded and the 93rd 11 wounded in the affair. The Maulvi managed to escape. Once the British had battered down the temple doors, "The defenders who had not gone off with the Moulvie were shot, sabred or bayoneted," wrote Thomas Kavanagh, "and we found on the floor the warm but lifeless body of Shurf-ood-dowlah, the Prime Minister of the rebel government."[81] This senior rebel's death is frequently chalked up as another British atrocity in modern histories, but the Maulvi and the Prime Minister were not friends (and he may even have committed suicide), and there was no reason for Kavanagh or others not to own up to the killing.

The Lucknow operations had lasted for 20 days, but the city had finally been returned to British control. There had been a period of nine days during these operations, noted Private Thomas Malcolm, 10th Foot, when the men were "not allowed to take off our belts and boots. We were not even permitted to wash our faces, so constantly did we keep watch over the foe."[82] The Raj had trumphed nevertheless. Sir Colin Campbell had retaken the city with a loss of 19 officers and 108 men killed, 55 officers and 540 men wounded and 120 missing, together with 51 Nepalis killed and 287 wounded. A terrible enough butcher's bill but low compared to the more than 3,000 Indians in the city who had died for Oudh. Campbell had also captured 127 heavy guns. Lord Canning called it "a great success" and "won at so little cost of valuable lives". The dead might not have concurred.

It is worth remembering that besides the 100,000 or so armed insurgents, the British had faced a civic population who hated them – out of fear, pride and other reasons. Majendie tells the story of a "wrinkled hag", bent double, who used to lurk near the Iron Bridge gathering rags. She was found dead on 17th March. On examination, a partially burnt piece of cotton, "like a candle-wick" was found close to her hand and beside it, a bamboo containing a slow-match. This led in turn to a carefully laid train of gunpowder and several barrels waiting to be detonated. There was no mark on the old woman's body and she may have had a stroke or heart attack. "What wrongs her feeble hands strove to avenge will never be known, what tragedy embittered her flickering life, history will never discover."[83]

"Thus Lucknow had been taken, but the foe had not been crushed, nor even punished, and they were free to reassemble elsewhere in their thousands and tens of thousands,"[84] wrote a very disgruntled James McLeod Innes. In contrast, a modern military historian, Dr Tony Heathcote, wrote: "Campbell's recovery of Lucknow deserves to be recognised as one of the British Army's greatest feat of arms."[85] The old general had done as his political master, Lord Canning, had demanded and against his preferred military strategy, he had put the enemy leaders to flight and scattered their army to the winds. With the great cities of Delhi and Lucknow safely back in British hands, it would now only be a matter of time before the last of the rebels was vanquished.

Soldiers in Campbell's army felt quite sanguine about matters. On 15th March, Ashton Warner told his mother in a letter, "The quiet that now pervades this place is something extraordinary … the thing is now finished off, I really think, and a few columns to march over the country, will settle the whole thing."[86] In a similar vein, John Chalmers wrote to a friend on 21st March:

Last night we fired the last shot at Lucknow… Days ago we had the palaces and all the entrenchments, but the Commander-in-Chief is rather a slow old gentleman and objects to taking any place until it is taken for him by some straggling party walking into it by mistake or something of that sort. The rebel army must have walked off with a loss of 3000 men killed and most of their guns taken from them, but they have not gone in a body, and I think they are not likely to act together in any great force again… We hope to get back to the Punjaub at once, but our men have such lots of plunder, I do not know how we are to go. I have a few good pearls and a shawl or two myself… I did not know there was such a city in India. I have seen nothing to equal the Kaisar Bagh Palace anywhere… I think the row is now over as as troops are concerned, although there will be lots of work for police."[87]

11

Captains and Kings

Oudh, India, Great Britain and Canada,
March 1858–August 1940

The fighting was over, the city won back by the British with the sword, but Lucknow lay under a miasma as the rotting and bloated corpses of rebels, obscenely swollen, floated down the sluggish waters of the Gumti. In the streets, burial parties gathered together the thousands of dead bodies; at least the victims were easy to find by the thick clouds of black flies that swarmed overhead.

The city also looked a mess – much of the great earth walls thrown up by the insurgents still stood alongside the ditches scattered with the dead. The massive bombardment by Campbell's artillery, and to a lesser extent by the rebels themselves, had left craters, smashed buildings and piles of rubble everywhere. A British officer, Charles Gordon, went for a walkabout:

The streets along which the 10th had so recently forced its way to the Kaiser Bagh presented a scene of utter devastation: walls blackened, loopholed, shattered with shot-holes of various sizes, the buildings roofless and tenantless, except by dead bodies gashed or torn by bullets, their cotton-wadded clothing burning, sickening, odours therefrom contaminating the air; heaps of debris everywhere, furniture, utensils and dead bodies, all mixed up together; breaches made by heavy guns to make way for advancing infantry, round shot by which they had been effected; domes, at one time gilded and otherwise ornamental, but now dilapidated and charred; costly furniture, oil paintings, once of great value, glass and china, strewed about, and everywhere to be seen; ornamental garden lakes black from gunpowder cast into them; the gardens trodden down, mosaic work of cisterns broken into fragments.[1]

Another officer, T. H. Stisted, 3rd Light Dragoons, wrote at the end of March that Lucknow was "completely deserted ... not a roof left on any house."[2] Eventually, Campbell forced shopkeepers to re-open only by threatening the direst of consequences if they remained closed.

Though Sir Colin's losses had been modest, there were still many wounded to deal with. Some lucky soldiers were cared for in regimental hospitals, while others had to lay in a general field hospital at the Dilkusha on floor pallets, some wounded, some suffering burns, "many groaning in their agony, others placidly bearing their sufferings, a few unconscious to pain, the death rattle in their throats."[3] Short funerals took place all over the city. Arthur Lang attended one for Captain A. J. Clerke, Royal Engineers, and 12 of his men, all placed in one grave under the gently waving cypress trees of the Kaisarbagh gardens.

No contemporary account mentions the residents of Lucknow, or how the insurgents coped with burying their dead or caring for their sick and wounded, of lost fathers, husbands, sons. Their names are not recorded anywhere, but we can be certain that thousands must have been mourned.

It was not until 18th March that order was restored at the Kaisarbagh. Prize Agents were set up to value and sell the loot. Rosie Llewellyn-Jones, in her study of the Uprising, suggests that there was an agreement, "probably between the Governor-General and the Nepalese leader", allowing Jung Bahadur's Gurkhas to get "their choice of plunder before the Prize Agents took over."[4] The agents, in fact, seem to have been particularly inefficient at Lucknow and many soldiers were able to sell their loot, or return to England with it. As late as July 1858 a new Commissioner, Sir Robert Montgomery, was complaining that "There is no authority... Any man who chooses places a badge on his arm, and plunders on his own account."[5]

Gradually, a police presence was restored as one man tried to bring order out of chaos. This was Robert Napier, Campbell's senior engineer, who produced as early as 26th March a "Memorandum On The Military Occupation Of Lucknow". This was a blueprint for the city's reconstruction. The document called for the clearing away of all habitations near military posts. These posts were to be set up in several main buildings, major streets broadened, new roads driven through and around the suburbs so that troops could be speedily brought to any point. Crucial to the plan was the old Machhi Bhawan fortress, which commanded two of the city's main bridges. This was to be restored and garrisoned and new roads, like spokes, would radiate outwards through the city. Napier proposed razing "every building and garden-enclosure not reserved for military purposes existing between the Martinière and the Gumti."[6] Any place that interfered with this scheme – be it a cemetery, a house or a religious building – was to be ruthlessly levelled.

Unfortunately for the inhabitants, engineers started very quickly to implement Napier's plan and they soon found themselves living amid frenetic demolition and construction work, dust and debris. For 30 years, riding roughshod over religious and cultural objections, troops were also billeted in the Great Imambara; Shia Moslems had to accept the sight of these men drinking alcohol, eating pork and trampling all over the most important religious shrine in the city. It was not until 1916 that a senior British architect, Sir Patrick Geddes, would write a report condemning Napier's new roads as "unbeautiful" and "costly". Huge chunks of Nawabi Lucknow had been lost. By then the Macchi Bhawan had long gone, replaced by what is today the King George's Medical University.

Lucknow reconquered, the Uprising rolled on in increasingly small and desperate encounters between the remaining insurgents and a powerful foe. Some felt the war was made longer than it needed to have been by Lord Canning, who wrote what became known as the Oudh Proclamation. He drafted and sent it to Campbell on 3rd March to be made public as soon as the city fell. On the one hand, the document advised against more general hangings and shootings in favour of mass transportation for rebels, but on the other, the Governor-General argued that only six landowners had remained faithful to the Government and so, with just a few exceptions, all the land in Oudh would now be confiscated; estates to be handed back in time against good behaviour by landowners. The Oudh Proclamation was then, and ever has been, roundly criticized. Such harshness seemed destined to create a long and bitter guerrilla war, since the taluqdars had lost everything. Even tough old British officers thought it went too far. Russell noted how the Proclamation "is looked upon by all men here, political and military, as too harsh and despotic... I have not heard one voice raised in its defence."[7] Naturally enough, the taluqdars were quick to offer their allegiance and in large numbers, but Russell saw a "scowling, hostile look" upon the faces of the ordinary people, while merchants "bow with their necks, and salaam with their hands, but not with their eyes."

Even before Canning's words had been proclaimed there was unrest all over Oudh. It seemed vital to nip this in the bud and Sir Colin told the Governor-General in June that Lucknow was still in danger of being threatened by rebel armies. A new spat developed between the two men, as Canning wanted Sir Colin to turn his attention to Rohilkhand where pro-British Hindus had complained of anti-British Moslems based at Bareilly. So, on 7th April, a large British column that included three Highland regiments as well as the hardy 4th PNI set off west of Oudh to restore order. Commanding this army was Robert Walpole, the least respected of Campbell's generals, considered by many officers to be a "great dolt" as one called him. At a mud fort named Ruiya, the brigadier needlessly wasted the lives of over 100 of his men, while the rebels slipped out of the fort's back door overnight. One of those killed was the much loved Brigadier Adrian Hope. On the day after the fight the bodies of the slain, many of them mutilated, were recovered. There was talk of lynching Walpole among the 93rd Highlanders, bitter at their losses and Hope's death. "Officers considered him insane," wrote William Forbes-Mitchell, or worse, "a coward."

Bareilly was taken after a bloody fight by Campbell against fanatical Moslem *ghazis* (holy warriors). Elsewhere, another white-haired and tough general, Sir Hugh Rose, with his Central India Field Force, had in April 1858 successfully besieged Jhansi and its courageous young Rani, then marched across burning deserts to re-take Calpee, Gwalior, and a series of stupendous hill forts, all under a blazing summer sun.

So it was not until the start of October 1858 that Sir Colin was able to focus all his attention on re-claiming Oudh. Throughout his Lucknow campaigns the old general had frequently run great personal risks; this good fortune finally ran out on Boxing Day when he led his advanced guard of guns and cavalry at a place called Burodiah. Galloping across some broken ground, the C-in-C's horse put its foot in a hole and threw the rider. He tried to sit up, blood running down his face, but could not stand; he had dislocated his shoulder. Returning to their base 20 miles away, the column found no tents pitched as the baggage had still not arrived. It was bitterly cold. Campbell sat on a small bedstead, his arm in a sling, surrounded by Baluchi cavalrymen. One tired soldier flung himself down on the bed, full-length, but was dragged off by his comrades. "Don't you see, you fool, that you are on the Lord Sahib's charpoy?" they shouted. But Sir Colin interceded on the native trooper's behalf: "Let him lie there; don't interfere with his rest."[8] Then the general took his seat on a piece of wood.

The Oudh Winter Campaign of 1858-59 was a short one, but the punitive operations worked: hundreds of hill forts were destroyed, about 150 heavy guns captured and 150,000 armed men, of whom about 35,000 were ex-sepoys, were quelled. The victor, who had by now been raised to the peerage as Lord Clyde of Clydesdale, explained his strategy:

The march of each column, the commencement of each attack, was guided from headquarters, and watched with the utmost care and accuracy. The different commanders ... all depended the one on the other... Although from the nature of the contest there were no great battles, the number of small affairs was very considerable; and the endeavour was made successfully ... on no occasion did it happen that any commander was under the necessity of fighting against odds which he could not easily overcome.[9]

The Great Uprising was rapidly drawing to a close and with it the lives of several of the main participants in the Lucknow campaigns. Nana Sahib, his chief advisor, Azimullah Khan, Begum Hazrat Mahal and her son, Birjis Qadr, all headed into the swampy lands of the Nepali Terai. For half a century, the hunt for the Nana would continue. Occasionally, some crazed old man or ex-rebel was dragged before a magistrate on the supposition that he was the real "Butcher of Cawnpore". It is now generally agreed that he probably died in Nepal within three years of the massacre that had brought him infamy; today, this former arch-villain is now one of the heroes of modern India, any crimes whitewashed or forgotten, his defiant stand against British rule being prominently noted.

On 1st November 1858, a proclamation from Queen Victoria was read aloud at Allahabad. It transferred India from the hands of "John Company" to those of the Crown. The real British Raj had begun. Lord Canning was henceforth a Viceroy ruling in the monarch's name. The Begum of Oudh, to her credit, made a strong and sarcastic reply to the Queen's Proclamation "Everything is written, and yet nothing is written," she fumed, "Let no subject be deceived by this proclamation." The document changed nothing of any importance. Her greatest anger was articulated concerning the Proclamation's assertion that religious laws would be observed for all:

> To eat pigs and drink wine, to bite greased cartridges, and to mix pig's fat with flour and sweetmeats, to destroy Hindoo and Mussulman temples on pretence of making roads, to build churches, to send clergymen into the streets and alleys to preach the Christian religion, to institute English schools and to pay people a monthly stipend for learning the English sciences, while the places of worship of Hindoos and Mussulmans are to this day entirely neglected; and with all this, how can the people believe that religion will not be interfered with? The rebellion began with religion, and, for it, millions of men have been killed.[10]

In Nepal, the Begam asked Jung Bahadaur for help. He refused and threatened to hand her over to the British, then relented and allowed her and a small entourage to stay. Her supporter, Raja Lal Singh, was caught and hanged. Her lover, Mammu Khan, was dismissed late in 1859 "for want of courage and devotion".

"The months passed, the years passed," wrote P. J. O. Taylor, "and the Begam refused to surrender."[11] The death of her son, the boy-king, changed nothing, certainly not her hatred for the British. Yet she had gained the respect of her enemies; the London *Times* reported at the end of 1858 that "Like all the women who have turned up in the insurrection, she has shown more sense and nerve than all her generals together." By 30th January 1860, the same newspaper was reporting that the only rebels who still held out were Prince Feroze Shah, a cousin of Bahdaur Shah II, and the Begum of Oudh. She was supposed to be living in the Terai with less than 1,500 supporters, "half-armed, half-fed and without artillery". Brave, stubborn, articulate and unforgiving, this last enemy of the Raj never did surrender and died in Nepal in 1879.

The British love irony; when Brigadier Jwala Pershad, who had negotiated and lied to General Wheeler at Cawnpore about safe passage, then helped plan the Satichura Ghat Massacre, was finally caught, he was hanged close to the spot where his men had gunned down the garrison.

Death was also waiting for the Maulvi Ahmadullah Shah, who had escaped from Lucknow in March. He was by now calling himself "King of Hindustan" and "God's Deputy". A reward of 50,000 rupees, dead or alive, was on his head. He led his followers against a small British garrison at Shahjahanpur, seizing the fort and turning the guns on his enemies holed up in the local jail, but a superior force turned up and the Maulvi fled again. On 5th June, he tried to enter the fort at Powain, a few miles from Shahjahanpur, but the Raja closed the gates in the nick of time. Historian Michael Edwardes:

> The Maulvi, who was riding a war elephant, ordered its driver to smash down the gate. The animal's head hit the gate with a loud crash, and it was already shaking on its hinges, when one of the defenders – the raja's brother, it was said – shot the Maulvi dead. The defenders then rushed out and cut off the Maulvi's head. Seeing their leader killed, the Maulvi's men broke and ran. Wrapping the severed head in a cloth, the raja set off almost immediately for Shahjahanpur... When he arrived he found the magistrate and some British friends sitting down to their evening meal. Without hesitating, the raja marched into the dining-room and produced a spectacular entree. Opening the cloth, he rolled the bloody head of the Maulvi on the floor. Next day it was set up on a pike over the police station.[12]

The Raja collected the reward in full. Today Ahmadullah Shah is another of India's heroes, but it was the Victorian historian, George Malleson, who wrote the Maulvi his most sympathetic epitaph: "He had not stained his sword by assassination, he had connived at no murders: he had fought manfully, honourably, and stubbornly in the field against the strangers who had seized his country, and his memory is entitled to the respect of the brave and true-hearted of all nations."[13]

A number of British characters in our tale also passed away while the Uprising was still being fought. They include Robert Loveday Inglis, whose beautifully written letters on wafer thin sheets of paper I found a fascinating delight at the British Library. Worn out by fever, he died at Allahabad on 29th December 1857. Another lieutenant who never recovered from the effects of the siege was the chirpy Lieutenant Hay. He died at sea on 6th June 1858 without ever seeing the mother who kept and re-read his letters for half a century. Another sad loss was Captain Peel V.C. of HMS *Shannon*; his wound at Lucknow had not seemed life-threatening, but he fell victim to smallpox contracted, it was believed, from someone who had lain in the doolie that had taken him to hospital. He was nursed at Cawnpore by Chaplain Moore and his wife, but gradually slipped away and died on 27th June 1858. He was only 33 years old. Another captain, Oliver Jones, wrote how he was a man "simple and unostentatious in his manner, friendly and conciliatory to all, upright and honourable in his heart".[14]

Another fatality, another gunshot wound, but a different continent; Lieutenant Danvers, who slogged to Lucknow with Havelock and had his horse shot from under him, recovered sufficiently to be sent on to China where British operations began near Canton in the summer of 1858. After an attack on a fort, the men were expending their ammunition when a shot rang out. A musket ball had gone straight through Danvers' body. He was less than a month past his 25th birthday. After seeing so much fighting in India, it seemed an unfair way to die.

Two of our main protagonists died just three years apart, though in very different circumstances. Tantia Tope was the last rebel general to fight on. He was arguably the brightest strategist among the insurgents, but after the Satichura Ghat Massacre he was another man with a price on his head. Finally he was caught, tried and executed on the parade ground at Sipree on 18th April 1859. He had been captured with the help of Man Singh, Raja of Narwar. A witness described Tantia Tope's end:

> His execution was announced to take place at 4pm... A considerable number of natives were scattered all over the plain; and any little elevation commanding a view of the scaffold was thickly studded with white- clad spectators... He expressed the wish that, as they were about to take his life, the Government would see to his family in Gwalior. Major Reade read the charge and the sentence that he be

hanged by the neck until he was dead. The *mistree* then knocked off the leg irons. He mounted the rickety ladder with as much firmness as handcuffs would allow him; was then pinioned and his legs tied, he remarking that there was no necessity for these operations; and he then deliberately put his head in the noose which, being drawn tight by the executioner, the fatal bolt was drawn. He struggled very slightly, and the *mehtars* were called to drag him straight... After the troops left, a great scramble was made by officers and others to get a lock of hair.[15]

Very different was the passing of Charles Canning, who had been at the British political helm from the beginning of the Uprising to its end. He died in London on 17th June 1862, worn out and with a broken heart. He never recovered from the loss of his effervescent wife, Charlotte, who had died in India eight months earlier, almost at the end of their time there. He was buried with some pomp in Westminster Abbey near the grave of his father.

The abbey became the last resting place, nine months later, of Sir James Outram, whose chest, after a lifetime of smoking big cigars, could not handle a nasty attack of bronchitis. One of the mourners of both men was Lord Clyde, already ailing and subject to bouts of depression; he died on 14th August and lies interred in a plain tomb with a simple inscription, also in Westminster Abbey. It was a well deserved honour; he had fought for his country on the plains of Spain and the rugged passes of India's North-West Frontier, in the creeks of China and the plains and hills of Oudh. During the Uprising, despite criticism of his slowness, he never risked a soldier's life unnecessarily, showed considerable skill as a strategist and restored much of India to British control. One year later, it was the turn of Martin Gubbins, the neurotic Commissioner who penned one of the best accounts of the Lucknow siege. Depressed and far from from well, he committed suicide at Leamington on 6th May 1863.

Many of our cast of characters returned to the United Kingdom and enjoyed long lives and honours. Until the 1st World War the survivors of the main siege at Lucknow, and those who relieved them, held annual dinners. For many years the chairman of the association was Major-General John Ruggles, colonel of the 19th Punjab Native Infantry; as a young lieutenant he had looked after the church during the early days of the siege. Doctors Fairweather, Munro, Wise and Fayrer all left memoirs, the latter survivor of the siege becoming a surgeon to the royal family.

One who was no scribe was "Hellfire Jack" Olpherts V.C. This daredevil of the horse artillery lived until 1902, growing increasingly eccentric over the years. His last words were typical of the old warhorse: "I'll show them how a Christian can die. Put out the light."[16]

The careers of some took odd turns. Vivian Majendie published his memoirs, some of the most honest and brutal recollections of the Uprising, then rose to become an artillery colonel and the British Government's resident expert on explosives; at Victoria Station in 1884 he defused a fiendish clockwork bomb planted by Fenians. He died in 1898. On 30th December 1897, Harry Havelock V.C. (now called Havelock-Allan) was killed by an Afridi sniper's bullet near the Khyber Pass. He had been expressly told not to leave camp on his own. One suspects though that Harry – and even his father – might have approved of this end, reunited in some Valhalla.

Two of the leading soldiers who helped the British win at Lucknow, cavalryman Hope Grant and engineer Robert Napier, went on to greater glory. Grant, expert horseman, martinet and violincello player, became C-in-C of the British troops in China during the second war with the Celestial Empire. He died in 1875. Rather unfairly, Grant was denied a peerage, but Napier was not; he had led the expedition to save British and European hostages in Abyssinia in 1868-69. He died in harness, full of honours, as Lord Napier of Magdala, in 1890. One old comrade said that he had "no faults save a refusal to see any wrong in any man he liked."[17]

The two men whose stars rose the highest after Lucknow were the energetic staff officer, Frederick Roberts, and Garnet Wolseley, who had captured the Moti Mahal and welcomed Campbell's relieving force in November. Both became C-in-Cs of the British Army and today their statues stare at one another across Horse Guards Parade. As the years rolled on, both field-marshals developed super-egos and great rivalries, Roberts lauded by his "Indians" and Wolseley his "Africans" within the army. In reality, they both wanted the best for their country and an institution they loved equally. Memory loss affected Wolseley in later years and by the time of his death in 1913 his days of glory, 30 years earlier, were all but forgotten. Roberts, however, a well-loved public figure, died in harness in 1914 after contacting a virus whilst visiting Indian soldiers on the Western Front.

What of the some of the 'ordinary' people in this story? The Lucknow schoolboy, Edward Hilton, became author of the city's best guide-book. Thomas Kavanagh V.C. had a see-saw life not made any easier by his ego and temper; he was made a civil judge with a fat £2,000 a year salary, but by 1876 was in debt with 13 children to support. Faced with compulsory retirement on a salary of £500 a year, he returned both his V.C. and Mutiny medals in a sulk. He was on his way to England to argue for a better pension when he died at Lord Napier's house on Gibralter in 1882. And Private Henry Metcalfe who had fought through the siege with his dog, Bustle, became a drill instructor in Macclesfield and died aged 80 in 1915.

The siege was as much a story of brave women as it was of heroic men. Lady Julia Inglis lived on for another 42 years after her husband's death. Her adventures had continued after the siege because she set out for England in the SS *Ava* and was shipwrecked off Pigeon Island, 12 miles from the coast of Ceylon, on 16th February 1858. "Johnny was delighted when the waves broke over the ship," she wrote of her son, "and his merry laugh sounded sadly in my ears, for I thought a watery grave awaited each of us."[18] The passengers and crew spent an uncomfortable night in the ship's boats before being rescued. Julia died surrounded by her children in Beckenham in 1904.

Tragedy continued to stalk the unhappy life of Katherine Bartrum who had waited on the Residency parapets for her husband Robert, only to hear that he had been killed hours earlier. Her infant son, Bobbie, grew weaker and she was advised to take the long four-month sea journey to England via the Cape in the hope that it might restore him to good health. Katherine was cheered by the thought that Mrs Polehampton would be on board helping to nurse sick soldiers. She and Bobbie boarded the SS *Himalaya*, but Bobbie grew weaker. Before the ship departed the little boy died on 11th February 1858. Katherine was distraught. "I have nothing else left," she wrote. Life goes on; Mrs Bartrum buried her infant son beneath a giant mango tree in the burial ground on the Lower Circular Road, Calcutta, then set sail for England. She remarried fairly quickly and bore her Nottingham physician husband three children before dying of pulmonary tuberculosis in March 1866.

Better fortune smiled on Katherine's fellow travelling companion and widower, Mrs Emily Polehampton, wife of the Residency's chaplain. In 1859 she married again and her new husband, Colonel Henry Durand, was a hero of the Uprising and duly became a major-general and knight. Lady Emily was stepmother to Durand's brood of children.

Lastly, we should not forget Amelia Horne, the girl saved from massacre at Cawnpore by a rebel trooper and who eventually ended up in Lucknow. As Campbell's troops entered the city in March she was dragged away by Trooper Mohammed Ismail Khan to his village. Much of the way she had to walk until her feet were bloody. Other ex-sepoys treated her with contempt: "You are cunning," one said, "Cunning like a monkey. The British are monkeys."[19] A month passed of Amelia's new captivity, but her captor was weighing his chances. Finally, he decided to release her provided that she wrote a plea in his favour. She did so and soon found herself hurrying down the road to Allahabad. Here she caused a stir at a police outpost, "a small dark peasant girl announcing vehemently that she was a Christian, whose great-uncle lived in Allahabad."[20] Amazingly, perhaps, Amelia stayed on in India and almost 60 years later was still living in the dingy riverside suburb of Howrah, Calcutta, "giving piano lessons to a world that had forgotten all about the mutiny", the Cawnpore massacres and the Siege of Lucknow.

The survivors, like Amelia, slowly passed away, the annual Lucknow Reunion Dinners stopped, though into the 1930s newspapers would occasionally mention how many of them were left alive. The last British soldier to fight in the Indian Uprising, George Christie, died aged 98 in 1939. A year later, the final survivor, who also happened to serve at Lucknow, passed away. This was Charles Palmer, the nine-year-old son of Colonel Charles Palmer of the 49th B.N.I., who had commanded the Machhi Bhawan at the start of the siege. This La Martinière schoolboy ran errands and helped his brother-in-law Lieutenant Ralph Ouseley on the battlements. It was Charles's 19-year-old sister, Suzanne, who died in agony after her leg was blown off at the start of the siege. He was sent to England after the relief and finished his education at Sherborne. Returning to India he became a civil engineer specialising in canal construction. An attempt at managing a brick-making business in Adelaide failed and Charles returned to India, yet again working on canals, notably a major section of the Lower Ganges Canal. His famine relief work in 1896 netted him the C.I.E. In 1900 he retired as head of the public works department and ten years later emigrated to Canada, ending his days as a farmer at Duncan on Vancouver Island. He died there on 18th August 1940 aged 92 and lies buried in a simple churchyard close to some stupendous beaches and spectacular Pacific breakers, a very long way from Lucknow.

A stone cross covered in lichen records that he fought at the "Defence of Lucknow". At the bottom, almost covered in dead leaves, are four simple words: "Fight the good fight."[21]

Epilogue
Britain and Uttar Pradesh, India
The Present Day

Seventeen decades after the Great Uprising, known to generations as the Indian Mutiny, it is all but forgotten in the United Kingdom; imperial history is little taught in schools and in universities the current view is that the Empire was a vile conceit run purely for the exploitation of its subject peoples. History lovers have the subject sidelined as somehow caused by polluted cartridges and dealt with by brutal repression. What more to be said? In India, the young learn of the First War of Independence and the subject has a clear resonance as a major step towards freedom from foreign domination. Indian academics generally accept the importance of the Great Uprising, but are split as to its causes and objectives, most especially whether it represented a national struggle for liberation, as several suggest, or was, as Ramesh Majumdar, a leading historian thought, neither a national revolt nor conspiracy.

On 13th September 1947, fast approaching Nehru's midnight hour of freedom, a highly secret ceremony was held at dusk in the grounds of the Lucknow Residency. A local British major-general and his officers were drawn up to salute the Union Jack as it was lowered for the first time in 90 years by its caretaker, Warrant Officer Ireland. It had been a unique situation, this honouring of the British flag, flown night and day, a symbol of the great fighting there and, in time, of the strength of the Empire itself. The flag was carefully folded and along with the one that had flown on the ramparts of Fort William, Calcutta, was despatched out of India to Britain by Field-Marshal Sir Claude Auchinleck (where it can still be seen today in the library of Windsor Castle). Even this was not enough for the British; that same night, a party of sappers were despatched, commando-style, to sneak into the Residency grounds, cut down the metal flag staff and lay cement over its base. Only then did the British depart Lucknow.

That flag had taken on if not a sacred, then certainly a mystic, character, the ultimate symbol of the British Raj. Poet laureate Alfred, Lord Tennyson, immortalised it thus in 1878:

> Shot through the staff or the halyard,
> but ever we raised thee anew.
> And ever upon the topmost roof our
> banner of England blew.

If the flag was sacred then so was the old Residency and its grounds. Writing at the turn of the 20th century one of the participants, Thomas Lewin, a humble subaltern back in 1857, wrote: "The walls of that Residency, pitted by balls, and shattered by cannon-shot, are, to my mind, the grandest monument of the supremacy of our race that India furnishes."[1]

A statement perforce that will enrage many today. Fast forward to 2024; today the cities of Lucknow and Cawnpore bear no resemblance to the places lived in and fought over in 1857. Both are mighty industrial hubs of a modern technological giant, lorries rumble along wide arterial roads, there are internet cafes and air-conditioned shopping centres and the populations have spread far beyond the old city boundaries. They have been referred to as the Manchester and Leeds of modern India respectively.

Wheeler's Entrenchment at Cawnpore, where so many died, still exists, though the area is overgrown with grass and people are warned to keep well away from the dark tunnels believed to be the home of cobras and other snakes. The pleasant sun-dappled track through the trees down to the Satichura Ghat has not changed at all and the fisherman's temple itself, despite some modern additions, is still recognizable as the spot where the British tried to climb into the boats, only to be shot down in their hundreds. Young Indians often come here as part of their marriage festivities and instead of the sounds of gunfire and screams are heard instead the sitar and songs.

Perhaps the biggest surprise is near where the dreadful Bibighar once stood. Here the British had laid out a park of remembrance, once the most sacred spot in the whole Empire, where natives were not permitted, and all carriages had to have muffled wheels so as not to disturb the serenity. A stone angel by the Victorian sculptor Marochetti stood on the spot of the infamous well. Today, the place is still a park, though traffic rumbles along close by, and the angel has been replaced by busts of Nana

Sahib Peshwa and Tantia Tope. A British element still survives; the spot is a favourite area for local schoolboys to play cricket. Few, if any, ever realise what took place there and the remains of the dead lay undisturbed beneath the cement.

The fierce fighting at Lucknow destroyed, along with Napier's traffic schemes, much of what had been the most beautiful city in India. The Kaisarbagh today gives no clue to its former size and gives little sense of its glory, yet the Sikanderbagh stands and was described by one recent British visitor as "atmospheric". On the outside wall of the garden (accessible through the hospital next door), is the spot where the British broke through and a monument to HM 93rd Highlanders. More astonishing perhaps is the Martinière building, still a school with Hodson's grave in its grounds and a wall plaque to the boys who fought in the siege. One 21st-century writer noted how "The boys of the school greet passers-by with that old fashioned courtesy that used to be thought British. If E. M. Forster was right and the last English gentleman will be an Indian, there's a good chance he'll have come from the Martinière."[2]

The Banner of England no longer flies in the Residency grounds, but an army of gardeners still keeps the place immaculate. Here, time has stood still to some extent and we are back in the 1880s. Sightseers, many of them foreign tourists, stare with little comprehension at the red brick ruins, the scarred wall tablets and tombs, set amid the perfectly manicured lawns and low hedges as guides hurry them along. I am happy to report that the Residency and its gardens remain a delight for the military historian, just as much as they are for the parties of Indian schoolchildren who are probably more interested in the parakeets in the waving palm trees than hearing of how their brave Awadhi ancestors besieged the sahibs and memsahibs. Considering the desecration of so much of the past in India – not just its British past – it is to the great credit of the Indian Government that the Lucknow Residency remains a beautiful place in a bustling modern city.

One incongruous aspect of this beautiful park is that for young Indian courting couples, the shady ruins and walks provide a perfect place to talk of romance, hold hands and, who knows, even steal a quick kiss. It is said that locals avoid the area at night; the place, they say, is haunted and the superstitious have no desire to encounter these ghosts. If those spirits exist, I think them benign. Some of the fiercest fighting of the Uprising took place here, it was the scene of terrible suffering and countess deaths on both sides. But I think, if the reader will forgive this sentimental remark, that Sir Henry Lawrence – the same Lawrence who loved children and liked nothing better than to perch his infants on his head in the bath – would be pleased to think that today, young people are happy in the Residency grounds. Teenagers who died in the fighting, such as Suzanne Palmer, or young Ensign Charles Dashwood, would surely smile to see courting couples in the ruins. One can almost hear the voluable Italian, Signor Barsotelli, chuckling in heaven as he clinks a glass with Monsieur Deprat.

And the brave Indian insurgents? They are also buried here in their thousands. I think they, too, would be pleased to see the young of a free and prosperous India enjoying this place.

All are at peace now, these Hindus, Moslems and Christians who lived, fought and died according to their times. It has ever been so. *Dulce et decorum est pro patria mori.*

Appendix A

List of the Insurgents in Lucknow Prior to Campbell's Relief

Regiment	Strength
Regt. of Captains Soobah Singh & Akipal Singh	700
Regt. No 8 Rightwing Capt. Gajadhar Singh	700
The Nadir Shahie Regt: Seetul Singh Adjt.	400
The Right Wing of Akhtari Regt: Capt. Bhowani Singh	950
Barlow's Regt. (6th Oudh Locals): Capt. Umrao Singh	700
The Akhtari Regt: Capt. Fida Hussain	600
The Volunteers (37th N. I.): Capt. Gauri Shanker	750
The 'Bole'Reg.t (22nd N. I.): Capt. Rajman Tiwari	700
Left Wing of Burbury's Regt. (8th Oudh Locals): Capt. Mukhodom Baksh	700
Left Wing of Roberts's Regt.	600
Right Wing of Roberts's Regt.	550
Regt. No 9: Capt. Gajen Singh	600

King's Regiments	
Regt. of Agha Hussain, Salar (general)	400
Regt of Jafir Ali, Salar	350
Regt. of Sheik Ali Bagar, Salar	400
Regt. of Bahadur Ali, Salar	250
Regt. of Mir Nagi, Ali Khan, Salar	762
Regt. of Mirza Shehar Yar, Salar	882
Remains of other regiments, approximately	2,556

Cavalry

Regt. No 12: Capt. Hari Singh	700
Regt. No 15	800
Regt. No 11	600

King's Cavalry

Tahwar Khan Rissaldar's Regt.	500
The Tircha Regt.	700
The Maiman-i-Shahi Regt	700
The Messurah Regt.	900
Ali Buksh Khan's Regt.	800
Mahomed Akbar's Regt.	900
The Regiment No 9	1,000
The New Regt.	120

Taluqdars' Troops

Raja Hardat Singh Bahadur	00
Raghunath Singh of Rajpur	200
The Ikauna Men	240
The Changapur Men	150
Hardat Singh of Churda	300
The Tepurdha Men	100
The Balrajkumars	200
The Shahpur Men	100
Kishandatt Pandey's Men	1,200
Sadun Salgunge	1,000
Bhinga Men	300
Tulsipur Men	500
Nanpara Men	400
Raghunath Singh of Baiswara	1,000
Raja Shanker Singh of Tiloi	80
Sheo Shankar Singh Jorapur	500
Lal Bahadur Sipath Salar of Kalukunkur	1,000
Rampur Katowalah Men	400
Beni Madhao Singh	1,000
Raja Man Singh	7,000
Raja of Amethi	2,500
Raja Sahaj Ram of Banthra	2,000
Raja Gurbux Singh of Ramnagar	2,500
Raja Nawab Ali Khan of Mahmudabad	2,200
Raja Baljandur Singh of Palpur	1,500
Surujpur Burhilah	2,000

List of the Insurgents in Lucknow Prior to Campbell's Relief

Baley Dube of Amooah	100
Umrao Singh of Mowhah	1,000
Umrao Singh of Ajuldhukwa	500
Jai Narain Singh of Dhorahrah	300
Balapur Rao Khairabad	800
Isanagar, Jai Prakash	500
Miscellaneous	300
Breakdown	
#Sepoys:	7,950
#Oudh Regts.	5,600
#Cavalry	7,720
#Taluqdars' Men	32,080

	53,350*

*Source: Captain Carnegie, Intelligence News of 15 December 1857

Appendix B

British Armies Attacking Lucknow

1. Havelock's Relief Army
   Commanding: Brig-Gen. Henry Havelock

   Cavalry
   European Volunteer Cavalry & 12th Bengal Irregular Cavalry   = 168

   Infantry
   1st Infantry Brigade (Brig. J. G. Neill, 1st Madras European Fusiliers)
   5th Foot (Northumberland Fusiliers)
   64th Foot (2 companies)
   84th Foot
   1st Madras European Fusiliers

   2nd Infantry Brigade (Brig. W. Hamilton, 78th Highlanders)·
   78th Highlanders
   90th Foot
   Ferozepore Regiment   = 2,729

   Artillery
   Artillery Brigade (Brig. G. L. Cooper, Bengal Artillery)
   3/8 R.A. (2nd Captain F.C. Maude)
   No 12 F.B. 2/3 Bengal Artillery (Captain W. Olpherts)
   No 3 H.F.B. 1/5 Bengal Artillery (Brev-Maj. V Eyre)   = 282

                                                                            3,179

2. Campbell's Relief Army (Nov. 1857)
   Commanding: General Sir Colin Campbell
   Second-in-command: Brig. J. H. Grant

   Cavalry Brigade (Brig. A. Little, 9th Lancers)
   9th Lancers (2 squadrons)
   Military Train (2 squadrons)
   Detachments of:
   1st, 2nd, 5th Punjab Cavalry & Hodson's Horse

   Infantry
   3rd Infantry Brigade (Brig. E.H. Greathed, 8th Foot)
   8th Foot
   Detachments of:
   5th, 64th and 90th Foot & 78th Highlanders
   2nd Punjab Infantry

   4th Infantry Brigade (Brig the Hon A. Hope, 93rd Highlanders)
   53rd Foot
   93rd Highlanders
   4th Punjab Infantry

   5th Infantry Brigade (Brig D. Russell, 84th Foot)
   23rd Foot
   82nd Foot

   Engineers
   Royal Engineers (one company)
   Detachments of Bengal Sappers & Miners, Madras Sappers & Miners,
   Sikh Pioneers

   Artillery Brigade (Brig. W. T. Crawford R.A.)
   4/5 R.A.
   5/13 R.A.
   6/13 R.A.
   1/1 & 2/3 Bengal Horse Artillery
   E troop Madras Horse Artillery
   No 17 F.B. 3/1 Bengal Artillery
   Detachment of 1/5 Bengal Artillery
   Naval Brigade HMS *Shannon* (Captain W. Peel V.C.)

3. The Army of Oudh (Feb. 1858)
   Commanding: General Sir Colin Campbell

Cavalry Division (Brig. J. H. Grant, 9th Lancers)

1st Brigade: (Brig. A. Little)
9th Lancers
Military Train
2nd Punjab Cavalry
Detachment of 5th Punjab Cavalry
Wale's Horse

2nd Brigade: (Brig. W. Campbell)
2nd Dragoon Guards
7th Hussars
Volunteer European Cavalry
Detachment of 1st Punjab Cavalry
Hodson's Horse

Infantry
1st Division (commanding: Maj-Gen. Sir J. Outram)

1st Brigade (Brig. D. Russell, 84th Foot)
5th Foot
84th Foot
1st Madras European Fusiliers

2nd Brigade (Brig. C. Franklyn, 8th Foot)
78th Foot
90th Foot
Ferozepore Regiment

2nd Division (commanding: Brig. Sir E. Lugard, 29th Foot)

3rd Brigade (Brig. W. Hamilton, 78th Highlanders)
34th Foot
38th Foot
53rd Foot

4th Brigade (Brig the Hon. A. Hope, 93rd Highlanders)
42nd Highlanders
93rd Highlanders
4th Punjab Infantry

3rd Division (commanding: Brig. R. Walpole, Rifle Brigade)

5th Brigade (Brig R. Douglas, 79th Foot)
23rd Foot
79th Highlanders
1st Bengal European Fusiliers

6th Brigade (Brig. A. H. Horsford, Rifle Brigade)
2nd & 3rd battalions, Rifle Brigade
2nd Punjab Infantry

Engineer Brigade (Brig. R. Napier, Bengal Engineers)
4th & 23rd companies Royal Engineers
Bengal Sappers & Miners
Sikh Pioneers

Artillery Divsion (commanding: Major-General Sir A. Wilson, Bengal
 Artillery)
Field Artillery: Brig. D.E.Wood R.H.A.
Siege Artillery: Brig G.R.Barker R.A.

E & F Troops Royal Horse Artillery
1/1, 2/1, 2/3 & 3/3 Bengal Horse Artillery
5/12, 3/14, 6/13, 8/2, 3/8, 6/11, 5/13 Royal Artillery
No 12 F.B. 2/3 Bengal Artillery & siege artillery 4/1, 5/1, 3/5, 4/5 &
 recruits
A/3 Madras Artillery

Naval Brigade of HMS *Shannon* (Captain W. Peel V.C.)

Endnotes

Prologue

1. Case, DAY BY DAY, p 20.
2. Polehampton, MEMOIR, pp 86-87.
3. In his diary Polehampton says James was shot in the arm, but Gubbins says the leg and Dr Fayrer, who dealt with the injury, is adamant that it was the knee-joint.
4. Innes in his account of the siege says Lawrence "ordered" food to be served out. Yet the problem is I cannot find this corroborated in other accounts and Innes was not there.
5. Forrest, HISTORY, Vol I, p 231.
6. Ibid.
7. Rees, PERSONAL NARRATIVE, p 88.
8. Tuker, METCALFE CHRONICLE, p 28.
9. NAM 1993-11-10 – letter of William Case to his mother.
10. Tuker pp 29-30
11. Rees p 80
12. Jones was recommended for a Victoria Cross but sadly died of cholera before the official warrant was made.
13. Cubbitt served throughout the siege, receiving his VC from Queen Victoria on 4th January 1860. For the next 19 years he served with the Lucknow Regiment, becoming its lieutenant-colonel. He married a sister of James Hill-Johnes, another Mutiny VC winner. He died in 1903 and has a fine headstone in St Peter's churchyard, Frimley, Surrey.
14. Joyce, ORDEAL, pp 6-7.

1 The Road to Chinhat

1. Lawrence. LAWRENCE, p 239
2. Moon, THE BRITISH DOMINION, p 647
3. Mount, TEARS, p 370
4. Lee-Warner, LIFE OF, Vol II, p 205
5. Pemble, THE RAJ, p 91
6. Sleeman, RAMBLES, p 322
7. Ibid. JOURNAL, p 397
8. "Scandalous and hysterical" says Mount, Llewellyn-Jones agrees, though the late Sir Penderel Moon thought Sleeman's report was only "slightly exaggerated".
9. Lee-Warner Vol II, p 319
10. Adams, MAKERS, p 340
11. Mount p 443
12. Baird, LETTERS, p 369
13. Mount p 444
14. Kaye, MUTINY Vol I p 96
15. Mukherjee, AWADH p 36
16. Taban essay, "The Coming Of The Revolt In Awadh" in Moosvi, FACETS p 14
17. Pemble p 145
18. David, THE BENGAL ARMY, pp 170-171
19. Hibbert, THE GREAT MUTINY, p 218
20. Lunt, FROM SEPOY TO SUBEDAR, p 161
21. Moon p 667
22. White, INDIAN REMINISCENCES, p 83
23. Stokes, ENGLISH UTILITARIANS, p 46
24. FSUP Vol II p 298
25. Kaye Vol I p 327
26. Holmes, HISTORY, p 246
27. Hibbert p 219
28. Ibid
29. Lee, BROTHERS, p 338
30. Morrison, LAWRENCE, p 300
31. Danvers, LETTERS, p 57
32. NAM 1993-11-10
33. David, THE BENGAL ARMY, p 213
34. Mukherjee, MANGAL PANDEY, p 64
35. Fayrer, RECOLLECTIONS, p 129
36. Llewellyn-Jones, GREAT UPRISING, p 105

37. Germon, JOURNAL, pp 27-28
38. Hibbert p 219
39. Edwardes, SEASON, p 36
40. Innes, LUCKNOW, p 77
41. Mukherjee, AWADH, pp 65-66. Saul David discerns a more widespread pattern of revolt in his book *The Bengal Army and The Outbreak Of The Indian Mutiny.*
42. Rees p 19
43. Case, DAY BY DAY, p 16
44. Bush, WARNER LETTERS, p 57
45. Edwardes & Merivale, LIFE OF, p 577
46. Hibbert p 223
47. Anderson, PERSONAL JOURNAL, p 10
48. Hayes left a widow and five children at Lucknow.
49. Ruggles, RECOLLECTIONS, p 49
50. NAM 1964-11-60 – McLeod Innes Unpublished Account
51. Hodge, TRAVELS, p 101
52. NAM 1964-11-60
53. Edwardes, SEASON, p 40
54. Anderson pp 28-29
55. Edwardes & Merivale p 591
56. Rees p 38
57. Daly, MEMOIRS, p 121
58. Lawrence p 247
59. Lee, BROTHERS, p 345
60. Case p 22
61. Edwardes, BOUND, pp 117-119
62. Harris, A LADY'S DIARY, pp 46-47 * both chaplains were Oxford men; Harris was in fact senior to Polehampton but seems to have been happy to serve as his assistant at Lucknow on the basis that the other man was there first.
63. Inglis, SIEGE OF LUCKNOW, p 30
64. Case, pp 46-47
65. Morrison p 307
66. Ibid p 318

2 'Neath Shot and Flame

1. Mrs Soppitt was born Erina L'Amour Weatherhead Malcolmson, daughter of a Bombay Army surgeon. Her brother became Major-General John Malcolmson and as colonel of the Sind Horse his behaviour at the disastrous Battle of Maiwand during the 2nd Afghan War led to his court-martial for cowardice, though he was acquitted.

2. William Oxenham of HM 32nd was the first man of the regiment to win a VC for helping to extricate Capper from the ruins. He had served 15 years with the regiment and was from Devon. The odd thing is that Capper felt that he owed his life primarily to Anderson and lobbied for him to get a VC, but the recommendation was not looked at by the War Office until 1868. It was turned down on the basis that a time limit for applications had passed. Oxenham left the army in 1862, re-married and died back in Devon in 1875 of meningitis. The family sold his VC in 1910 for £70 and it is now in the regimental museum. I am happy to relate a smart headstone to his memory was erected in Pinhoe Cemetery, Exeter, in 1993.

3. Morrison p 323

4. FSUP Vol II p 113

5. Rees pp 116-118

6. Edwardes, SEASON, p 54

7. I am following what Mrs Huxham says in her Narrative and several other women say the second storey, but Mrs Brydon in her diary says Miss Palmer was seated near the venetian doors on the ground floor.

8. Hay, DIARY, pp 9-10

9. Innes, LUCKNOW, p 102

10. Joyce pp 29-30

11. Morrison pp 325-326

12. Harris p 78

13. Joyce p 43

14. Lawrence p 256

15. NAM-1973-03-24

16. Case p 81

17. Taylor, FEELING, p 39

18. Ibid quoting Otto Trevelyan

19. Fayrer p 131

20. The clock was a fake, simply a dial painted on a surface.

21. Anderson p 59

22. Taylor, FEELING, p 52

23. Gubbins, ACCOUNT, pp 204-205

24. Taylor, FEELING, p 84

25. Wilson says that Polehampton was shot on the 7th but the victim says the 8th – and he ought to have known!

26. Wilson, DIARY, p 53

27. NAM-1957-06-17

28. Hay p 14

29. NAM-1973-03-24

30. Anderson p 65

31. Edwardes, JOURNAL GERMON, p 58

32. Harris p 81
33. Hibbert p 240
34. NAM-1964-11-60
35. Tuker p 37
36. NAM-1964-11-60
37. Gubbins pp 212-214
38. ILN 26th September 1857
39. Wilson p 60
40. Polehampton's goods fetched 700 rupees at auction (about £7000 today)
41. Edwardes, SEASON, p 103
42. Rees p 153
43. WJW/1 – Author's Collection
44. Fayrer p 177
45. Holmes, HISTORY, p 270
46. NAM-1964-11-60
47. Joyce pp 113-115
48. Hay pp 18-19
49. Joyce pp 117-118
50. Ibid p 137
51. Harris p 85
52. Edwardes, JOURNAL GERMON, p 75
53. Fayrer p 180
54. Ruggles p 63
55. Forrest, HISTORY, Vol I p 300
56. Ibid p 303

3 A Fossil Turned into Pipe Clay

1. Maude, MEMORIES, Vol I, p 39
2. Pollock, WAY TO GLORY, pp 161-162
3. Wright, WARRIORS, p 137
4. Brock, HAVELOCK, p 138
5. Sir Patrick Grant is buried in the Brompton Cemetery in West London. Many years ago I was looking in the long grass at some of the military tombs and managed to stub my toe on the corner of his memorial.
6. Pollock pp 150-151
7. Campbell, MEMOIRS, Vol I p 282
8. Maude Vol I p 39
9. Hibbert p 199
10. Collier p 133
11. Maclagan, CLEMENCY CANNING, p 46
12. Allen, BURNING PLAIN, p 70

13. Pollock p 152
14. David, INDIAN MUTINY, p 232
15. Collister, HELLFIRE JACK, p 77
16. Spencer, PERSONAL REMINISCENCES, p 40
17. BL Mss Eur. LYVEDEN PAPERS F/231/5
18. Kaye, SEPOY WAR, Vol II p 236
19. Allen p 60
20. Dawson, SQUIRES, p 43
21. Holmes p 211
22. David, INDIAN MUTINY, p 231
23. Hibbert p 200
24. Campbell Vol I pp 281-282
25. David, INDIAN MUTINY, p 235
26. Pandey, VISION, p 189
27. Kaye, LIVES, Vol I p 373
28. Staff Officer, REMINISCENCES, 45
29. Kaye, SEPOY WAR, Vol II p 269
30. David, INDIAN MUTINY, p 227
31. Heathcote, PEARSON LETTERS, pp 46-47
32. David, INDIAN MUTINY, p 239
33. Kaye, LIVES, Vol I p 374
34. Sen, EIGHTEEN FIFTY-SEVEN, p 154
35. Pollock p 157
36. Heathcote, PEARSON LETTERS, p 47
37. Maude Vol I p 34
38. Ibid p 36
39. Swanson, MY JOURNAL, p 17
40. Barker, LETTERS, p 52
41. McKenzie, MY LIFE, pp 34-35
42. Maude Vol I p 41
43. Pollock p 164
44. Sherer original Journal quoted in Ward, OUR BONES, p 394
45. Pollock p 165
46. Groom, WITH HAVELOCK, pp 26-27
47. North, JOURNAL, pp 40-41
48. Forrest, HISTORY, Vol I p 375
49. Forrest, STATE PAPERS, Vol II p 86
50. Maude Vol I pp 42-43
51. Holmes, SAHIB, pp 339-340
52. Forrest, HISTORY, p 376
53. "Line of metal" meant that Maude aimed straight across the groove in the gun's breech to the foresight in its muzzle. The breech was broader than

the muzzle so that the piece would be fired with a slight elevation. A good gunner knew precisely what "line of metal" would represent for various types of cannon.

54. Pollock p 168
55. Sherer, MEMORIES, Vol I p 186
56. Forrest, HISTORY, pp 377-378
57. Maude Vol I p 46
58. Sherer Journal in Ward p 397
59. He died of exhaustion on 22nd August
60. Marshman, MEMOIRS, p 296
61. Ibid p 298
62. Pollock 172-173
63. There is a memorial tablet to Renaud in Christ Church, Warminster, Wiltshire, with words that seem almost ironic if they were not so sincere – "Fight the good fight." The major's two medals for the Persian War and Relief of Lucknow, given posthumously, were sold at auction in 2017 and fetched £3,000.
64. NAM 1959-03-10
65. Pollock pp 175-176
66. Kinsley, DEVILS, pp 31-32
67. Maude Vol I p 53
68. Forrest and Pollock say 4 heavy guns, Innes says 3.
69. Kinsley pp 33
70. Pollock p 178
71. Kinsley p 37
72. Pollock p 180
73. Kinsley p 38
74. Collier p 178
75. NAM 1959-03-105
76. Forrest, HISTORY, Vol I p 389
77. Kinsley p 34
78. Heathcote, PEARSON LETTERS, p 50
79. Pollock p 185
80. Marshman p 314
81. Poor Shepherd' adventures are fascinating but unfortunately there is not space enough in this book to cover them. They belong to the Siege of Cawnpore and the reader is directed to Andrew Ward's superb study – see bibliography. Shepherd authored one of the best books on the siege and massacres. He died relatively poor and in obscurity aged 66 in 1891.
82. Ward p 428
83. Collier p 183
84. Forbes, HAVELOCK, p 114

85. Ward p 429
86. Crump, PICTORIAL RECORD, p 2
87. Wright, THROUGH THE INDIAN MUTINY p 131
88. Blomfield, LAHORE TO LUCKNOW p 121
89. Mukherjee, SPECTRE OF VIOLENCE, pp 72-73
90. Pollock p 188
91. Maude Vol I p 78
92. Pollock p 191
93. Forrest, HISTORY, p 319
94. Pollock p 195
95. Bogle survived his wounds and retired from the army as a major in 1868. He died 22 years later and has a large memorial in Effingham churchyard, Surrey.
96. Pollock p 196
97. Ball, HISTORY, Vol II p 18
98. CALCUTTA REVIEW Vol XXXII p 33
99. North p 112
100. Heathcote, PEARSON LETTERS, p 56
101. Forrest, HISTORY, pp 491-492
102. Groom p 60

4 Terriers in Rat Holes

1. Edwardes, SEASON, p 112
2. Ibid p 113
3. NAM 1987-06-29
4. Ibid
5. Taylor, FEELING, p 102
6. "So useless was this operation of spiking that ere the party had been four hours within the works, both guns were again battering the Brigade Mess with undiminished effect." – Gubbins p 267
7. Fforde pp 47-55 and Hibbert p 249
8. CSAS Cambridge – BOILEAU PAPERS – Extract from "A Lady's Diary Of The Siege Of Lucknow" by Mrs Boileau
9. Hilton, TOURIST'S GUIDE, p 81
10. Edwardes, JOURNAL GERMON, pp 84-85
11. Parry, SIEGE, p 43
12. Hay pp 30-32
13. Rees p 206
14. Joyce p 188
15. Macmillan, WOMEN, p 95
16. Hilton p 91

17. Gubbins pp 282-283
18. Hay p 35
19. Joyce p 213
20. Ibid p 214
21. Ibid pp 215-216
22. Bartrum, REMINISCENCES, p 40
23. Inglis, SIEGE, p 146
24. Forrest, HISTORY, Vol I p 324
25. NAM 1987-06-29
26. The Indian chronicler, Roshan Taqui, says Fulton's assailant was an ex-ressaldar named Najeebuddaula. Clearly he was a good shot.
27. BL Mss Eur ROBERT LOVEDAY INGLIS LETTERS F693/1
28. Fayrer p 216
29. Rees p 220
30. Inglis p 142
31. Ibid p 143
32. Hay p 44
33. Joyce p 226
34. Ibid pp 229-230
35. Edwardes, JOURNAL GERMON, p 97
36. Bartrum p 43
37. Robinson, ANGELS, p 178
38. Fynmore, JESSIE BROWN, Notes & Queries, IIS IV p 416. Forbes-Mitchell is the only participant in the Mutiny who claims to have heard this story while at Lucknow. It is almost certainly apocryphal.
39. Joyce p 232
40. Some writers talk of 87 days, starting on first full day of 1st July 1857, others such as Michael Joyce, or Lieutenant Hay, (who was there), write of 88 days. It seems to me that the siege started the minute troops returned from Chinhat around noon on the 30th June and is thus 88 days.

5 Lambs to the Slaughter

1. Heathcote, PEARSON LETTERS, pp 63-65
2. Forrest, HISTORY Vol I p 495
3. Ibid, SELECTIONS, Vol II p 173
4. Ibid, HISTORY, Vol I p 496
5. Barker p 66
6. Forrest, HISTORY, Vol I p 498
7. Pollock p 210
8. Barker p 66

9. Pollock p 210
10. NYCRO/ZDG HAVELOCK PAPERS
11. Forrest, HISTORY, Vol I p 502
12. Ibid
13. Marshman p 357
14. Forrest, HISTORY, Vol I p 503
15. Heathcote, PEARSON LETTERS, p 69
16. North pp 136-137
17. Forrest, HISTORY Vol I pp 505-506
18. Marshman p 363
19. NAM 1959-03-105
20. Kaye, LIVES, Vol I pp 380-381
21. NAM 1959-03-105
22. Hibbert p 211
23. London Times, 16th October, 1857
24. BL Mss Eur EWART PAPERS – B267
25. NAM 1976-04-10
26. Barker p 67
27. NAM 1959-03-105
28. Heathcote, PEARSON LETTERS, p 71
29. Ibid
30. Barker p 69
31. Pollock p 218
32. Ibid p 219
33. Goldsmid, OUTRAM, Vol I p 42
34. Maclagan p 122
35. SRO – WADE LETTERS
36. Barter, SIEGE, p 106
37. Pollock p 219
38. NAM 1992-10-27
39. Ibid
40. Pollock p 219
41. Ibid p 222
42. BL Mss Eur MASON PAPERS – C330
43. Barker p 73
44. Danvers p 98
45. Home, SERVICE MEMORIES, p 108
46. Barthorp & Anderson, TROOPS, p 23
47. Ibid
48. BL Mss Eur NEILL PAPERS – 422
49. Danvers p 99
50. Ibid

51. NAM 1957-05-10
52. BL Mss Eur MASON PAPERS – C330
53. Forbes, HAVELOCK, p 194
54. Swanston p 37
55. JSAHR Vol XLIII No 176 p 205
56. Ibid p 204
57. Maude & Sherer Vol II p 283
58. Swanston p 38
59. Ibid p 39
60. Home p 116
61. BL Mss Eur MASON PAPERS C330
62. Danvers p 103
63. Forrest, HISTORY, Vol II p 31
64. Collister p 105
65. Johnson, SOLDIER'S LIFE, p 174
66. Dawson p 64
67. Danvers p 104
68. BL Mss Eur MASON PAPERS – C330
69. Delavoye, 90TH REGIMENT, p 140
70. Swanston p 41
71. Marshman p 406
72. Grant was promoted to sergeant and later joined the Metropolitan Police serving in Holloway until his death in 1874. Buried in a pauper's grave at Highgate, the Commissioner of the Metropolitan Police unveiled a new headstone in 2008.
73. BL Mss Eur NEILL PAPERS – 422
74. Maude & Sherer Vol II p 290
75. Kinsley pp 46-47
76. Ibid
77. Ibid p 48
78. Maude & Sherer Vol II p 291
79. Kinsley p 49
80. Ibid
81. Wright, WARRIORS, p 78
82. Kinsley p 50
83. Ibid p 41
84. Collister p 109
85. Kinsley p 55
86. Sources differ on when exactly Olpherts was wounded; Home says it happened after the enemy guns had been taken and while he was congratulating the men, who thought he was a sitting target.

87. Kinsley p 55
88. LondonTimes, 23rd March, 1890
89. Kinsley p 54
90. Pollock p 232
91. Despite later being made Consul-General at Warsaw and a military knight of Windsor, Maude had serious financial problems in later life and had to sell his VC to an American collector, an action "much regretted" by the C-in-C. Buried in Windsor Cemetery, he left an estate in 1900 of just £63.15.06. Holmes died in 1872 and is buried in All Souls Cemetery, Halifax – his grave unmarked and cemetery sadly overgrown. Boulger served in the Egyptian War of 1882 and was made an honorary colonel of the 84th. He died in 1900 and has a fine headstone in Ballymore R.C. churchyard, Co. Kildare. Mylott died in 1878 and was placed in a pauper's grave in Anfield Cemetery, Liverpool, but happily was given a new stone in 1994. Macpherson rose to be a general and led the Indian Contingent to Egypt in 1882 but died of fever in Burma in 1886. He is buried in the British Military Cemetery, Rangoon. Jee rose to become Deputy Surgeon-General. He died aged 80 at his home in 1899 and has a fine headstone at Ratcliffe R.C. College, Queniborough, Leicestershire. McMaster died of a heart attack in 1872 barely 18 months after his marriage; he is buried in Belfast City Cemetery. Olpherts died aged 81 in 1902 as Colonel Commandant of the Royal Artillery. His VC group is on display in the National Army Museum and his grave is in Section N of Richmond Cemetery.
92. Apparently, on orders from above the guns were not spiked. The insurgents later recovered them from the canal and within a few days they were once again being used against the British.
93. Kinsley pp 67-68
94. Ibid p 71
95. Ibid p 72
96. Ibid p 60
97. JSAHR Vol XLIII No 176 p 206
98. NAM 1957-05-10
99. In retrospect, it seems a little odd that the whole force did not follow Moorsom's route, which might have saved several lives. It has to be assumed that the directness of just following one long street, successful if accomplished quickly, explains why it was the chosen route.
100. There is some confusion between sources as to whether these men were killed; Forrest says they were, but Danvers tells us, more happily, all three recovered, and adds that the worst wounded man, who had three bayonet wounds and one sword cut on his upper body, was sitting up in hospital a few days later.

6 Enter Sir Crawling Camel

1. Goldsmid, Vol II, p 240
2. Johnson p 184
3. Collister p 116
4. Anon. "Havelock's Indian Campaign" in Calcutta Review Vol XXXII pp 39-40
5. Duffy died in 1868 and sadly lies in an unmarked grave in Glasnevin Cemetery, Dublin.
6. Awarded the VC, Bradshaw died on 9th September 1861 aged just 31 and is buried at Thurles, Co. Tipperary.
7. Home p 123
8. Forrest, HISTORY, Vol II p 58
9. Both Ryan and McManus got the VC and were made sergeants; the former died at Cawnpore in March 1858, the latter of smallpox at Allahabad in 1859.
10. Like many old soldiers with a VC, Hollowell ended his days as a commissionaire for a store in Oxford Street. The war correspondent, Archibald Forbes, interviewed him for his books on the Mutiny. He died in 1876 and lies in the Brookwood Cemetery, Surrey.
11. After receiving his VC, Surgeon Home went on to serve in the 2nd Anglo-Chinese War, the Maori Wars and the 1873 Ashanti War. He got the KCB and died at his home in London in August 1914. He has a fading headstone in Highgate Cemetery.
12. Collier pp 280-281 based on Bartrum's journal.
13. Maude & Sherer Vol II p 311
14. Harris pp 123-124
15. Case p 210
16. Innes, LUCKNOW, p 225
17. BL Mss Eur INGLIS LETTERS F693/1
18. Rees pp 252-253
19. Dawson p 73
20. NAM 1966-02-62
21. Hilton p 109
22. BL Mss Eur MASON PAPERS C.330
23. Swanston pp 39-50
24. Collier p 290
25. Joyce p 277
26. Inglis pp 158-159
27. Forrest, HISTORY, Vol II p 82
28. McKenzie, MY LIFE, pp 60-61
29. Edwards, SEASON, p 232

30. NAM 1973-03-24
31. Ibid 1975-10-31
32. Kinsley pp 102-103
33. Outram, CAMPAIGN, p 321
34. Taqui, LUCKNOW 1857, pp 166-167
35. Taylor, A STAR, pp 218-219
36. Danvers pp 118-120
37. Collier p 289
38. Kavanagh, HOW I WON, pp 67-68
39. Knight, MARCHING, pp 111-112
40. Joyce p 292
41. NAM 1975-05-10
42. Dawson p 77
43. Tuker p 57
44. Fitchett, Soppitt appendix
45. Shadbolt, LIFE, Vol I p 406
46. Wright, WARRIORS, p 66
47. Campbell Vol I p 283
48. Wolseley, STORY, Vol I p 250
49. Surtees, CHARLOTTE CANNING, p 244
50. Allen p 75
51. Maclagan p 23
52. BL Mss Eur CANNING PAPERS – letters to Vernon Smith of 5ᵗʰ & 9ᵗʰ June and 20ᵗʰ July 1857
53. Shadwell Vol I p 437
54. Ramsay, RECOLLECTIONS, Vol I p 269
55. Wright, WARRIORS, p 238
56. Fortescue, HISTORY, Vol XIII p 275
57. Greenwood, SCOTTISH LION, p 339
58. Douglas & Ramsay, PANMURE PAPERS, Vol II p 439
59. Majendie, PANDIES, p 71
60. Gordon-Alexander, RECOLLECTIONS, p 31
61. Alison, "Lord Clyde's Campaign In India" in Blackwood's Magazine October 1858 p 483
62. Hare, NOBLE LIVES, Vol II p 292
63. Forbes-Mitchell, REMINISCENCES, p 179
64. Trevelyan, COMPETITION WALLAH, p 300
65. Moon p 739
66. Hare Vol II p 312
67. Watson, GREAT INDIAN MUTINY, p 56
68. Barter p 76
69. Roberts, FORTY-ONE, Vol I p 259

70. Barter p 78
71. Roberts, FORTY-ONE, Vol I p 262
72. Roberts, LETTERS, p 73
73. I have accepted Barter's story of the impatient infantry being urged on by an Irish private since it has the ring of truth. He mentions nothing of cowardice but the cavalry officers in their accounts imply strongly that the infantry held back that day – one wrote, "They could not be got to look round a corner or advance in any way."
74. Anson became a colonel, an M.P. and married an Earl's daughter. He died in 1877 and is buried in the British cemetery at Grasse.
75. This VC winner died in Marylebone on 1ˢᵗ August 1859.
76. Blair died of smallpox at Cawnpore in 1859; Donohoe is buried at Donaghmore, Co. Meath.
77. Kells became a proud VC-wearing Yeoman of the Guard; he died in 1905 and is buried in Lambeth Cemetery.
78. Diamond died in 1892 at Masterton, New Zealand, Fitzgerland in India in 1884.
79. Campbell, Vol I, p 257
80. Anson, WITH H.M. 9ᵀᴴ LANCERS, pp 177-178
81. Holmes p 392
82. Bourchier, EIGHT MONTHS, p 95
83. Roberts, FORTY-ONE, Vol I p 270
84. Raikes, NOTES, p 70
85. Roberts, LETTERS, p 77
86. Holmes p 393
87. Forrest, HISTORY, Vol II pp 95-96
88. Lee-Warner, HENRY WYLIE NORMAN pp 178-179
89. Heathcote, MUTINY, p 161
90. Blomfield pp 114-115
91. Freeman was wounded badly at Bareilly in 1858 but received his VC from the hands of the Queen. He died in 1913 aged 80 and is buried in Abney Park Cemetery, Stoke Newington.
92. He is buried in Kensal Green Cemetery.
93. He was killed a few weeks later on 2ⁿᵈ January 1858.
94. Ewart, STORY, Vol II p 53
95. Blomfield p 123
96. Hay pp 51-53
97. Harris p 84
98. Swanston pp 50-51
99. Pemble p 213
100. Collier p 246
101. Greenwood p 354

102. Wright, WARRIORS, p 121
103. Roberts, FORTY-ONE, Vol I pp 298-299
104. Forrest, HISTORY, Vol II, p 119
105. Shadwell, Vol II, p 5

7 One Corner of Hell

1. Hibbert p 332
2. Collier p 296
3. Kavanagh, HOW I WON, p 84
4. Ibid p 86
5. Ibid p 87
6. Forrest, HISTORY, Vol II p 129
7. Mukherjee, AWADH, p 95
8. Collier p 308
9. Wolseley, STORY, Vol I p 194
10. Shadwell Vol I p 455
11. Forrest, HISTORY, Vol II p 130
12. Hibbert p 337
13. Barter p 97
14. Forbes-Mitchell REMINISCENCES p 33
15. Gough, OLD MEMORIES, pp 154-156
16. Hugh Gough later fought in the Abyssinian War 1868 and commanded the cavalry of the Kurram Field Force in the 2nd Afghan War. He died in 1909.
17. Wolseley Vol I p 296
18. Gordon-Alexander, RECOLLECTIONS, p 48
19. Shadwell Vol II p 5
20. Llewellyn-Jones, FATAL FRIENDSHIP, p 153
21. Blomfield p 137
22. Forbes-Mitchell p 40
23. Wright, INDIAN MUTINY, p 143
24. Collier p 314
25. Watson and Probyn remained firm friends after both received the VC. Watson died in his 90th year in 1919. Probyn became in due course a revered member of the Royal Household and Colonel of the 11th (King Edward's Own) Lancers (Probyn's Horse). He died in 1924 and is buried in Kensal Green Cemetery. His VC was bought by an anonymous bidder at auction in 2005 for £160,000.
26. Blomfield pp 137
27. Ewart, STORY, Vol II p 72
28. Greenwood p 361

29. Herford, STIRRING TIMES, p 72
30. Roberts, FORTY-ONE, Vol I p 315
31. Jones-Parry, MEMORIES, p 186
32. Blomfield p 138
33. Collier p 315
34. Ibid p 316
35. Roberts, FORTY-ONE, Vol I p 320
36. Wright, INDIAN MUTINY, p 145
37. Wise, DIARY, p 169
38. Wright, INDIAN MUTINY p 146
39. Collier p 319
40. Ibid p 318
41. Forrest, HISTORY, Vol II p 146
42. Herford p 75
43. Roberts, FORTY-ONE, Vol I p 324
44. Ibid p 325
45. Ibid p 326
46. In the Lucknow Despatches it was written that Gokul Singh "will be duly rewarded, but Parrett and Chhina state that "no trace" of his being raised to the Order of Merit has been found. He was, however, appointed to the lesser Order of British India and raised to Subedar-Major rank.
47. Thirty-four of the gallant 4th Punjabis got the Order of Merit for service that day. Mokurram Khan continued to show special gallantry in Rohilkhand and raised to the Order of Merit, 2nd class.
48. Hibbert p 340
49. Blomfield p 139
50. Norfolk Records CUB 137/4
51. Wright, INDIAN MUTINY, p 148
52. Roberts, LETTERS, pp 103-104
53. Forbes-Mitchell p 58
54. Wright, INDIAN MUTINY, p 148
55. Ewart Vol II p 81
56. Forrest, HISTORY, Vol II p 156
57. Ibid p 157
58. Forbes-Mitchell pp 72-73
59. Salmon duly became Admiral of the Fleet Sir Nowell Salmon and died in 1912. Harrison was not so lucky; his Indian Mutiny wounds and malaria weakened him and he died at his London home in 1865.
60. Hall continued to serve in the Royal Navy until 1876 when he retired to Nova Scotia with petty officer rank. He died there on 25th August 1904. He has a splendid memorial in the grounds of Hantsport Baptist Church.

61. Verney, DEVIL'S WIND, p 77

62. NAM 1987-01-22

63. Watson p 77

64. Kinsley p 107

65. Ibid p 109

66. The longest living of the Sikanderbagh VCs was Private John Dunlay (or Dunlea) who died in 1890. John Paton, who found the gap in the Shah Najeef wall, moved to Australia, held various senior appointments in the prison service and lived until 1st April 1914, aged 81. The actual number of awards is a hot topic among medal collectors, since the figure quoted includes some acts of bravery with no specific date that took place between 26th September and 22nd November. Author Brian Best, an authority on Mutiny VCs, credits 16 only to the 16th of November 1857.

67. NAM 1987-01-22

68. Forbes-Mitchell p 88

69. Wolseley Vol I p 306

70. Lee-Warner, MEMOIRS, p 187

71. Wolseley Vol I p 311

72. Lehmann, ALL SIR GARNET, p 66

73. Kavanagh p 116

74. Lehmann p 67

75. Knollys, INCIDENTS, p 192

76. The incident gave rise to Thomas Jones Barker's famous painting, "The Relief Of Lucknow" which is now in the National Portrait Gallery, London. It was done six years after the event and while the artist tried to get the uniforms right, it should not be taken as accurate. Lord Wolseley wrote that "there is a theatrical air about the picture, which represents everyone looking clean and tidy, which none of us certainly did look."

8 Windham Takes a Gamble

1. Joyce p 328

2. Shadwell, Vol I, p 455

3. Forrest, HISTORY, Vol I p 189

4. Maclagan p 149

5. Roberts, FORTY-ONE, Vol I p 342

6. Knollys, LIFE, VolI p 296

7. This story appears in Rees and was used by Collier. The historian Michael Edwardes said it was untrue, but I have used it since it is very much in keeping with Campbell's character.

8. BL Mss Eur INGLIS LETTERS F693/1
9. Edwardes, JOURNAL GERMON, pp 120-121
10. BL Mss Eur INGLIS LETTERS F693/1
11. Collier pp 332-333
12. Edwardes, GERMON JOURNAL, pp 124-125
13. NAM 1973-03-24
14. Greenwood p 374
15. Inglis p 153
16. Hibbert p 349
17. Gubbins p 416
18. NAM 1957-05-10
19. Broehl, CRISIS, pp 169-170
20. Forrest, SELECTIONS, Vol II p 381
21. Gordon-Alexander p 148
22. Knollys, LIFE, Vol II p 303
23. Pollock p 252
24. Marshman p 441
25. Pollock p 252
26. Roberts, FORTY-ONE, Vol I pp 357-358
27. Edwardes, GERMON JOURNAL, pp 127-129
28. Harris p 172
29. Shadwell Vol II p 23
30. Wolseley Vol I p 323
31. Roberts, LETTERS, pp 106-107
32. ____, FORTY-ONE, Vol I p 320
33. Inglis p 197
34. Forrest, SELECTIONS, Vol II p 373
35. Wolseley Vol I p 324
36. BL Mss Eur JOHNSON JOURNAL A1611
37. Norfolk Records WINDHAM LETTERS MC 135/171-85
38. Ibid
39. Ward p 478
40. Holmes p 417
41. PP No 6 p 147
42. Ibid p 175
43. Adye, DEFENCE, p 22
44. NAM 1976-04-10
45. Oliver pp 27-29
46. Forrest, HISTORY, Vol II p 202
47. Ibid
48. Ibid p 203
49. Holmes p 422

50. Thomson p 235
51. BL Add Mss 37151 MOORE DIARY
52. Ward p 483
53. NAM 1976-04-10
54. London Times, 2nd February, 1858
55. Lewin p 13
56. Holmes p 424
57. Forrest, SELECTIONS, Vol II p 407
58. Maude & Sherer Vol II p 385
59. McKenzie p 80
60. Munro, RECORDS, Vol II p 225
61. Shadwell Vol II p 30
62. Knollys, LIFE, Vol I p 307
63. Mackay, FROM LONDON, Vol II p 285
64. Fayrer p 242
65. Inglis p 200
66. Lewin p 17
67. London Times, 11th February, 1858
68. Gordon-Alexander p 280
69. Inglis p 221
70. Allen p 89
71. Martin, INDIAN EMPIRE, Vol VIII p 474
72. Ewart Vol II p 108-110
73. Blomfield p 147
74. Verney, DEVIL'S WIND, p 85
75. Forbes-Mitchell p 140
76. Verney, DEVIL'S WIND, p 98
77. Holmes p 428
78. Maude & Sherer Vol II p 394
79. Greenwood p 392
80. Gordon-Alexander p 187
81. Broehl p 176
82. Roberts, FORTY-ONE, Vol I p 372
83. Angelsey Vol II p 169
84. BWRA 0016/06 ROBERTSON BOOK II p 38-39
85. NAM 1979-05-51
86. BL Add Mss 37151 MOORE DIARY
87. Norfolk Records WINDHAM LETTERS MC 135/171-85
88. Ibid
89. Ibid
90. Wright, INDIAN MUTINY, p 161
91. Gordon-Alexander p 184

9 Potting Ducks and Hanging Rebels

1. Pemble p 222
2. Gordon-Alexander pp 195-196
3. Duff, REBELLION, p 232
4. Verner, MILITARY LIFE, Vol I p 171
5. Forrest, HISTORY, Vol II p 243
6. Jones, WINTER CAMPAIGN, p 71
7. Forrest, HISTORY Vol II p 245
8. Verney, SHANNON'S BRIGADE, p 60
9. Anson p 222
10. It was bad luck for George Younghusband. He had diced with death on several occasions and in the cavalry chase at Agra he had fallen down a well while on horseback. He was not so lucky at Khudnaganj.
11. Knollys, LIFE, Vol I p 319
12. Roberts, FORTY-ONE, Vol I pp 385-386. The incident led to him receiving the coveted Victoria Cross.
13. Verney, SHANNON'S BRIGADE, p 62
14. Greenwood p 395
15. Verney, SHANNON'S BRIGADE, p 63
16. Ibid p 65
17. Jones p 89
18. Seaton, FROM CADET, Vol II p 261
19. Trotter, HODSON, p 269
20. Holmes p 616
21. Verney, SHANNON'S BRIGADE, pp 67-69
22. Shadwell Vol II p 65
23. David p 335
24. Forrest, HISTORY, Vol II p 255-256
25. Gordon-Alexander p 214
26. Hibbert p 355
27. Wright, INDIAN MUTINY, p 164
28. The incident won Innes a well deserved VC. He had a long life and wrote two books on the Uprising including, up to now, the only full military study of the Oudh campaign, though seen entirely from his perspective. He was highly critical of Inglis and others in his personal papers, though not in his books. He died at his home in Cambridge on 13th January 1907. His gravestone can be seen in the City Cemetery, Section A.
29. NAM 1976-04-10
30. Forrest, HISTORY, Vol II p 274
31. Goldsmid Vol II p 285
32. PP – Further Papers No 8 Relative To The Insurrection In The East Indies p 19

33. Herford p 92
34. Ibid p 105
35. BL Mss Eur COLLINS PAPERS 059
36. Wolseley Vol I p 333
37. BL Mss Eur COLLINS PAPERS 059
38. Herford p 108
39. Forrest, HISTORY, Vol II p 285
40. Harrison, RECOLLECTIONS, p 35
41. Forrest, HISTORY, Vol II p 289
42. Cardew, HODSON'S HORSE, p 78
43. Heathcote, PEARSON LETTERS, p 95
44. Forrest, HISTORY, Vol II pp 291-292
45. Robertson, PERSONAL ADVENTURES, p 252
46. NAM 1975-10-31
47. Maclagan p 1818
48. JUSI of I, July 1932, Wilson Letter CLV
49. Wilkinson-Latham, CORRESPONDENT, p 59
50. Russell, DIARY, Vol I pp 170-171
51. Forrest, HISTORY, Vol II p 302
52. Ibid p 303
53. Maclagan p 173

10 The Last Battle

1. Majendie p 140
2. Russell Vol I pp 227-230
3. Chalmers, LETTERS, pp 45-46
4. Oliver p 41
5. Llewellyn-Jones, UPRISING, p 121
6. Daly p 200
7. Forrest, SELECTIONS, Vol III p 465
8. Greenwood p 403
9. Ibid
10. Holmes p 439
11. Wright, INDIAN MUTINY, p 169
12. Russell Vol I pp 253-254 & 257
13. Anon. *Blackwoods Magazine*, July 1858, "The First Bengal European Fusiliers At Lucknow"
14. Russell Vol I p 279
15. Chalmers p 56
16. Macgregor, LIFE, Vol I p 73
17. BL Mss Eur D581

18. Hibbert p 359
19. Majendie p 187
20. Hay, LUCKNOW, pp 83-84
21. Forrest, SELECTIONS, Vol III p 479
22. Vibart, MUTINY, p 185
23. Forrest, HISTORY, Vol II p 328
24. Awarded the VC, Butler received it from Queen Victoria on 8th June 1859. He later served on the N.W. Frontier of India, retired as an honorary major and died at his home in Camberley on 17th May 1901. He is buried in St Michael's churchyard.
25. Blomfield p 162
26. Ibid pp 162-163
27. Chalmers p 66
28. Herford p 127
29. Maude & Sherer Vol II p 421
30. *Bombay Times*, 24th March, 1858
31. NRO CUB 1374
32. Forrest, HISTORY, Vol II p 339
33. Blomfield p 163
34. Forbes-Mitchell p 210
35. NLS Mss 2234
36. NAM 1959-03-146
37. Ibid
38. NAM 2009-06-02
39. NAM-03-146
40. NAM 1968-07-043
41. Bush p 213
42. BL Mss Eur 047
43. BL Mss Eur 022
44. NRO CUB 1234
45. Medley, CAMPAIGNING, p 179
46. Mount p 536
47. Russell Vol I p 323
48. Forrest, HISTORY, Vol II p 353
49. Russell Vol I p 337
50. Blomfield pp 165-166
51. Herford p 135
52. Verney, DEVIL'S WIND p 137
53. NAM 1976-06-43
54. Russell Vol I p 334
55. Ibid pp 329-330
56. Ibid p 333

57. Reeves, ARMY DOCTOR, p 86
58. Forrest, HISTORY, Vol II p 356
59. Greenwood p 410
60. Jocelyn, MUTINY, p 353
61. Wood, REVOLT, p 276
62. Collister p 142
63. Majendie p 210
64. Hibbert p 363
65. Majendie p 223
66. Ibid p 224
67. Knollys, LIFE, Vol I p 346
68. NAM 2006-06-14
69. Kavanagh p 140
70. Ibid p 151
71. NAM 2009-06-02
72. Russell Vol I p 343
73. Hay p 115
74. Russell Vol I p 343
75. Mackenzie, MEMOIRS, p 195
76. Strange, GUNNER, p 194
77. BL Mss Eur 059
78. Edwardes, BATTLES, p 136
79. NAM 1966-05-07
80. Mackenzie p 201
81. Kavanagh p 195
82. Caine, BARRACKS, p 87
83. Sen p 243
84. Innes, REVOLT, p 225
85. Heathcote, MUTINY, p 180
86. Bush p 212
87. Chalmers p 70

11 Captains and Kings

1. Gordon, RECOLLECTIONS, pp 133-134
2. JSAHR Vol XLIII, Sept 1965, p 144
3. Gordon p 133
4. Llewellyn-Jones, UPRISING, p 148
5. Oldenburg, LUCKNOW, p 64
6. Ibid pp 32-33
7. Russell Vol I p 357
8. Ibid Vol II p 370

9. Shadwell Vol II pp 371-372
10. Rizvi, FSUP, Vol II p 529
11. Taylor, STAR, p 223
12. Edwardes, RED YEAR, p 109
13. Malleson, HISTORY, Vol II p 544
14. Buried in the old British cemetery, Cawnpore; sadly, the headstone and grave site are long gone, buried beneath modern-day rebuilding. There are, however, several memorials to him in Great Britain.
15. Ball Vol II p 602
16. Collister p 174
17. Wright, WARRIORS, p 201
18. Inglis p 220
19. BL Mss Eur HORNE MANUSCRIPT 41488
20. Collier p 343
21. St Peter's Church, Duncan, Vancouver Island, British Columbia.

Epilogue

1. Lewin p 23
2. Spilsbury, INDIAN MUTINY, p 353

Select Bibliography

Original Documents

The Black Watch Regimental Association (BWRA) Diary of Private Walter Robertson 0016/06

British Library, India Office Records (BL)
Diaries of Lieutenant Arthur Lang, Bengal Engineers – Add Mss 43818-43825
Diary of Captain Edward Mason, 5th Northumberland Fusiliers – Mss Eur C330
Diary of Chaplain Moore at Cawnpore – Add Mss 37151
Diary of Lieutenant Sidney Hand, 82nd Foot – Add Mss 3249
Johnson Journal – BL A1611
Journal of Brigadier James Neill – Western Manuscripts R.P. 626/2
Letters of Brigade-Surgeon Francis Collins, 5th Fusiliers – Mss Eur 059
Letters of Captain Francis Sitwell, adc to Outram – Mss Eur Photo Eur 357
Letters of Ensign Wynyard Warner & Lieutenant Ashton Warner, Bengal Army – Mss Eur C190
Letters of Lieutenant R.L.Inglis, Bengal Army – Mss Eur F693/1
Letters of Mrs Janet Wells besieged at Lucknow – Mss Eur F444
Lyveden Papers – Mss Eur F231/5
Manuscript of Amy Horne – Mss Eur 41448
Memoir of Madeline Jackson – IOR Neg 11666
Mutiny Papers of William Mansfield, Lord Sandhurst – Mss Eur D174
Papers & Diary of Katherine Bartrum – Mss Eur A67 & A69
Papers of Captain Robert Biddulph R.A. – Mss Eur Photo Eur 047
Papers Of Charles, Lord Canning – Mss Eur F231
Papers of David Money, private secretary to Outram – Mss Eur C124/19-38
Papers of J.W. Adair – Mss Eur C295

Papers of Lieutenant Frederick Ames, Rifle Brigade – Mss Eur B236
Papers of Lieutenant George Cracklow, B.H.A. – Mss Eur 9900/26
Papers of Lieutenant John Oliver R.A. – Mss Eur A66
Papers of Sergeant William Burnett R.A. – Mss Eur C824
Papers of Surgeon William Dicken with Nepalese Contingent – Mss Eur C366
Papers of Trooper T. Palmer, 7th Hussars – Mss Eur D581
Telegrams and letters of Brigadier James Neill – Mss Eur Photo Eur 422

Cambridge University Centre of South Asian Studies (CSAS)
Papers of Boileau family including "A Lady's Diary of the Siege of Lucknow" by
  Mrs Boileau
Papers of Captain Gore Lindsay, Rifle Brigade

National Army Museum (NAM)
Diary of Captain T. Wilson during Siege of Lucknow – 1957-02-22
Diary of Lieutenant William Elles – 2009-03-12
Diary of Major G. Bingham, 64th Foot – 1959-03-105
Diary of Major G. Hume, 38th Foot – 2008-06-02
Diary of Sergeant James Taylor, 93rd Highlanders – 1979-05-51
Diary of Trooper T. Cope, F Troop, R.H.A. – 2007-10-21
Documents relating to Hodson's death – 1959-03-146
Letter by unknown cavalry officer written after capture of Lucknow – 1966-05-07
Letter of George Lawrence to his mother from Cawnpore – 1964-11-60
Letter of Lord Walter Kerr, Naval Brigade HMS *Shannon* – 1987-01-22
Letter of Lt-Colonel William Case 32nd Foot, to his mother – 1993-11-10
Letter of Private Gabriel Spiers, Rifle Brigade – 2012-06-09
Letter of Trooper John Moss, F Troop, R.H.A. – 2011-08-10
Letters of Asst-Surgeon A. Bradshaw, Rifle Brigade – 1966-02-62
Letters of Lieutenant E. Chamier, aide to Outram – 1975-10-31
Letters of Lieutenant H. Stansfield, 8th Bengal Native Infantry – 1976-06-43
Letters of Lieutenant J. Bryce, Bengal Artillery – 2005-11-161
Letters of Lieutenant N. Graeme, 90th Foot – 2009-06-10
Letters of Lieutenant S. Chamier R.A. – 1976-04-10
Letters of Lieutenant W. Fletcher, 40th Bengal Native Infantry – 1957-06-17
Letters of Lieutenant William Hargood, 1st Madras Fusiliers – 1952-06-10
Letters of Major-General Sir Archdale Wilson – 1967-04-83
Letters of Sgt-Major W. Dalziel, Bengal Army – 2009-06-02
Manuscript letter book of Sir Henry Lawrence – 1977-11-230
Manuscript of Lieutenant Montagu Hall, 1st Madras Fusiliers – 1957-05-10
Manuscript of Mrs Huxham during Siege of Lucknow – 1973-03-24
Notes & sketch plans by Lieutenant William Moorsom – 1956-08-16
Papers of Captain George Fulton during Siege of Lucknow – 1973-11-30

Papers of Lt-General Sir James Outram including "Notes On The Campaign" by
   Sir H Havelock – 1985-07-22 & 1992-10/127
Papers of Sgt-Major H. Greenhow, Bengal Army – 1992-06-2
Private Account of Events By Lieutenant J. McLeod Innes – 1964-11-60

National Library of Scotland (NLS)
Journal of Captain Frederick Burroughs, 93rd Highlanders – MSS 2234-35

Norfolk Records Office (NRO)
Letters of Major-General Sir Charles Ashe Windham – MC 135/171-185
Papers of Major Frank Astley Cubitt – CUB

North Yorkshire County Record Office (NYCRO)
Papers of General Sir Henry Havelock and General Sir Henry Havelock-Allan
   V.C. – ZDG

Royal Cornwall Museum (RCM)
Letters of Captain John Edmonstone, 32nd Foot

Suffolk Record Office (SRO)
Letters of Lieutenant J. Wade, 90th Foot – 1062-12
Letters of Sir Charles Fraser, 7th Hussars – HA11/A16/1

Wellcome Medical Library (WML)
Diary of Surgeon Anthony Home V.C. – RAMC/268

Author's Collection
Extracts from the recollections of the Siege of Lucknow by James Parry,
   uncovenanted gentleman of the Delhi Bank
Manuscript account of Surgeon James Fairweather, 4th Punjab Infantry

Printed Works

Official Publications
British Parliamentary Papers 1857-59:
Mutinies In The East Indies
Mutinies In The East Indies (Supplement To The Papers Presented July 1857)
Appendix To Papers Relative To Mutinies In The East Indies (Inclosures in
   Nos 1, 3, 5 & 6)
Appendix To Papers Relative To Mutinies In The East Indies (Inclosures In
   Nos 7 To 19)
Further Papers Relative To The Mutinies In The East Indies

East Indies (Mutinies) – 3 papers

Mutinies In India – Letters From The Court Of Direrctors Of The East India Company To The Governor-General Of India In Council

Further Papers (No 4) Relative To The Mutinies In The East Indies

Further Papers (No 5) Relative To The Mutinies In The East Indies

Appendix (A) To Further Papers (No 5) Relative To The Mutinies In The East Indies (Inclosures In No 1)

Appendix (B) To Further Papers (No 5) Relative To Mutinies In The East Indies (Inclosures In Nos 2,3 & 4)

Further Papers (No 6) (In Continuation Of No 4) Relative To Mutinies In The East Indies

Supplement To Papers (No 6) Relative To Mutinies In The East Indies

Further Papers (No 7) (In Continuation Of No 5) Relative To Mutinies In The East Indies

Further Papers (No 8) (In Continuation Of No 6) Relative To Mutinies In The East Indies

Further Papers (No 8A) Relative To The Insurrection In The East Indies

Further Papers (No 9) (In Continuation Of No 7) Relative To The Insurrection In The East Indies

East India (Punjab) Papers Relating To The Mutiny In The Punjab

Other Official Works

Cardew (Lt. F.G.). *A Sketch Of The Services Of The Bengal Native Army To The Year 1895.* Superintendent Government Printing. Calcutta 1903.

Forrest (G.W.) ed. *Selections From The Letters, Despatches And Other State Papers Preserved In The Military Department Of The Government Of India 1857-58.* 4 vols. Superintendent Government Printing, Calcutta 1912.

Rizvi (S.A.A.) ed. *Freedom Struggle In Uttar Pradesh: Source Material.* 6 vols. Information Department, Uttar Pradesh. Lucknow 1959-61

Sen (S.N.). *Eighteen Fifty-Seven.* Government of India. Delhi 1957.

Books

Adams (W.H.D.). *The Makers Of British India.* London 1894.

Adye (Lt-Col. J.). *The Defence Of Cawnpore By The Troops Under The Orders Of Major-General Charles A. Windham, C.B.* London 1858.

____(Gen. Sir J.). *Recollections Of A Military Life.* London 1895.

Aitchison (Sir C.). *Rulers Of India: Lord Lawrence.* Oxford 1892.

Allen (C.). *A Glimpse Of The Burning Plain: Leaves From The Indian Journals Of Charlotte Canning.* London 1986.

____*Soldier Sahibs: The Daring Adventurers Who Tamed India's Northwest Frontier.* London 2000

Anderson (Capt. R.P.). *A Personal Journal Of The Siege Of Lucknow.* London 1858.

Anglesey (Marquess of). *A History Of The British Cavalry Vol II 1851-1871.* London 1975.

Anon. *Narrative Of The Indian Revolt: From Its Outbreak To The Capture Of Lucknow By Sir Colin Campbell.* London 1858.

Anon. (Katherine Bartrum). *A Widow's Reminiscences Of Lucknow.* London 1858.

Anon. (A Member Of The Garrison – J.C. Parry). *The Siege Of Lucknow.* Calcutta 1858.

Anon (Staff Officer – E. Thurburn) *Reminiscences Of The Indian Rebellion Of 1857-1858.* Privately printed. London 1889.

Anon. (A Member Of The Original Residency Garrison). *Reminiscences Of 1857: Or The Defence Of Lucknow.* Lucknow 1891.

Anon. *General The Rt. Hon. Sir Edward Lugard GCB; PC 1810-1898.* Privately printed. Boscombe nd (c.1925).

Ansari (I.H.) & Qureshi (H.A.). *1857 Urdu Sources.* Lucknow 2008.

Anson (H.S.) ed. *With H.M. 9th Lancers During The Indian Mutiny: The Letters Of Brevet-Major O.H.S.G. Anson.* London 1896.

Atkins (J.B.). *The Life Of Sir William Howard Russell CVO; LLD.* 2 vols. London 1911.

Baird (J.G.A.) ed. *Private Letters Of The Marquess Of Dalhousie.* Edinburgh 1911.

Ball (C.). *The History Of The Indian Mutiny: Giving A Detailed Account Of The Sepoy Insurrection In India.* 2 vols. London 1859.

Barker (Gen. Sir G.D.) *Letters From Persia And India 1857-1859.* London 1915.

Barter (Capt. R.). *The Siege Of Delhi: Mutiny Memories Of An Old Officer.* London 1984.

Barthorp (M.) & Turner (P.). *The British Army On Campaign 1856-1881.* London 1988.

Barthorp (M.) & Anderson (D.). *The British Troops In The Indian Mutiny 1857-59.* London 1994.

Battye (E.D.). *The Fighting Ten.* London 1984.

Beckett (I.). *The Victorians At War.* London 2003.

____ ed. *Wolseley And Ashanti: The Asante War Journal & Correspondence Of Major-General Sir Garnet Wolseley 1873-1874.* Army Records Society vol 28. Brimscombe Port 2009.

Bence-Jones (M.). *Palaces Of The Raj: Magnificence And Misery Of The Lord Sahibs.* London 1973.

____*The Viceroys Of India.* London 1982.

Best (B.). *The Victoria Crosses That Saved An Empire: The Story Of The VCs Of The Indian Mutiny.* Barnsley 2016.

Billington (M.F.). *Women In India.* London 1895.

Bleby (Lt-Comm. A.). *The Victorian Naval Brigades.* Dunbeath 2006.

Blomfield (C.) ed. *Lahore To Lucknow: The Indian Mutiny Journal Of Arthur Moffatt Lang.* London 1992.

Bonham (Col. J.). *Oude In 1857: Some Memories Of The Indian Mutiny.* London 1928.

Bourchier (Col. G.). *Eight Months Campaign Against The Bengal Sepoy Army During The Mutiny Of 1857.* London 1858.

Brock (Rev. W.). *A Biographical Sketch Of Sir Henry Havelock KCB.* London 1858.

Broehl (W.G.). *Crisis Of The Raj: The Revolt Of 1857 Through British Lieutenants' Eyes.* Hanover 1986.

Brooks (R.). *The Long Arm Of Empire: Naval Brigades From The Crimea To The Boxer Rebellion.* London 1999.

Bryant (Sir A.). *Jackets Of Green: A Study Of The History, Philosophy And Character Of The Rifle Brigade.* London 1972.

Bryant (M.). *Wars Of Empire In Cartoons.* London 2008.

Buckland (C.E.). *Dictionary Of Indian Biography.* London 1906.

Bush (J.). *The Warner Letters: The Experiences Of Two English Brothers During The Indian Rebellion Of 1857-1859.* New Delhi 2008.

Caine (Rev. C.) ed. *Barracks And Battlefields In India.* New Delhi 1985.

Campbell (Sir G.). *Memories Of My Indian Career.* 2 vols. London 1893.

Cantlie (Lt-Gen. Sir N.). *A History Of The Army Medical Department.* 2 vols. Edinburgh 1974.

Cardew (Maj. F.G.). *Hodson's Horse 1857-1922.* Edinburgh 1928.

Case (Mrs). *Day By Day At Lucknow: A Journal Of The Siege Of Lucknow.* London 1858.

Chalmers (Col. J.). *Letters Written From India During The Mutiny And Waziri Campaigns.* Edinburgh 1904.

Chaudhuri (S.B.). *Theories Of The Indian Mutiny 1857-59.* Calcutta 1965.

Chick (N.) ed. *Annals Of The Indian Rebellion 1857-58: Containing Narratives Of The Outbreaks And Eventual Occurrences And Stories Of Personal Adventures.* London 1974.

Clowes (Sir W.L.). *The Royal Navy: A History* Vol VII. London 1903.

Cobban (J.M.). *The Life And Deeds Of Earl Roberts VC; KG; KP; GCB; GCSI; GCIE, Field Marshal And Commander-in-Chief.* 4 vols. Edinburgh 1901-02.

Collier (R.). *The Sound Of Fury: An Account Of The Indian Mutiny.* London 1963.

Collister (P.). *'Hellfire Jack V.C.': The Life And Times Of General Sir William Olpherts, VC; GCB 1822-1902.* London 1987.

Cooper (L.). *Havelock 1785-1857.* London 1957.

Cope (Sir W. H.). *The History Of The Rifle Brigade.* London 1877.

Creagh (Sir O.M.) & Humphris (E.M.). *The Victoria Cross 1856-1920.* Chippenham 1995.

Crump (Lt. C.W.). *A Pictorial Record Of The Cawnpore Massacre*. London & Calcutta 1858.

Cunningham (Sir H.S.) *Rulers Of India: Earl Canning*. Oxford 1892.

Daly (Maj. H.). *Memoirs Of General Sir Henry Dermot Daly GCB; CIE*. London 1895.

Danvers (R.W.). *Letters From India And China During The Years 1854-1858*. Privately printed. London 1898.

David (S.). *The Indian Mutiny 1857*. London 2002.

____*Queen Victoria's Wars: The Rise Of Empire*. London 2006.

____*The Bengal Army And The Outbreak Of The Indian Mutiny*. New Delhi 2009.

Dawson (Capt. L.). *Squires And Sepoys 1857-1958*. London 1960.

Delavoye (Capt. A.M.). *Records Of The 90th Regiment: With A Roll Of Officers From 1795 To 1880*. London 1880.

Dodd (G.). *History Of The Indian Revolt*. London 1859.

Dodgson (D.S.). *General Views And Special Points Of Interest In The City Of Lucknow: From Drawings Made On The Spot By D.S.S. With Descriptive Notices*. London 1860.

Douglas (G.) & Ramsay (G.). *The Panmure Papers*. 2 vols. London 1908.

Duff (A.). *The Indian Rebellion: Its Causes And Results In a Series Of Letters*. London 1858.

Edwardes (Maj-Gen. Sir H.B.) & Merivale (H.). *Life Of Sir Henry Lawrence*. New York 1873.

Edwardes (M.) ed. *Journal Of The Siege Of Lucknow: An Episode Of The Indian Mutiny*. London nd (c. 1957).

____*Battles Of The Indian Mutiny*. London 1963.

____*Bound To Exile: The Victorians In India*. London 1969.

____*Red Year: The Indian Rebellion Of 1857*. London 1973.

____*A Season In Hell*. London 1973.

Elliott (Maj.) & Knollys (Lt-Col.). *Gallant Sepoys And Sowars*. London c.1882.

Elsmie (G.R.). *Field-Marshal Sir Donald Stewart GCB; GCSI; CIE*. London 1903.

Ewart (Lt-Gen. J.A.). *The Story Of A Soldier's Life: In Peace War & Mutiny*. 2 vols. London 1881.

Farwell (B.). *Queen Victoria's Little Wars*. New York 1985.

Fayrer (Surg-Gen. Sir J.). *Recollections Of My Life*. Edinburgh 1900.

Fforde (Maj. C. Del W.) ed. *The Lucknow Siege Diary Of Mrs C. M. Brydon*. Privately published. Okehampton 1979.

Field (Col. C.). *Britain's Sea Soldiers: A History Of The Royal Marines*. 2 vols. Liverpool 1924.

Fitchett (W.H.). *The Tale Of The Great Mutiny*. London 1903.

Forbes (A.). *Havelock*. London 1891.

____Henty (G.) & Griffiths (Maj. A.). *Battles of the Nineteenth Century.* 7 vols. London 1896-1901.

Forbes (Mrs H.). *Some Recollections Of The Siege Of Lucknow (1857).* Axminster 1904.

Forbes-Mitchell (Sgt. W.). *Reminiscences Of The Great Mutiny 1857-59: Including The Relief, Siege And Capture Of Lucknow, and The Campaigns in Rohilcund And Oude.* London 1897.

Forrest (G.W.). *A History of The Indian Mutiny.* 3 vols. Edinburgh 1904.

____*The Life of Lord Roberts KG; VC.* London 1914.

Fortescue (J.W.). *A History Of The British Army Vol XIII.* London 1930.

Fraser (T.G.) & Harrison (A.T.) ed. *The Graham Indian Mutiny Papers.* Belfast 1980.

Fulton (Capt. G.W.W.). *Biographical Memoirs: With His Private Journal Of His Own Part In The Siege Of Lucknow.* Privately published. Napier 1913.

Gardyne (Lt-Col. C.G.). *The Life Of A Regiment: The History Of The Gordon Highlanders From 1816 To 1898.* London 1929.

Gimlette (Lt-Col. G.H.D.). *A Postscript To The Records Of The Indian Mutiny: An Attempt To Trace The Subsequent Careers And Fate Of The Rebel Bengal Regiments, 1857-1858.* London 1927.

Goldsmid (Maj-Gen. Sir F.J.). *James Outram: A Biography.* 2 vols. London 1881.

Gordon (Sir C.A.). *Recollections Of Thirty-Nine Years In The Army.* London 1898.

Gordon-Alexander (Lt-Col. W.). *Recollections Of A Highland Subaltern: During The Campaigns Of The 93ʳᵈ Highlanders In India Under Sir Colin Campbell, Lord Clyde, In 1857, 1858 And 1859.* London 1897.

Gough (Gen. Sir H.). *Old Memories.* London 1897.

Govett (B.). *Discontented Soldier: The Letters Of Surgeon-Major Frederick Dalzel, Bengal Army, From India 1852-1864.* Privately published. London 1975.

Greenhow (H.M.). *Notes Medical And Surgical, Taken During The Late Siege Of Lucknow.* Calcutta 1858.

Greenwood (A.). *Victoria's Scottish Lion: The Life Of Colin Campbell, Lord Clyde.* Brimscombe Port 2015.

Groom (N.). *The Union Jack: The Story Of The British Flag.* London 2017.

Groom (Lt. W.T.). *With Havelock From Allahabad To Lucknow 1857.* London 1894.

Greet (C.S.). *Six Years 1856-1861: The Diaries Of Edward Welch Of Arle.* Cheltenham 1987.

Gubbins (M.R.). *An Account Of The Mutinies In Oudh And Of The Siege Of The Lucknow Residency.* London 1858.

Hannah (W. H.). *Bobs: Kipling's General.* London 1973.

Hare (A.J.C.). *The Story Of Two Noble Lives.* 3 vols. London 1893.

Harris (Mrs G.). *A Lady's Diary Of The Siege Of Lucknow: Written For The Persual Of Friends At Home.* London 1858.

Harrison (Gen. Sir R.). *Recollections Of A Life In The British Army During The Latter Half Of The Nineteenth Century.* London 1908.

Hay (Lt. D.). *Diary In The Form Of A Letter Written To His Mother During The Siege Of The Residency At Lucknow, 1857.* Privately printed. Edinburgh 1911.

Hay (S.). *Historic Lucknow.* Lucknow 1939.

Headley (J.T.). *The Life Of General Havelock KCB.* London 1859.

Heathcote (T.A.). *The Indian Army: The Garrison Of British Imperial India, 1822-1922.* London 1974.

____ed. *The Indian Mutiny Letters Of Colonel H. P. Pearson CB: August 1856–March 1859.* Leeds 2008.

____*The Military In British India: The Development Of British Land Forces In South Asia 1600-1947.* Barnsley 2013.

Herford (Capt. L.S.A.). *Stirring Times Under Canvas.* London 1862.

Hewitt (J.). *Eye-Witnesses To The Indian Mutiny.* Reading 1972.

Hibbert (C.). *The Great Mutiny: India 1857.* New York 1978.

Hilton (E.H.). *The Tourist's Guide To Lucknow.* Lucknow 1907.

Hodge (W.). *Travels In India During The Years 1780, 81, 82, 83.* London 1783.

Hodson (Rev. G.H.) ed. *Twelve Years Of A Soldier's Life In India.* London 1859.

Holloway (J.). *Essays On The Indian Mutiny.* Privately printed. London 1865.

Holmes (R.). *Sahib: The British Soldier In India 1750-1914.* London 2005.

Holmes (T.R.). *A History Of The Indian Mutiny: Fifth Edition Revised.* London 1904.

Home (Surg-Gen. Sir A.D.). *Service Memories.* London 1912.

Hughes (Maj-Gen B.P.). *The Bengal Horse Artillery 1800-1861.* London 1971.

Hughes (D.). *The Mutiny Chaplains.* Salisbury 1991.

Inglis (Maj-Gen. Sir J.). *Reports On The Engineering Operations During The Defence Of Lucknow.* Woolwich 1861.

Inglis (Hon. Julia). *The Siege Of Lucknow: A Diary.* London 1893.

Innes (Lt-Gen. J. M.). *Lucknow & Oude: In The Mutiny.* London 1895.

____*The Sepoy Revolt: A Critical Narrative.* London 1897.

____*Rulers Of India Sir Henry Lawrence: The Pacificator.* Oxford 1898.

James (D.). *Lord Roberts.* London 1954.

James (L.). *Raj: The Making And Unmaking Of British India.* London 1897.

Jocelyn (Col. J.R.J.). *The History Of The Royal And Indian Artillery In The Mutiny Of 1857.* London 1915.

Johnson (Maj. W.T.). *Twelve Years Of A Soldier's Life.* London 1897.

Jones (Capt. O.J.). *Recollections Of A Winter Campaign In India 1857-58.* London 1859.

Jones-Parry (Capt. S.H.). *An Old Soldier's Memories.* London 1897.

Joyce (M.). *Ordeal At Lucknow: The Defence Of The Residency.* London 1938.

Joynson-Cork (B.). *Rider On A Grey Horse: A Life Of Hodson Of Hodson's Horse.* London 1958.

Kavanagh (T.H.). *How I Won The Victoria Cross.* London 1860.

Kaye (J.W.). *Lives Of Indian Officers: Illustrative Of The History Of The Civil And Military Services Of India.* 2 vols. London 1867.

____*A History Of The Sepoy War In India, 1857-1858.* 3 vols. London 1876.

____ & Malleson (Col.). *History Of The Indian Mutiny Of 1857-8.* 6 vols. London 1889-91.

Keene (H.G.). *A Handbook For Visitors To Lucknow.* Calcutta 1875.

Kinsley (D.A.). *They Fight Like Devils: Stories From Lucknow during The Great Indian Mutiny, 1857-58.* London 2001.

Knight (I.) ed. *Marching To The Drums: From The Kabul Massacre To The Siege Of Mafikeng.* London 1999.

Knollys (H.) ed. *Life Of General Sir Hope Grant: With Selections From His Correspondence.* 2 vols. Edinburgh 1894.

Kochanski (H.). *Sir Garnet Wolseley: Victorian Hero.* London 1999.

Lamb (J.B.). *Jingo: The Buckskin Brigadier Who Opened Up The Canadian West.* Toronto 1992.

Lawrence (J.). *Lawrence Of Lucknow: A Biography.* London 1990.

Lee (H.). *Brothers In The Raj: The Lives Of John And Henry Lawrence.* Oxford 2002.

Lee-Warner (Sir W.). *Life Of The Marquis Of Dalhousie.* 2 vols. London 1904.

____*Memoirs Of Field-Marshal Sir Henry Wylie Norman GCB; GCMG; CIE.* London 1908.

Lehmann (J.). *All Sir Garnet: A Life Of Field-Marshal Lord Wolseley.* London 1964.

Lewin (Lt-Col. T.H.). *A Fly On The Wheel: Or How I Helped To Govern India.* London 1912.

Llewellyn-Jones (R.). *A Fatal Friendship: The Nawabs, The British And The City Of Lucknow.* Delhi 1985.

____*The Great Uprising In India 1857-58: Untold Stories, Indian And British.* Woodbridge 2007.

Longford (E.). *Victoria R.I.* London 1964.

Low (C.R.). *History Of The Indian Navy (1613-1863).* 2 vols. London 1877.

____*Soldiers Of The Victorian Age.* 2 vols. London 1880.

____*General Lord Wolseley (Of Cairo).* London 1883.

____*Major-General Sir Frederick S. Roberts Bart VC: A Memoir.* London 1883.

Lunt (J.) ed. *From Sepoy To Subedar: Being The Life And Adventures Of Subedar Sita Ram, A Native Officer Of The Bengal Army, Written And Related By Himself.* London 1970

Macgregor (Lady) ed. *The Life And Opinions Of Major-General Sir Charles Metcalfe Macgregor KCB; CSI; CIE.* 2 vols. Edinburgh 1888.

Mackay (Rev. J.A.). *From London To Lucknow.* 2 vols. London 1860.

Mackenzie (Col. A.R.D.). *Mutiny Memoirs: Being Personal Reminiscences Of The Great Revolt Of 1857.* Allahabad 1892.

Maclagan (M.). *Clemency Canning: Charles John, 1ˢᵗ Earl Canning.* London 1962.

Macmillan (M.). *Women Of The Raj: The Mothers, Wives And Daughters Of The British Empire In India.* London 1998.

Macmunn (Lt-Gen. Sir G.). *The Indian Mutiny In Perspective.* London 1931.

____*The History Of The Sikh Pioneers.* London nd (c. 1935).

Majendie (Lt. V.D.). *Up Among The Pandies.* London 1859.

Majumdar (R. C.). *The Sepoy Mutiny And The Revolt Of 1857.* Calcutta 1963.

Mansfield (H.O.). *Charles Ash Windham: A Norfolk Soldier (1810-1870).* Lavenham 1973.

Marshman (J.C.). *Memoirs Of Major-General Sir Henry Havelock KCB.* London 1860.

Martin (R.M.). *The Indian Empire: With A Full Account Of The Mutiny Of The Native Troops.* 3 vols. London 1859-61.

Mason (P.). *A Matter Of Honour: An Account Of The Indian Army, Its Officers And Men.* London 1974.

____*The Men Who Ruled India.* London 1985.

Maude (Col. F.W.) & Sherer (J.W.). *Memories Of The Mutiny.* 2 vols. London 1894.

Maurice (Maj-Gen. Sir F.) & Arthur (Sir G.). *The Life Of Lord Wolseley.* London 1924.

McKenzie (Capt. T.). *My Life As A Soldier.* St John 1898.

Mecham (C.H.) & Couper (G.). *Sketches And Incidents Of The Siege Of Lucknow: With Descriptive Notes.* London 1858.

Medley (Capt.G. J.). *A Year's Campaigning In India: From March, 1857 To March, 1858.* London 1858.

Miles (A.H.) & Pattle (A.J.). *Fifty-Two Stories Of The Indian Mutiny: And The Men Who Saved India.* Hutchinson 1895.

Misra (A.). *Nana Sahib And The Fight For Freedom.* Lucknow 1961.

Moon (Sir P.). *The British Conquest And Dominion Of India.* London 1989.

More (S.B.). *The 1857 Jihad.* New Delhi 2009.

Moosvi (S.) ed. *Facets Of The Great Revolt 1857.* New Delhi 2008.

Morrison (J.). *Lawrence Of Lucknow 1806-1857.* London 1934.

Mount (F.). *The Tears Of The Rajas: Mutiny, Money And Marriage In India 1805-1905.* London 2015.

Mukherjee (R.). *Awadh In Revolt 1857-1858.* New Delhi 1984.

____*Mangal Pandey: Brave Martyr Or Accidental Hero?* New Delhi 2005.

____*Spectre Of Violence*: *The 1857 Kanpur Massacres*. New Delhi 2007.

____ & Kapoor (P.). *Dateline 1857*: *Revolt Against The Raj*. New Delhi 2008.

____*The Year Of Blood*: *Essays On The Revolt Of 1857*. New Delhi 2014.

Munro (Surg-Gen.). *Records Of Service And Campaigning In Many Lands*. 2 vols. London 1887.

Napier (Lt-Col. Hon. H.D.). *Field-Marshal Lord Napier Of Magdala GCB GCSI*. London 1927.

Napier (Maj-Gen. Sir R.), Harness (Col.) & Lennox (Lt-Col.). *Reports On The Engineering Operations At The Siege Of Lucknow In March 1858*. Woolwich 1861.

North (Maj.). *Journal Of An English Officer In India*. London 1858.

Oldenburg (V.T.). *The Making Of Colonial Lucknow 1856-1877*. Princeton 1984.

Oliver (Maj-Gen. J.R.). *Campaigning In Oude Etc.* Privately published. London 1860.

Outram (Lt-Gen. Sir J.). *Lieut-General Sir James Outram's Campaign In India 1857-1858*: *Comprising General Orders And Despatches Relating To The Defence And Relief Of The Lucknow Garrison, And Correspondence Relating To The Relief Up To The Date When That Object Was Effected By Sir Colin Campbell*. Privately published. London 1860.

Ouvry (Col. H.A.). *Cavalry Experiences And Leaves From My Journal*. Lymington 1892.

Owen (A.). *Recollections Of A Veteran Of The Days Of The Great Indian Mutiny Of 1857*. Lahore 1915.

Pandey (S.). *Vision Of The Rebels During 1857*: *Aspects Of Mobilization, Organization And Resistance*. New Delhi 2008.

Parrett (C.) & Chhina (R.). *The Indian Order Of Merit Vol I 1837-1860*. Brighton 2010.

Parry (D.H.). *Britain's Roll Of Glory*: *Or The Victoria Cross*. London 1906.

Pati (B.) ed. *The 1857 Rebellion*. New Delhi 2007.

Paul (B.J.). *The Greased Cartridge*: *The Heroes And Villains Of 1857-58*. New Delhi 2011.

Pearse (Maj. H.) ed. *The Crimean Diary And Letters Of Lieutenant-General Sir Charles Ash Windham*: *With Observations Upon His Services During The Indian Mutiny*. London 1897.

Pemble (J.). *The Raj, The Indian Mutiny And The Kingdom Of Oudh 1801-1859*. Hassocks 1979.

Polehampton (E.) & Polehampton (T.S.) ed. *A Memoir, Letters And Diary Of The Rev. Henry S, Polehampton MA, Chaplain Of Lucknow*. London 1858.

Pollock (J.C.). *Way To Glory*: *The Life Of Havelock Of Lucknow*. London 1957.

Raikes (C.). *Notes On The Revolt In The North-Western Provinces Of India.* London 1858.

Rait (R.S.). *The Life Of Field-Marshal Sir Frederick Paul Haines.* London 1911.

Ramsay (B.). *Rough Recollections.* 2 vols. Edinburgh 1882.

Raugh (H.E.). *The Victorians At War 1815-1914: An Encyclopaedia Of British Military History.* Santa Barbara 2004.

____*The Raugh Bibliography Of The Indian Mutiny 1857-59.* Solihull 2015.

Rees (L.R.R.). *A Personal Narrative Of The Siege Of Lucknow: From Its Commencement To Its Relief By Sir Colin Campbell.* London 1858.

Reeves (N.) ed. *An Army Doctor In The Indian Revolt 1857-58: The Diary Of Assistant Surgeon Henry Kelsall, HM 20ᵗʰ Regiment Of Foot.* Nedlands 1984.

Richards (D.). *Cawnpore And Lucknow.* Barnsley 2007.

Roberts (F.). *Letters Written During The Indian Mutiny.* London 1924.

____(FM. Lord). *Forty-One Years In India: From Subaltern To Commander-in-Chief.* 2 vols. London 1897.

Robertson (Col. J.P.). *Personal Adventures And Anecdotes Of An Old Officer.* London 1906.

Robinson (J.). *Angels Of Albion: Women Of The Indian Mutiny.* London 1996.

Rowbotham (Comm. W.B.). *Naval Brigades In The Indian Mutiny 1857-58.* London 1948.

Ruggles (Maj-Gen. J.). *Recollections Of A Lucknow Veteran 1845-1876.* London 1906.

Russell (W.H.). *My Diary In India In The Year 1858-59.* 2 vols. London 1860.

Sandes (Lt-Col. E.W.C.). *The Military Engineer In India.* 2 vols. Chatham 1933.

____*The Indian Sappers And Miners.* Chatham 1948.

Schofield (V.). *The Highland Furies: The Black Watch 1739-1899.* London 2012.

Schawohl (E.). *A Guide To The Lucknow Residency.* Privately published. Lucknow 2018.

Seaton (Maj-Gen. Sir T.). *From Cadet To Colonel: The Record Of A Life Of Active Service.* 2 vols. London 1866.

Sen (S.N.). *Eighteen Fifty-Seven.* Calcutta 1957.

Sewell (Col. J.W.). *A Record Of The Life And Times Of Captain Bernard McCabe.* Privately printed. Oxford nd (c. 1980).

Shadwell (Lt-Gen.). *The Life Of Colin Campbell, Lord Clyde.* 2 vols. Edinburgh 1881.

Sharar (A.H.). *Lucknow: The Last Phase Of An Oriental Culture.* Delhi 1989.

Shepherd (J.W.). *A Personal Narrative Of The Outbreak And Massacre At Cawnpore During The Sepoy Revolt Of 1857.* Lucknow 1886.

Sheppard (E.) ed. *George, Duke Of Cambridge: A Memoir Of His Private Life.* 2 vols. London 1907.

Sheppard (Maj. E.W.). *The Ninth Queen's Royal Lancers 1715-1936.* Aldershot 1939.

Sleeman (W.H.). *A Journey Through The Kingdom Of Oude In 1849-50.* London 1858.

____*Rambles And Recollections Of An Indian Official.* London 1893.

Small (M.) ed. *Told From The Ranks: Recollections Of Service During The Queen's Reign By Privates And Non-Commissioned Officers Of The British Army.* London 1897.

Smith (R.B.). *Life Of Lord Lawrence.* 2 vols. New York 1883.

Spencer (M.). *Personal Reminiscences Of The Indian Mutiny.* Clifton (c. 1916).

Spiers (E.M.). *The Scottish Soldier And Empire 1854-1902.* Edinburgh 2006.

Spilsbury (J.). *The Indian Mutiny.* London 2007.

Srivastava (K.B.). *The Great Indian Revolt Of 1857: Flames, Fire And Freedom.* New Delhi 2007.

Stark (H.A.). *The Call Of The Blood: Or Anglo-Indians And The Sepoy Mutiny.* Rangoon 1932.

Stokes (E.). *The English Utilitarians And India.* Oxford 1959.

____*The Peasant And The Raj: Studies In Agrarian Society And Peasant Rebellion In Colonial India.* Cambridge 1978

____*The Peasant Armed: The Indian Revolt Of 1857.* Oxford 1986.

Strange (Maj-Gen. T.B.). *Gunner Jingo's Jubilee.* London 1893.

Stuart (B.). *Harry Bell: Being Part Of A Family History.* London 1955.

Stubbs (Maj-Gen. F. W.). *History Of The Bengal Artillery 1800-1861.* 3 vols. London 1877-1905.

Surtees (V.). *Charlotte Canning.* London 1972.

Swanston (Maj-Gen.). *My Journal: Or What I Did And Saw Between The 9th June And 25th November, 1857.* Uxbridge 1890.

Swiney (Col. G. C.) ed. *Historical Records Of The 32nd (Cornwall) Light Infantry: Now The 1st Battalion Duke Of Cornwall's Light Infantry, From The Formation Of The Regiment In 1702 Down To 1892.* London 1893.

Swinson (A.) & Scott (D.) ed. *The Memoirs Of Private Waterfield, Soldier In Her Majesty's 32nd Regiment Of Foot (Duke Of Cornwall's Light Infantry) 1842-57.* London 1968.

Tacqui (R.). *Lucknow 1857: The Two Wars At Lucknow – The Dusk Of An Era.* Lucknow 2001.

Taylor (A.C.). *General Sir Alex Taylor GCB; RE.* 2 vols. London 1913.

Taylor (P.J.O.). *Chronicles Of The Mutiny And Other Historical Sketches.* New Delhi 1992.

____*A Star Shall Fall: India 1857.* New Delhi 1993.

____*A Feeling Of Quiet Power: The Siege Of Lucknow 1857.* New Delhi 1994.

____*A Companion To The 'Indian Mutiny' Of 1857.* Delhi 1996.

____*What Really Happened During The Indian Mutiny: A Day-By-Day Account Of Major Events Of 1857-1859.* New Delhi 1997.

Thackeray (Col. Sir E.T.). *Biographical Notices Of Officers Of The Royal (Bengal) Engineers.* London 1900.

____*Reminiscences Of The Indian Mutiny (1857-58) And Afghanistan (1879).* London 1916.

Thomas (R.D*.). Outram In India: The Morality Of Empire.* Milton Keynes 2007.

Thompson (E.). *The Other Side Of The Medal.* London 1925.

Thomson (Capt. M.). *The Story Of Cawnpore.* London 1859.

Thomson (W.P.L.). *The Little General And The Rousay Crofters: Crisis And Conflict On An Orkney Estate.* Edinburgh 2000.

Thornton (Dep. Surg-Gen. J. H.). *Memories Of Seven Campaigns: A Record Of Thirty-Five Years' Service In The Indian Medical Department In India, China, Egypt And The Sudan.* London 1895.

Toomey (T.E.). *Heroes Of The Victoria Cross.* London 1895.

Trevelyan (O.). *The Competition Wallah.* London 1864.

Trotter (Capt. L.J.). *A Leader Of Light Horse: A Life Of Hodson Of Hodson's Horse.* London 1901.

____*A Life Of General Sir James Outram Bart: The Bayard Of India.* Edinburgh 1903.

Tuker (Lt-Gen. Sir F.) ed. *The Chronicle Of Private Henry Metcalfe: HM 32nd Regiment Of Foot.* London 1953.

Valbezen (E. De). *The English And India: New Sketches.* London 1883.

Verner (Col. W.) & Parker (Capt. E.D.). *The Military Life Of George, Duke Of Cambridge.* 2 vols. London 1905.

Verney ((Lt. E.H.). *The Shannon's Brigade In India: Being Some Account Of Sir William Peel's Naval Brigade In The Indian Campaigns Of 1857-58.* London 1862.

Verney (Maj-Gen. G.L.). *The Devil's Wind: The Story Of The Naval Brigade At Lucknow.* London 1956.

Vibart (Col. E.). *The Sepoy Mutiny: As Seen By A Subaltern.* London 1898.

Vibart (Maj. H.M.). *The Military History Of The Madras Engineers And Pioneers From 1743 To The Present Time.* 2 vols. London 1883.

Ward (A.). *Our Bones Are Scattered: The Cawnpore Massacres And The Indian Uprising Of 1857.* New York 1996.

Watson (E.S.). *Journal India: With HMS Shannon.* Kettering nd (c.1870).

Weston (Maj. C.S.). *Private Memoranda Of The Second Punjab War Of 1848 And Of The Mutiny In India, 1857.* Privately published. Npp. Nd (c. 1915)

White (Col. S.D.). *Indian Reminiscences.* London 1880.

____*A Complete History Of The Indian Mutiny.* Weston-Super-Mare 1885.

Whitehead (J.). *Thangliena; A Life Of T. H. Lewin.* Kiscadale 1992.

Wilkinson (Maj-Gen. O.) & Wilkinson (Maj-Gen. J.). *The Memoirs Of The Gemini Generals: Personal Anecdotes, Sporting Adventures And Sketches Of Distinguished Officers.* London 1896.

Wilkinson-Latham (R.J.). *From Our Own Special Correspondent: Victorian War Correspondents And Their Campaigns.* London 1979.

____ & Embleton (G.A.). *The Indian Mutiny.* London 1977.

Wilson (Capt. T.F.). *The Defence Of Lucknow: A Diary.* London 1858.

Winton (J.). *Hurrah For The Life Of A Sailor! Life On The Lower Deck Of The Victorian Navy.* London 1977.

Wise (J.). *The Diary Of A Medical Officer During The Great Indian Mutiny Of 1857.* Cork 1894.

Wolseley (F.M. Visc.). *The Story Of A Soldier's Life.* 2 vols. London 1903.

Wood (Sir E.). *The Revolt In Hindustan 1857-59.* London 1908.

____*British Battles On Land And Sea.* 2 vols. London 1915.

Wright (Rev. C.H.H.) ed. *Memoir Of John Lovering Cooke: Formerly Gunner In The Royal Artillery, And Late-Lay Agent Of The British Sailors Institute Boulogne.* London 1873.

Wright (W.). *Through The Indian Mutiny: The Memoirs Of James Fairweather, 4th Punjab Native Infantry, 1857-58.* Brimscombe Port 2011.

____*Warriors Of The Queen: Fighting Generals Of The Victorian Age.* Brimscombe Port 2014.

Wylly (H.C.). *Neill's Blue Caps.* 3 vols, Aldershot 1925.

Yalland (Z.). *Traders And Nabobs: The British In Cawnpore 1765-1857.* Wilton 1987.

____*Boxwallahs: The British In Cawnpore 1857-1901.* Wilton 1994.

Yule (H.) & Burnell (A.C.). *Hobson-Jobson: The Anglo-Indian Dictionary.* Concise Edition. Ware 1996.

Journals and Newspapers

Army Quarterly
Bombay Times
Blackwood's Magazine
Calcutta Review
Colburn's United Service Magazine
Illustrated London News
Journal of the Society for Army Historical Research
Journal of the United Service Institution of India
Soldiers of the Queen
The Times of London

Websites

reflectionsonthelucknow residency.blogspot.com
victorianwarsforum

By the same author

A British Lion in Zululand: Sir Garnet Wolseley in South Africa
A Tidy Little War: The British Invasion of Egypt, 1882
Battle Story: Omdurman 1898
British Murder: A Compendium, 1901-2000
Manipur Mischief: Rebellion, Scandal and the Dark Side of the Raj, 1891
Through the Indian Mutiny: The Memoirs of James Fairweather, 4th Punjab
   Native Infantry, 1857-1858
Warriors of the Queen: Fighting Generals of the Victorian Age

Index

Also available from Amberley Publishing

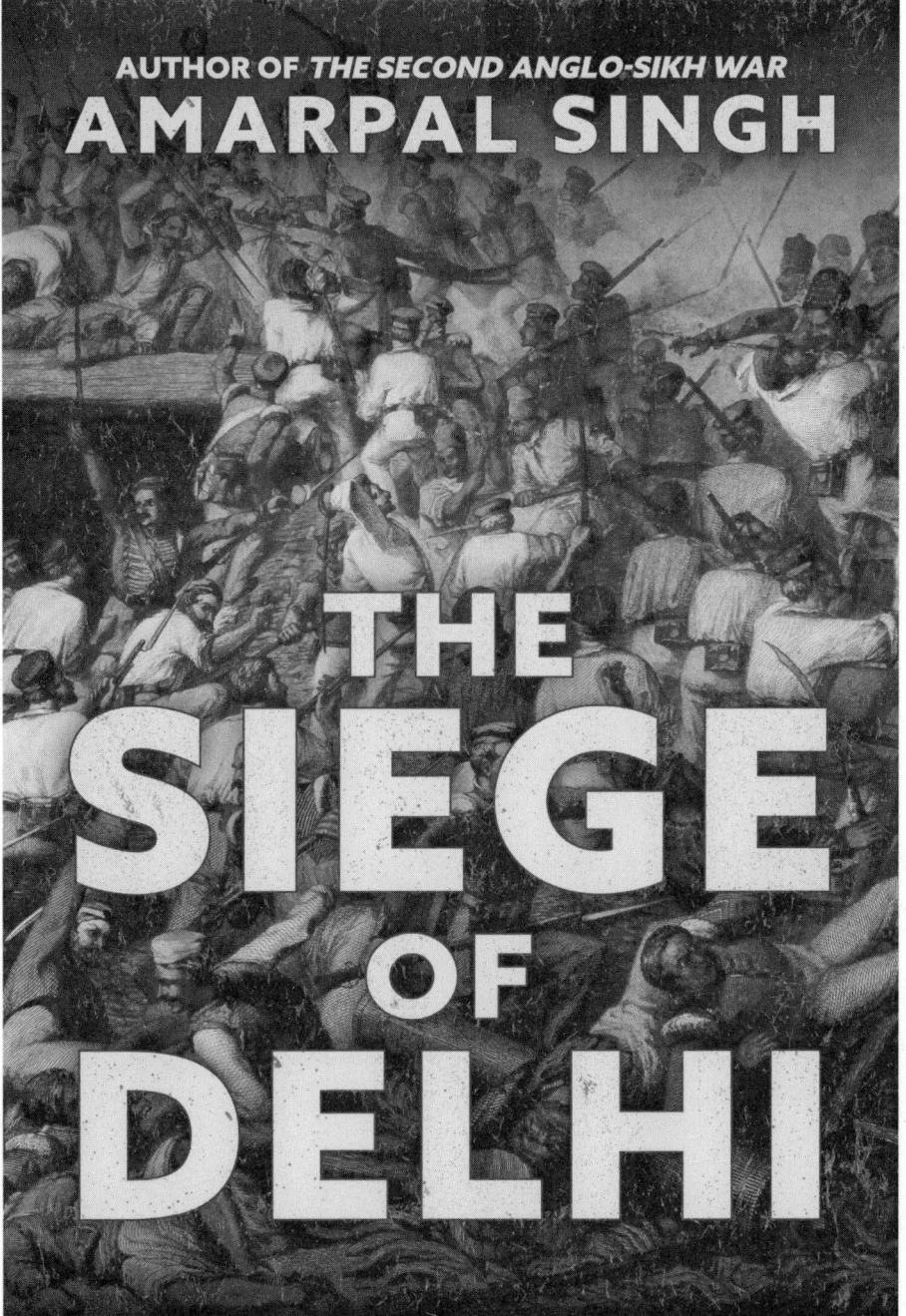

AUTHOR OF *THE SECOND ANGLO-SIKH WAR*
AMARPAL SINGH

THE SIEGE OF DELHI

Available from all good bookshops or to order direct
Please call **01453–847–800**
www.amberley-books.com